BIG DATA ANALYTICS IN MARKETING

BIG DATA ANALYTICS IN MARKETING

Editor

ANIL KULKARNI

BLOOMSBURY PRIME

First published, 2017

BLOOMSBURY PUBLISHING INDIA PVT. LTD.
New Delhi London Oxford New York Sydney

ISBN: 978-93-86826-84-8

Published by Bloomsbury Publishing India Pvt. Ltd.
DDA Complex LSC, Building No. 4, 2nd Floor
Pocket 6 & 7, Sector C
Vasant Kunj, New Delhi 110070

Laser Typeset by FORTUNE GRAPHICS, Naraina, New Delhi

Digitally Printed and bound in India by Replika Press Pvt. Ltd.

CONTENTS

PART TWO: METHODS

ACKNOWLEDGEMENTS

The thought of holding conferences in the Marketing area for academicians came up about four years ago. The first such conference Innovations in the Teaching of Marketing was held on January 14, 2012. The second, *Big Data Analytics for Marketing* was held on February 21-22, 2015. Ashita Aggarwal (Associate Professor and Head of Marketing Department, SPJIMR) had asked me to organize the conference and choose a theme. That is when the thought of Big Data came up and we decided to call for papers from both academicians as well as practitioners.

The conference from which this book is drawn received papers from 9 academicians and 16 practitioners. Besides the paper presenters there were more than 80 academicians and practitioners who attended the conference. I would like to extend my grateful thanks to all the authors and their organizations for taking the time and putting in the effort on a topic of great current interest. The papers had to be revised and due to the willing co-operation of the authors in doing so, the quality of this book has been enhanced. The list of authors and their organizations is given in an appendix at the end of the book.

The conference was possible because of the support and funding from SPJIMR and the personal support from Sesha Iyer (Professor and Advisor to the Dean, SPJIMR). The marketing faculty helped unstintingly, especially Ashita Aggarwal and Renuka Kamath (Professor and PGEMP Chairperson, SPJIMR). I must also thank Michigan State University (MSU) for joining in and collaborating with us in organizing this conference. Vallabh Sambamurthy (Eli Broad Professor and Chairperson Accounting and Information Systems

Broad College of Business, MSU) not only helped in getting MSU's participation and funding but actively participated in designing the conference, giving the concluding session and being a panel chair over the two days of the conference. I must also thank my colleague Prem Chandrani (Professor and Head of Finance Department, SPJIMR) for putting us in touch with Professor Sambamurthy.

My thanks are due to many others in managing the conference. It is not possible to list all of them but let me mention a few. Firstly, I am grateful to Suraj Commuri (Associate Professor, School of Business, SUNY Albany) for helping in conceptualizing, designing, and giving the concluding session and being a panel chair. Thank you to Sunil Lakdawala (Visiting Faculty, SPJIMR) and Mr. Anil Srinivasan (Consultant) for chairing the panel. I'd like to extend my gratitude to Mr. Clifford Patrao of IBM for giving the opening address and Mr. Arun Chearie of SAS. My colleagues Abbasali Gabula (Deputy Director, External Relations and Admin, SPJIMR) and Jagdish Rattanani (Editor, SPJIMR) managed the Public Relations around the event and I'm thankful to them for doing justice to the task.

I must also thank all faculty members from other departments who gave us their enthusiastic support and attended the conference. I must thank the administration team of SPJIMR which managed the logistics of the conference. I must thank students from PGDM and PGPM programmes who volunteered in helping to manage the conference. I am mentioning a few names; Anant, Devavrat, Vishakh, Manika, Foram, Monisha, Aditi, Anmol, Akshhay, Milton, Nikhil and others.

My special thanks to Anshul Garg for being around and helping on a daily basis from conceptualizing to executing the conference. I must also thank Almas Shaikh in this regard. Lastly, thanks to Harneet Jayakar and Sudhindra Gadag for relentlessly managing and following up the publication of this book.

INTRODUCTION

Big Data in the field of marketing is becoming mainstream. Today there is a persistent flow of data all around us – be it at the industry, firm, or customer level. Marketing analytics probe complex data aggregated across several periods, sources and various types, whether quantitative, textual or image. Explosive volumes of data are now available continuously.

In conventional analysis, independent variables were chosen based on their hypothesised causal relationships with the dependent variables. Now the volume, variety and velocity with which data is available it is sometimes enough for purposes of decision making to establish a correlation between independent and dependent variables leaving the cause and effect understanding for post decision analysis. This has resulted in various decisive shifts – from how advertising is targeted to how media are purchased; from how pricing is set to how prospects are retargeted; from how product reviews are ordered to which hash tags are used. The emergence of new streams of revenue as well as new business models around big data in marketing has also heralded a vigorous debate about the best practices, opportunities, trade-offs, and the strategic implications of big data in marketing.

It is against this backdrop that this conference aimed to showcase current thought and stimulate discussions about the role, application, and relevance of Big Data in Marketing.

We received 25 papers in all from a mix of industry practitioners (16) and academicians (9). They have been organized under two themes viz. Analytical Methods and Application Areas of Marketing. The papers under the Application Area theme are about Integrated Marketing, Segmentation, Brand Management, Promotion, Pricing, Online Marketing, and Customer Relationship Marketing. The Analytical Methods theme contains papers on Modelling Techniques, Predictive Modelling, Sentiment Analysis and Data Management.

OPENING ADDRESS

BIG DATA AND ANALYTICS FOR MARKETING

Clifford Patrao
Director and Leader – Business Analytics & Strategy
IBM India/South Asia

KEY FORCES CHALLENGING MARKETERS

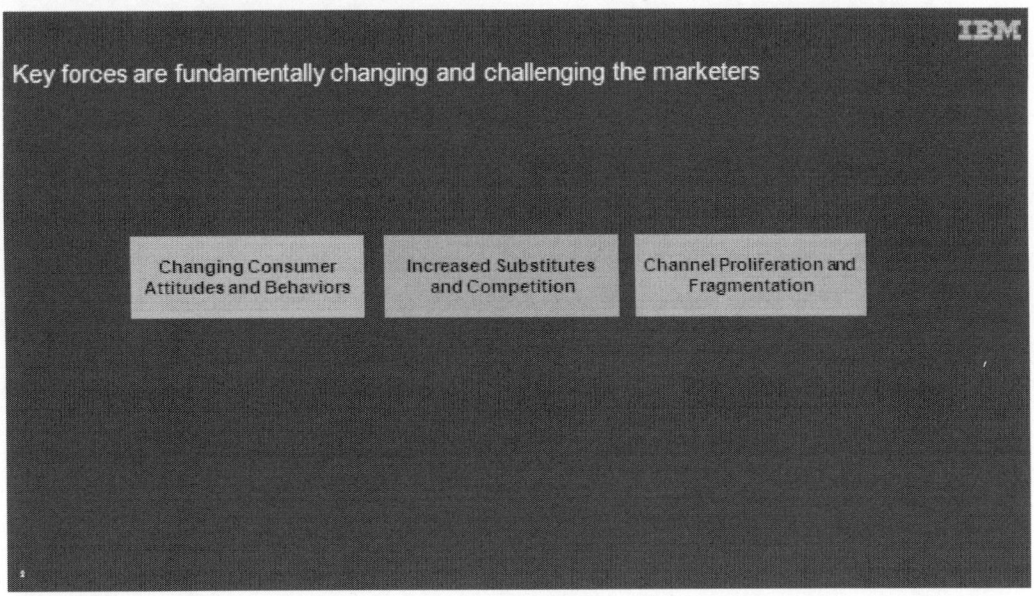

We, at IBM, do a study on consumer behaviour every alternate year in 12 countries, including India. This study is something that marketers need to watch out for because it looks at how consumer attitudes and behaviours are changing, which helps them decide what they need to do in their own spheres. We distilled the results of the study into three factors:

- Consumer attitiudes and behaviors are changing
- There is an increase in the number of substitutes and competition
- There is a proliferation of channels

Although this study is oriented towards consumer businesses, it can be extrapolated and applied to various degrees in other businesses as well.

Changing Consumer Attitudes and Behaviors

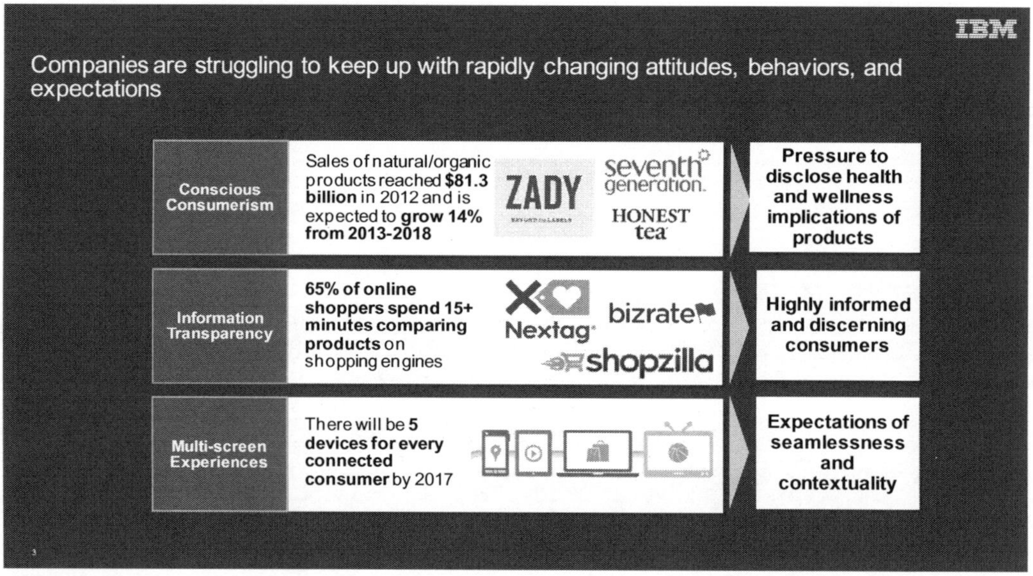

The changing consumer attitudes and behaviors can be attributed to the fact that consumers are getting a lot of information from various sources, not only from the company. In the earlier days, companies had a message and a medium (advertisement, promotions, etc) through which they communicated the brand values to the consumers. This was the only/ primary source through which consumers got to know about the company, the product, the brand, etc. However, now, consumers are no longer dependent on the company's communications. There are multiple sources through which they are becoming aware about what the product stands for, what the brand values are and so on. In a global CEO study we did about 4 years ago, we found a very strong consumer orientation towards sustainability. That is the first time we said that the company can do well while it does good. Now, consumers have started asking about the product, its origin, how it was made, etc, and this is becoming a very important factor for companies. If a product is perceived as having good values from a sustainability perspective, consumers are oriented towards the product. With the advent of apps that tell the consumer about the product, its composition, where and how it has been made, it has become easy for consumers to know more about the product.

There are various sites through which consumers can compare products to evaluate which one is better from a price perspective, features perspective and so on. This is becoming an increasingly important way of finding out about the product. Also, it is not only sequential. For example, a consumer walking into a retail store will actually be checking about the product on his mobile phone. So, consumers are now being able to assess the product on multi-channel, multi-device platforms.

Increased Number of Substitutes and Competition

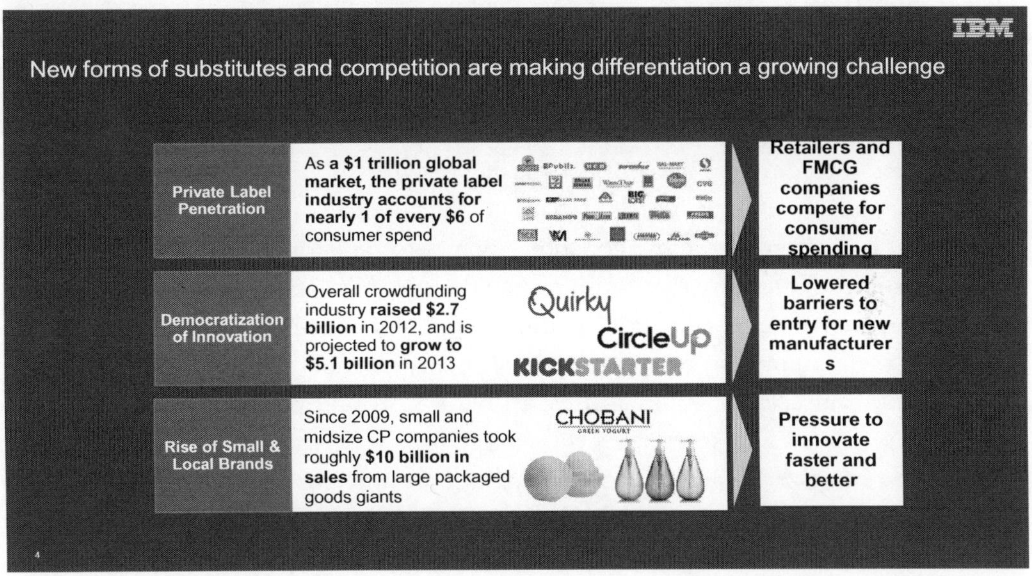

Earlier, if you were a large company you had the muscle power to spend money on marketing, research, etc. and that was an entry barrier for smaller companies. But now these barriers are disappearing. The availability of funding is increasing such that even the smaller companies have access to capital. Secondly, smaller companies have various avenues, like social media, through which they can reach out to people. Being a large company having muscle power is no longer an entry barrier for companies. Competitors need to keep this in mind as they are increasingly facing competition from companies they thought they could never compete with.

Channel Proliferation and Fragmentation

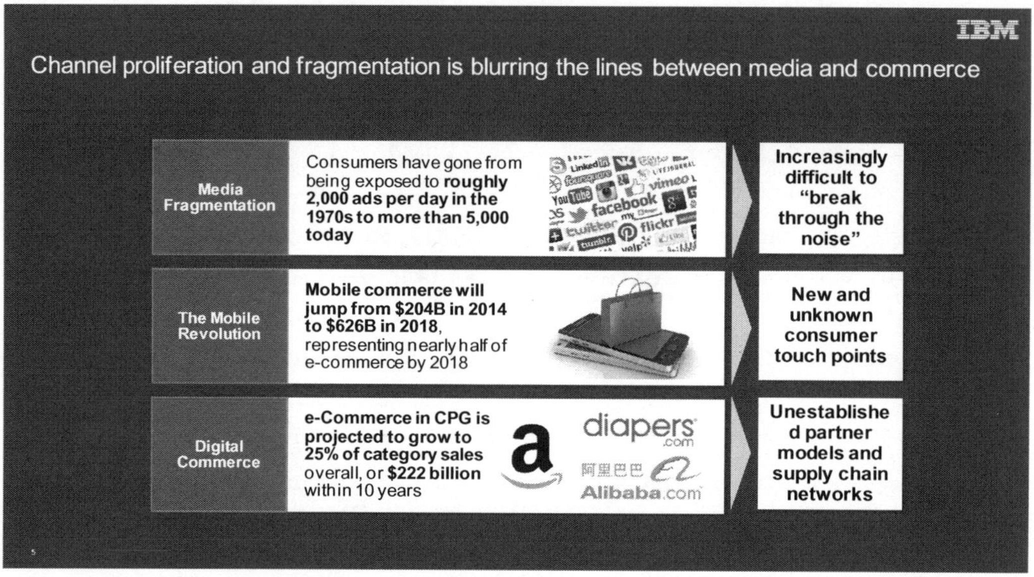

The third factor is the large number of channels that are proliferating now, the latest being e-commerce. As a marketer, with such a large number of channels and consumers alternating from channel to channel, you need to be able to reach out to the consumer where the consumer wants to be – a tablet, a store, a call centre. You also need to ensure that you provide the same experience across all channels. I had a personal experience regarding this when I had a problem with my refrigerator. I went to the manufacturer's website and wrote them an email saying that I have a problem and to please come and address it. I got a prompt response saying that your mail is appreciated and someone will respond within 3-4 days. I waited 4 months, but got no response. So here is a channel that consumers can come to but the experience is not the same. I then called up the call centre and someone came in in the next two days and addressed the problem. So, as the channel proliferation increases, you have to ensure that you have consistency in the message and the experience that you are giving across the channels as well.

We call India a mobile-only, not a mobile-first, country. This is because there is so much mobile penetration and most of the innovations happening are around the mobile front. With the impending increase in broadband hopefully in the next couple of years, we should see a lot more advances in this area. Thus, how to use the mobile as a device to connect with and respond to consumers is a key focus area going forward.

KEY FOCUS AREAS FOR MARKETERS

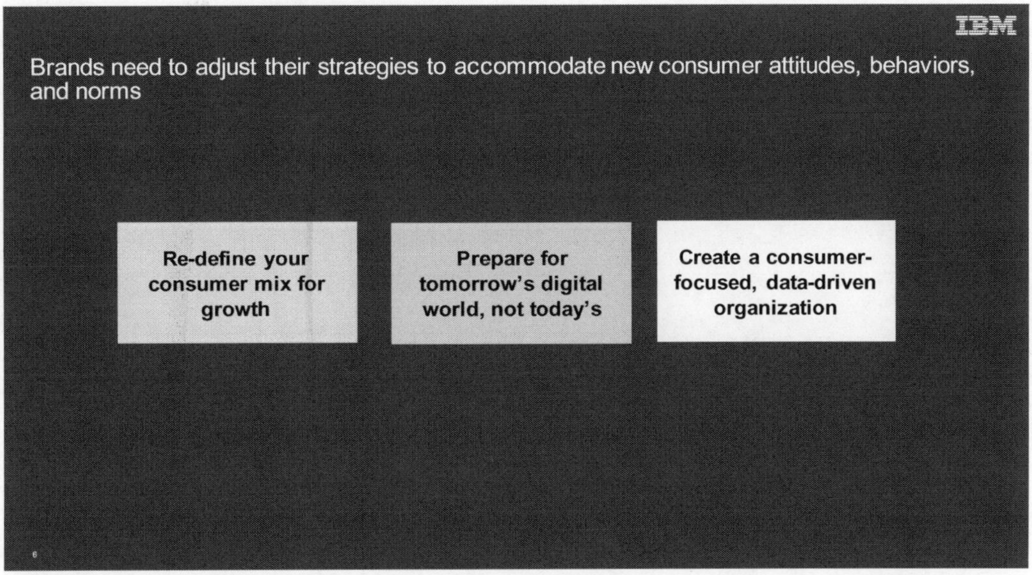

As a result of the study, the three areas that we felt that marketers should focus on are:

- Re-defining your consumer mix for growth
- Preparing for tomorrow's digital world, not today's
- Creating a consumer-focused, data-driven organization

First, have you really understood your changing consumers, not in a traditional sense through market research and segmentation, but from a digital perspective? There are certain consumers who like sharing information with brands and then there are consumers who avoid any digital presence with a brand. So, marketers need to understand such consumers and respond and engage with them in the digital world of tomorrow. The study says 'digital world of tomorrow' because even today marketers use the digital world to understand what the consumer sentiment is but what they really need to do is engage with consumers in the digital world, which is the digital world of tomorrow. For example, as of yesterday I received 100 emails in my personal inbox out of which I only read 5, which means 95% of the emails I receive are not relevant to me. But there is a lot more data available out there. My bank knows how much I earn, where I spend, how much I spend, where I invest, how much I invest, because I have a credit card. But is my bank using all this information to give me relevant contextual information offers? The answer is not yet. Another example is my telecom company which knows the kind of money I spend in communication, the kind of influence that I have, who I talk to, how often I talk, how many people connect in to me, where I go, what sites I see. But do I get information that is very relevant to me? The answer is not yet. These are areas where probably we will see advances as we go forward.

WANING BRAND LOYALTY

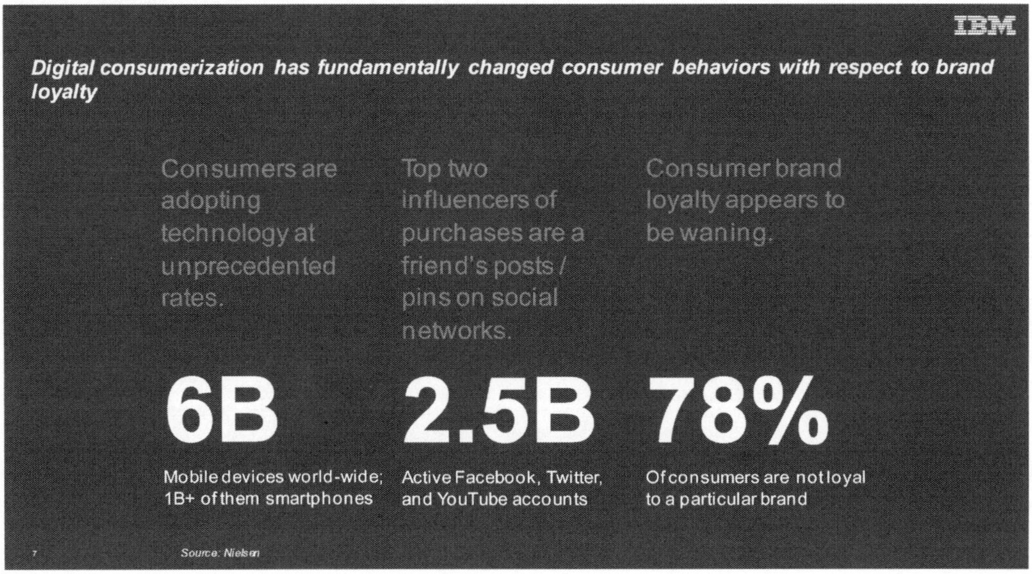

This digital consumerization has led to a couple of things mentioned above. One of them is brand loyalty which is seen to be coming down, 78% of consumers are not loyal to any particular brand. This poses a challenge for marketers about how to engage consumers and keep them loyal. Loyal in this world is not defined in the traditional way as a consumer who buys your product every now and then, but is a consumer who is ready to engage, communicate, share and get information with you as a brand. There is a little change in the definition of loyalty and if marketers can use that information to then engage with consumers, we have a winner.

THREE IS : INSTRUMENTED, INTERCONNECTED, INTELLIGENT

About a decade ago, we at IBM spoke about the smarter planet, defined by the three Is: Instrumented, Interconnected and Intelligent. When the ads came out, many of us in India thought this to be a little too futuristic as the direction seems to be good but one doesn't really know when these things will come to us. But over the last couple of years, organizations have pushed boundaries and the three Is. With the internet of things coming in we see a lot more instrumentation happening. For example, my car manufacturer knows how much and how I am driving. The experiments that are happening in India with automotive manufacturers relate to getting a lot of information about driving, driving capabilities and preferences.

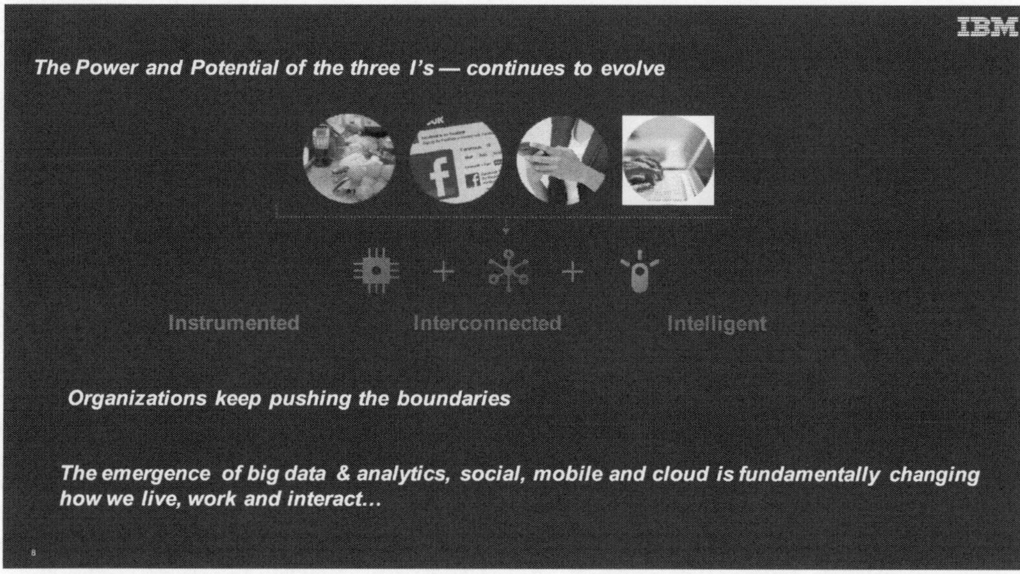

Today, when you go to a bank to carry out a simple transaction like putting your ATM card in the machine, withdrawing money and coming out, you sometimes see a static marketing message on a screen in the ATM. We at IBM are working with one of the banks in India, the bank wants to personalize this message according to the profile and behavior of the consumer so that it is relevant to the consumer. We are seeing that in India, brands want to give out a contextual message at every touch point that the consumer is engaging with the brand. Again in the telecom area, service providers have information about where you are, if you're entering a mall then they can use location based information to give offers that are relevant to you.

CHANGING ROLE OF THE CMO

This is all changing the role of the CMO and the marketer. This is again drawn from one of the studies we did which said that the role of marketers is changing from knowing the customer to actually creating a segment of one customer i.e. treating each and every consumer as an individual and therefore being able to send contextual messages to each of them. The second point is about using all the information you have about the consumers to engage with them. When a consumer receives messages that are relevant to him/her the consumer starts to feel that you are different from others. The third point is about communicating the brand message. Earlier the brand message was communicated assuming everyone is seeing that message, but now that message should be felt and experienced across various touch points with the consumer, and to do this the company's culture really needs to become one with the brand. Looking at these three imperatives for a CMO, it is evident that big data plays a significant role in all of them. Because combining customer data along with social media interaction and behavior data along with call centre data will enable marketers to understand their consumers better.

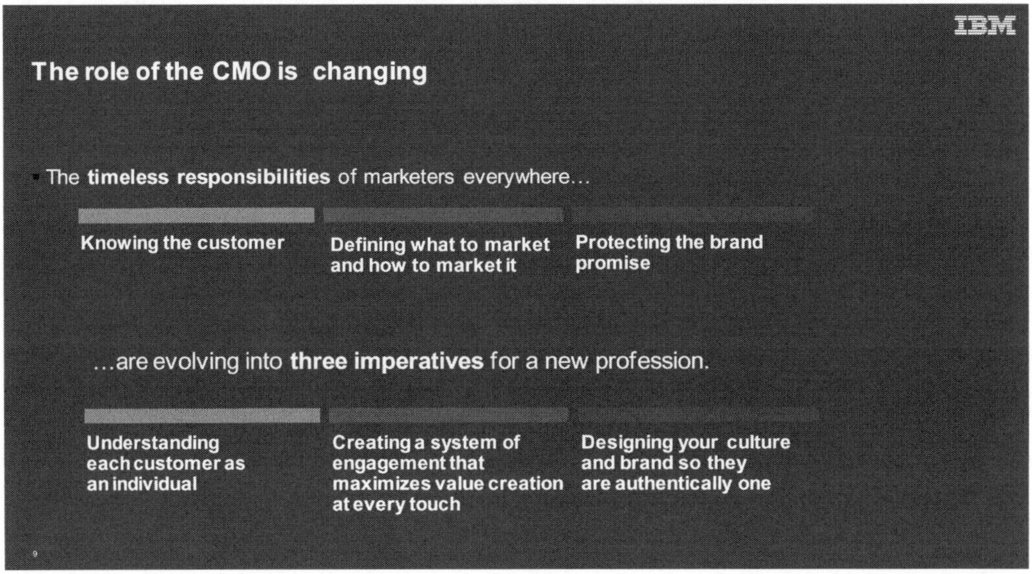

We were working with an FMCG company in India and the challenge that they face, ironically, is that they don't understand the consumer very well. Being a fast moving consumer goods company, they know their distributors and dealers very well but not their consumers, which they have realized is a severe disadvantage. They are now trying to understand who their consumer is and in doing so they are trying to create an online presence and an engagement platform, for example Coke. Now consumer companies in India are also trying to know their consumers better but they are late as the e-commerce and e-tail companies understand the consumers much better.

CHANGE FOR COMPANIES

What is really changing for companies in terms of big data? Data is available in plenty but the real question is: are marketers able to use that information to create a competitive advantage of knowing their customers much better than their competitors? Secondly, decision making was centralized earlier but now data is not

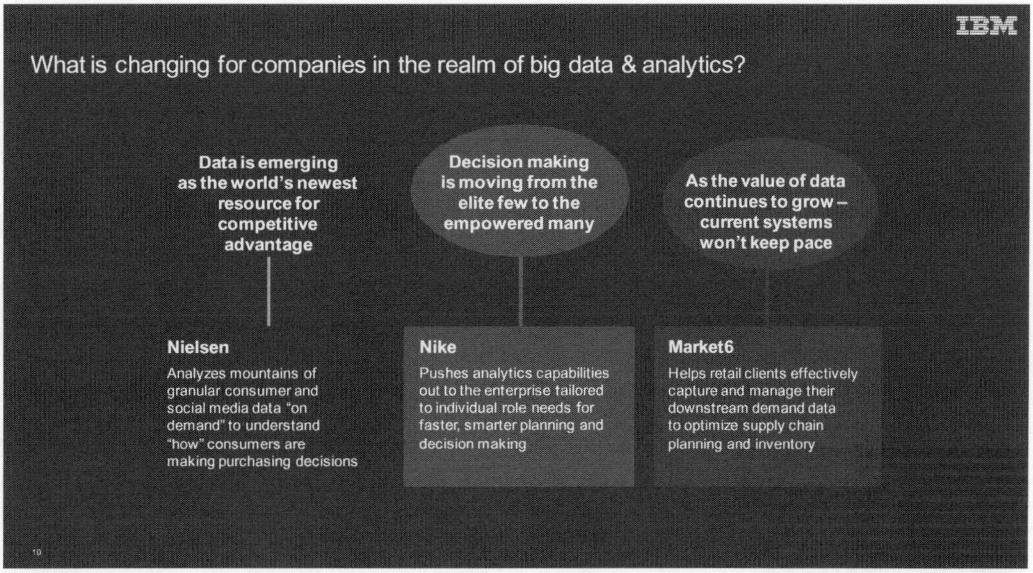

available only for a few. Now as a culture, organizations can have decision making which is spread out across the organization since information can now go out to people who can take the decision in real-time. Thirdly, there is a lot of data available and companies have not really used this data to streamline their business operations. For example, when we used supply chain engagements with clients, we used to work on sales and operations planning cycles which were about a month long. With the demand information or demand forecast you can decide what and where to produce and what and from whom to order, which is a monthly cycle. Now, you get demand data real-time every hour because of the online presence. But is this information being used to change the way you work? Many companies are not using this daily demand information. So, having got this data to make decisions is a huge area of advantages that companies can explore.

PARADIGM SHIFTS ENABLED BY BIG DATA AND ANALYTICS

Leverage More Data

With the advent of big data analytics, the things that we have done in the past need to differ from the way in which we will do things and a few paradigms have to change. I still see companies practicing the traditional ways of doing things although they have entered a new era. Companies have a lot of data but are they leveraging it? In the world of big data analytics, you can leverage more data as opposed to small segments of the data.

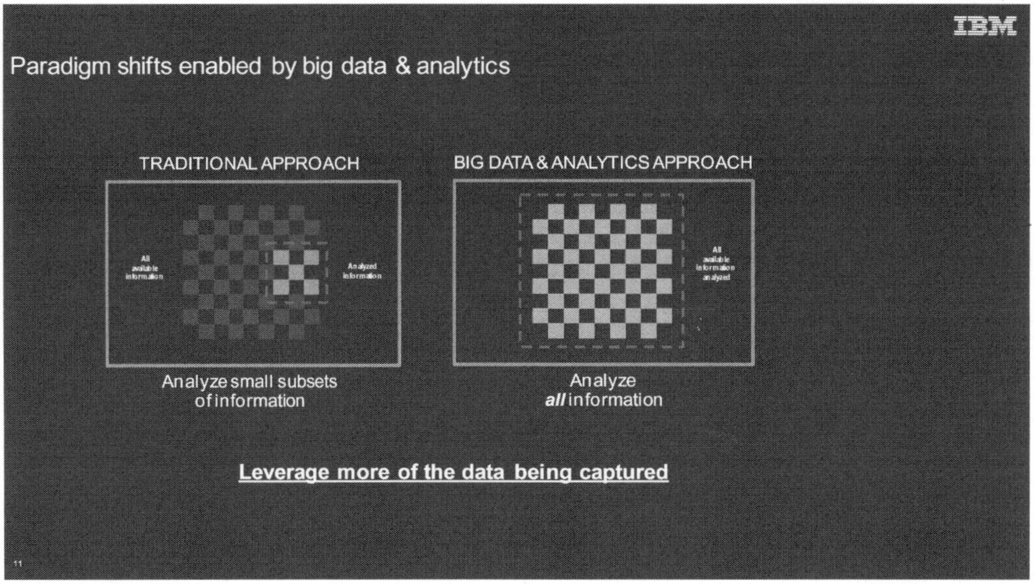

Reduce Effort Required to Leverage Data

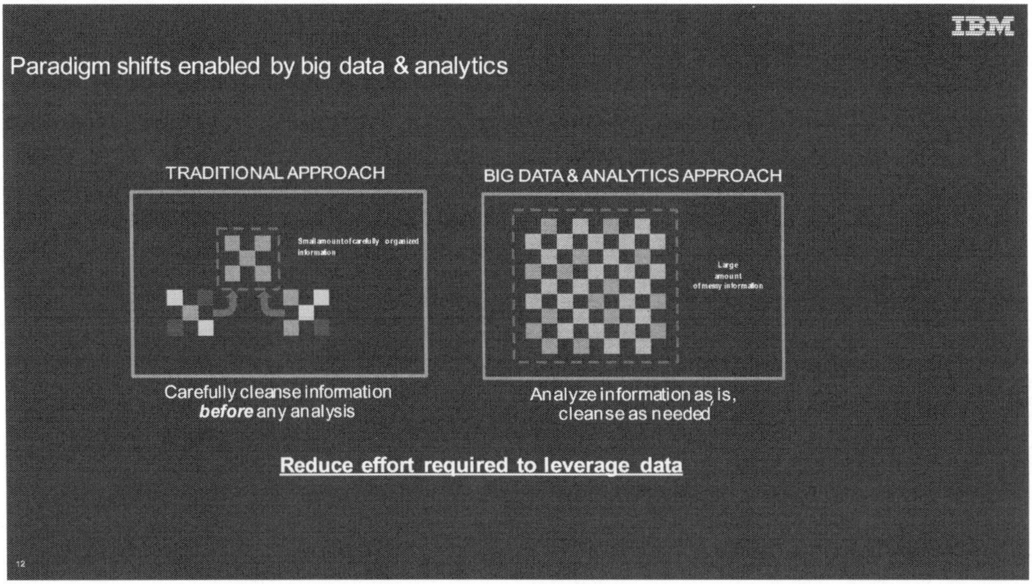

Also, you don't need the data to be clean since big data analytics deals with data which is structured or unstructured, in various formats like text, video or voice. Therefore, you don't really need to wait for a process in which you are cleaning the information, getting into a data mart and then using it.

Data Leads the Way

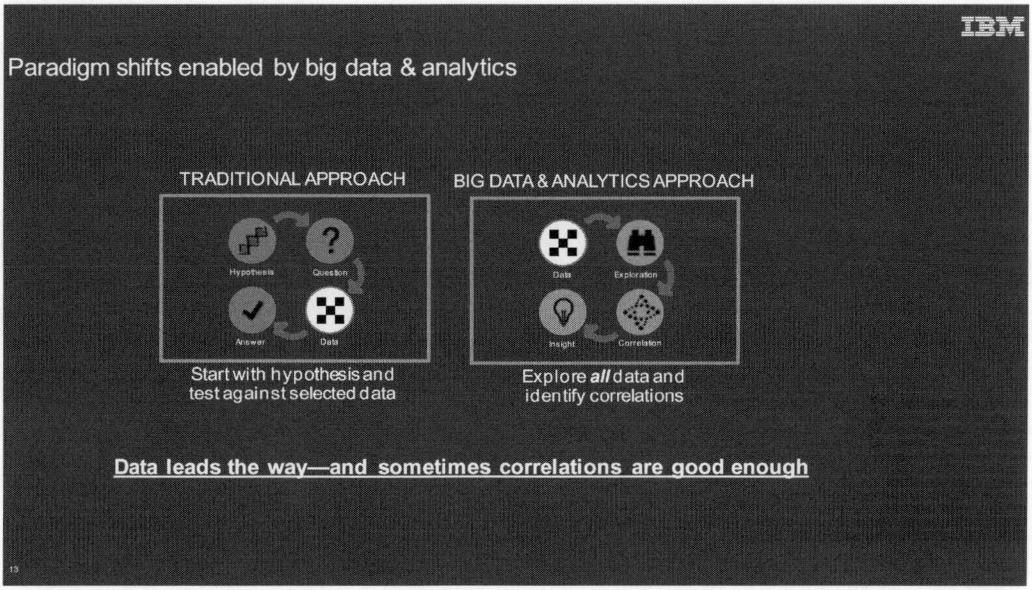

In the traditional approach, in order to understand what to analyze, you first had a hypothesis according to which you collected and examined the data and found out whether the hypothesis is true or not. But in the world of big data, that is not necessary. You can put all the data together and see what it gives out. IBM is working with one of the life insurance companies where they engage with the customer once a year because of the annual premium payment. The challenge they face is that about 30-50% of the policies lapse wherein people pay the first year and don't pay after that and the company needs to understand how they can identify such people, their propensity to lapse and contact those customers and prevent this from happening. This company needs to put together the information they have about the consumer, the kind of policies they already have, etc and see what correlation throws up. Then the company can start targeting customers according to this correlation through their marketing campaigns in terms of renewals, etc.

Leverage Data as it is Captured

Big data analytics is completely on real-time and there is no lag between the data being available. You're wasting time if you wait for all the data to be available, analyze the data and then take action. Now, action is warranted real-time and big data helps in a large way to get real-time information out there.

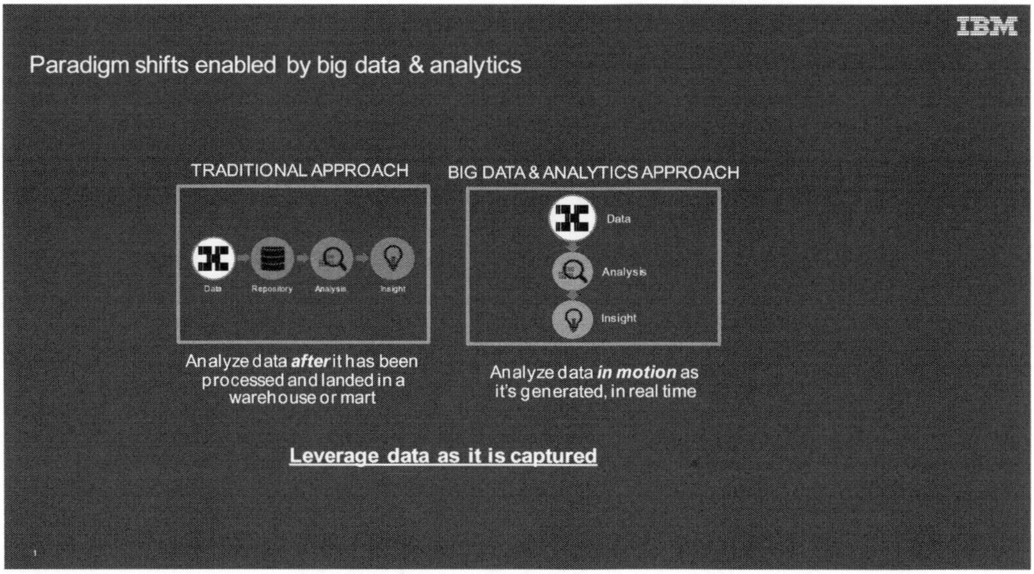

Predict and Decide the Best Course of Action

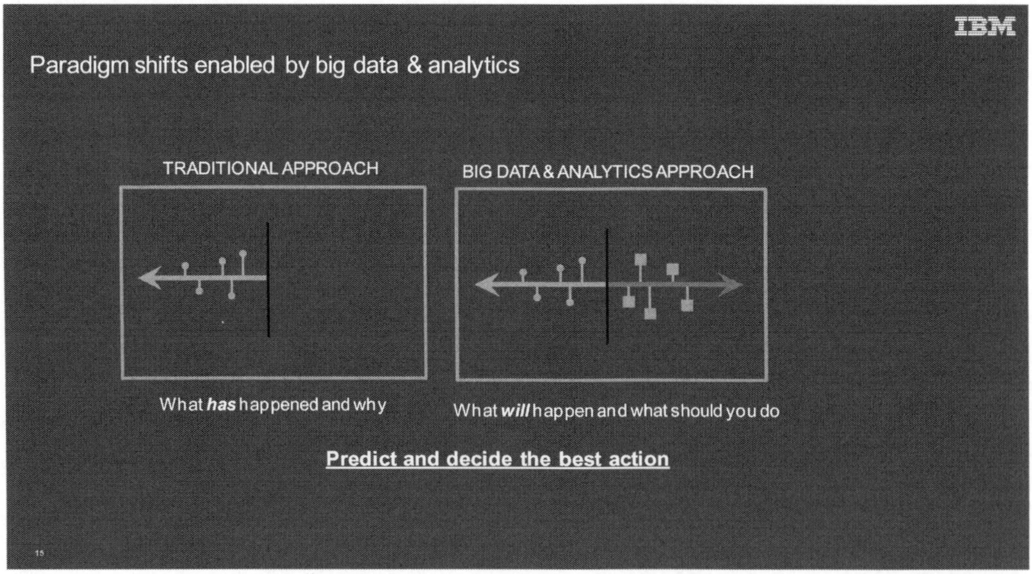

It is not only essential to understand what has happened, it is also essential to be able to predict what you should do. There are predictive models available that tell you if this was happening in the past then this is what you could do. We at IBM are working with a pharmaceutical company. The customers of pharmaceutical companies are doctors. Doctors spend very little time with medical reps, two minutes on an average. In those two minutes the medical rep rattles off whatever he has to and the doctor picks up whatever he has to. So we need to figure out what is the best way to engage a doctor: seminar, medical rep, mobile app, email, etc by seeing what the propensity of different doctors who respond to these is. This is where we are using predictive modeling and deciding the best action.

Intuitive Analytics for Everyone

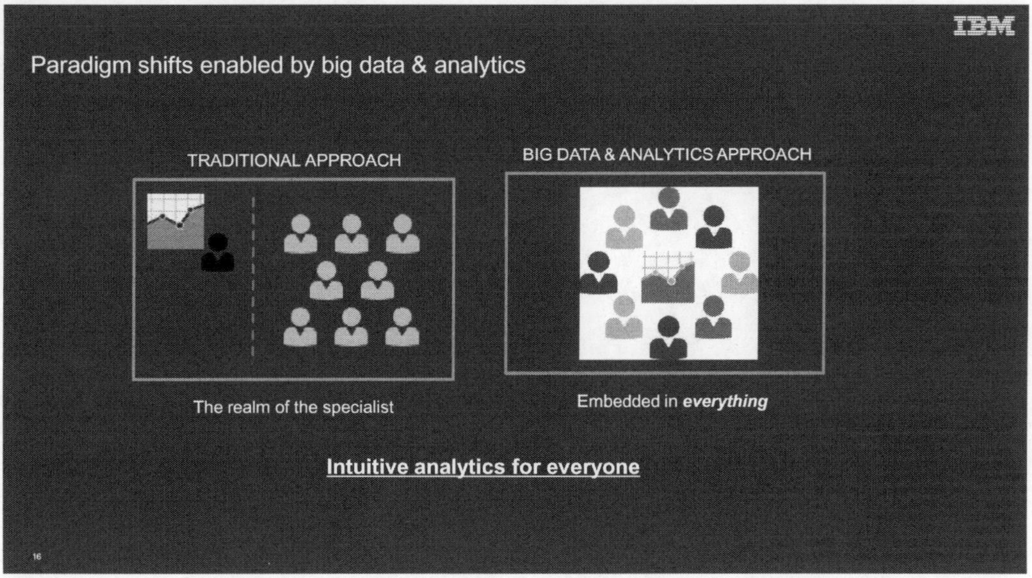

Big data analytics is for everyone and is not only limited to certain people. This makes it more widespread and thus builds a culture where the organization is data dependent and data oriented. You can use this information, embed it in everything and see how it works, which the traditional way did not allow you to do.

Cognitive Computing

Cognitive computing is an area which is very dear to IBM and we have been using Watson for it. In Asia Pacific for example we are working with Watson in banking to help them with using information, in system learning and recommending what you should do with a wealth advisor. In the US, Watson is being used a lot in health care where the number of journals published is so large that the doctors really can't keep abreast with them. If all this information is fed into a super computer and the super computer learns all of this it is likely to diagnose that there is a problem earlier than a doctor. Watson is now being used in the US, albeit on a scale of pilots, on experiments on what we can do. This is the way forward where you get a lot of information; get it into a system which learns it as the information comes and predicts what happens.

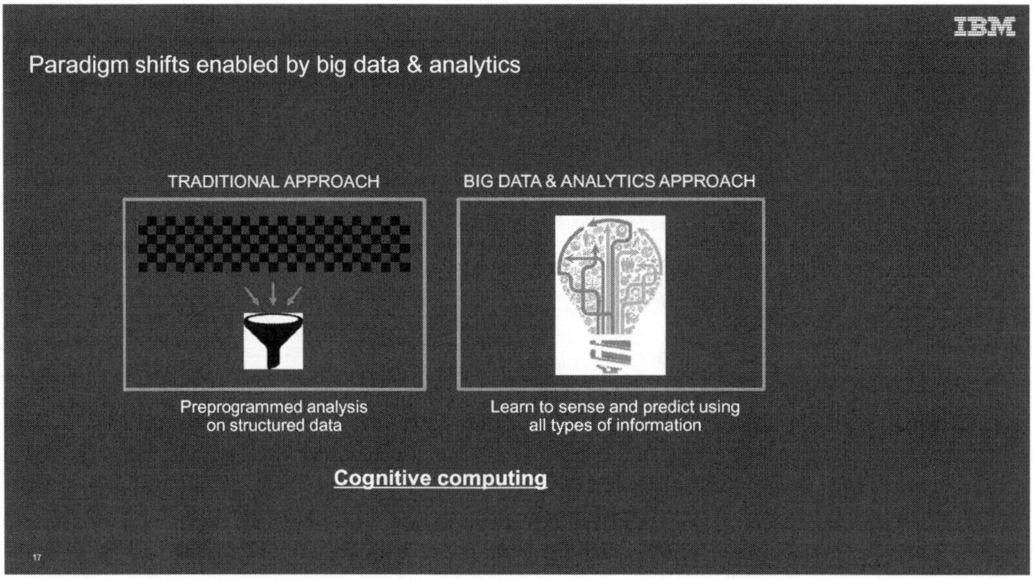

Analytics as and When it is Needed

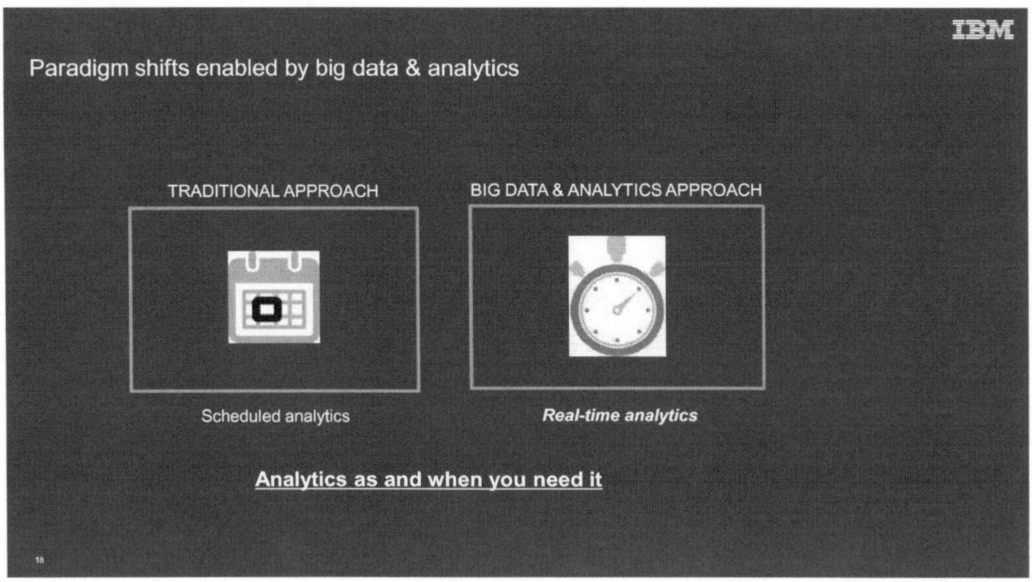

The paradigm shifts that are happening require a shift in the way in which organizations are used to taking decisions as well. The data and the technology to use this data to get insights is there, but in order to use that it is critical for organizations to change the way they take decisions and respond.

BIG DATA IN MARKETING – LEADERS FROM LAGGARDS

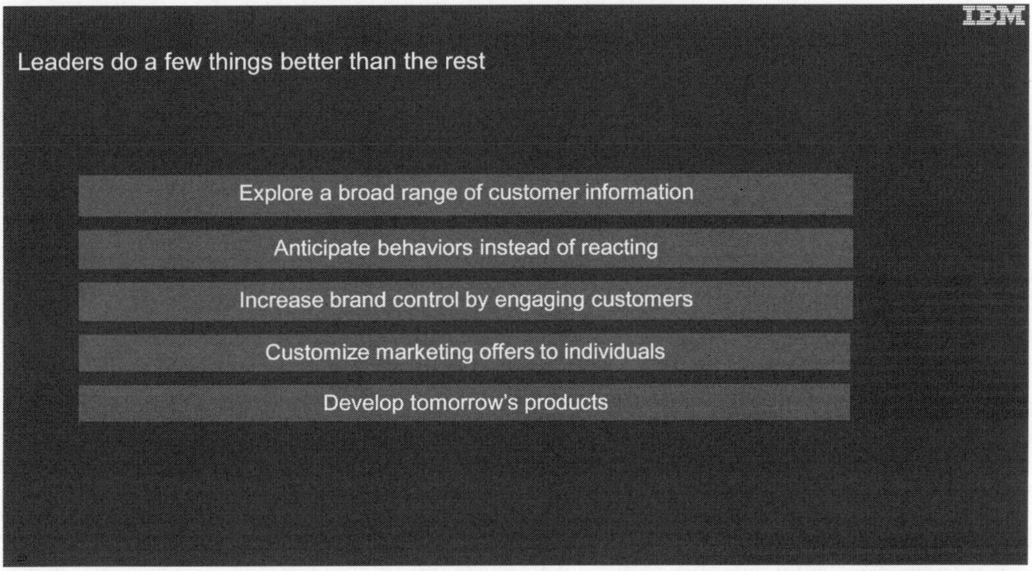

Below is a list of characteristics that separate leaders from laggards with a specific focus on big data and marketing:

- Leaders look at a wider range of information as compared to the laggards. This information is obtained through the use of social media, blogs, understanding consumer behavior by their online presence, click stream analysis and so on. Using a wide range of information to capture consumers is likely to give marketers a better insight on the consumers.
- As a marketer, when you try to address consumers you want to anticipate their response by taking steps before they actually react. Leaders try to predict that they will get a certain response from their consumer who has a particular type of behavior and then leverage on that. This is possible only if you understand the consumer at such a deep level that you can take these decisions.
- Social media is a double-edged sword; you can use it for getting things to go viral which can impact and damage the brand very quickly. But it can also be used to engage with consumers and understand from them. One of our FMCG clients was launching a product and wanted to understand what the sentiment on that product is. The moment they launched the product they started understanding the sentiment, the buzz, the kind of noise it was creating, what people were saying

about it and they were able to tweak their marketing message accordingly. Thus sensing what the buzz is, on the go they were able to create a very successful launch of the product.

- Similarly, it is important to create offers which are relevant to an individual. We work with one of the banks in India that runs a large number of campaigns flooding their consumer base with various offers that keep coming in. One of the problems they face is that the response rate is very low. What they needed to do is decide what offer they are going to send to a consumer based on how he has responded to previous offers. We started working on a mechanism in which if the consumer doesn't respond to an offer, the bank does not flood him with 10 more. Thus, companies and consumers are both moving in a direction where they are trying to interact on an individual basis.
- A lot of product ideas could come from satisfied consumers, and marketers need to ensure that they are able to tap that and use it internally as well. This requires collaboration between various functions of an organization.

CONSUMERS' COMFORT WITH SHARING PERSONAL INFORMATION

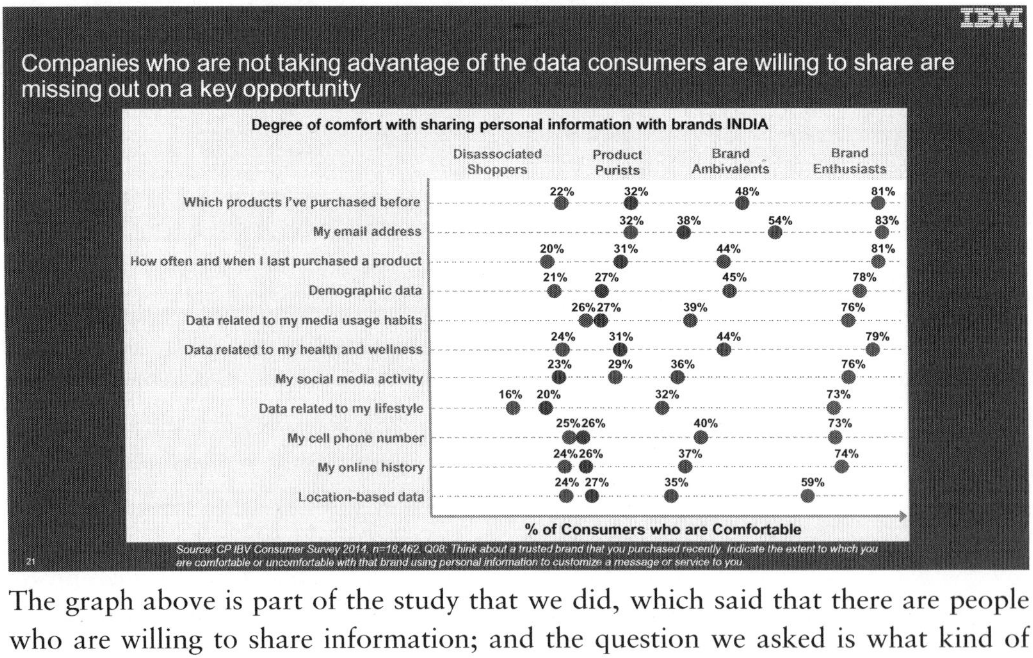

The graph above is part of the study that we did, which said that there are people who are willing to share information; and the question we asked is what kind of information they are willing to share. The brand enthusiasts comprise one fourth of the population, the brand ambivalents about one third of the population and the product purists about one-third of the population. This clustering was done based on the analysis of various factors that we did. As the name suggests the brand enthusiasts are the ones who really want to engage with the brand. And the other extreme is the dissatisfied shopper who does not want to engage with the brand. Consumers are willing to share a lot of information with products and brands that they trust. Companies that are not taking advantage of this are going to lose out; they are not going to be able to make decisions based on all the information available.

TYPICAL BARRIERS FACED

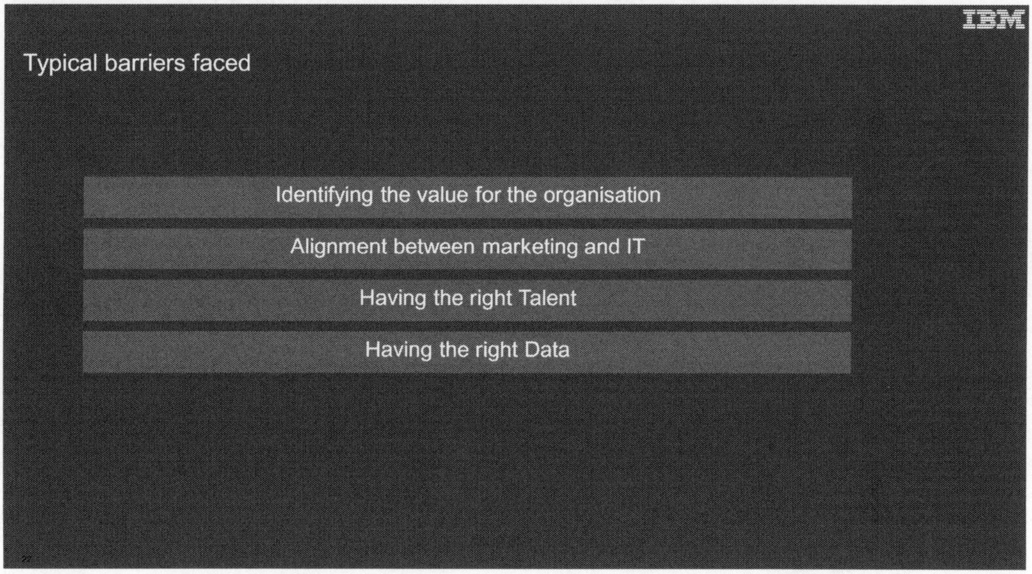

Some of the challenges and practical issues we face when we meet clients are listed below:

- There are some companies that don't know if big data analytics is of any value to their organization. In India, there are companies that say they haven't found the perfect use case to use big data for marketing. This challenge is not from the marketer alone, it is also from convincing the rest of the organization.
- The second challenge is how an organization aligns the marketing and IT functions because a lot of marketers don't understand technology. Although big data is seen as a domain of IT, it doesn't really need you to understand technology.
- Organizations are so tied up in what they are doing today that they really don't have the wherewithal to focus on talent. Again with big data they don't need to really have everything since there are collaborative models they can work with.

- A lot of organizations want to know if having the right data is important and if garbage in and garbage out still holds true in the big data scenario. Companies have started appointing CDOs, Chief Data Officers, whose role is to think about what data they have and leveraging it, what data they need which they probably don't have today. Coming back to the pharmaceutical industry example in India, we don't have information about which doctor prescribes what medicine to a consumer, unlike the developed markets where this information is available. Here, companies go to the chemist and probably do a retail audit to see the doctors' prescriptions. The question is if companies don't have the data, then what are the ways in which they can get the data?

BIG DATA AND ANALYTICS FOR EXTRAORDINARY MARKETING – A FEW EXAMPLES

Micro-Market Campaign Management

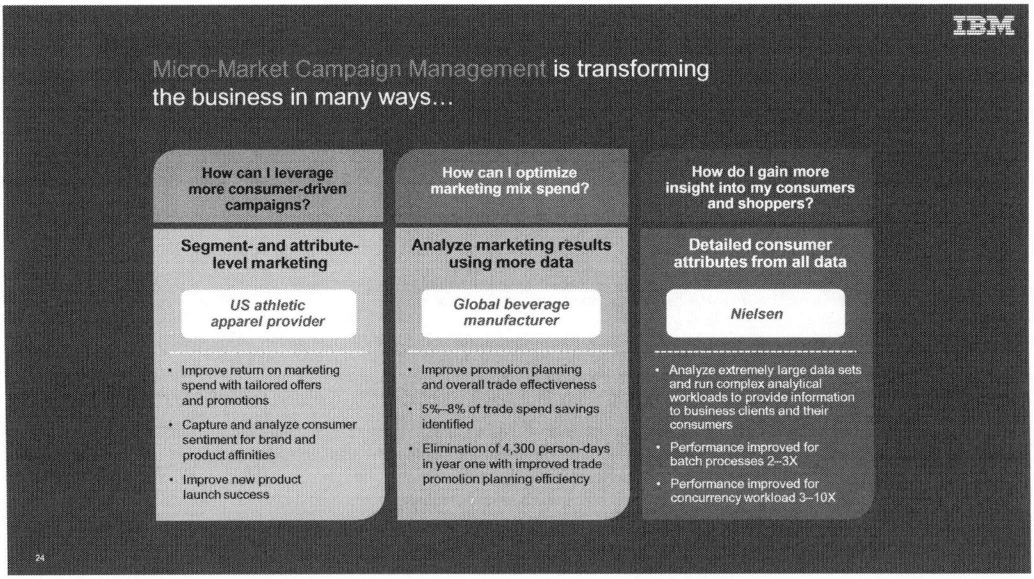

One of the biggest uses of big data analytics is the ability to micro-segment and give offers to the consumer accordingly. We at IBM have gone to the extreme of saying micro-segment of one, but even if it is not a segment of one, you can give relevant offers to the consumer through big data. India is picking up on this, especially companies from the banking and telecom industries, since they have a lot of consumer data and are trying to leverage that.

Optimized Promotion Effectiveness

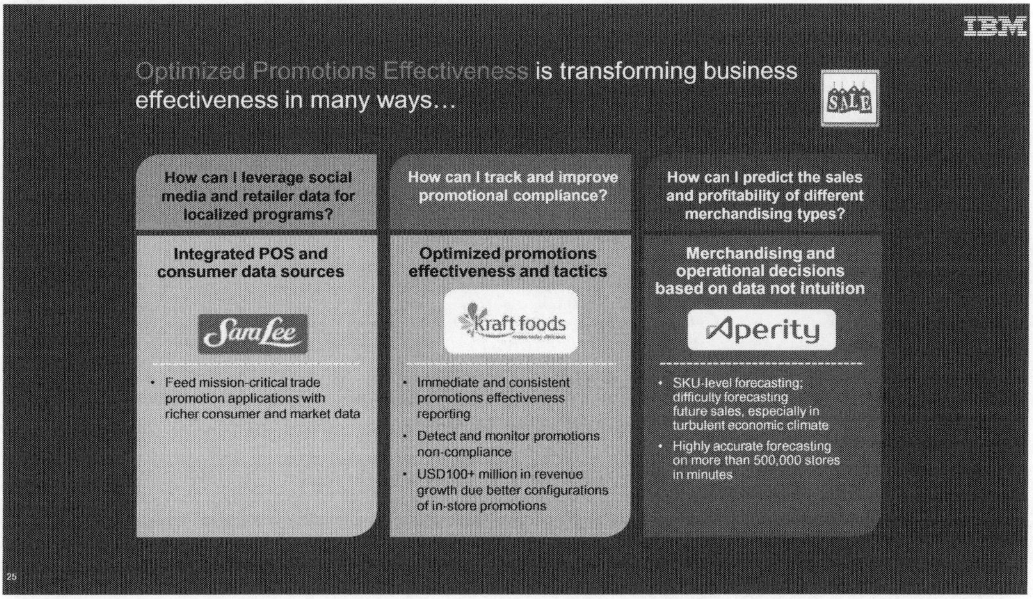

The second example is about promotions, checking the effectiveness of promotions and the marketing mix. A few years back, digital data started becoming relevant in India and marketers realized that they need to start using digital channels for marketing in addition to the other channels. They needed to then decide how to change their marketing mix, how much to spend on digital, how to calculate the ROI on digital spends. In one of the case studies of this conference, a retail company started using local information like the local buzz, local sentiment, and local discussions to understand what products they should stock in the store. They analyzed social media data to figure out what is being spoken about to start populating the required SKUs in the local stores.

Real-Time Demand Forecast

Real-time demand forecast is an area that Indian companies have not leveraged. Companies have information about demand and they can use this information to ensure they don't have a stock-out. This is will ensure right inventory planning and can be used for downstream planning as well. This area has a lot of potential but we haven't seen much movement in this area.

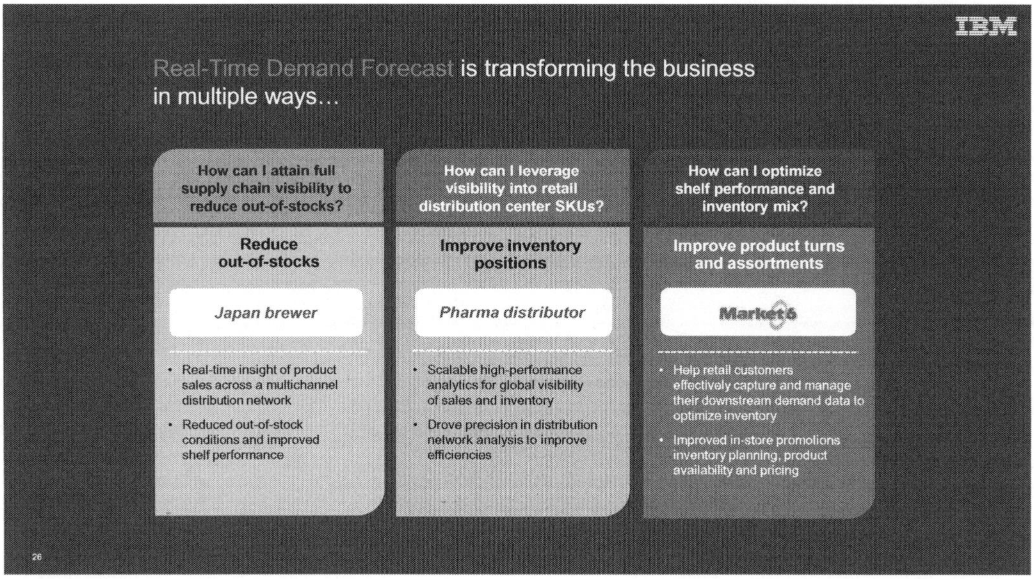

PATH TO SUCCESS WITH BIG DATA AND ANALYTICS IN MARKETING

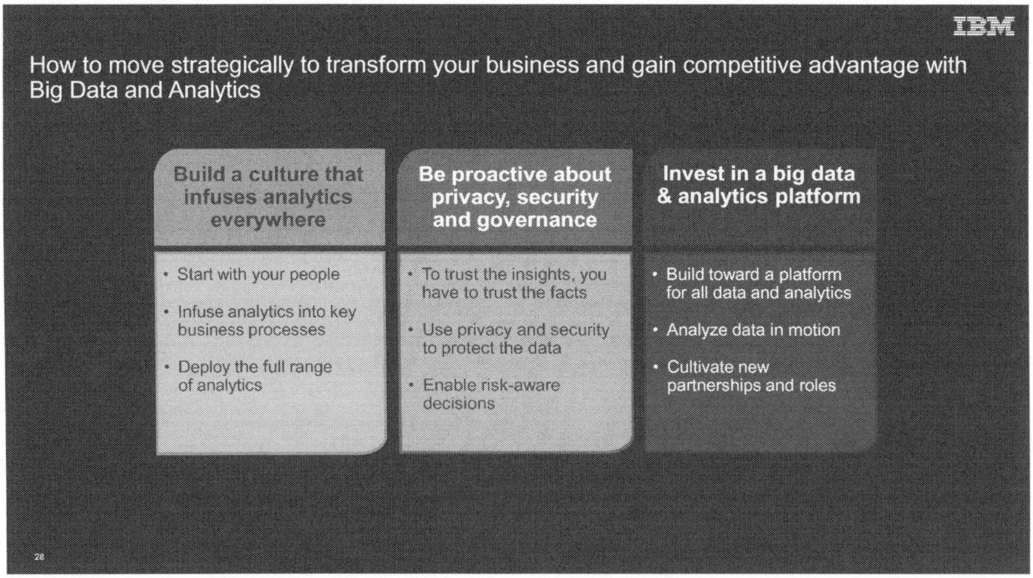

The path to success with big data analytics in marketing

- Building a culture of using analytics in all functions. Companies that are not even using the data that they have today can start looking at using it and eventually enriching it.

- Privacy and security are the biggest concerns with respect to big data. As we saw in the previous chart, consumers are willing to share information with brands that they trust. When relationship managers leave one bank and go to the other, they have all the information about customers of the previous bank. This is a huge concern and customers will start logging out of a company that does not respect their privacy. Our CMO was presenting a study in the US where he raised a case study of a retail company that gave some coupons to a consumer saying we know you are pregnant and you will need these but that consumer hadn't told anyone that she was pregnant.
- Two years ago there was a question if big data is just a buzz word but today, no one questions the relevance of big data any longer. It is not a buzz word and it is important for organizations create the right platform where they can use information that will enable them in taking decisions.

The biggest change in marketing is going to come from the way companies are using data to tailor and communicate their messages to customers. Companies now have the data and the technology to do this, it is only the ability of the organization to leverage this to make the right decisions which is preventing this.

PART ONE

APPLICATION AREA

PART
ONE-A

INTEGRATED MARKETING

Measuring ROI on marketing spends has always plagued marketing managers. However, technological progress has led to the development of ROI measurement techniques in the decision science space. Another challenge is that of the lack of integration; strategies are myopic and silo-like. The paper, "Long Term and Short Term Impact of Marketing Drivers (Integrated Marketing ROI)" presents a ROI framework built on a time series regression model on nested Key Performance Indiactors (KPIs) which accommodates all KPIs and the inter-dependence between them. The methodology provides an integrated view of data sources to generate business insights on lead indicators and forecast business results in different scenarios within an integrated system.

In the paper "Turn Big Data into Big Ideas – Panasonic" an exhaustive environment analysis of the consumer electronic industry and an internal analysis of Panasonic's marketing strategy and implementation is done. Panasonic's brand equity is also qualitatively evaluated through brand reach, brand power and brand attitude association.

The paper "Big Data Analytics for Marketing" looks at how unstructured big data that are not traditionally analyzed can be used effectively for deriving business insights – specifically for the Sales and Marketing function in the telecom industry. It discusses how to build a 360 degree view of a customer through the traditional internal data sources as well as external, unstructured or semi-structured data sources which can be synthesized together to get a comprehensive, multi-faceted, "derived view" of a customer. The paper also discusses more use cases such as Precise Marketing, Location Monetization, Churn Identification, Prediction and Prevention.

CHAPTER ONE

BIG DATA ANALYTICS FOR MARKETING

Anthony Thomas and Satish Mittal

INTRODUCTION

The term "big data" is slightly a misnomer – as if it suggests the data that we analyzed so far are small (it isn't) or that it only takes on the challenge posed by sheer volume (in fact, volume is just one of the challenges). Traditionally, organizations have utilized structured data arising out of transactions in various business functions like sales, marketing, billing, finance, supply chain, etc., to support business decision making. We have so far ignored huge volumes of unstructured data e.g. information coming from business partners, customer surveys, interaction with call center agents, emails, real-time events, weblogs and social media – this is big data which accounts for more than 80% of all enterprise data for an organization.

The present paper will examine why it is high time that organizations should start using big data for meaningful insights – we shall investigate deeper in the Sales and Marketing domain of the Telecom Industry. We shall highlight the type of (big) data that are largely not analyzed so far and how they can add additional insights through use cases. The Figure 1 illustrates how big data has evolved over time.

Clearly Volume, Variety and Velocity are three necessary characterizations for big data – in real life, any of their combination can lead to big data scenario. A host of innovations, combined with affordable high-capacity processing power, have made it feasible to sift through Big Data and unify it with other more standard enterprise data. Before moving on to the use case, let us examine why it is becoming increasingly hard for organizations to ignore this wealth of information called big data.

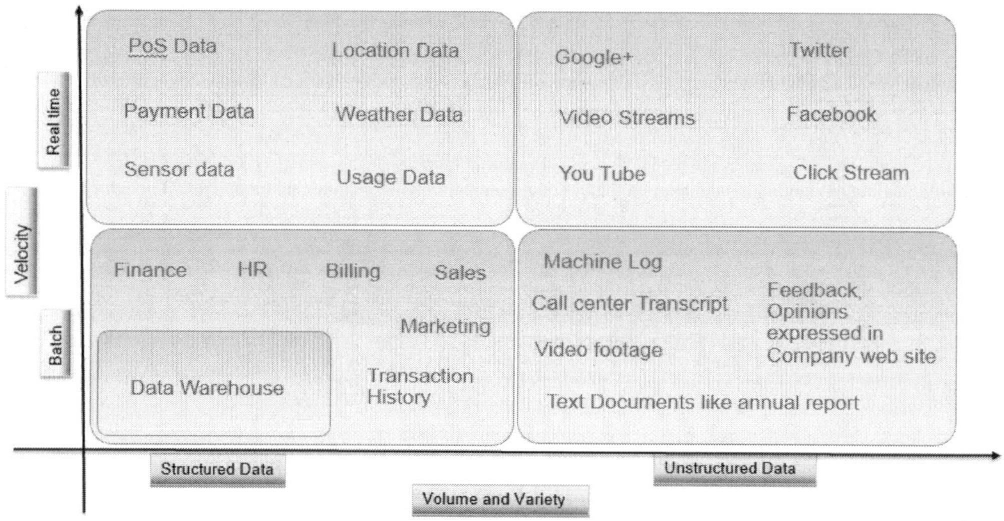

Fig. 1

WHY BIG DATA IS BECOMING SO IMPORTANT

Data Deluge

The Internet has changed the way we communicate and consume services. The explosion of data is driven by customer demand for more low-latency services which are interactive, integrated and audio/video intensive. To add to this, the world has seen unprecedented innovation in the area of Devices, Network and related Equipment in the last few years. Smartphones, mobile broadband, social media interactions, video-based services have all contributed to the data deluge. Smartphones (e.g. Apple iPhone, Android OS based devices, Samsung Galaxy, etc.) and other mobile devices (tablets) have vastly improved the web surfing experience and the same has raised expectation from a mobile device. This has resulted in increased consumption of media and content-based services leading to bandwidth consumption.

Given the massive global growth of the Internet and its increasing importance, it has become an inescapable tool for service and consumer companies. Figure 2 shows emerging types of data and new age business expectations which are changing the modern day data architecture.

Few companies can ignore the ubiquity of the Internet especially for two reasons. First, it has become a cost effective channel for companies to interact with customers.

It provides a platform where companies can link with customers and prospects build brand and sell their products.

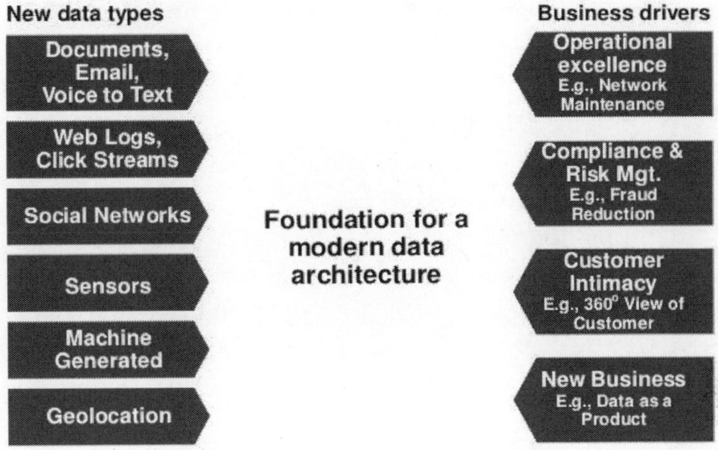

Fig. 2

Secondly, Internet is a gold mine for extracting customer intelligence. A person's daily Internet journey can reveal their interests, communications and the purchases they make. Just to substantiate the fact, internet usage has increased from an average of 5.2 hours a week in 2001 to 19.6 hours in 2012 in USA.

Key Numbers

A few numbers are quoted below to highlight the growth of Internet coverage and its usage:

- Internet Penetration
  - 25% of the global population is on the internet – roughly 2 billion internet users
  - Internet penetration in China is expected to increase from 42% in 2012 to 52% in 2016
  - According to Sky TV, about 80 percent of its video content is consumed over Wi-Fi networks
- Data Volume
  - 5 Exabyte every 10 minutes in 2013
  - 20 billion RFID tags
  - 5 Petabytes of location data every 100 days for a large CSP
  - 30+ Petabytes of user generated data in Facebook
  - Data network traffic from smartphones will multiply 50 times by 2016

  - A European operator claims its data traffic is getting doubled every 6 to 8 months
  - Volume of data doubles every 18 months
- Data Velocity
  - Mobile data growth compounded 78%, projected to 10.8 Exabyte per month in 2016
  - Online advertisement bidding process in 80 milliseconds
  - 250 billion emails/day
  - 200 million tweets/day
  - 100 billion Google searches/month
  - 1 hour of video uploaded at YouTube/second
- Data Variety
  - Structured, unstructured text, voice, video, RFID tags, maps, seismic data, medical events
  - Call center conversations and chat sessions in many languages
- Usage in Sales and Marketing
  - 70% of Internet users use Internet search as their primary source of information
  - 64% of Internet users rely on online recommendations when buying as if everyone is an influencer
  - 57% of organizations are more likely to adopt social tools in next couple of years

Approach towards Analytics is Changing

As the nature of data is changing, new horizons for analytics are also opening up. The following table is a snapshot of how Big Data Analytics has changed the paradigm of legacy analytics.

Table 1

Storage Cost	High	Low
Analytics	Offline	Real-time
Data Loading Speed	Low	High
Data Loading Time	Long	Average 50%-60% faster
Data Discovery	Minimal	Critical
Data Variety	Structured	Unstructured
Volume	Gigabyte, Terabyte	Petabyte, Exabyte, Zettabyte
Velocity	Batch	Real-time
Administration Time	Long	Average 60% faster

Category	*Legacy Analytics*	*Big Data Analytics*
Complex Query Response Time	Hours/days	Minutes
Data Compression Technique	Not matured	Average 40-60% more data compression
Support Cost	High	Low

Finally, we need to remember that the ultimate goal of big data is to combine "big" and "existing" data from all possible information sources to produce a holistic, transparent, all-encompassing view of a customer or household based on all their interactions with the organization and socially.

Exploring its Relevance in the Telecom Industry

Buyer's Market

The Telecommunication Industry is currently experiencing severe competition where the margin of error is very small. In certain countries there are so many telecom options that 78%/87% straightaway avoid a Communication Service Provider (CSP) for poor experience based on hearsay, whereas 73%/85% share poor experiences with friends and family in mature and emerging markets respectively, as shown in Fig. 3.

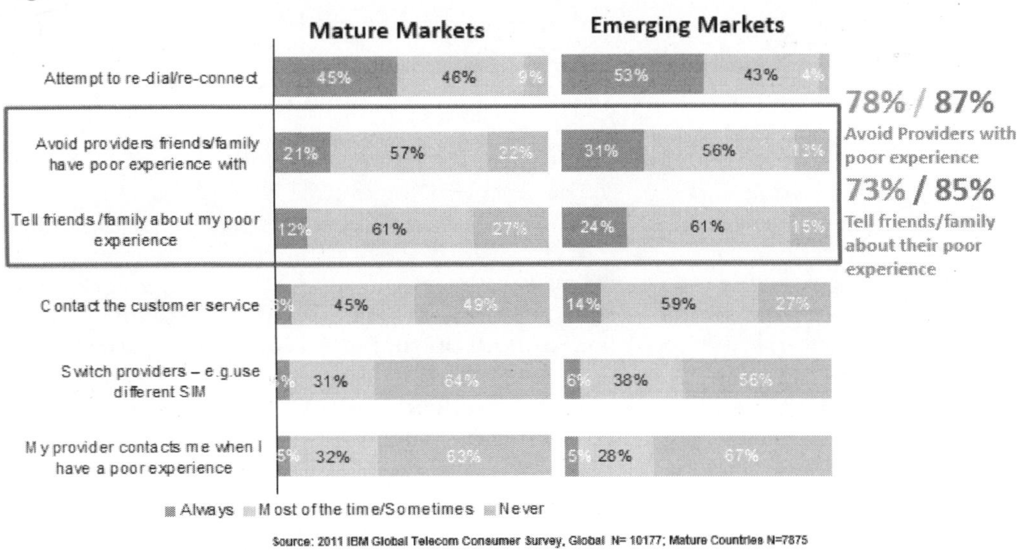

Fig. 3

As more and more human movements and activities are getting "recorded", it has become a race against time to process and analyze data from multiple sources to outsmart competitors. Big data is an essential ingredient for E2E Telecom processes –

right from winning a customer, serving a customer to optimal network management. The following is a snapshot on how the analytics use cases have changed with the advent of big data:

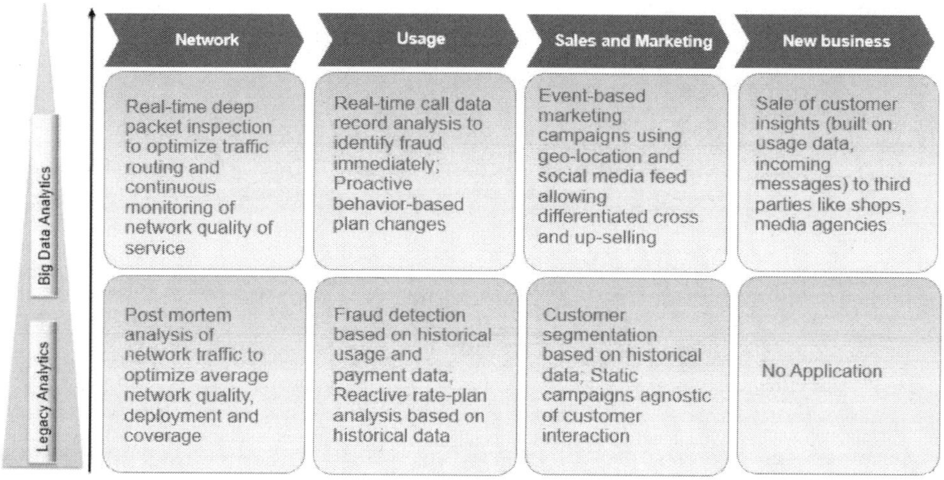

Fig. 4

Typical Use Cases

Some more use cases except Sales and Marketing ones for big data analytics are mentioned below to substantiate the fact that it is hard to ignore big data. We shall explore Sales and Marketing use cases in the next section in greater detail.

Table 2

Network	Optimizing routing and quality of service by analyzing network traffic in real time	Radio Access Network (RAN) congestion has become a major problem for mobile operators. This is because the data traffic on mobile networks is growing exponentially with the introduction of powerful smartphones and data-intensive multimedia services. Since network resources are limited through spectrum allocation, this data growth is increasingly causing rewsource shortage and consequently reducing subscriber quality of experience. Big data analytics can help identify the location for congestion and help allocating higher priority to tier-1 customers. For cable TV viewers, Set-Top Box messages can be analyzed in real-time to detect video degradation quality causes like Network node (switch/router), Set-Top Box firmware/hardware or Channel encoding errors etc. If the CSP network node topology is mapped with Google Maps, exact geographical location can be identified on a real time basis

Subject Area	*Use Case Title*	*Use Case Description*
	Intelligent Network Planning	Inorganic growth (like acquisition) for many CSPs had led to the expansion of network but the same resulted in poor capacity utilization. Big data analytics can help predicting the demand and necessary network change by identifying potential stress points integrating with geo-spatial maps.
	Proactive maintenance	OPEX consumes 30-40 percent of revenue and it is even higher for some CSPs. Network operations alone account for about 45 percent of this expenditure. This can be reduced by predicting network resource life in a timely manner. They emit signals of wear and tear and by using big data analytics, one can identify the patterns and do the necessary maintenance before it completely breaks down.
Fraud	Analyzing call data records in real time to identify fraudulent behavior immediately	CSPs can utilize a big data-driven advanced analytics infrastructure to detect in real time abnormal subscriber consumption, fraudulent cases; malicious applications download and save operators from revenue spill. Pattern matching can be effectively employed to match live customer events with past patterns and alert major variances, drive blocking of transactions or invoking some revenue assurance fixes on real time basis.
Customer	Improved Customer Experience through Unified Solution	Service providers have traditionally operated in silos e.g. Provisioning, CRM, billing, fulfillment, Inventory, service management, network management and different generations of network architecture (2G, 3G, 4G, LTE etc.), each holding different types of data, in different formats and with different business goals. By 'correlating' these data using Big Data platform, the CSPs can look for a unified solutions and paint a complete picture of customer experience
	Preemptive Customer Care	Linked to 'Proactive maintenance' use case as the CSP can plan to inform customers using their preferred channel about any "supply shortage" due to some planned maintenance.
	Identify and utilize Influencers	Identify Influencers by performing Social Network Analytics. If an Influencer churns, the probability of his/her follower multiplies manifold. Strategy should be to keep such subscribers "happy" to prevent churn and also utilize their influence in the social network to woo subscribers from competitors.

Subject Area	*Use Case Title*	*Use Case Description*
New Business	Match Demand & Offering	CSPs can track customers' interest by listening to their social interactions, Internet access, downloads etc. They can share this information with merchants (like malls, shopping centers, supermarkets etc.) who can match wish list of subscribers with merchant offerings on the fly. In the longer run, this can help merchants sell their products, conduct precise campaigns and create a more robust and efficient market place for buyers and merchants.
	Package Design for Specific OTT	Over the top (OTT) Applications like "WeChat", "WhatsApp" are posing a great challenge to the conventional CSPs. Rather than, going into a competition mode, OTTs and CSPs can join hands to promote respective offerings. CSPs can include certain OTT applications as part of their data plans (e.g., unlimited Facebook, unlimited YouTube, Music Streaming etc.) and in turn the OTT content provider can share the cost with the CSP.
	TV Advertising	Grocery/Merchandise purchase behavior and CSP profile together can drive Television Advertising. Internet viewing, mobility, TV viewing, etc., from CSP can drive intelligent campaigns to deliver coupons by the Grocery/Merchandise
	Big data as a service to advertisers, retail, logistics, marketing firms hospitality etc.	Tier 1 operators are seriously considering monetization of big data. They are updating customer privacy policy to accommodate selling aggregate customer data or anonymous information. AT&T, Verizon are some of the early players in the field. The cable industry is also producing a huge amount of data. Set top boxes are emitting customer, network and viewership information which can be very useful in targeted advertisements and the development of personalized content services.

Internal Vs. External Data

Let us take a look at the types of data that are potentially available to the CSPs. Whether there are marginal changes on internal type of data (data that are generated through various transactions within CSP and the same is stored in CSP), there have been huge surge in the external data (data that can be acquired from a secondary source). These data might be combined to create new business opportunities, improve customer care and reduce fraud, etc.

Table 3

Internal data				
Network events Network CDRs (on and off network) Inventory Volume of data traffic Location-specific data User handset data Technical fault data	Product catalog Product life-cycle data Product and platform costs Innovation road map Product usage Critical products Product delivery management	Customer devices Option preferences Sales channel data ARPU classification Response rate of marketing campaigns Segmentation data Usage patterns Subsidy levels	Order data Contract data Fault handling data - Problem type - Resolution time and rates - Repeated faults Call center logs Termination reasons	Call detail records Tariff data Usage history Customer account data Payment data
External Source				
EJL Wireless Research International Data Corporation European Competitive Tele-communications Association World Broadband Information Service Fiber to the Home Council Europe	Gartner 451 Research iSuppli Corporation ComScore Data Mine European Information Technology Outlook	eMarketer newsletters Acxiom marketing data Ovum Forrester Nielsen metric GfK TNS Infratest ITU country case studies	Social media data (e.g., Twitter, Facebook) BuddeComm TelegeoGraphy GlobalComms database Merrill Lynch Wireless Matrix	Credit Karma ITU World Tele-communication Experian TeleGeography yearbook OECD Communications Outlook

DIVING DEEP INTO THE SALES AND MARKETING DOMAIN

Let us take a look at the possibilities of exploiting this data deluge and use of Big Data Analytics to boost the Sales and Marketing function in the Telecom sector. The backbone of any Sales and Marketing lies in understanding its customers (precisely who they are and what their needs are). So we shall describe building a 360 degree view of a customer in detail. We shall also discuss the following use cases subsequently:

- Churn Identification, Prediction, Prevention & SNA
- Precise Marketing

- Location Monetization

Building a 360 Degree View of a Customer

Let us explore how big data can provide additional insights to the present all round view of a customer. The following information is available to most operators from internal structured data sources:

- Customer Demographics (gender, age, marital status, education, occupation, location)
- Customer usage behavior (e.g. Data, SMS, Voice, Video consumption, time of the day, Install base)
- Customer Interaction (Customer Care history, Trouble Ticket, Service Request, Payment and mode)
- Customer participation (Marketing campaigns and loyalty programs)

Now let us look at the internal/external unstructured or semi-structured data like Event Logs, Social media platforms. The following information can be tapped in:

- Number of visits to Telco's web site, visit duration, subject of searches, Customer Care transcripts to have a deeper understanding of what customer wants
- Web histories, using cookies or other forms of anonymous tracking
- Opinions, interests expressed in the public domain as on You Tube, Facebook, etc.
- Clickstream on telecom's E-Commerce site (succession of mouse clicks, order in which the pages were viewed, at what point user has abandoned the transaction, etc.)

The above-mentioned types of data can be synthesized to get following "derived views" of a customer:

- Socioeconomic class (e.g., prefers the newest, high-end devices, Lifestyle brands)
- Non-telecom behavior (with increasing trend of authenticating customers over mobile number, most of customer service organizations (e.g. Bank/ Online shopping/utilities/travel, etc.) sends regular alerts or event based communication over mobile as SMS. These can help identifying Lifestyle brands, Financial Institutions that the person is associated with)
- Product Portfolio

- Influence in their network (e.g., Leader, Follower (based on Social Networking Analytics (SNA) or XDRs))
- Network with off-net users (e.g., makes or receives frequent calls to those using a different service provider)
- Relationships (Family, Head of the Family)
- Interests (e.g., gaming, music or video downloads, time spent on social media portals, web-sites visited, apps downloaded and consumed)
- Telco product and channel preference
- Last 6 months' value (provided to the CSP)
- Propensity to churn (e.g., predictive modeling)
- Customer Life Time Value
- Life changing events (Marriage, Going to College, Shifting base etc.)
- Intent to buy non-Telco products (different approach for purchasing fast food or fridge or house)

The following diagram provides a schematic view of a customer, which will provide the basis for extracting further insights:

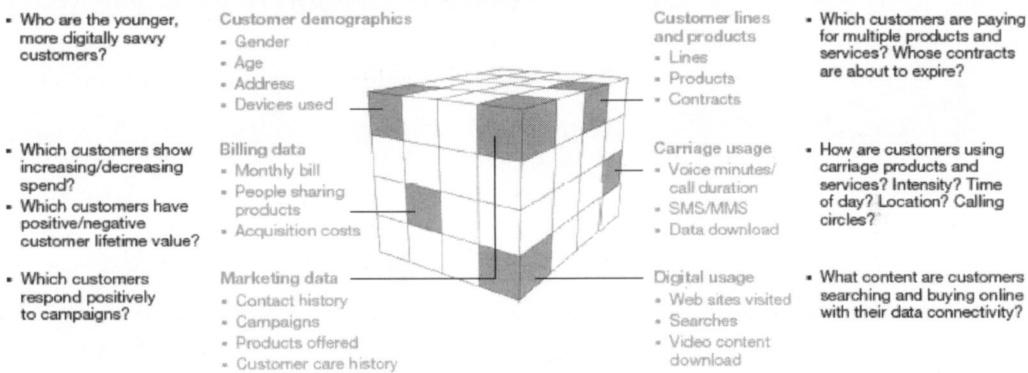

Fig. 5

Source: April 2013, 'Crunch time: Using Big Data to boost Telco marketing capabilities', McKinsey Report on Marketing & Sales

Churn Identification, Prediction, Prevention

Acquiring a new customer is 6 times more difficult than retaining a customer. So it is important for Sales and Marketing department to identify possible churners beforehand to come up with offers that can prevent churn. So far we have looked at the following data to predict a churn:

- Diminishing Usage
- Frequent complaints to Customer Care

- Prolonged poor quality of network in an area

The big data driven advanced analytics solution can identify possible churn almost in real time by combining the following data with the churn propensity score achieved from above-mentioned data:

- Churn of an Influencer/Leader whom this customer follows
- Expression of problems (Rate plan, QoS, Billing, etc.) in the public domain
- Churn in the family especially head of the family

Some associated use cases are described below:

- **Multi-SIM prediction**: One can identify subscribers who are buying SIM cards from other CSPs (either for roaming or for better time based plan) by reviewing their call or surfing patterns. The CSP can offer them more appealing rates or product bundles, roaming offerings based on travel plan.
- **Rotational churn identification**: Identify subscribers who are habitual churners. They take a service in order to take advantage of promotions applicable to new customers and then leave. This will also help minimizing revenue leakage since many such customers do not even pay. The Sales and Marketing can plan to create a profile for "right acquisition" i.e. who are expected to stay at least 6 months.
- **Churn location**: All CSPs are not equally strong in all locations with respect to Network performance. People from "weakly" connected areas seem to churn more frequently than the "strong" ones. Identify and send more attractive offers in locations that have a higher churn rate.
- **Influencer Identification**: Leaders are 1.2 times more likely to churn compared to non-leaders. And when the leaders churn, additional churns become almost 20 times more likely. So it is pertinent to identify them and prevent their churn.

Identify disseminating leaders (connected to their group using outgoing calls) and authority leaders (connected through a larger proportion of incoming calls). SNA can further strengthen this concept by diving into the billions of opinions expressed in the public domain to see who are leaders and followers socially.

Combining this information with the CRM systems, CSPs can take care of their experience enhancement, churn reduction and revenue growth.

- Leaders can be advocates for selling products and services to the followers
- Also, if one can track relationship with off-net users, the same can be used for a possible "churn in" using their influence.

Finally, big data and advanced analytics have changed the paradigm of BI approach of only looking back at old records to looking forward with current data in a predictive and preventative fashion. Correlation and Corroboration of data from multiple sources in near real time can help determining "What behaviors will trigger churn?" and "What actions can prevent a churn?"

Precise Marketing

Mobile devices follow their owner and reveal a lot about their owner's interests through surfing pattern and applications used over the phone. This wealth of data can be analyzed in conjunction with conventional structured data to design intelligent personalized campaigns. Few examples are given below:

- Based on the current device being used, there can be up-sell propositions for devices (may be jointly with the device retailer/manufacturer)
- Push up-sell proposition for Plans, VAS, Apps etc. suitable for the handset
- Track surfing of competitor's web site and provide counter offers to products searched
- Personalizing "path to transaction" by analyzing clickstream data, which can maximize sales conversion rate
- Customer preferences and behavior could enable the recommendation of attractive price plans and add-ons, such as sports add-ons for fans and free audiobook offers for commuters
- Using insights into customer behavior and usage, develop new products and services (either personalized or for certain segments)
- Big data has left its mark on Digital Marketing as well. CSPs are undertaking context aware advertising campaigns by sending personalized SMS/MMS advertisements and vouchers and realizing better return for their marketing spend. SingTel had acquired Amobee, a mobile advertising firm in 2012 to provide targeted offerings across smartphones and feature phones.

Location Monetization

Big data analytics allows analysis of location-based data that enables CSPs to better target users by applying geo-fencing or location-based advertising. In the scenario below, a subscriber sends a "like" on Facebook for a camera that her friend had bought. Seeing an opportunity, the Telco sends a "promo code" for buying the camera (as arranged with the retailer) as soon as the person reached in a 2 KM vicinity of the retailer. The similar approach can be applied to food joints, sports merchandise and other retailers.

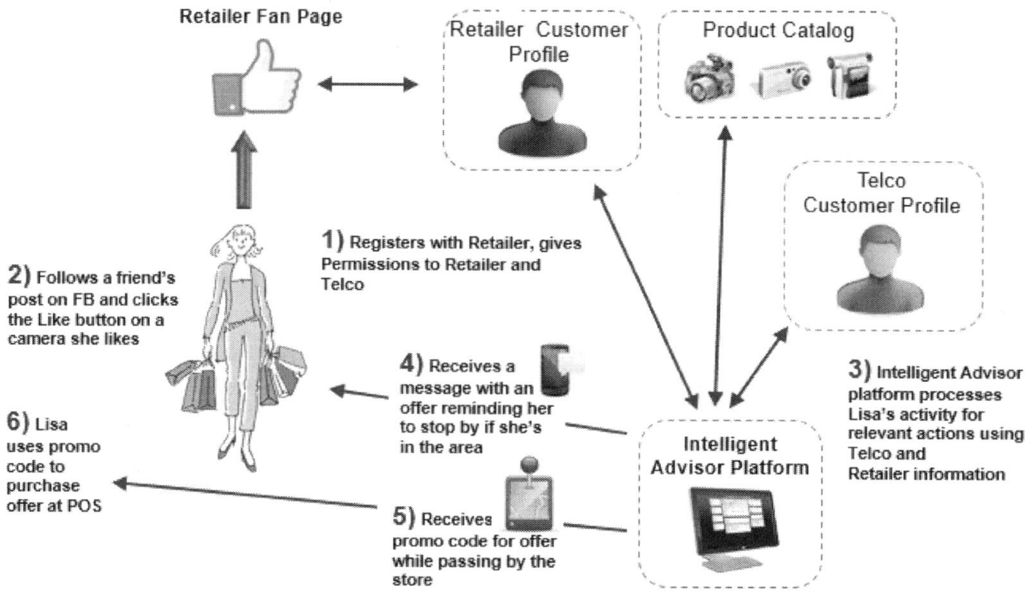

Fig. 6

IMPLEMENTATION APPROACH

Conventional thoughts of having a massive data warehouse churning out pre-defined analytics at regular time intervals are going through changes. Data is now being treated as a corporate asset and Chief Data Officer, Data Scientist roles (who can correlate data elements from various source systems to provide a consistent view and can provide data monetization ideas) are evolving in organization chart. Enabled by schema on read, Big Data allows gobbling up all data in its original format and storing them in cheap and unlimited storage. Centralized data governance programs are adopted by most organizations to deal with Data Quality, Availability, Integrity and Confidentiality. Figure 7 highlights the changes.

The methods and technologies for ingesting, managing, and analyzing both structured and unstructured data in real time had really set the expectations high. This is particularly true in the telecom sector. Most CSPs have analytics programs to use their internal data to boost the network efficiency, customer experience and drive profitability. But success of big data depends on how we can combine much larger amounts of information to increase revenue and profit across the entire telecom value chain, from product development to network operations to marketing, sales, and customer service through monetization of the data.

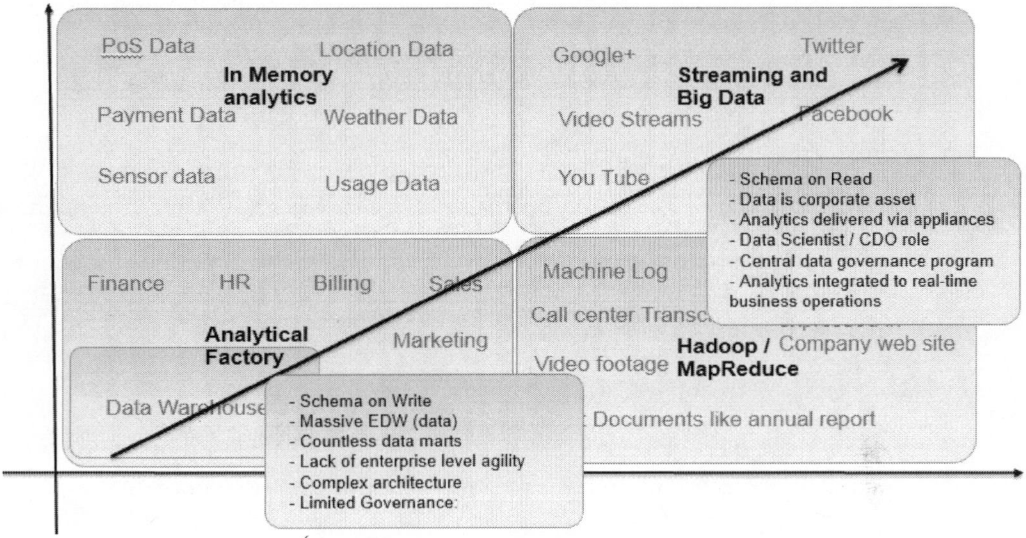

Fig. 7

Unfortunately, not many Big Data implementations have lived up to the high expectations. Most companies in every industry including Telecom are employing a top-down approach by focusing on specific business problems that big data can solve and then gathering the data needed to solve them. But the business problem often surpasses the capacity of available data and also the process of gathering the right data is poorly executed by many companies.

To avoid this problem, companies should adopt the inverse approach i.e. viewing the opportunity from bottom up. In this scenario, one examines the data currently available and identifies the monetization opportunities and business problems that the data can solve. Our recommendation will be to adopt bottom up approach through pilot programs and keep the expectation reasonable. The team should analyze available data and explore with the help of any additional structured or unstructured data to create actionable insights and then test the efficacy of the results in real life.

This tactic will offer a

- concrete launching pad
- more realistic assessment of the benefits of big data

better understanding of what is actually needed in the long term – a roadmap.

CHALLENGES WITH BIG DATA

There are plenty of challenges in implementing a big data platform for any organization. These are discussed in detail below:

Data Security and Privacy

Data privacy must be addressed to the satisfaction of the consumers. Two extreme views are coming to the front, needless to say that both are bad for business:

- the conservative view is to stop mingling of personally identifiable information with social media
- the liberal view does not pay heed to customer privacy preferences at all.

There are many questions to be answered related to security/privacy:

- Can Telco data be correlated with social media to get an improved profile of the customer (both from technical point of view and ethics point of view)? And can the same be used for
  - Acquisition
  - Product Introduction
  - Campaigns/responses
  - Care – assisted/self-care
  - Loyalty and churn management
- How about sharing these profiles with third parties? Aggregation, Anonymization are some of the possibilities
- Could we buy third party data and correlate with CSP information?
- Under what conditions can we interact with the customer and provide added value to improve product, promotion or price?
- How about Analytics in the Cloud? Can we ship CSP CRM data to a third party cloud?
- How to be compliant with privacy laws of the land?

Data Quality

Enormous volumes of customer, financial and operational data exist in the secondary sources; however more data does not guarantee good data. A few basic principles for safeguarding quality and trustworthiness of data are as follows:

- Subscribe data from reputed data providers like government agencies, market researchers, statistical survey etc.
- Avoid using free data, rather subscribe to the data provider to ensure quality data at the right time

- Validate external data with respect to standard reference data as appropriate
- Use industry standard data capture tools and data exchange format to ensure no loss of data quality during data transmission

For various external sources, especially from social media, data comes in huge volumes and at great speed. The organizations should have a robust Data Governance mechanism in place to make sure that data ingested are worth it.

Selection of Tools and Technologies

This area is still evolving and is yet to be matured. The organizations should carefully evaluate both functional and non-functional requirements against capability and maturity level of tools before adopting them. The organizations should prepare a blueprint for enterprise level Big Data Tools and Technology to ensure a seamless experience across the organization.

High Expectations from Big Data

As discussed in the preceding chapter, many Big Data implementations have failed to live up to high expectations. The Organizations should adopt a "Start small, Scale fast" approach i.e. start with building pilot components and comprehend issues with Big Data Security, Big Data Quality, Big Data Lifecycle Management, Tools etc. during its implementation. Based on this experience, the organizations should prepare the Big Data Analytics Roadmap and Big Data Governance strategy.

CONCLUSION

The big question is - how much can CSPs benefit from "big data"? Every CSP is looking for new avenues for increasing revenues and profits during the current period of stagnancy and saturation. But few have shown the abilities to make the most of this new technology so far. Operators seeking to make initial inroads with big data are adopting the usual top-down approach which starts with a business problem and then hunts for the data that can solve it. Instead, operators should adopt a bottom up approach starting with the data at hand and experiment with it to reveal connections and correlations.

Below is the Organization Maturity Matrix:

Table 4

Maturity Level	*Characteristics*

Breakaway	A company which is generally considered to be the best in their execution of key business strategies, thereby able to exhibit the characteristics of an agile, transformational and optimized organization. Key predictive performance indicators are used; modeling for outcomes and information is utilized enterprise wide for multi-dimensional decision-making.
Differentiating	A company whose execution of key business strategies through utilization of information is viewed as generally better than most other companies; creating a degree of sustainable competitive advantage. Management has the ability to adapt to changes to the business to a degree and measure business performance. Business leaders and users have visibility to key information and metrics for effective decision-making.
Competitive	A company which has capabilities generally in line with the majority of similar companies and has growing ability to make decisions on how to create competitive advantage. It is also the starting point to establish some consistency in key business metrics across the enterprise.
Foundational	A company which has capabilities to gather key information but requires a high degree of manual efforts to gather information. Information is not consistently available or utilized to make enterprise wide business decisions.
Ad-hoc	A company which is just starting to develop the capability to gather consistent information in key functional areas; generally falling well behind other companies in the corresponding sector. Information beyond basic reporting is not available. Generally needs time consuming, manual efforts to gather information needed for day to day business decisions

Big Data Analytics is bringing unprecedented changes to organizations across industries. In order to climb up the ladder from ad-hoc to breakaway (as per the Organization Maturity Matrix), CSPs need to act fast and embrace Business solutions, Technical solutions and an Implementation approach as summarized below:

Business Solutions

- Network Analytics, Campaign Management, Profile and Location Monetization
- Significant business value by tapping and conquering volume, velocity and variety
- New applications, new business models, new partnerships

Technical Solutions

- Overall architecture integrates with current DW platform using a three layer architecture – conversation, orchestration, discovery
- Significant technological advancements happened in the last couple of years in each of these areas as well as their integration.

- Big data is not a substitute for DW rather it is supposed to complement a DW

Implementation Approach

- Start small and Scale fast – start with a pilot experiment in bottom up manner
- Establish a road map based on current and target maturity levels
- Should treat Data Security, Quality and Governance very seriously

The operators that can adopt new agile strategies into their organizational DNA faster to gain a "first mover advantage".

BIBLIOGRAPHY

Banerjee, Ari. (December 2013). *Big Data & Advanced Analytics in Telecom: A Multi-Billion-Dollar Revenue Opportunity*. (Report sponsored by Huawai for www.heavyreading.com) Retrieved from www.huawei.com/ilink/en/download/HW_323807

Dietrich, Brenda L., Plachy, Emily C., & Norton, Maureen F. (2014). *Analytics across the Enterprise*. IBM Press/Pearson plc.

Hazan, Eric, & Banfi, Francesco. (August 2013). Leveraging big data to optimize digital marketing. Retrieved from: http://www.mckinsey.com/client_service/marketing_and_sales/latest_thinking/leveraging_big_data_to_optimize_digital_marketing

Hürtgen, Holger, Natarajan, Samba, Spittaels, Steven, Vetvik, Ole Jørgen, & Ying, Shaowei. (April 2013). *Crunch time: Using Big Data to boost Telco marketing capabilities*. (McKinsey Report on Marketing & Sales). Retrieved from: https://www.mckinsey.com/.../mckinsey/.../Telecoms/.../RecallNo21_Big_D...

Zikopoulos, Paul, & Eaton, Chris. (2011). *Understanding Big Data: Analytics for Enterprise Class Hadoop and Streaming Data*. McGraw Hill Education.

CHAPTER TWO

LONG TERM AND SHORT TERM IMPACT OF MARKETING DRIVERS (INTEGRATED MARKETING ROI)

Sunder Muthuraman, Manoj Kumar, T. Sujit Kumar Dora, Kavya Madhava and Thayagarajan Subramanian

BACKGROUND

Close to accurate measurement of ROI has always been a challenge for marketers. Various methodologies and approaches have helped decision makers to take informed decisions. The evolution of technology in the last two decades has accelerated the development in the decision science space.

However with multiple studies being conducted in silos the strategies are myopic and poor in ROI in the era of big data and tighter budgets. To illustrate, Awareness, Consideration, Loyalty and imageries are tracked by market research team, Social interactions on the web are analysed by digital team, and the CEO is challenged with "top line" i.e. revenue. If these are not integrated the attributions from market research and marketing investments will be limited.

The methodology provides an integrated view of the data sources, direct/indirect; slow/fast moving; research/transactional variables KPIs. This helped the marketers generate better insights, know their lead indicators and plan optimum resource deployment in consumer targeted activities.

Business Challenge

Establish an integrated view of all the external factors, buzz, brand equity research data, consumer targeted activities, and resultant Business KPI (Sales) and generate insights and forecast business results under different scenarios.

Short term and long term effect of all marketing inputs (price, distribution, advertising, promotions, etc.) is quantified which is usually relegated as a base sales/ base demand in traditional forecasting models and science.

Objectives

Provide a single integrated view of multiple time series data of marketing investments, consumer buzz, external factors, and market research and business results for

(a) Insight generation on lead indicators
(b) Forecast business under different scenarios in integrated system

An Illustration of the Framework

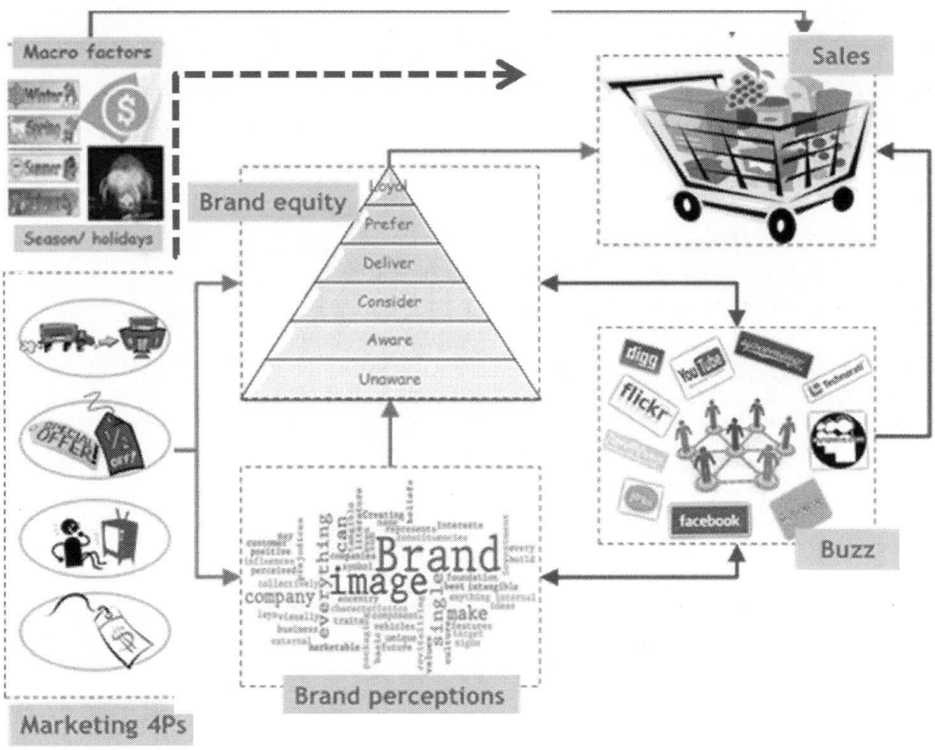

Fig. 1

Approach and Methodology

Understanding the consumer purchase model will provide clear focus area for marketing decisions. We are proposing an estimation technique that will provide feasible solutions involving multiple independent as well as dependent constructs.

Integrated marketing ROI is a framework built on **advanced statistical technique, Time series regression on nested Key Performance Indicators (KPIs)** to accommodate all the key KPIs and the inter-dependencies that exist. This process (Nested KPI regression) is the unique aspect of the framework with its ability to capture both fast moving and slow moving impact. In the traditional marketing mix models the slow moving driver impacts are generally represented as the base without helping in marketing decisions.

A brief note and estimation process is outlined here.

All this while all marketing models, either MMM or Awareness, have been focusing on a single KPI only, i.e. marketing or advertisement. An integrated view is a must considering the inter-dependencies between multiple KPIs.

A basis for quantifying the attributes that drive the brand equity (Brand health pyramid):

- We expect the model to provide sharper directions on marketing investments and the attributes that marketing needs to focus on.
- The opportunity is to address what has been eluding marketers - take an integrated view of ROI on the path to purchase.

The Model Structure

- $y_t = c + \sum_{s=1}^{L} B_s Y_{t-s} + u_t$ (With endogenous variables only)
- In effect, written entirely in terms of "y" because everything in the system is presumed to be jointly endogenous.

- This is a system of equations, where there are as many equations as variables, k.
- yt is understood to be a vector, the value of each of the variables at time t. Bs is a matrix of regression parameters, k by k.
- For situations involving other independent variables the functional form will be as below

  $$y_t = c + \sum_{s=1}^{L} B_{sYt-s} + \sum_{f=1}^{L} B_{fxt-f} + u_t \text{ (With exogenous variables included)}$$

  Source: Monogan, 2010

- Consider the case of a 3 variable system. The notation will be

$$\begin{bmatrix} y_{1t} \\ y_{2t} \\ y_{3t} \end{bmatrix} = \begin{bmatrix} c_1 \\ c_2 \\ c_3 \end{bmatrix} + \sum_{s=1}^{L} \begin{bmatrix} \beta_{11}^{(s)} & \beta_{12}^{(s)} & \beta_{13}^{(s)} \\ \beta_{21}^{(s)} & \beta_{22}^{(s)} & \beta_{23}^{(s)} \\ \beta_{31}^{(s)} & \beta_{32}^{(s)} & \beta_{33}^{(s)} \end{bmatrix} \begin{bmatrix} y_{1t-s} \\ y_{2t-s} \\ y_{3t-s} \end{bmatrix} + \begin{bmatrix} u_{1t} \\ u_{2t} \\ u_{3t} \end{bmatrix} + \sum_{s=1}^{L} \begin{bmatrix} \beta_{11}^{(s)} & \beta_{12}^{(s)} \\ \beta_{21}^{(s)} & \beta_{22}^{(s)} \\ \beta_{31}^{(s)} & \beta_{32}^{(s)} \end{bmatrix} \begin{bmatrix} X1 \\ \\ X2 \end{bmatrix}$$

Data Requirement

Step	*Data Requirement*	*Periodicity*
	A. Retail audit from Nielsen or equivalent source • Sales volume • Sales volume • Numeric/Weighted distribution B. Brand Score (consumer panel) C. Penetration D. Media (TV GRP, Print spends, OOH) by campaign	Weekly/Monthly for 3 years

Process in Detail

1. **Preliminary data analysis:** The data harmonization and Exploratory Data analysis stage will be very important considering the many layers of the data (Multiple Independent and dependent constructs)
   (a) If the number of KPI variables we want to include in the path is high (which is quite possible) then we will face issues of degrees of freedom
   (b) In this case we will use Bayesian estimation process to address the issues of degrees of freedom
   (c) Variables Setting: The first step is to identify the Endogenous and Exogenous variables (KPIs)
   (d) Set the Path Among the KPI variables: There is a need to identify the Path, and one or a combination of methods can be used to identify the Path relationships between the KPIs
      - Grangers Causality test to check hypothesis on Path
      - BMA (Bayesian Model Average)
      - Multivariate/OLS regressions
2. **The IMR model building process:** Once the data is harmonized and the Path is identified,the next stage is about setting the model process
   (a) As in other models- Application of transformations which apply the business learning (for example – the carry over effect in case of Media / reduction of curve using power transformations where incremental benefits are reducing...) are applied

(b) In addition – from business learning Priors can be set in the path when reasonable effect of a variable is known on second (Only if Bayesian estimation is used)

3. **The interpretation:** It is not the interpretation of a single model but reading of results involves summarizing and interpretation of the models or stacks of models of KPIs calling for a system of results.

The summarization will have the following:

1. Path of purchase
2. Strength of relationship between KPIs
3. Cross effects

Sample Model Summary

Path Diagram

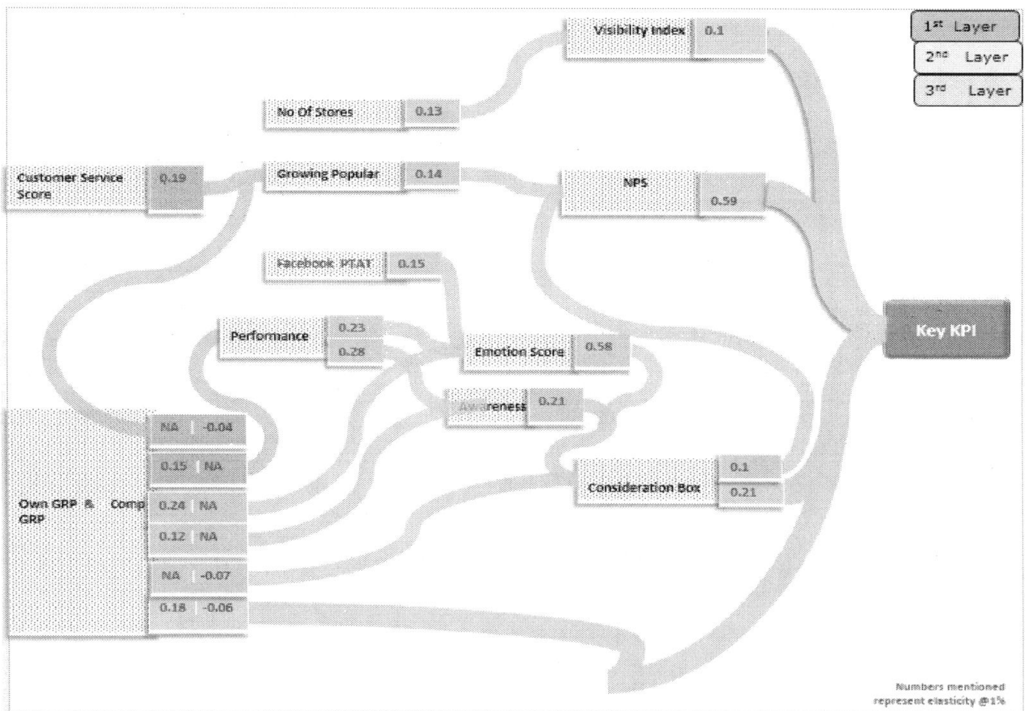

Fig. 2

The above figure represents a sample model summary with 3 layers of impact on the key KPI. There are 4 drivers that have an immediate or direct impact on the key KPIs. Some of the drivers in turn get impacted by other drivers represented in the 2nd and 3rd layer.

The key achievement of the framework is the way it captures the impacts of key drivers in multiple layers. E.g. media in this case not only impacts sales but also have significant impact on key perception variables and hence have long-term impact. The aggregated impact of media in general is close to 3 times of the impact captured through the Marketing Mix Models.

The framework also captures the time-bound impact of any driver on the KPIs using the "Impulse Response Function".

Sample Impulse Response Results

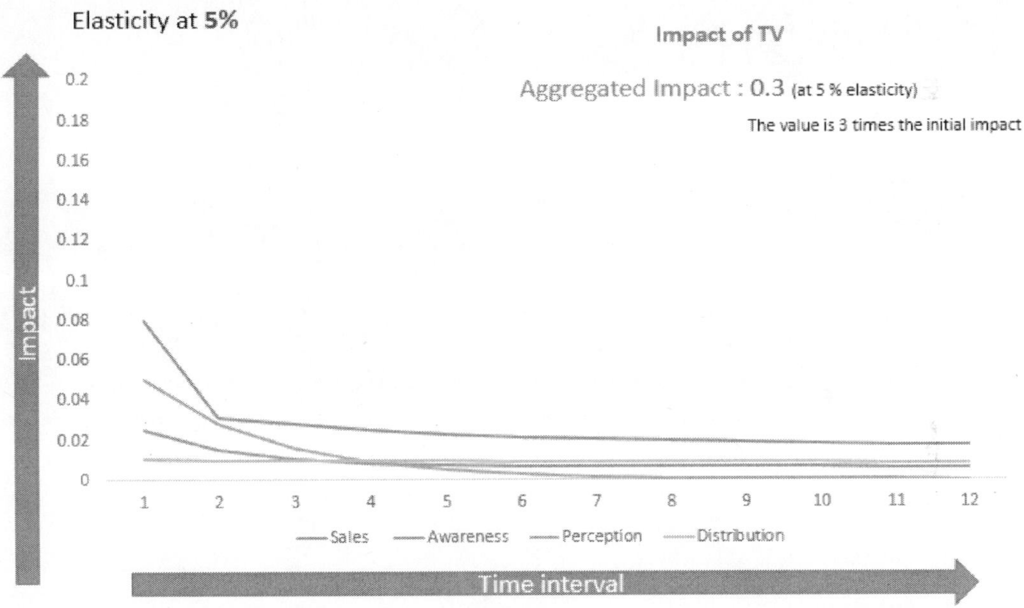

Fig. 3

REFERENCE

Monogan, Jamie. (2010). *Vector Autoregression.* (presentation). Washington University. St. Louis. November 15 & 17, 2010. Available at: http://artsci.wustl.edu/~jmonogan/teaching/ts/14var.pdf

CHAPTER THREE

TURN BIG DATA TO BIG IDEAS – PANASONIC

Mansi Arora Madan

ABSTRACT

Brand management and marketing space today are being driven by a new kind of analytics called Big Data. It is a totally new kind of customer engagement that brands and marketers must achieve. Its implication is that companies need to use Internet sources based intelligence and advanced analytics to predict market scenario and consumer behavior. Big data analytics provides the capability of mining and structuring the multitudes of data being generated on the Internet, mass media and social media in a format which could be analyzed. Thus the intelligence gathered could be processed and inferences derived in the real time increase the information value manifold.

Recognizing the relevance of the subject, the paper discusses the strategic tactics of Panasonic. The research focuses on the strategic management of Panasonic. The study is an investigation of the relationship between effective leadership behavior and successful strategy implementation of Panasonic in the electronics industry. The research conducts an exhaustive analysis on the consumer electronic industry and prevailing environmental conditions thereby giving a vivid picture of the company's SWOT profile. The main research problem was to make an in-depth analysis of its marketing strategy and implementation. The research method was a qualitative analysis of their company data, annual reports and management interaction to evaluate their Brand Equity. The quantitative data has been collected through empirical observations to diagnose the success rate of strategic tactics of Panasonic in engaging the Indian Smart Consumer. The paper showcases the application of strategic tools like GE-Nine cell matrix to understand their tactics at corporate, business-unit and functional level for hands on success in marketing.

Keywords: Strategic, Brand Equity, Consumer Durables, Customer.

INTRODUCTION

India is the fifth largest economy in the world and has the second largest GDP among emerging economies. Owing to its large population, the potential consumer demand is almost unlimited and consequently under appropriate conditions, strong growth performance can be expected. With the continuous inflow of disposable income and the advancement of technology, the need for varied consumer durable goods is increasing. This in turn is leading to strong competition among the different consumer durable brands available in the country, and also the price gaps between the same consumer goods of different companies are narrowing down. Day by day these goods are becoming cheaper. The rural and urban market of consumer durables has been growing at a rate of around 15% on an average.

The electronics industry in India dates back to the early 1960s.It took off around 1965 with an orientation towards space and defence technologies. This was rigidly controlled and initiated by the government. This was followed by developments in consumer electronics mainly with transistor radios, black &white TVs, calculators and various audio products. Until 1984, the electronics sector was primarily government owned. The late 1980s witnessed a rapid growth of the electronics industry due to sweeping economic changes, resulting in the liberalization and globalization of the economy. The economic transformation was motivated by two compelling factors – the determination to boost economic growth, and to accelerate the development of export-oriented industries, like the electronics industry.

The electronics industry has recorded very high growth in subsequent years. By 1991, private investments – both foreign and domestic – were encouraged. The easing of foreign investment norms, allowance of 100 percent foreign equity, reduction in custom tariffs, and de-licensing of several consumer electronic products attracted a remarkable amount of foreign collaboration and investment. The domestic industry also responded favorably to the policies of the government. The opening of the electronics field to the private sector enabled entrepreneurs to establish industries to meet hitherto suppressed demand.

KEY CATEGORIES

The Indian Consumer Durables Segment can be segmented into three Groups

White Goods	*Brown Goods*	*Consumer Electronics*
• Air conditioners • Refrigerators • Washing machines • Sewing machines • Watches and clocks • Cleaning equipment • Other domestic appliances	• Microwave ovens • Cooking range • Chimneys • Mixers • Grinders • Electronic fans • Irons	• TVs • Audio and video systems • Electronic accessories • PCs • Mobile phones • Digital cameras • DVDs • Camcorders

RESEARCH OBJECTIVES

- To conduct an exhaustive analysis on the consumer electronics industry and prevailing environmental conditions.
- To draw a vivid picture on the company's SWOT profile.
- To understand its marketing strategy and implementation.
- To analyze customer behaviour towards the brand
- To detail the relationship between effective business strategy and successful strategy implementation of Panasonic in the electronics industry.
- To evaluate the brand equity of Panasonic

RESEARCH METHODOLOGY

Primary Research

- Original information has been directly gathered through a Questionnaire based survey and in-Depth interviews amongst the Panasonic users in Delhi NCR and a few prominent cities of Punjab like Ludhiana, Jalandhar, Nawan Shehar, Gorayan, Kartarpur, Moga, Barnala, Amritsar and Chandigarh. The questionnaire was shared through emails and face to face interaction to obtain the consumer responses.
  Sample size: 10,000 respondents
- Also included is the direct Q&A session with Mr. Sarthak Seth, Head- Brand and Marketing Communications, Panasonic India Pvt. Ltd.
- Information from their PR agency-Genesis

Secondary Research

Existing information has been obtained through available sources, which includes:

- Information on the internet
- Existing market research results
- Existing data from their own stock lists and customer database
- Sustainability Report 2012-13 provided by Panasonic

DATA ANALYSIS AND PRESENTATION

The objective is to comprehend and assess opinions of different consumers towards the consumer electronic products. More stress is given to features, appearance, cost or any other feature of the electronic products. Quantitative data is presented in graphical form and thematic analysis is used to present qualitative data.

To meet the above objectives, it becomes imperative to study the 4Cs – Circumstances, Company, Competition and Customer.

Circumstances

India is expected to become the fifth largest consumer durables market in the world, the market is expected to reach US$ 12.5 billion by FY 15 from US$ 7.3 billion in FY 12.

Urban markets account for the major share (65%) of total revenues in the consumer durables sector in India. Demand in urban markets is likely to increase for non essential products like LED TVs, laptops, split ACs, and beauty and wellness products. In rural markets, durables like refrigerators and consumer electronic goods are likely to witness high demand in the coming years as the Government of India plans to invest significantly in rural electrification.

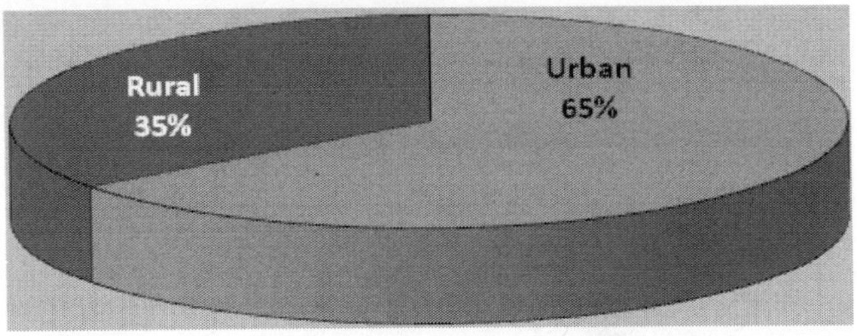

Fig. 1: Consumer Durables Market Share in India (FY 14)

100% FDI is allowed in the electronics hardware-manufacturing sector under the automatic route. The consumer durables sector raked in revenues worth US$ 7.3

billion in FY12. Growth has been healthy over the years, recording a compounding annual growth rate of 10.8 percent in FY03-12. The Consumer durable sector is expected to double at 14.8 percent CAGR to reach US$ 12.5 billion in FY 15 from US$ 6.3 billion in FY10.

The sector is expected to post a CAGR of 15% over 2010-15. Growth in demand from the rural and semi-urban markets is estimated to outpace demand from the urban market for consumer goods.

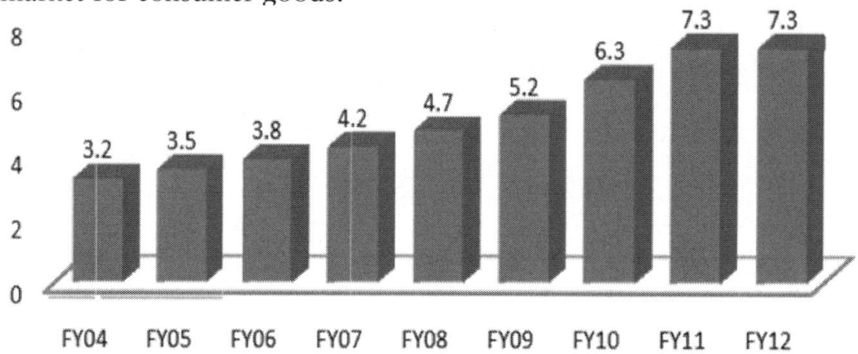

*Latest data as avaible

Fig. 2: Size of the Consumer Durables Market (USD billion)

Salient Budget Announcements for Electronics Design and Manufacturing 2014-15 TV Manufacturing

- BCD on LCD and LED TV panels below 19 inches reduced from 10 per cent to zero.
- BCD on Colour picture tubes for manufacture of cathode ray TV reduced from 10 per cent to zero.
- BCD on Specified parts of LCD and LED TV (including open cell, plate diffuser, film diffuser) reduced from 10%/7.5% to zero.

LED

Excise Duty on LED (Light Emitting Diode) driver and MCPCB (Metal Core Printed Circuit Board) for use in manufacture of LED lights and fixtures or LED lamp reduced from 12/10 per cent to 6 per cent.

Consumer Appliances

Excise duty on Reverse Osmosis membrane element for household type filters reduced from 12 per cent to 6 per cent and on Reverse Osmosis membrane element for water filtration or purification equipment (other than household type filters) based on reverse osmosis technology using thin film composite membrane reduced from 12 per cent to zero.

Industry wide Announcements Applicable for Electronics System Design and Manufacturing

Investment Allowance at the rate of 15 percent to a manufacturing company which invests more than 25 Crore in any year in new plant and machinery. This benefit will be available for 3 years, i.e. for investments made upto 31.3.2017. The scheme announced last year will continue to operate in parallel till 31.3.2015.

Promoting FDI

FDI in manufacturing is today on the automatic route. The manufacturing units would be allowed to sell their products through retail including e-commerce platforms without any additional approval.

Industry SWOT

Strengths

- The domestic market is entering a rapid growth phase, with projected double-digit growth of key products such as notebook computers and mobile handsets.
- Low rates of penetration for key products such as computers (2%) and mobile phones (43.5%).
- Rising incomes and GDP growth are increasing affordability.

Weaknesses

- Low incomes and huge digital inequalities.
- Large 'grey' market for illegal products.
- Relatively low level of demand for higher end products such as LCD TV and 3G phones.
- Infrastructure deficiencies, with only 20% of Indian houses capable of receiving broadband.

Opportunities

- Rapid growth in mobile subscriber penetration to 145% by 2015 will drive the booming mobile handset market.
- Big opportunity for expansion in under penetrated semi-urban and rural areas.

- Hardware sector set to grow faster after a number of government measures to encourage domestic manufacturing and new investment incentives under consideration.
- The government's efforts to get India connected to the modern world will provide the frame for electronics market development over the next few years.
- The ultimate goal of government policy is for 1bn computers connected to the internet – equivalent to the total number of PCs in the world today.

Threats

- Global economic slowdown may affect consumer spending.
- Moves to stimulate the hardware sector may have mixed results.
- Falling prices.

Company – Panasonic

Headquartered in Osaka, Japan, Panasonic Corporation is a leading global manufacturer of electronic products and solutions for consumer, business, and industrial needs based on innovative and energy-efficient technologies. Panasonic strongly believes in designing products and solutions that keep the environment in mind. To achieve this vision, the company develops energy-efficient, state-of-the-art products and encourages customers to live eco-conscious lifestyles with an aim to reduce carbon emissions in households and manufacturing units. Panasonic's global strategies are driven by the core business philosophy of being a responsible—and successful—corporate citizen and contributing to the progress and development of society at all levels. They are working to expand their business by creating products that meet local needs, a goal that requires the insights and skills of a local workforce. By designing and manufacturing products locally, Panasonic's know-how can be leveraged to solve local social and environmental challenges. They have recently formulated anew Sustainability Policy that outlines the development of a sustainable future through business, while being in harmony with society and the global environment. Emphasizing on steady business growth, innovation, local products to meet local needs, and equitable development, Panasonic will become a successful and socially responsible global enterprise.

Mission

"Recognizing our responsibilities as industrialists, we will devote ourselves to the progress and development of society and the well-being of people through our business activities, thereby enhancing the quality of life throughout the world."

Vision

"Through our business activities, we at Panasonic have long nurtured our "consumer electronics DNA." Making this DNA central to all of our activities and carrying it forth, we aim to continue to provide "better living" for our customers in the various spaces and areas where our customers go about their lives, such as their homes, communities, businesses, journeys, and automobiles."

Panasonic India

Panasonic commenced its operations in India in 1972 and has shown a remarkable growth over the past five years. Their business in India comprises of multiple sister companies, divisions and manufacturing units, through which they offer a wide range of products and solutions across consumer segments and industries.

The Indian Hierarchy

Mr. Daizo Ito, President, Panasonic India & Regional Head, ISAMEA
Mr. Manish Sharma, Managing Director, Panasonic India and South Asia
Mr. Sajeev San, Deputy Divisional Managing Director for Channel and Retail, Panasonic India
Mr. Suresh Kumar Bandi, Divisional Deputy Managing Director, AC Division, Panasonic India
Mr. Neeraj Bahl, Associate Director, AVD Sales, Panasonic India
Mr. Amitabh Reu, Head of Corporate Sales, Panasonic India
Mr. Santosh Das Gupta, Head of Customer Service, Panasonic India
Ms. Radhika Kalia, Head of Corporate Affairs & CSR
Mr. Sarthak Seth, Head Brand and Marketing Communications, Panasonic India

Panasonic Consumer Product Range

- TV
- Cameras and Camcorders
- Home Appliances
- Beauty Care Appliances
- Mobile Phones

Below are the Products and Revenue Charts from various products of Panasonic India:

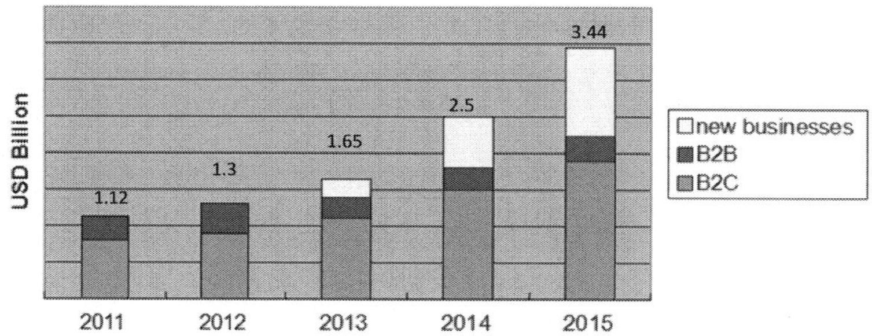

Fig. 3: Annual Revenue Chart

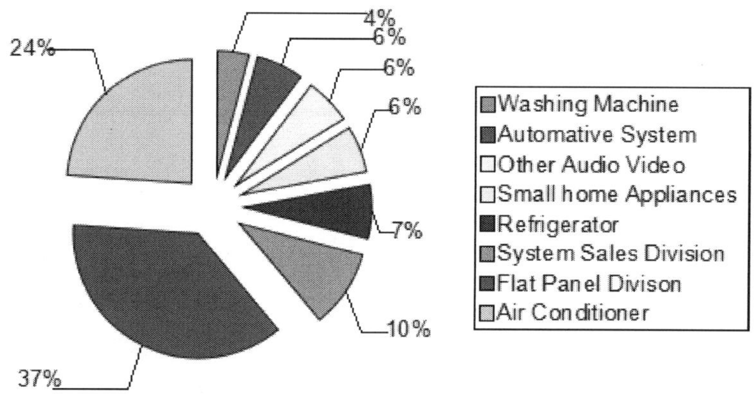

Fig. 4

Panasonic India also pursues localisation in the products it develops. They understand that Indian consumers have unique requirements that need specific focus. Through "Indovation"—that is, Indian-inspired innovation—they focus on developing products that specifically meet the needs of Indian consumers. In addition, their Volume Zone Market Research Centre team visits households in India and works towards marrying their insights with the strength of their technology expertise to develop locally inspired innovations that are integral to Indian life. Bringing product development and production closer to home, the factory, Technopark in Jhajjar, Haryana, was inaugurated in December 2012, to support the on-going efforts to be a positive force in the Indian society. In many aspects of everyday life, Panasonic products, services, and solutions are becoming a common sight. The goal is to deliver innovations that will not only be of service to individuals, but will also help in making new contributions to Indian society and businesses across India.

Panasonic India has outlined three core strategies for sustainable growth.

- The first strategy is to create new product categories in both consumer and business segments. This will be done by forging strategic partnerships.
- Secondly, to promote the India-led local management as well as to ensure

that our business grows its footprint in West Asia, Middle East and Africa, Panasonic India is realigning its business structure with the new direction that the company is taking.

- The third imperative is to pursue the strategy of autonomous management in India. This will be followed in product development originating in India as well as in new business incubation activities in the establishment of strategic partnerships.

Panasonic India will grow its business just as India's economy and society grow and expand. Panasonic is known, to prioritize products that are specially designed keeping the consumers' requirements and the environment in mind.

This growth must happen at all levels of Indian society, in rural and urban environments. For instance, approach to rural development aims to apply technology to socially beneficial goals, creating economically viable, sustainability-focused projects to improve the quality of life and state of infrastructure in many rural areas across India. These projects include renewable energy generation and storage, and introducing Panasonic Kiosks that can be used for long-distance education and medical diagnosis needs.

Panasonic has deep roots throughout India, with a broad array of companies and divisions that manufacture goods inspired by Indian needs. Panasonic India comprises of six group companies, four sales divisions and five manufacturing divisions in operations.

Panasonic SWOT

	Strength • International Presence • Innovation • R&D Focus • Strong Brand Image • Best Quality Products • Highly Trained Working Staff	*Weak* • Quality is higher than the price ratio
Opportunities • New Ways of Advertising • New features and Technology • Expansion of Products and Services • E-commerce	*SO* • Incorporation of latest technology in products and services • Applying innovative and creative ways to advertise the product by highlighting the product features • Enhancing online services by R&D	*WO* • Taking Advantage of E-commerce to make strong financial position • Application of cost effective technology

Threat	*ST*	*WT*
• Emerging Players in the market increase competition	• Patent the technology and make it a competitive advantage • Use cost effective technology to produce quality and affordable products	• Develop proactive approach in critical circumstances. • Use cost effective strategies for providing products at affordable cost.

Below are the inputs by Mr. Sarthak Seth, Head- Brand and Marketing Communications, Panasonic India Pvt. Ltd.

What training techniques are adopted by your company to build a delivering team of Staff members?

Panasonic is built on seven core values: Gratitude, Cooperation and team spirit, Fairness and honesty, Contribution to the society, Adaptability, Courtesy and humility and Untiring effort for improvement. The leadership values of Japanese management style are deeply enrooted in Panasonic's business culture which was created by Konosuke Matsushita. Panasonic's culture promotes a democratic leadership style of believing in ideas and creativity flowing freely and encouraging the team to communicate their views. Panasonic has a well-defined and thought through management structure to ensure effective and smooth implementation of business plans and strategies in order to drive growth and achieve business targets. Effective communication within the team, allowing a free environment involving all team members is the key to success.

With 13,000 employees working across facilities, Panasonic opens the door to a multitude of opportunities. We offer a demanding yet fulfilling work environment. Our challenging and rewarding assignments allow the employees to realize their full potential. Training opportunities include participation in company programs, attending external courses and on-the-job learning.

What kind of supply chain is followed by Panasonic?

In a time of increased outsourcing and responsibility with regard to Environment, Health and Safety, it is crucial that companies find the right supply chain configuration enabling them to create a network that is sustainable and effective in meeting customer expectations. Panasonic India believes in implementing a responsible supply chain that helps to connect people beyond our network and go home with design strategies that contribute to the creation of a better world. Our supply chain is based on the concept of "Responsible Corporate Citizen at each Step" and is designed to manage material issues that lead to lowering of risks, lower costs, and promotion of e social and environmental responsibility. We wish to inform our stakeholders about the processes that we have starting from sourcing of products to end of its life. We understand the impact of our business activities on the environment and society, and work with our suppliers to promote socially responsible procurement.

How do you approach to counter the new foreign entrants in the Indian Market?

The consumer electronics market in India is fairly competitive and price sensitive. At the same time, consumers have also become very conscious about the value for money aspect while making a purchase and do not necessarily go for the lowest priced products. We have been present in the market for a very long time now and understand that the products that work well in international markets like the United States and Europe need not work in India. To have an edge over the competitors, Panasonic has a focus on localization of products and technologies to suit the domestic requirements, by making 'Indovation' integral to its business strategy which means creating products in India for the Indian market. Localization is the key to our success for penetration in the Indian market place, and we aim to continue developing more India-specific innovations in various product categories.

Unlike other brands, we also focus on communicating the research, innovation advantage, and energy saving features which are integral to the products that not only reduce power bills but also preserve our habitat.

Established companies are coming down to low cost products, thus penetrating to fight for market share. How is Panasonic going to cope with it?

India is a diverse market and therefore it is hard to categorize the Indian buyer. Today, while there is a significant increase in the purchasing power, the consumers are looking for 'value options' which are increasingly becoming 'price plus', that is, an option which balances the variables of price, quality, convenience, consistency, innovation and shopping experience. They are not only looking for availability of products; they also want better experience and services.

Panasonic, in the recent past, has revamped its entire India strategy and expects to use the high-potential of this market as the arrowhead for future growth. The results are already coming in and almost all product categories are witnessing huge growth. Reassured by the overwhelming response, the company has drawn up plans to bring to India, a range of products from its international level of offerings, customized to suit the needs of the Indian consumer. Localization is the key to its business growth, and modification of business, products and content should satisfy both the language and cultural differences of the targeted market, in this case India. Keeping in mind the current market conditions in India, Panasonic has launched products across categories to cater to the Indian market. We continuously endeavor to develop and deliver the products best fitted for the Indian consumers without compromising on technology and quality.

What new products shall we expect from Panasonic?

Encouraged by tremendous growth, Panasonic is further investing in the B2B and B2C segments in India focusing on introducing a new range of innovative products, manufactured in accordance with the evolving needs of our customers.

- Panasonic's scope of operations has grown from televisions, premium home appliances and personal care to newer businesses such as mobile phones, water purifiers, entry-level home appliances, professional batteries and industrial products.
- The focus now will be more on niche businesses in the B2B segment, including auto parts, solar panels etc. which will play a stronger role.
- India Business Development Centre in Gurgaon leads the new business development activities based on market and consumer needs, especially on four key areas of water, non-electricity areas, food and remote area.
- Our diverse product portfolio in the B2B segment will help us grow as per our plan – focus on products from the ICT, security & surveillance, automotive, power generation and distribution, store solutions and display solutions etc.
- We will continue strengthening our new product range mainly in energy solutions, mobility, healthcare solutions, security-surveillance systems and solutions products. According to the above observations the GE-nine cell Matrix is given below.

	Business Strength			
	Strong	*Average*	*Weak*	
High	ACs	TVs	Mobile phones	Market Attractiveness
Medium	Washing Machines	Cameras and Camcorders	Microwave Ovens	
Low	Beauty Care Products	Refrigerators		

Competition

In recent years the electronics industry is growing at a brisk pace. The demand in the Indian market is growing rapidly and investments are flowing in to augment manufacturing capacity.

The Growth Drivers

Behind the impressive growth of the electronics industry is the robust and consistent growth in Electronic Hardware market of approximately 25 per cent due to a stable economy and large middle class of 350 million people.

Household Appliances Industry size (Rs. Billion)

Appliances	*FY'04*	*FY'09*	*FY'14*
Colour TV	68	110	185
Room Air Conditioners	23	47	95
Refrigerators	31	51	81
Washing Machines	11	21	36
Total	133	229	337
Five year CAGR	–	11.5%	11-12%

The Indian television market is the third largest TV market after the U.S. and China. It has seen a drastic change in the last decade.

The market which was once dominated by Indian players like Videocon, BPL and Onida is now dominated by MNC players LG, Samsung, Sony, Panasonic, Phillips and Toshiba.

Even technology wise, the market is clearly shifted towards LCD, LED and Plasma from CRT (Cathode Ray Tube) TVs.

The upper class and upper middle class has already shifted to the smart TV segment, now middle class segment is largely shifting towards LCD, LED and Plasma TVs.

Rising family income, different payment options, changing lifestyle, technological advancement, minimal price difference between CRT TVs and LCD, LED TVs have driven the shift towards LCD, LED and Plasma TVs segment.

Innovation, quick up gradation of technology, product composition, price, picture quality, sound quality, style and customer reviews are major influential factors in LCD, LED and Plasma TVs segment.

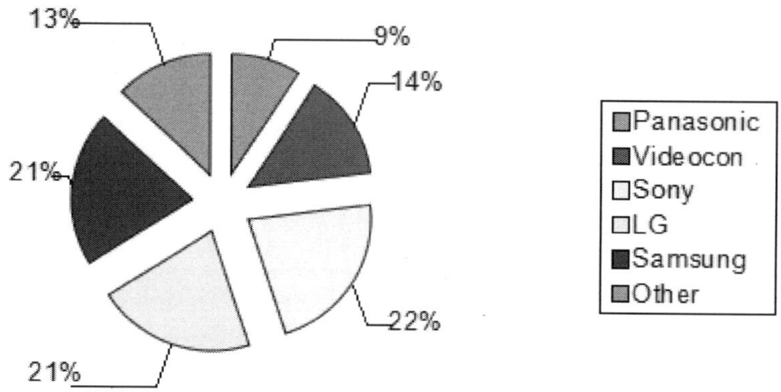

Fig. 5: Flat Panel TV Market Share

During 2006–13, the LCD, LED and Plasma TVs segment has shown a robust 76% growth rate in India. For the financial year 2012-13 this segment has sold more than 4.6 Million units, which account for Rs 105 Billion. The graph below clearly shows that LG, Samsung and Sony dominate the segment with more than 65% market share and are the top television brands in India in 2013.

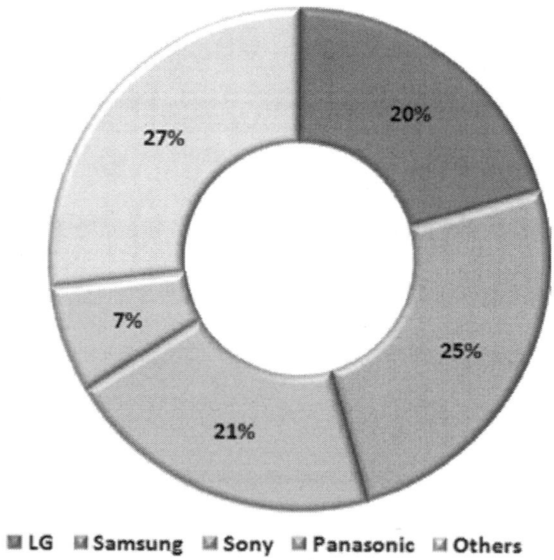

Fig. 6: Top Television Brands Market Share in India, FY 2012-13

Air conditioner Market

The air conditioning market is more competitive with many Indian and foreign players. Top Air conditioner brands in India are Voltas, LG, Panasonic, Daikin, Samsung, Godrej, Bluestar, Onida, Videocon and Whirlpool.

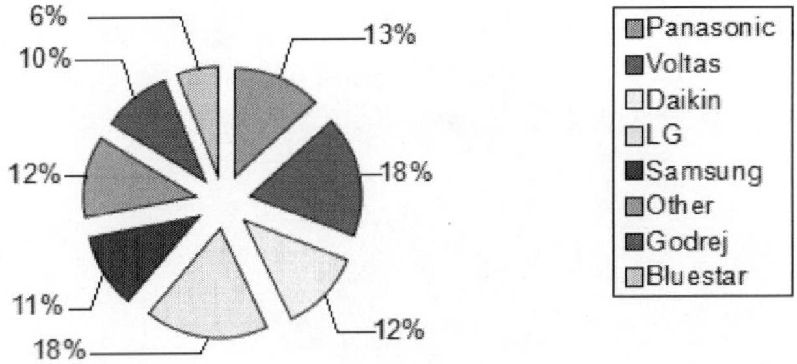

Fig. 7

Customers

USP	Depth and diversity of its research capabilities, manufacturing expertise, high quality and sophisticated products.
STP:	
Segment	Electronics semiconductors and home appliances
Target Group	Upper middle and upper class individuals
Positioning	The most desirable products in the market due to their high quality at a reasonable price

Survey Report

- Age Composition of the Respondents

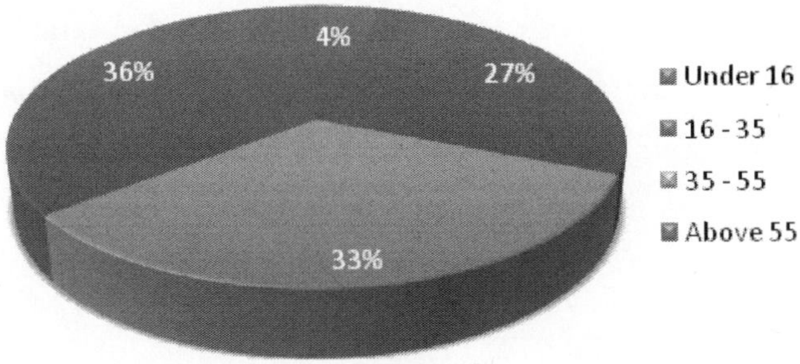

Fig. 8

- Gender of Respondents

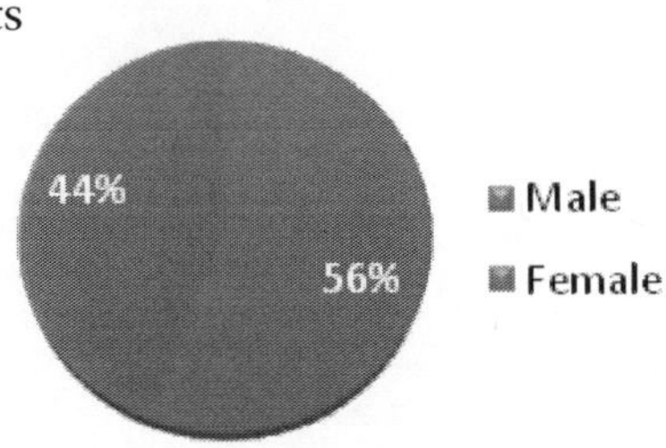

Fig. 9

- Occupation of Respondents

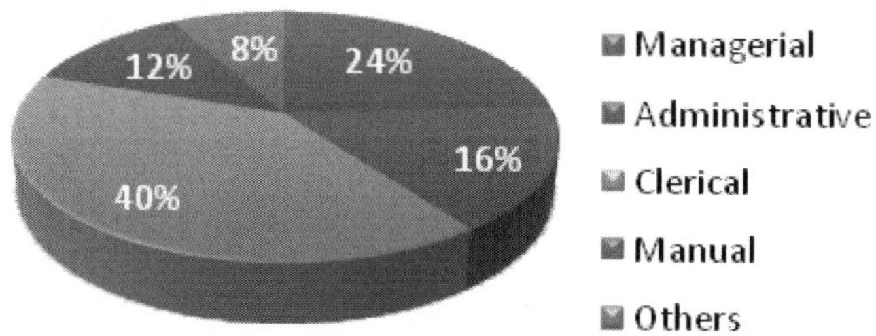

Fig. 10

- Category of Panasonic Products Purchased

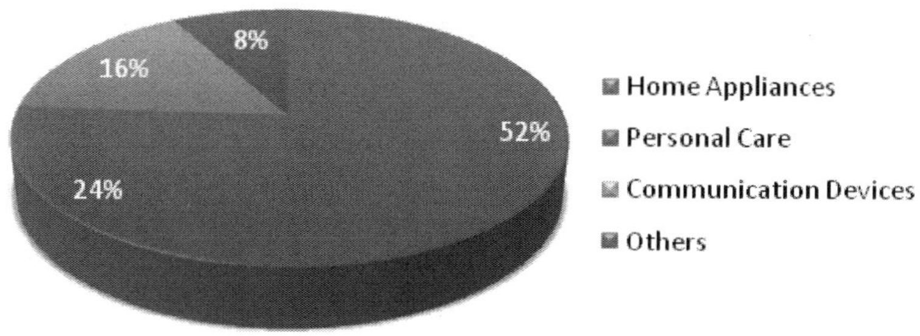

Fig. 11

- Quality of Products

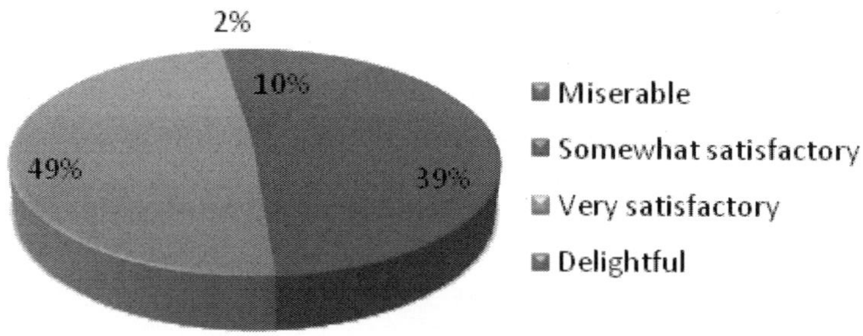

Fig. 12

- Price Value of Panasonic products

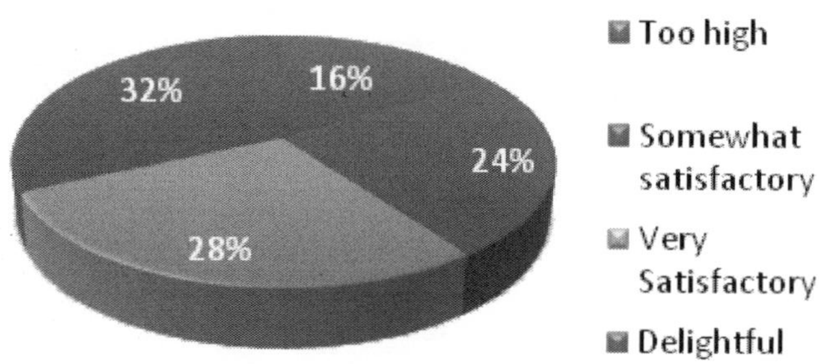

Fig. 13

- Purchase Experience of Respondents

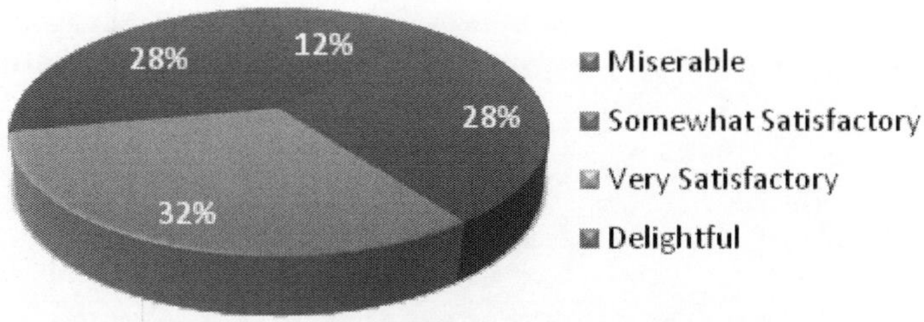

Fig. 14

- Installation or demonstration service

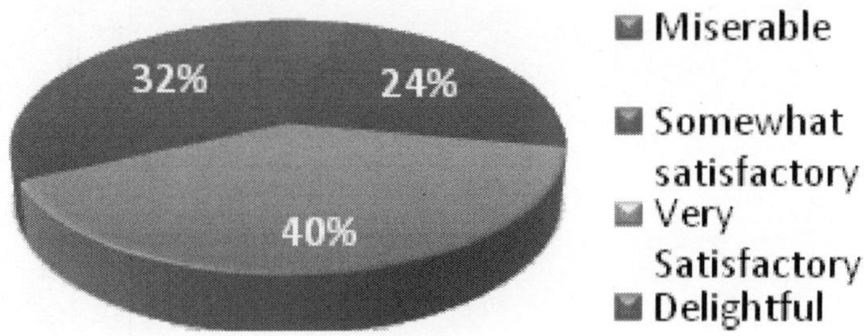

Fig. 15

- Experience of users of Panasonic Products

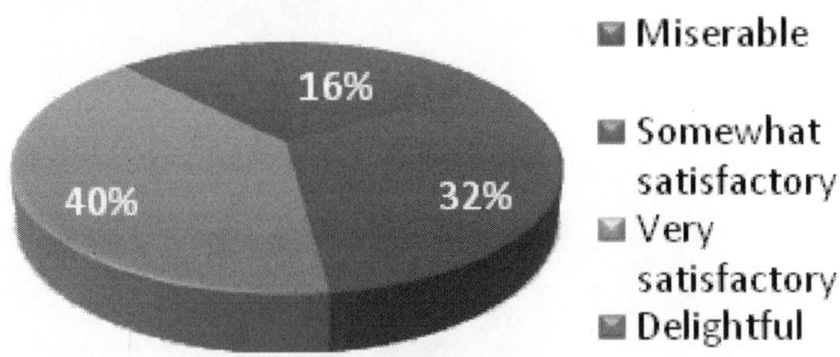

Fig. 16

- Point of Contact with Customer Care executive

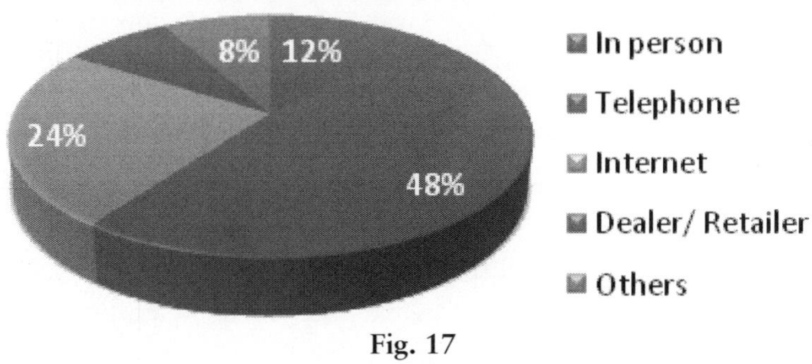

Fig. 17

- Problem Resolution

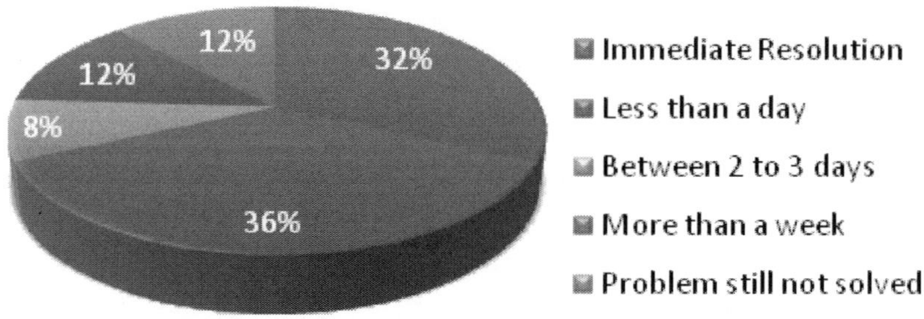

Fig. 18

- After Sales Service of Panasonic

Fig. 19

- Product Repurchase

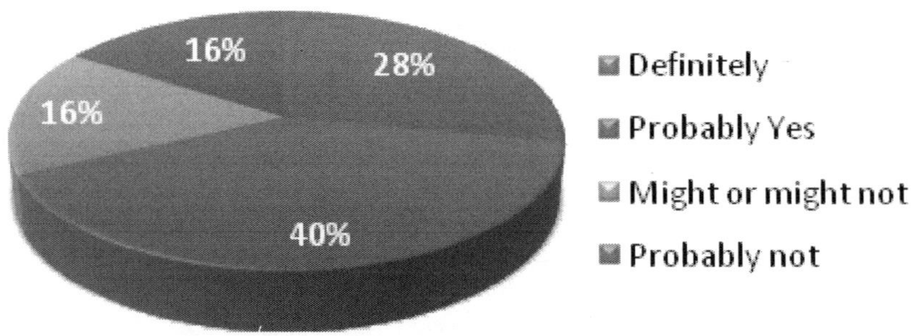

Fig. 20

FINDINGS AND INTERPRETATION

Respondents were asked to fill out the questionnaire to judge the relationship between their preferences of various factors while deciding on a brand over the other. Most of the Panasonic respondents had price as a barrier over the product features and preferred a product with value for money. Their behavior was seen in tandem with their positive responses towards the product quality, purchase experience, re-purchase agreement and after sales services.

Brand Equity

It is the sum total of learning about the brand by all stakeholders, including consumers, shareholders and employees. It includes all that people feel and think about the brand as a result of direct experience, word of mouth, moments of truth with the brand and the brands marketing activities. It constitutes a storehouse of future cash flow and profits.

Good measures of brand equity can give indications on the future profit trends. If brand equity is falling, it indicates trouble, however rising brand equity indicates future profits.

Brand Reach

Brand reach is evaluated through the awareness of the product range in the market. Panasonic has good brand reach with 9% of the total electronic market. According to our survey of 10,000 people Panasonic provides quality products and middle class people like to purchase Panasonic products. They also provide above average purchase experience and after sales services.

Brand Power

Brand power is analyzed through product differentiation of Panasonic towards other brand products. In the electronics industry technology has the most important role in differentiating the products.

Panasonic uses its 32" LED TV to capture the market share with all the high end feature like IPS panel for greater viewing angle, energy saving, and 3 ports for connectivity of other devices.

Panasonic's most selling ACs have all the new anti-bacterial filters and low energy consuming condensers with more cooling efficiency than before.

Brand Attitude

Brand attitude can be measured through the overall experience pattern of the consumer toward the Panasonic product line.

According to our survey out of 10,000 people 65% people had good experience and they are more likely to be the loyal customers and shop with Panasonic. Brand association also derives the attitude towards the brand.

Brand association could be derived with repeat customers. 80% respondents find quality to be satisfactory, 50% people consider Panasonic on satisfactory price.

On the basis of this and their purchase experience, overall 50% Panasonic customers will buy Panasonic products again.

Future Plans (Acc. to Sustainability Report)

The aim is to become India's largest electronics and durables brand. Mr. Daizo Ito, President of Panasonic India, envisions making Panasonic an Indian company in India. Under his aegis and able guidance, this vision comes through our strategy of Localisation. A key to our success, Localisation is reflected in our people, products, operations and in the way we conduct business. Panasonic India has a team that has an in-depth understanding of the Indian market. Our emphasis on being a company entrenched in Indian ethics and insights has prompted key Indian appointments in our leadership. Panasonic India's organisational culture and management practices echo the Localisation ethos. The organization thrusts on having the right person for the right job, irrespective of nationality, region, gender, or any other classification.

REFERENCES

Case Study of Panasonic Marketing [Essay]. Retrieved from http://www.ukessays.com/essays/marketing/the-case-study-of-panasonic-marketing-essay.php

Consumer Durable Industry. Shine.com retrieved from: http://info.shine.com/industry/consumer-durables/21.html

Hawkins, Dell, and Best, Roger J. *Consumer Behavior.* 7th ed. Tata McGraw Hill Education.

India Big Market for Consumer Electronics, wearable Tech. (2014). *The Economic Times*, Jan 6 2014

Kotler, Philip, Armstrong, Gary, Agnihotri, Prafulla Y., and Ehsan ul Haque. *Principles of Marketing*. 13th ed. Pearson.

Moorthi Y.L.R., Madanmohan, T.R. *Market entry and Sustenence strategies of Korean Firms in Indian Consumer Electronic Market: An Exploratory Study.* Indian Institute of Management, Bangalore

Nair, Suja R. (2011).*Conumer Beshavior.* Mumbai: Himalaya Publishing House.

Sharma, Manish (Director Panasonic India). Exclusive Interaction; *India Infoline News Service*, Mumbai; retrieved from http://www.indiainfoline.com/article/research-leader-speak/mr.-manish-sharma-director-marketing-panasonic-india-18657023_1.html

Shri Prakash (2010). *Theory of Consumer Behaviour.* New Delhi: Vikas publishing House.

Top Air conditioners brands in India – Growth and Market of Companies. (2014). *Currentweek.com;* April 20, 2014. Retrieved from: http://www.currentweek.com/top-air-conditioner-brands-in-india-growth-market-of-top-companies

Tsuga, Kazuhiro (2014). *A Brief Report on Consumer Durable Industry in India: Panasonic Business Strategy.* Corporate Catalyst India Private Limited, September 18 2013.

PART
ONE-B

SEGMENTATION/TARGETING

In light of the rising costs of customer acquisition and online marketing with decreasing conversion rates, behavioral targeting ads are a cost-effective way of appealing to prospective customers who have demonstrated some level of interest. Analyzing consumers' online behavior – which website they visited, how much time they spent on the page, what product they viewed, how close they were to making the purchase – with advanced data analytics provides marketers with promising sales leads enabling them to place relevant ads online. With the proliferation of Smartphones and tablets, mobile advertising has seen significant growth in the recent past. Marketers and advertisers have realized that the mobile phone is one of the major touch points in reaching potential customers. The big data generated by smartphones and other connected devices can uncover useful behavioral insights that can make mobile advertising efforts of marketers more focused and targeted.

In the paper 'Customer Classification in the age of analytics 3.0 using Machine Learning Techniques', Vibhati Sharma and Swaroop Johnson illustrate the use of standard mobile app data to reliably determine subscribers' gender through the use of Support Vector Machine algorithm. This study provides predictive insights to marketers and advertisers to focus their targeting efforts thereby increasing efficiency and responsiveness.

CHAPTER FOUR

CUSTOMER CLASSIFICATION IN THE AGE OF ANALYTICS 3.0 USING MACHINE LEARNING TECHNIQUES

Vibhati Sharma and Swaroop Johnson

ABSTRACT

This study provides evidence that Gender can be reliably predicted for Customer Classification from standard mobile device app usage data. A model can be built to accurately identify patterns and classify based on certain static parameters using Support Vector Machine algorithm of Machine Learning on a set of user data. By training and validating a model on a set of randomly collected user data, we were able to predict mobile users' gender with a mean accuracy of approximately 81%. The increase in data usage which stems from the advent of smartphones has heightened consumers' appetite for mobile apps available. Given the fast growing number of mobile phone subscriptions and availability of logs data to researchers, our study opens the door for exciting possibilities for targeted marketing and focused product planning particularly for marketers and advertisers. It potentially enables one to provide predictive insights based on behavioral data leading to efficiency and responsiveness to marketing efforts.

Keywords: Machine Learning, Customer Classification, Gender Prediction, Predictive Modeling, Behavioral Targeting, Support Vector Machine Algorithms, Consumer Behavior, Text Classification, Over-fitting.

INTRODUCTION

With the growing popularity of mobile usage among consumers, along with the recent advances in online marketing, behavioral targeting has offered a means of targeting customers with more relevance and accuracy. Behavioral targeting collects data on the browsing activities of consumers and the applications used, and places digital tags in the browsers of website visitors, using these tags to "track and aggregate consumer behavior". While the vast majority of the data is collected anonymously (with no information the person's identity), digital tags enable the creation of a digital dossier, where browsing history can be tagged to a particular individual. This data holds great implications for companies as customer classification is the starting point in strategic decision making. Behavioral metrics, which help in focused and targeted marketing, can be derived from browsing data, usage of apps, and internet buying behavior. Behavioral data can help marketers along the way as predictive insights based on behavioral data can lead to better efficiency in marketing, improve both purchase rate (first time and repeat purchase), and responsiveness to advertisements.

In recent years there has been an explosion in the usage of mobile devices, and interest in the subscriber's demographic, behavioral, and usage data amongst marketers. As of December 2012, India was home to 431 million internet capable devices, second only to China. (Webtrends, 2014) With the dramatic growth in mobile usage around the world and proximity with consumers, smartphones prove to be the latest touch point for understanding the user and uncovering usage patterns (Sundsoy, Bjelland, Iqbal, Pentland, de Montjoye, 2014). With customer queries, feedbacks, purchase intentions, trends and sentiments churning out tremendous volumes of transactional data; this data holds great potential in helping companies target and focus their advertising initiatives. Marketing strategists are increasingly seeking out new ways to create value by analysis of mobile data, and brands and advertisers are looking for more opportunities to get their messages in front of the right audience. The data collected can be mined by statisticians to find patterns in subscriber usage and ensure focused and targeted marketing. Smartphone data offers a relevant, agile and intelligent solution that drives targeted marketing.

Behavioral targeting with information on a consumer's online activity is aimed at predicting potential purchases, and is conducted by advertising networks. Advertising networks identify potential customers by observing the websites visited, duration of the visit, time spent on the website, pages viewed, and pages followed afterwards. Despite all the browsing information gathered it remains anonymous (as Personally Identifiable Information (PII) such as name, address, email Ids, and phone number were not collected) due to privacy reasons. Non-personal identifiable information is collected by numerous e-commerce sites without the user's consent, and forms the basis for advertisements, and mailers for targeted marketing.

Main Issues

With the growth in mobile usage, a new problem that has shaped up for marketers is the definition of privacy and what information can be legally collected, and shared. Privacy has been equated to autonomy of users, and has been synonymous with "fairness, independence, equality, and free choice" in the decision process. In the discrepancy between more powerful and less powerful parties to obtain information, privacy can ensure a level playing field. (Waldo, Lin, & Millett, 2007). And this represents an issue in tracking of consumers online anonymously as it undermines their autonomy. The only reason for absence of an individual's information browsing and other related behavioral data is abstinence from the online medium. (Conti, 2009).

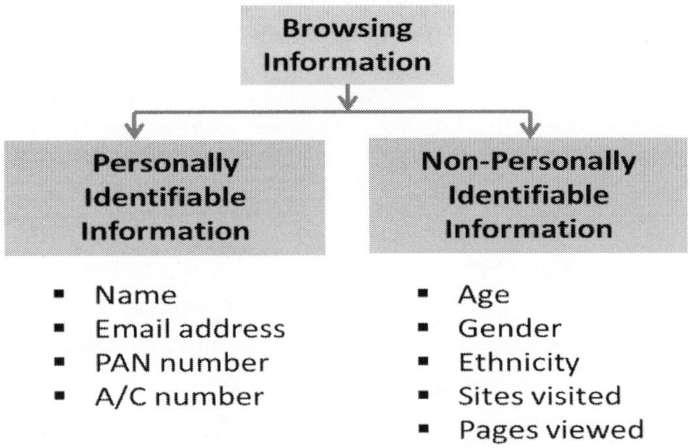

Fig. 1: A Depiction of the Broad Classification of Browsing Information

The ambiguity in the meaning of privacy is one difficulty for e-commerce sites in defining the boundaries of trust and privacy. This lack of agreement on the definition of privacy has existed for centuries, in numerous cultures across the globe and has remained elusive even today. Privacy guidelines today have been used to split a person's trail into personally identifiable information (PII) and non-personally identifiable information (non-PII) (Dwyer, 2009).

Privacy guidelines and controls are explicitly well defined for PII with "informed consent, adequate data security, and rules for data sharing are only explicitly spelled out". Under the defined rules for privacy you only need to control information through which you can be explicitly identified, and "as long as you are treated anonymously, then you have no privacy concerns" (Cohen, 2009).

The growing awareness of privacy risks has led to increase in blocking cookies, and this has reduced the effectiveness of behavioral marketing. Simultaneously approaches and methods for improving behavioral targeting have grown, and predictive methods to determine the demographics and interests of a person have grown. (Jensen, Sarkar, Jensen, & Potts, 2007).. Today with the advances in natural language processing techniques, and machine learning we are able to predict with greater accuracy the shopping patterns, and preference of consumers. Behavioral targeting has evolved to a series of techniques to "collect and organize click stream data, develop data warehousing structures, apply data mining algorithms to uncover consumer browsing patterns, and serve targeted ads matched to an individual". Today with the application of behavioral targeting, marketers are able to customize messages to individual consumers based on their "specific shopping interests, and characteristics like gender, age, and ethnicity". In this study, we use Gender as a means of classifying the customers for devising more efficient and effective marketing initiatives.

Artificial Intelligence Technique used and its Relevance to the Research

Machine learning represents two tasks, classification (if target variable is nominal) and regression (if target is numerical). Machine learning has been recommended when large scale data is available, and large scale deployment of machine learning has been shown to improve accuracy and speed in classification. Machine learning is a supervised learning technique which understands non linearity in data and generates a function mapping input to output. (Kotyuk, & Buttyan, 2012).

Machine learning algorithms can be broadly categorized into Supervised Learning Algorithms and Unsupervised Learning Algorithms. In a Supervised Learning Algorithm, the machine learns a mathematical function which could be applied to unseen data as the machine is trained with the training dataset, with a set of inputs to correspond to a particular output. On the other hand Unsupervised Learning Algorithms understand data in the structure, as there is no functional mapping of inputs to outputs.

Machine Learning allows rapid processing of "large amounts of customer centric data" including customer conversations in the form of calls, email, chat, etc. It ensures better profiling of customers to understand their needs thus enabling intelligent decision making through the use of computer algorithms. Combining Machine Learning techniques on structured and unstructured data can provide marketers, advertisers, network and media companies access to dispositional information about their customers to design customized offers and advertisements (Kotyuk, & Buttyan, 2012).

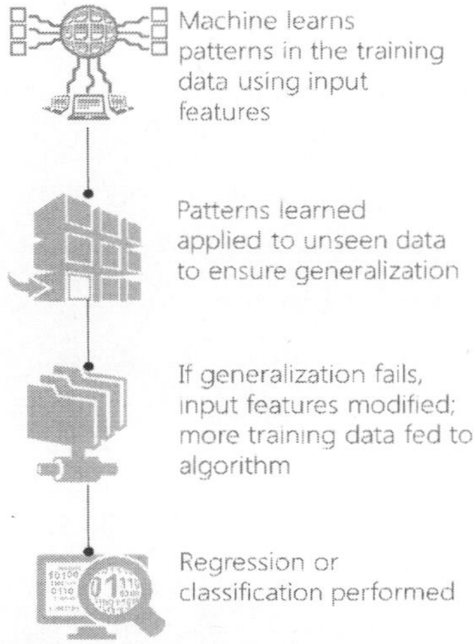

Fig. 2: Representation of the Machine Learning Process as Used for Conducting the Research

For this research, as we are dealing with a large amount of customer centric log data, we use a Supervised Learning Algorithm associated with Machine Learning for improving the overall accuracy and predictability of the model.

MANAGERIAL IMPLICATIONS OF THE RESEARCH AND PROBLEM FORMULATION

With the proliferation of smartphones and tablets, mobile advertising has seen significant growth in the recent past. Marketers and Advertisers are looking forward to leveraging this opportunity to identify different customer bases. Unlocking this opportunity requires a profound understanding of subscriber behaviors from big data generated by usage of smartphones, tablets and other connected devices.

Smartphone operating systems, such as Apple iOS and Google Android allow third-party developers to create mobile software applications on their systems. The increase in data usage that stems from the advent of smartphones has heightened consumers' appetite for the available mobile apps. By studying the different apps installed by the subscribers we can understand the gender of the mobile subscribers. This information can be used by advertisers in order to ensure focused and targeted marketing. A solution is required aiming to deliver a relevant, agile and intelligent system that drives targeted marketing.

METHODOLOGY

An individual's device usage data can have a number of data fields, for instance call log, call duration, visited Bluetooth devices, Apps usage, frequency of app download, battery usage etc. These data fields can be used for making a variety of predictions which can be as generic as the most widely used features or as specific as the most probable app to be downloaded next. These predictions are crucial for marketers to design their marketing approach using the knowledge of the consumer's psychology and behavior. Simple details like the gender of an individual or the demographic attributes can also divulge a lot of insight on consumer sensibility.

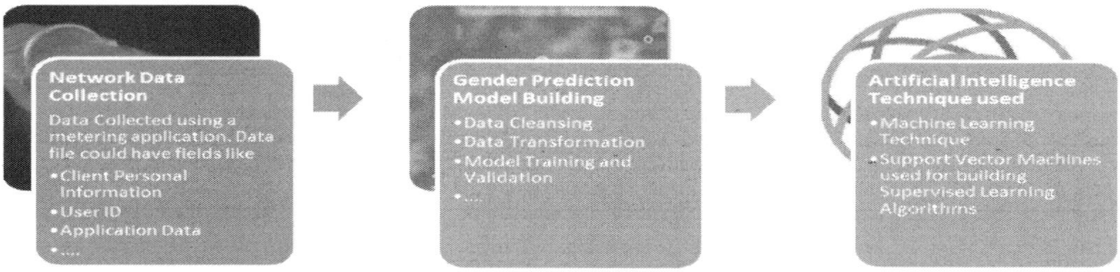

Fig. 3: Overall Methodology using Machine Learning Techniques

Essential Features of the Innovative Approach

The entire process of developing a model for gender prediction using machine learning can be broadly broken down into the following steps:

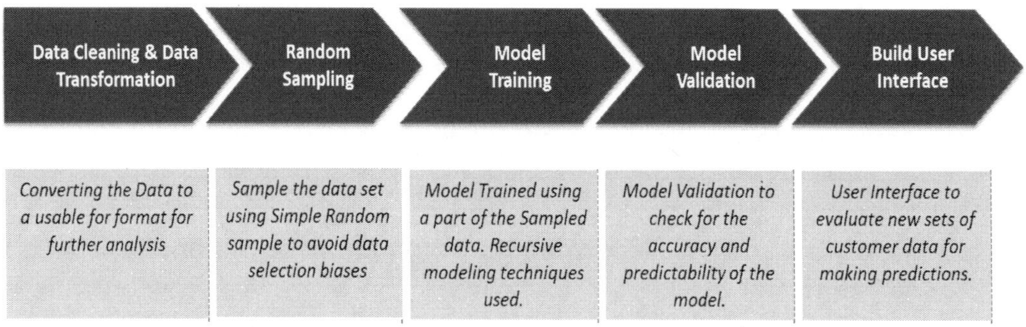

Fig. 4: Step-by-Step Approach for Model Building for Application User Gender Prediction

Data Preparation: Cleaning and Transformation

The first step involved was cleaning and transforming the raw data before processing it. This was done for early detection and removal of errors and inconsistencies from the data in order to improve the overall data quality. It involved removing duplicate data, fixing and amending badly-formatted, incorrect and incomplete data from the databases (Rahm, & Hong Hai Do. 2000). Post this, a customer Id was assigned corresponding to each customer. As a customer could have used multiple apps, the classification was based on the number of apps used by each user in each category. Some of the broad categories identified were Sports, Books, Entertainment, Healthcare & Fitness, Social Networking, News, Business, Games, Travel, Lifestyle, etc. Data cleansing and transformations were performed in order to ensure data could be fed to a supervised learning algorithm.

userid	stateName	telecircle	dateofBirth	Age	gender	education	occupation	employmentType	operatorName	connectionType	brandname	modelname	Goup	os	Town class
91125h09106	Maharashtra	Metros	1983-05-25	25-30 yrs	Male	SSC/HSC	Business	Businessmen/ Indus	idea	Prepaid	iBall	Andi 4.5h	M25-30 yrsM	Android	Metros (Mumbai, D
98003i06513	Maharashtra	Metros	1992-02-04	18-24 yrs	Female	Some Colleg	Not employed	Student	Airtel	Prepaid	Karbonn	A18	F<30Metros	Android	Metros (Mumbai, D
35261j77306	Maharashtra	Metros	1989-09-12	18-24 yrs	Male	Graduate/ P	Salaried Full-t	Supervisory Level	idea	Prepaid	Samsung	Galaxy Y Pro Duc	M<24Metros	Android	Metros (Mumbai, D
35946k49616	Maharashtra	A	1980-08-04	31-35 yrs	Male	Some Colleg	Business	Shop Owner	Tata Docomo	Prepaid	Samsung	Galaxy Y s5360	M31-35 yrsA	Android	More than 100000
35954l61036	Manipur	C	1966-06-05	40+ yrs	Female	Graduate/ P	Salaried Full-t	Officer/Executive (M	Airtel	Prepaid	Samsung	Galaxy Note	F>30C	Android	Less than 100000 (I
35261m5932	Meghalaya	C	1985-11-04	25-30 yrs	Male	Graduate/ P	Salaried Full-t	Officers/ Executive (	BSNL	Prepaid	Samsung	Galaxy Y Pro Duc	M25-30 yrsC	Android	Less than 100000 (I
35946n88328	Meghalaya	C	1992-01-01	18-24 yrs	Male	Some Colleg	Not employed	Student	Vodafone	Prepaid	Samsung	Galaxy Y s5360	M<24C	Android	Less than 100000 (I
35174o37598	MP_Chhattisgarh	B	1986-01-01	25-30 yrs	Female	Unknown	Unknown	Unknown	Vodafone	Prepaid	Samsung	Galaxy Mini S55	F<30B	Android	Less than 100000 (I
35302w5823	MP_Chhattisgarh	B	1995-01-01	18-24 yrs	Female	Unknown	Unknown	Unknown	BSNL	Prepaid	Samsung	Galaxy S Advanc	F<30B	Android	More than 100000
35445x17830	MP_Chhattisgarh	B	1994-01-01	18-24 yrs	Male	Unknown	Unknown	Unknown	idea	Prepaid	Sony	Xperia U	M<24B	Android	Less than 100000 (I
35466y48148	MP_Chhattisgarh	B	1986-01-01	25-30 yrs	Male	Unknown	Unknown	Unknown	idea	Unknown	Samsung	Galaxy Note II N	M25-30 yrsB	Android	More than 100000
35677z69391	MP_Chhattisgarh	B	1991-01-01	18-24 yrs	Female	Unknown	Unknown	Unknown	Airtel	Prepaid	LG	Optimus Black P	F<30B	Android	Less than 100000 (I
35851a94141	MP_Chhattisgarh	B	1985-01-01	25-30 yrs	Male	Unknown	Unknown	Unknown	Tata Docomo	Prepaid	SonyEricsson	XPERIA Neo	M25-30 yrsB	Android	More than 100000
35870b92469	MP_Chhattisgarh	B	1988-01-01	25-30 yrs	Male	Unknown	Unknown	Unknown	Tata Docomo	Prepaid	HTC	Wildfire S	M25-30 yrsB	Android	More than 100000
35923c01689	MP_Chhattisgarh	B	1994-01-01	18-24 yrs	Male	Unknown	Unknown	Unknown	Vodafone	Prepaid	Samsung	Galaxy Fit S5670	M<24B	Android	600000-999999 (Ti
35923e16760	MP_Chhattisgarh	B	1993-01-01	18-24 yrs	Male	Unknown	Unknown	Unknown	idea	Prepaid	Samsung	Galaxy Fit S5670	M<24B	Android	More than 100000
35925f77822	MP_Chhattisgarh	B	1995-01-01	18-24 yrs	Male	Unknown	Unknown	Unknown	Tata Docomo	Prepaid	Samsung	Galaxy Y s5360	M<24B	Android	Less than 100000 (I
35946g08262	MP_Chhattisgarh	B	1956-01-01	40+ yrs	Female	Unknown	Unknown	Unknown	Airtel	Prepaid	Samsung	Galaxy Y s5360	F>30B	Android	100000-199999 (Ti
91122h74602	MP_Chhattisgarh	B	1995-01-01	18-24 yrs	Male	Unknown	Unknown	Unknown	Tata Docomo	Prepaid	Micromax	A52	M<24B	Android	200000-599999 (T
35818i70534	Nagaland	C	1990-09-03	18-24 yrs	Male	Some Colleg	Not employed	Student	idea	Prepaid	LG	Optimus Net	M<24C	Android	100000-199999 (Ti
91115j85694	Nagaland	C	1989-07-17	18-24 yrs	Male	Some Colleg	Not employed	Student	Vodafone	Prepaid	Micromax	A73	M<24C	Android	100000-199999 (Ti
35270k41578	North East	C	1994-01-01	18-24 yrs	Male	Unknown	Unknown	Unknown	idea	Postpaid	Samsung	Galaxy Pocket	M<24C	Android	Less than 100000 (I
12560l22860	Orissa	C	1988-01-01	25-30 yrs	Male	Unknown	Unknown	Unknown	Reliance	Prepaid	Sony	Xperia X8	M25-30 yrsC	Android	Less than 100000 (I
35188m2643(	Orissa	C	1993-06-14	18-24 yrs	Male	Some Colleg	Not employed	Student	BSNL	Prepaid	Sony	XPERIA Neo	M<24C	Android	100000-199999 (Ti
35227n25432	Orissa	C	1975-01-01	36-40 yrs	Male	Graduate/ P	Salaried Full-t	Officers/ Executive (	BSNL	Prepaid	Samsung	Galaxy Y Duos S	M>36C	Android	Less than 100000 (I
35227o28845	Orissa	C	1994-01-01	18-24 yrs	Male	Unknown	Unknown	Unknown	BSNL	Prepaid	Samsung	Galaxy Y Duos S	M<24C	Android	600000-999999 (Ti
35227p76808	Orissa	C	1988-06-28	25-30 yrs	Male	Graduate/ P	Salaried Full-t	Officers/ Executive (	BSNL	Prepaid	Samsung	Galaxy Y Duos S	M25-30 yrsC	Android	600000-999999 (Ti

Fig. 5: Snapshot of the Data File Post Data Cleaning and Transformation Stage

Data Selection using Sampling Techniques

Once the frequency count for apps for each user in each category was defined, the next step was to sample the data randomly for the process of model building. An advantage of using simple random sampling as opposed to other forms of probability sampling techniques is that it reduces/ eliminates the potential for any kind of bias in the selection of cases to be included in the sample, which makes it highly representative of the population. Also since the cases selected are chosen using probabilistic methods, simple random sampling allows for drawing statistical inferences from the sample to the population.

Challenges Faced and Solutions

In this case since the data was obtained from the human population, so in order to avoid any potential bias in the sampling process, a total of 5592 users' data was selected using simple random sampling. This ensured that an adequate portion of the population data was used as part of the research. To apply the Supervised Learning Algorithms technique of Machine learning, the sample data set was broken down in the ratio of 7:3 for Model Training and Model Testing purposes i.e. 3915 and 1677 respectively. The training data was used to produce an inferred function which can be further used for mapping new examples. Defining the sample subset as Testing Set also helped in avoiding the problem of over-fitting.

A bottleneck which surfaced at this stage was the uneven distribution of classes in the training data in the form of male to female ratio of 7.4:1. This meant that since the data set was highly imbalanced and skewed towards the male population, the model would have a tendency to be overwhelmed by the majority class and ignore the minority class examples (Hara-czyk, 2010). Class imbalance could also lead to a problem where the model would "memorize" training data rather than "learning" to generalize from the trend.

Under normal conditions most models simply favor the male and correctly predict them at 98-99% accuracy while the female prediction accuracy remains at the 0-10% level. In an ideal scenario, there should be an even distribution of examples among classes in the training dataset so that the model can be trained properly using an unbiased data. This would also help in building a robust model which can effectively make accurate predictions for any distribution of data (Cao, Zhao, & Zaiane, 2013). Hence in order to predict the minority class better, more importance was given to the female class during model training by introducing a parameter named as weights (Hara czyk, 2010; Ben-Hur, & Weston, 2009).

Machine Leaning Algorithms and Parameters used

In machine learning, Support Vector Machine (SVM) is used for building supervised learning models which have associated algorithms that analyze data and identify patterns. In this case, the SVM algorithm was used for model building which assigned new sets of data into one of the two categories i.e. male or female, making it a non-probabilistic binary linear classifier (Kai-Bo Duan & Sathiya Keerth, 2005; Hsu, Chang, & Lin, 2010).

Further, for model building, certain control parameters were identified. The parameters were adjusted by optimizing performance on a subset (called a validation set) of the training set. The various parameters used were:

- Gamma
- Weights
- Cost

The most appropriate value for *Gamma* was selected by using a set of initial records.

As explained earlier, *Weights* were assigned to compensate for the irregularity in the male to female distribution of data. In order to solve the data imbalance issue, more importance was given to the females in the form of weights (assigned a value of 7).

Cross-Validation was used to train the model. For this, the training set is split into k smaller sets and the model is trained on k-1 subsets of the training set. The resulting model is then validated using the remaining subset (validation set) and this procedure is followed 'k' times. In this case, the value for Cross-validation was set as 9/10 indicating that the whole of the training data would be divided into 10 parts out of which the first 9 parts would be used for training and the last part would act as a validation set and this process would go on for 10 iterations (Cross-validation, n.d.; Guyon & Elisseeff, 2003). The performance measure, i.e. Accuracy in this case, was taken as the average of the values computed by running the model for 'k' iterations (Elkan, 2012).

Cost is the cost of constraints violation (default: 1)—it is the 'C'-constant of the regularization term in the Lagrange formulation (Data Mining Algorithms, n.d.).

Model Training and Validation

Post parameter adjustment and model training using recursive modeling on the parameters, the performance of the resulting function was measured on a Test set that was separate from the Training set. This step helped in validating the model and checking for any anomalies in model building. The data set was passed as an input to the model and the results were cross verified with the already known gender values corresponding to the Id.

The model was run on a Test dataset consisting of 1677 data points. Post this certain model parameters were modified and the model was again run on the dataset to reveal better results in terms of prediction accuracy.

RESULTS AND DISCUSSION

The analysis helped to understand the device usage pattern of different users based on gender. It suggested that there were strong patterns which helped to predict the gender of the users based on their mobile usage. As the trend of using different mobile apps increases, the advertisers aim to reap higher financial rewards with strategic marketing plans.

Model Results 1

Table 1: Model Results for Model Run on Test Dataset

Actual/Predicted	*Female*	*Male*	*Accuracy*
Female	177	32	84.69%
Male	401	1067	72.68%

Model Results 2

Table 2: Model Results for Model Run on Test Dataset Post Parameter Adjustment

Actual/Predicted	*Female*	*Male*	*Accuracy*
Female	167	42	79.90%
Male	346	1122	76.43%

The final model helped to:

- Achieve predictive accuracy of 79.90% and 76.43% for females and males respectively and an overall accuracy of 72.18%.
- Develop an integrated solution with a GUI to enable real time results to be obtained based on real time data feeds to the learning algorithm.

In order to access the model and use it for predicting gender, a user interface was built. Given below is a snapshot of the Interface along with the source input file and the destination output file path definitions. These can be modified to run the data kept at different locations in the system.

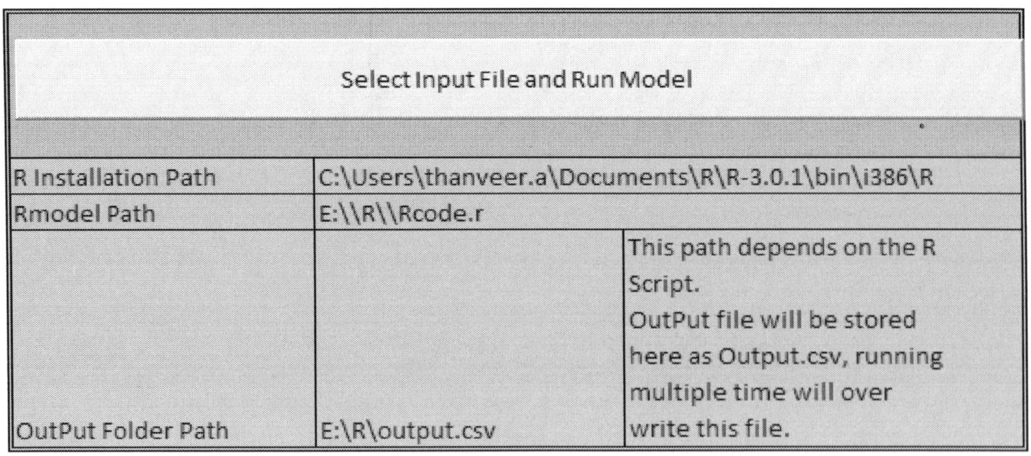

Fig. 6: User Interface for Accessing the Model

CONCLUSION

We classified customers based on Gender using machine learning techniques. We further outlined the major steps for data transformation and data cleaning and established the reason for selecting certain crucial parameters for model building. Furthermore, we provided an overview of the machine learning technique used and its relevance. We see several topics deserving further research.

Future Research

Based on the findings, the following represents the future scope:

(a) Conduct a detailed profile by industry as to the levels of use of behavioral targeting methods.
(b) Understand gender specific shopping patterns and responses to promotions by studying browsing patters
(c) Understand the gender specific risk taking, so as to understand the implications of the same in the Insurance, and Gambling Industry through behavioral research
(d) Conduct an extensive research so as to link browsing patterns to understand gender differences in preferences in brands

REFERENCES

Ackerman, M. (2000). The Intellectual Challenge of CSCW: The Gap between Social Requirements and Technical Feasibility. *Human-Computer Interaction 15*(2/3): 179-203.

Ben-Hur, Asa, & Weston, Jason (2009). A User's Guide to Support Vector Machines. In: O. Carugo, F. Eisenhaber (eds.). *Data Mining Techniques for the Life Sciences, Methods in Molecular Biology.* Ch 13, p. 223-239. Springer Verlag.

Cao, Peng, Zhao, Dazhe & Zaiane, Osmar (2013). *An Optimized Cost-Sensitive SVM for Imbalanced Data Learning.* Key laboratory of Medical Image Computing of Ministry of Education, Northeastern University, China, University of Alberta, Canada.

Cohen, N. (2009). As Data Collecting Grows, Privacy Erodes. *The New York Times*, February 16, 2009.

Conti, G. (2009). *Googling Security*, Pearson Education.

Cross-validation: evaluating estimator performance. Retrieved from: http://scikit-learn.org/stable/modules/cross_validation.html; accessed on 11th November 2014.

Data Mining Algorithms in R/Classification/SVM. Retrieved from: http://en.wikibooks.org/wiki/Data_Mining_Algorithms_In_R/Classification/SVM; accessed on 24th November, 2014.

Dwyer, Catherine (2009). Behavioral Targeting: A Case Study of Consumer Tracking on Levis.com. *Proceedings of the Fifteenth Americas Conference on Information Systems, San Francisco*, 2009.

Elkan, Charles (2012). *Evaluating Classifiers*. Retrieved from http://cseweb.ucsd.edu/~elkan/250Bwinter2012/classifiereval.pdf

Guyon, Isabelle & Elisseeff, Andre. (2003). An Introduction to Variable and Feature Selection. *Journal of Machine Learning Research 3*, 1157-1182.

Hara-czyk, Grzegorz (2010). *Predictive model optimization by searching parameter space.* Institute of Mathematics, Jagiellonian University, Poland.

Hsu, Chih-Wei, Chang, Chih-Chung, & Lin. Chih-Jen, (2010). *A Practical Guide to Support Vector Classification.* Department of Computer Science, National Taiwan University.

Jensen C., Sarkar C., Jensen C. and Potts, C. (2007). Tracking website data-collection and privacy practices with the iWatch web crawler. *Proceedings of the 3rd symposium on Usable privacy and security*, Pittsburgh, Pennsylvania, ACM, 2007.

Kai-Bo Duan & Sathiya Keerth, S. (2005). *Which Is the Best Multiclass SVM Method? An Empirical Study.* BioInformatics Research Centre, Nanyang Technological University.

Kotyuk, G.; Buttyan, L. (2012). A machine learning based approach for predicting undisclosed attributes in social networks. *Pervasive Computing and Communications Workshops (PERCOM Workshops), 2012 IEEE International Conference,* 19-23 March 2012. pp.361, 366.

Rahm, Erhard, & Hong Hai Do (2000). Data Cleaning: Problems and Current Approaches, *IEEE Bulletin of the Technical Committee on Data Engineering*, *23*(4).

Sundsoy, Pal, Bjelland, Johannes, Iqbal, Asif M, Pentland, Alex Sandy, & de Montjoye, Yves-Alexandre (2014). Big Data-Driven Marketing: How machine learning outperforms marketers' gut-feeling. *Social Computing, Behavioral-Cultural Modeling & Prediction Lecture Notes in Computer Science* Volume 8393, 2014, pp 367-374.

Webtrends (2014). *Database Marketing with Online Behavioral Data Made Simple.* Webtrends White Paper, 2014.

Waldo, J., Lin, H.S. and Millett, L.I. (2007). *Engaging Privacy and Information Technology in a Digital Age.* Washington, DC, National Academies Press.

PART
ONE-C

BRAND MANAGEMENT

Brand management is the practice of managing all aspects of a brand, from tangibles such as logo and package design to the intangible tenor of the emotions a consumer experiences when purchasing a brand product or service. The approach to strategically manage brands has transformed over the last few years with increasing social media usage, social media interactions and online consumer transactions. This colossal increase in customer interactions across multiple touch points coupled with increased connectivity and speed of information dissemination creates enormous amounts of data thereby posing challenges for firms to create, maintain, change or manage their brands in the digital era. Organizations need the ability to access, aggregate and analyze these volumes of data in order to manage their brands. The following papers are a part of understanding this movement and the ongoing process of managing the customer 'conversations'.

In their paper, 'A Brand Equity Construct Using Social Media And Consumer Research', Ayan Ghosh and Archana Menon explore an aspect of brand management in the Personal Computers market. They demonstrate the use of social media mining and surveys to construct a framework for tracking brand equity composed of brand awareness, brand assessment, brand judgment, and brand affinity.

The erosive impact of heavy discounting and frequent promotions on brand value is explored in S. Ravi Kumar's paper, 'Don't Let Your Brand Become a Commodity'. Regression modeling is used to identify the maximum number of discounts and discount depth that a marketer can offer to maximize sales without putting its brand equity at risk.

A new approach to sentiment analysis is discussed in the paper 'What People Are Saying About Your Brand When You're Not Looking: A Distinctive Approach to Social Media Sentiment Analysis'. Social media conversations provide marketers with a chance to tap into the unbiased, candid and unadulterated thoughts of consumers and understand their 'true' sentiment towards a brand. While most sentiment analysis techniques can be inaccurate due to a pre-defined dictionary and binary scores, this paper proposes a methodology overcoming these limitations through which the entire spectrum of consumer sentiments can be uncovered.

CHAPTER FIVE

A BRAND EQUITY CONSTRUCT USING SOCIAL MEDIA AND CONSUMER RESEARCH

Ayan Ghosh and Archana Menon

ABSTRACT

This paper explores an approach to track the Brand Equity of PC brands using triangulated results from social media mining and consumer surveys. The Brand Equity framework used in this tracker is constituted in four stages, namely, Brand Awareness, Brand Assessment, Brand Judgment and Brand Affinity. This framework can be used to assess the performance of PC brands to see how they fare with reference to each other on a quarterly basis and distinguishes itself from competing approaches through higher reach, lowest costs and most recent data on consumer sentiments.

PROBLEM STATEMENT

The PC market is undergoing a tectonic shift; regional players are shifting focus to global markets, new low cost players are beginning to gain market share in emerging markets, brands that were previously perceived as smartphone makers are now recognized as mainstream computing device makers, and established global PC manufacturers are struggling to hold on to their forte. In this scenario, it becomes important to constantly monitor the performance of a brand in comparison to competing PC brands. Historically, brand trackers have relied on primary research and consumer surveys. But the results from these trackers often suffer from a time lag, low sample size and high implementation costs.

OUR SOLUTION

In this digital age, there is a wealth of information available from social media conversations, which can be mined to gather meaningful insights. Enterprises of all kinds are investing millions of dollars on Online Marketing and Social Media campaigns to engage with the new age customer and increase the digital footprint. The resultant data is humongous and unstructured, calling for powerful mining tools. However, social media mining scores over traditional market research on multiple points including reach, cost, sample size, time, etc. Also, online conversations are often unprompted, which removes the respondent/ interviewer biases associated with traditional market research. Thus, social media mining is fast becoming one of the most important arms of next gen market research. The consumerization of big data analytics tools will add further impetus to this trend as it would allow for mining of near real-time data at much lower costs. In our solution we highlight a best practice where we marry the best of both worlds - consumer research and social media mining.

According to Keller's Customer Based Brand Equity model (CBBE), there are four steps to build a strong brand, which involves establishing brand identity, brand meaning, brand response and brand relationship. The CBBE model depends on six brand-building blocks, namely salience, performance, imagery, judgments, feelings, and resonance, for building a successful brand (Keller, 2008, p. 69). We take a similar approach to assess the brand equity of PC brands. (Please refer to Figure 1)

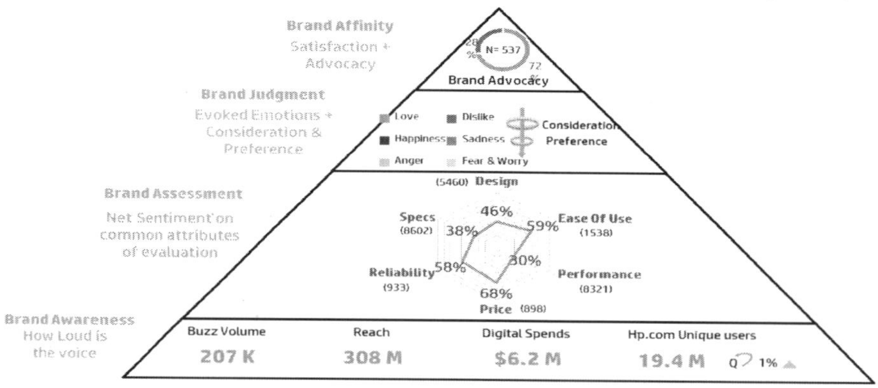

Fig. 1: Brand Equity Outline Example

Each brand is evaluated across four stages using metrics defined primarily through social media aggregation, supported by consumer survey results.

1. **Brand Awareness:** Buzz Volume & Reach (from social media), Digital Spends and Web Site Traffic (from syndicated research).

Buzz volume is the total number of posts and Reach is the total number of mentions (the no. of people who comment, retweet etc.) for the primary keywords, measured by the social listening tool. Digital Spend is the number of dollars spent on online advertising by each of the brands being studied. Website Traffic is the number of unique visitors for the company websites.

2. **Brand Assessment:** Net sentiment for 'Design', 'Ease of Use', 'Reliability', 'Price', 'Performance' and 'Specs' pertaining to computing.

   The Net Sentiment is the 'Absolute Difference between positive and negative sentiments defined as a percentage of the total sentiment bearing conversations'. The social media monitoring tool used for the analysis categorizes positive and negative sentiments to give the Net Sentiment score.

3. **Brand Judgment:** Emotions evoked (Mentions expressing 'Love', 'Happiness', 'Anger', 'Dislike', 'Sadness' and 'Fear & Worry') and Conversion Ratio, defined as Brand Consideration by Preference (from consumer survey).

   Emotions are measured by assessing the % of positive sentiment (for Love, Happiness) and % of negative sentiment (Anger, Dislike, Sadness, Fear & Worry) among the total number of sentiment bearing conversations.

4. **Brand Advocacy:** Satisfaction (Net Promoter Scores from consumer survey) and Advocacy (for or against the brand, from social media).

   The NPS scores are measured through a consumer research among the installed base customers and are refreshed on a quarterly basis, whereas the Brand Advocacy is expressed as the % of positive and % of negative sentiments (those who say they would recommend (in favor of the brand) and those who say they would not recommend (against the brand).

The brand tracker is refreshed on a quarterly basis to understand how the brands are faring with reference to each other as well as over the previous quarter,

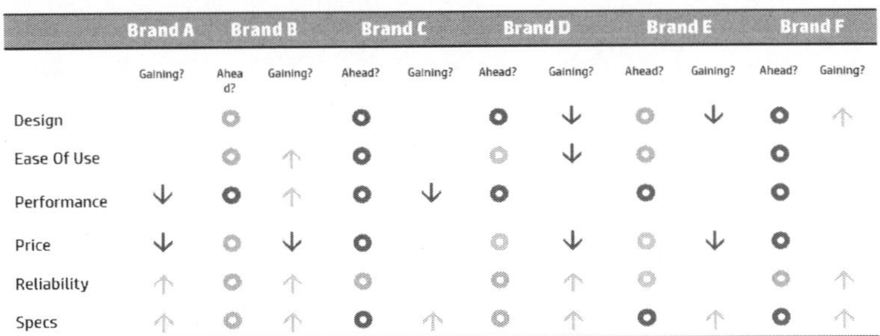

Competition significantly ahead, No significant difference between with Competitor, Significantly ahead of competition, Brand losing significantly over last quarter, Brand gaining significantly over last quarter

Fig. 2: Brand Assessment Summary

at each step of the brand equity process (Please refer to Figure 2). The difference in net sentiment (%) across quarters and across brands within a quarter for 'Design', 'Ease of Use', 'Reliability', 'Price', 'Performance' and 'Specs' are tested for statistical significance at a confidence level of 99%.

Though the current version of the tracker requires manual intervention, especially in defining keywords for different metrics, ongoing research in the field of Natural Language Processing is expected to improve efficiencies through automation.

CURRENT STATUS

Combining social media metrics and listening helps to arrive at key themes that help business understand the broad movements, i.e. new product line launches, specific features in demand etc., that affect and guide customer sentiment for respective brands and help formulate strategies that would help HP win in this digital world.

The solution has been used by the Customer and Market Insights team to compare the performance of brands across quarters vs. other brands and forms a part of a quarterly update that is rolled out to the Consumer Personal Systems business.

COMPETITIVE APPROACHES

Most brand trackers in use today are based on online surveys. The results from survey based trackers are easily quantifiable and it is also possible to get device level metrics (For example, HP Convertible PCs vs. Lenovo Convertible PCs) with higher accuracy. However, social media trackers fare better in terms of recency of data, sample size and cost. Moreover, this tracker captures the finer nuances of a brand, including emotions and imagery as well. Above all, triangulating results from different sources allow us to improve the business adoption of this solution.

NEXT STEPS

Current analysis is based on customer conversations on social media and the listening tools (based on keywords) are not able to source all comments from review sites like amazon.com, best buy etc. Capturing reviews from these sites using a web crawler and advanced NLP tools can give considerable inputs at a product level as well.

REFERENCE

Keller, K L. (2008). *Strategic Brand Management: Building, measuring and managing Brand Equity.* Upper Saddle River, NJ: Pearson Prentice-Hall.

CHAPTER SIX

DON'T LET YOUR BRAND BECOME A COMMODITY

S. Ravi Kumar

ABSTRACT

Over aggressive promotional deals and frequent promotions can erode brand loyalty as consumers get used to buying products at a lower price. The profit margin of a manufacturer is impacted in the long term because the brand value is eroded. Many brands are in trouble because management takes a short-term approach to boost sales by deep discounting and increasing the frequency of discount. The use of price as an incentive encourages consumers to focus on price as a differentiator rather than product quality or other brand attributes. The more people buy on deals, the more profitable the promotion will appear, unless allowance is made for any consequent fall in baseline sales resulting from such activities. If marketers ignore the erosion of baseline sales and continue to fund "profitable" price promotions, they risk turning loyal brand buyers into price shoppers who may come to find store brands an even better deal. A manufacturer should know how many promotions he should make in a calendar year and what is the depth of the discount he should be giving so that brand equity is not impacted. The frequency of discounts and depth of discount a manufacturer can give would change depending on the category.

This paper looks at proposing an analytical approach to identify the maximum number of discounts and depth (percentage) of discount a manufacturer can give so that the brand equity is not eroded, while trying to maximize sales without losing out on margin because of brand erosion.

Keywords: Brand Equity, Excessive Discounting, Frequency of Discounts, Impact of Promotions.

BACKGROUND – A DEAL CAN ALWAYS BE BEATEN BY A COMPETITOR

The most powerful value contribution of a strong brand is the ability to demand and defend higher prices than competitors. Value is the relationship between quality and price. Perceived quality takes time to build but it can be destroyed quickly by indiscriminate discounting for short term gains. While consumers may not have prices etched in memory, they usually have a good feel for a product's price relative to competitive products. Discounting is a temporary price reduction intended to increase sales over the short term, the perception of quality is not fixed as firmly in the mind of the consumer as the producer might think. For an established brand, discounting can have an adverse effect on value. Consumers don't view Quality and Price separately, they are interrelated. Research has shown that deep discounts do cause the consumer to believe that something is wrong. Frequent discounting lowers the value of the brand because of an almost subconscious reaction by the consumer who believes that quality also has been compromised.

Strong brands should avoid the vicious cycle of frequent deep discounts, if one is a part of it, then it is better to get out of it as soon as possible. A brand which has developed equity realizes no benefit over long term due to frequent sales and may be suicidal because in the interest of short terms gains they lose out on the margin in longer term. Customers tend to rely more on established brands to simplify the purchase task and reduce purchase risk. Maintaining a strong brand will bring many competitive advantages and results in financial returns in future. How far can a manufacturer go and where should he stop so that it is not seen as a brand whose quality has been compromised. A brand should just do the optimum number of discounts and do the right depth of discount so that it is perceived as a brand whose quality has not been compromised. We have proposed an approach to find out the maximum number of discounts and depth of discount a manufacturer can give so that the brand equity of the product is not compromised.

CLASSIC EXAMPLE OF WHAT EXCESSIVE DISCOUNTING CAN DO FOR A BRAND

Vlasic was one of most loved brands in America's kitchen cupboards for about 50 years; in the late 1990s it had started discounting its pickles by offering them in gallon – size jars. Wal-Mart began selling the product for an abysmally low $2.99

– a price so low that Wal-Mart made up 30% of Vlasic's business. This abysmally low gallon jar cannibalized Vlasic's other channels and shrank its margins by as high as 25%. When Vlasic asked for pricing relief, Wal-Mart refused an immediate price increase. In 2001, Vlasic filed for bankruptcy.

APPROACH

We are doing this study for a premium packaged food manufacturer in the U.S. The price gap is the difference in price between the product of interest, which in this case is price of the premium product and the price of the private label brand in the same category. The additional premium that a person is willing to pay for the premium brand is a measure of brand equity. The data that we have captures two different prices:

1. **Actual Price** – Actual selling price of the product, price inclusive of the promotions/discounts.
2. **Base Price** – Base Prices are estimated by extrapolating from periods when there are no price reductions or other kinds of promotions. In a way, it is the price the customer is generally used to paying for the product. This price is always greater than or equal to Actual Price.

The variation in Base Price is less as it is a smoothed price and does not change frequently, suggesting the brand equity does not change frequently, the change is slow and steady and changes over a period of time. Base Price Gap is the difference in Base Prices between the premium brand and the private label brand. This is the measure of equity in terms of price.

DRIVERS OF BRAND EQUITY FROM DATA PRESPECTIVE

- **Advertising GRPS:** The current brand equity of the product is a function of its advertising expenses in the past. Advertising has a long term impact on the brand though it also influences short term sales. Brand knowledge is created over time by all kinds of marketing communications such as advertising and promotion programs. We have used GRPS as a proxy for Advertising Expenses.

  Gross Rating Points = Reach * Frequency.

  GRPS is the product of the percentage of the target audience reached by an advertisement; times the frequency they see it in a given campaign (frequency × % reached)

Reach is defined as the size of the audience who saw the advertisement at least once in a given period. Frequency is the number of times the advertisement has been seen by an average person or household during a given time period.

This data is available for different media channels like TV, Online (Web), and Print. We have used only TV GRPS for this study, as the manufacturer did not use online and print as much. Advertising Expenses can be a proxy for GRPS but when both the variables are available, it is better to use GRPS, as they are not always linearly related. This is because sometimes the manufacturer is able to get a better discounted deal from the media channel, as a result even if more and more GRPS are pumped in the market, expenses do not increase commensurately in the same fashion.

- **R&D Expenses:** Companies focusing on product innovation and having a good R&D backbone generally tend to have higher brand equity. These companies are backed by strong R&D work on enhancing the packaging, enhancing the customer experience, increasing the self-life of the product and releasing different variants to cater to the health conscious market. For this study we have got the quarterly level data on the amount spend in dollars. This is one of the important drivers for enhancing customer experience and thereby increasing the brand equity.
- **Store Level Sensitivity:** Trading areas populated by more elderly people, larger percentage of Hispanic and African-American consumers tend to be both more price sensitive and more prone to purchasing private labels. The private label is usually more sensitive to changes in prices then the premium brand. The price gap which we are using as a proxy for brand equity should be less in these regions from the premium brand point of view, or the premium brand should completely avoid these markets unless the population in these regions is large enough to ignore.
- **Depth of Discount:** Like it or not discounting can be a sign of weakness and can hurt the brand image in the long run though it increases short term sales.
- **Frequency of Discounts:** It can lead to damage in brand equity and reduction in profitability in long run. Though price promotions increase sales in the short run, in the long run it can hurt brand image and the product might be perceived to be of a lower quality which is not able to differentiate itself from a regular private label brand and would be forced to sell at a lower margin. In our analysis we have used frequency of off season discounts.
- **Sales Ratio:** The last thing one would want is that though the brand equity in terms of the price gap is maintained, the premium brand is selling less then what it was selling previously. For example, if the gap was $5 previously and instead

of selling 100 units of packaged food, if the premium brand is selling just 70 units, this means that less and less consumers are willing to pay a higher price for this brand. The Sales Ratio is a derived variable (Volume Sales of Premium Brand/Volume Sale of Private Label Brand). This ratio should not decrease from a premium brand's point of view.

Most of the parameters discussed above have a lagged impact, meaning the money that has been splurged in advertising a year back will show an impact on brand equity now. The manufacturer is able to leverage the past advertising spend now by being able to charge additional premium without impacting his revenue. The same logic holds good for R&D Expenses. While both Advertising and R&D expenses will have a positive impact, the lagged Depth of Discount and Frequency of Discounts will have a negative impact now on brand equity.

DATA

Data Level: 4 Years Store Level Data at a monthly level for 500 stores
Data Source: Point of Sales (POS)
Tool Used: SAS

Key Variables	*Level*	*Usage/Type*
Current Base Price	Store Month	
Price Elasticity /Store Level	Store Month	
Depth of Discount	Store Month Level	Lagged
R&D Expense	National Quarterly Level	Lagged
Advertising GRPS	National Monthly Level	Lagged
Sales Ratio	Store Month	
Frequency of off Season Discounts	Monthly Level	

DATA CLEANSING AND DIAGNOSITCS

- **Missing value treatment:** Given we had adequate data we removed the rows where the price information and discount information was not populated.
- **Outlier treatments:** Proc Univarate in SAS was used to identify the outliers. The top 5% and bottom 5% of the observations in terms of price based on the frequency were removed.
- **Creating mean centered and modeling dataset:** Once the data has been cleaned and once outliers are removed, we are ready to create the regression dataset. The regression dataset differs from the raw store-week data in that it is **mean-**

centered by store. This means that, in the modeling dataset, each variable is set equal to its value in the store-week dataset *minus the mean value for that variable in each store.* This ensures that we are measuring the impact of changes over time within the same store and not, for example, that of different prices across different stores in the same week.

PROPOSED SOLUTION

The solution proposed is a regression model.

Dependent Variable

Base Price Gap as a proxy for Brand Equity

Independent Variables

Price Elasticity/Store Level
Depth of Discount
R&D Expense
Advertising Expenses
Sales Ratio
Frequency of off Season Discounts

The regression model is a statistical procedure used to find relationships among a set of variables. We have used a multiple linear regression with the following form:

Base Price Gap/Brand Equity per Unit = $\alpha + \beta_1$ (Advertising GRPS) + β_2 (Price Elasticity) + β_3 (R&D Expense) + β_4 (Depth of Discount) + β_5 (Frequency of discounts) + β_6 (Sales Ratio)

RESULTS AND INTERPRETATION

	Coefficients
Intercept	8.860713552
Advertising GRPS	0.010034319
Frequency of Discounts	–0.238714325
R&D Expenses	0.198301482
Avg. Depth of Discount	–1.947372714

R Square = 84%

All these above variables came out significant at a significance level (alpha level) of 5 % (0.05). **Sales Ratio** did not stay in the model, check was done to make sure if the sales ratio has not dipped.

- R&D Expenses have a bigger impact on the Brand Equity than the Advertising Expenses, intuitively it makes sense, the more the company spends on innovation and enhancing the packaging, the more it is able to charge a premium.
- Depth of Discount has a more detrimental impact on the brand equity than the Frequency of Discounts, the company should be more cautious on the percentage of discount it is giving.

Once we get the coefficients, the manufacturer has to take a call on how much gap needs to be maintained (in terms of the price) so that the brand equity is not eroded. Once the numbers are fed in the equation for Advertising GRPS, R&D Expenses, the manufacturer would get to know how much depth of discount and frequency of discounts one should be giving so that the gap is maintained.

- The Company wanted to maintain its Advertising GRPS at around 150 GRPS
- The Company wanted to maintain its R&D Budget at $2.4 Million per quarter

The manufacturer wanted to maintain the Brand Equity/ gap of $10 and wanted to see what could be its frequency of discounts in a year and depth of discount.

The company can create different scenarios for different values of Frequency of Discounts and Depth of Discount based on the regression equation and choose the one that makes most sense for it.

Examples of Scenarios

2 Discounts and 17% Discount

$$10.03 = 8.860 + 0.010034(150) -0.2387(2) + 0.1983(2.4) + -1.9473(0.17)$$

3 Discounts and 19% Discount

$$9.75 = 8.860 + 0.010034(150) - 0.2387(3) + 0.1983(2.4) + -1.9473(0.19)$$

4 Discounts and 21% Discount

$$9.47 = 8.860 + 0.010034(150) - 0.2387(4) + 0.1983(2.4) + -1.9473(0.21)$$

3 Discounts and 15% Discount

$$9.83 = 8.860 + 0.010034(150) - 0.2387(3) + 0.1983(2.4) + -1.9473(0.15)$$

We recommend that the manufacturer should go with the last scenario of 3 discounts in a year and can stretch up to 15% in terms of depth of discount in average. The reason to go with the last scenario was because the Brand equity measured in terms of Gap is very close to what the manufacturer wanted and the Gap is just below $10. The manufacturer can also go with the 1st scenario which maintains the brand equity at around the same level of $10.03, the only reason why this is not the preferred scenario is because the gap is slightly above 10 and breaching this psychological threshold of $10 could have negative impact on the volume sales.

REFERENCES

Barsky, Robert, Bergen, Mark, Dutta, Shantanu, and Levy, Daniel (2001). *What Can the Price Gap between Branded and Private Label Products Tell Us about Markups?* NBER Working Paper No. 8426. Retrieved from: http://www.nber.org/papers/w8426.pdf

Blattberg, R.C., R. Briesch, and E.J. Fox (1995). How Promotions Work. *Marketing Science, 14*(3): G122-G132.

Fong, Nathan M., Simester, Duncan I., and Anderson, Eric T. (2011). *Private Label vs. National Brand Price Sensitivity: Evaluating Non-experimental Identification Strategies.* Retrieved from: http://sites.temple.edu/nmfong/files/2011/11/nathan_fong_jmp.pdf

Li, Hai Hong (2007). *Impact of Price Promotions on Customer-based Brand Equity with a Proxy Measure,* pp. 1–60. Retrieved from: http://spectrum.library.concordia.ca/975778/1/MR40981.pdf

Volpe, Richard James (2010). *National Brand and Private Label Pricing and Promotional Strategy.* III1, pp. 1–35. Retrieved from: http://ageconsearch.umn.edu/bitstream/60986/2/10181.pdf

CHAPTER SEVEN

WHAT PEOPLE ARE SAYING ABOUT YOUR BRAND WHEN YOU'RE NOT LOOKING: A DISTINCTIVE APPROACH TO SOCIAL MEDIA SENTIMENT ANALYSIS

Sameer Malhotra, Anand S. Rao and Joseph D. Voyles

ABSTRACT

Tapping into the rich consumer dialogue in social media allows companies a unique advantage over conducting traditional market research: the opportunity to gain insights from consumers' unadulterated and spontaneous thoughts, and assess their 'true' sentiment towards a brand or product. However, harnessing meaningful and specific insights from the vast volume of data generated has proved to be challenging. Most social media sentiment analysis techniques compromise the accuracy of a sentiment model as they rely on pre-defined 'classifiers' or 'dictionaries' that are limiting; develop less granular 'binary scores' that do not measure the full range of consumers' attitudes toward a subject; and do not account for context, introduced through subtleties of human language and writing styles.

PwC has developed a fast, simple and discerning methodology for social media sentiment analysis that (a) measures the full width of the sentiment spectrum, (b) allows for key words to emerge based on consumer usage patterns (versus pre-defining them), and (c) identifies and integrates the contextual background for the unstructured dialogue. Our approach utilizes natural language processing (NLP) to detect 'token' sentiments, identify the textual content and recognize the arrangement patterns of the words/phrases, and then aggregates these token scores to come up with a granular 'overall sentiment score' that sits on a broad continuum that captures the range of negative to positive emotion.

This accurate, time-effective and uncomplicated methodology (no probabilistic classifiers or training-based algorithms in the back end) allows marketers the ability to extract key trending consumer themes, sentiment drivers and the specific contexts related to the on-going social conversation. This allows them to not only detect changing customer preferences and perceptions in near-real time, but also to 'sense' unmet needs and proactively participate in and powerfully influence the consumer dialogue, positioning them at the leading edge of the industry.

INTRODUCTION

Businesses have started acknowledging sentiment analysis as an important methodology to leverage non-traditional sources such as blogs, social media, mails etc. to unmask hidden information and insights. Sentiment analysis attempts to answer a very essential question: 'What do people like?'. Its applications include understanding employee sentiments, estimating the influence of a marketing campaign and identification of pain points in business strategies. There are numerous approaches and vendors that perform sentiment scoring with varying levels of accuracy and complexity. However, most of these have limited application due to lack of business context, dependency on training data, lack of granularity, etc. But despite these issues, sentiment analysis has been increasingly used in the recent times as a technique to analyze unstructured data or open text. Research also supports the same. Dhar & Chang (2009) in their research have shown that music sales are positively correlated with the volume of blog posts about an album.

PwC has developed a fast and flexible methodology to predict the 'goodness' of open text on a 10 point scale. The underlying goal behind this exercise was to help companies answer questions like 'what people are interested in?', 'how is my brand or product being perceived?', 'what is my competitor doing better than me?' etc., and to introduce the buyer to an objective methodology for research and comparison of products. In order to achieve this, we developed a scoring algorithm using some of the popular sentiment analysis and natural language processing techniques. The approach was then tested on multiple online datasets including movie review databases, airline rating websites and social media portals. Although different data from different sources showed different levels of accuracy in scoring, the overall polarity match was over 90%, which is extremely competitive when compared with many of the traditional sentiment scoring services in the market.

Throughout the development, the focus was on keeping the procedure simple enough so that it can be used with ease, yet effective so that it can be used to solve business problems. Although the current methodology is limited and fails to understand the industry specific contexts and sentiment details, it does allow for manual customization to improve accuracy in industry specific scoring. The customization comes in 2 ways: manually modifying/updating the taxonomy to reflect industry specific sentiment, and adding user-defined rules to the calculation logic.

THEORY

With the vast amount of online data being produced every day, sentiment classification has grown as one of the upcoming topics over the past few years. Traditionally, the focus has been on classifying large text, like reviews (Pang, Lee & Vaithyanathan, 2002) and blog posts (Mishne, 2005). Sentiment analysis using machine learning based classifiers by Pang et al. (2002) has been a baseline technique for many other works in this field.

Despite substantial research, there are several challenges in the business application of social media sentiment analysis. The sheer size of data and the unstructured nature of the open text are two major hurdles in this space. The nature of data includes the level of language complexity as well as the quality of content, and the noise in the data. These vary across regions and data sources and create hindrance in the process of development of a universal sentiment analysis algorithm. However, there have been several attempts to incorporate these irregularities and complexities into scoring models and methods.

In this section, we shall elaborate on some of the methods and concepts that were used in our exercise.

Defining Sentiment

Though sentiment is a complex human emotion that describes multiple states of mind, popular research assumes sentiment to be a measure of how much good or bad feeling is conveyed by a given text.

The above definition is subjective as the good/bad nature is difficult to quantify due to lack of proper standards. Also, as the size of text increases and it becomes more complex, there are bound to be multiple sentiments corresponding to multiple fragments of the text. Combining those individual emotions to come up with a single representative sentiment is also a difficult task. Some of these complexities are intrinsic to the language, such as sarcasm or use of pun words, whereas some are more context specific and depend on the topic of conversation, author's history and region etc. In a lot of cases, the text fragments may appear to have sentiments associated with them but the intent of the overall statement is to put forward a neutral opinion. A general rule of thumb to identify such statements is to see if they could ever appear as a newspaper headline on the front page, or as a sentence in Wikipedia.

Sentiment Analysis

Sentiment analysis can be defined as the use of natural language processing, text analysis and computational linguistics to identify and extract subjective information in source materials (Wikipedia). The aim of sentiment analysis is to determine the attitude of the author in the context of the conversation or topic of discussion.

The most basic form of sentiment analysis involves categorizing the text as positive or negative. This is often referred to as the *sentiment polarity* of the text. Pang (2002) and Turney (2002) did some of the early work in this field where they applied different methods to detect polarity of movie and product reviews respectively. While some researchers believe in bucketing text into only positive and negative groups, and treating the border line cases as neutrals, others are of the opinion that neutral texts are a separate group in itself and hence the bucketing logic should treat neutral as a separate addition to positive and negative buckets.

A more complicated but more impactful way is to produce a sentiment scale (–5 to +5) or a star rating (0 to 5). The advantage of such methods is that they quantify not just the polarity, but also the *intensity* of the sentiment. Snyder & Barzilay (2007) did an extensive research in this area to predict ratings based on restraint reviews.

In further advanced analysis techniques, *subjectivity* of the text sentiment is also determined in addition to the polarity and intensity. How subjective/objective the text is relates to the ambiguity in the meaning of the words that contribute to the text sentiment. As described by Su & Markert, 2008), the subjective nature of any text depends on the meaning of subjectivity used when annotating text. The text is ultimately classified into two categories: subjective or objective.

In our approach, we have limited the analysis to identify the polarity and intensity of sentiment.

Analysis Methodologies

In this section, we shall discuss the different methods of sentiment analysis, and the different granularity levels at which sentiment scoring is done. Based on the level at which scoring is done, different approaches are classified as:

- **Document Level Scoring:** The complete document (article, post, review or blog etc) is assigned a single sentiment score which is indicative of the overall emotion of the complete content of the document. Apart from the sentiment calculation itself, the step of combining individual sentiments of different sections of the document is an additional level of complexity.
- **Sentence Level Scoring:** Sentence level scoring is a more granular scoring approach in which every sentence in the data is given an independent sentiment score. This scoring generally creates high accuracy results as individual sentences usually carry simple unidirectional sentiments. The downside is that in scenarios where sentences are contextually linked, scoring does not reflect the actual sentiment of the text.
- **Entity Level (Aspect Based) Scoring:** Entity level scoring relates to calculating the overall sentiment associated with a particular entity (object, brand or process, etc.) across the entire text. In involves detecting all possible references to the entity, calculating the sentiment relating to every reference, and combining the individual sentiments to come up with an overall entity sentiment. Detection of entity references is done using text classification algorithms. It is a really powerful approach as it allows businesses to pin-point attributes, services or products that are less appreciated than others.

Each of the above can be done using different algorithms or methods. These methods can broadly be classified as:

Lexicon Based Methods

In a basic lexicon or keyword based approach, text is classified on the basis of the presence of certain unambiguous words such as happy, sad, afraid, bored, etc. (Ortony, Clore, & Collins, 1988). These words are called *affect* words as they have affinity to a particular emotion. Some relatively developed methodologies also account for arbitrary words that were not a part of the original affect words. This is done by assigning a probable affinity to these words based on their occurrence with the original affect words.

In our analysis, we have leveraged a very basic form of lexicon based sentiment analysis technique in which each affect word is associated with a stationary sentiment score. This allowed us to not only categorize the text, but also to score it. To score a given text, all scores associated with the affect words in it are modified as per the context and rolled up using a mathematical formula. The result is a numeric score in the range of –5 to +5.

Statistical Methods

These methods use complex *machine learning* techniques to automatically identify positive or negative nature of the text. Some of the popular processing techniques are:

- **Probabilistic Classifier:** A Naïve Bayes classifier and decision tree classifier are two popular machine learning based classification techniques. Classifiers take decisions based on rules that they learn using a training dataset (supervised learning). In sentiment analysis, classifiers require to be trained on a pre-scored dataset in order to identify what is good versus what is bad. These training datasets comprise of text which is already classified into categories, hence called scored or tagged data. It is important to not have neutral texts in the training data as it can bias the classification and create skewed results.
- **Latent Semantic Analysis (LSA):** LSA is a natural language processing technique which analyses the relationships between a set of text documents by producing a set of concepts related to the same (Wikipedia). The underlying principle behind the algorithm is that words with similar meaning will occur in similar pieces of text. The text is converted into a mathematical matrix of word frequencies and the similarity between words is calculated. Text is classified as good/bad based on how similar the words in the text are to affect words.
- **Support Vector Machines (SVMs):** SVMs are supervised learning models with associated learning algorithms that analyze data and recognize patterns, used for classification and regression analysis. They also require training data to understand the linguistic behavior and categorize text based on the patterns observed in the training data.

Research shows that for analyzing large documents of text such as blogs, such methodologies are more effective than the lexicon based approach. For our analysis, we tried and tested some of the above techniques as part of our experiments but due to limitations like biases in the training data, huge training time, etc. these approaches were found to be less effective.

APPROACH

PwC has tried to make the algorithm exhaustive by testing it on data from multiple online sources, having varying degrees of complexity.

Preprocessing of Data

Free text or unstructured data in its raw form is inevitably associated with various data quality issues. Some basic ones include presence of URLs, phone numbers, dates etc in the text which increase processing time. Other more complicated issues involve presence of ambiguous words (For example the word 'like') that can tamper with the results. As part of our algorithm the first step was to remove noises in the data. This was divided into the following steps:

Data Cleaning

All non-ASCII characters, URLs and websites, special characters and numbers were removed from the raw text.

Data Standardization

All text was converted to lower case for uniformity. Also, some phrases in the text contained words that carried a different sentiment than the overall phrase itself. For example, 'right' usually is associated with a positive sentiment but in the phrase 'right across' it is a neutral word. It was important to replace such ambiguous phrases with similar meaning neutral language in order to improve the accuracy of the algorithm. However, this was a manual effort and the list of ambiguous phrases was heavily dependent on the data being analyzed. After a few iterations of analysis, the following substitutions were identified as significant and were hence added to the data standardization process in order to remove ambiguous phrases from the text:

- 'kind of' was replaced by 'similar to'.
- 'hard work' was replaced by 'hardwork'.
- 'right now' was replaced by 'now'.
- 'not to mention' was replaced by 'also'.
- 'right across' was replaced by 'across'.
- 'not at all' was replaced by 'not'.
- the title 'Miss' was replaced by 'Ms'.
- 'right away' was replaced by 'at the time'.

Although there were certain noises in the data that depended on the source of data as well, after performing the above general steps, the data was ready for analysis.

Selecting the Approach

The following analysis options were explored:

Naïve Bayes Classifier

The classifier was trained on 10,000 positive and 10,000 negative tweets (Go, Bhayani, & Huang, 2009). During the training process, every word is assigned a probability that it might be positive or negative based its occurrences in the positive and negative training data.

Let $n(W, X)$ = Number of times word W appears in the data X,
$t(X)$ = Total number of tweets in the data X,
$t(W, X)$ = Total number of tweets in the data X which have the word W.

Then the probability that a given word W is positive is given by

$$P(W^{+}) = n(W, T^{+}) / n(W, T)$$

where T is the complete training data and T^{+} is the positive training data.

Using Bayes' theorem, the probability that a text D, containing words W_1, W_2, $W_3 \ldots W_n$ is positive can be written as a function of the probabilities of each W_i being positive. Mathematically,

$$P(D^{+} \mid \{W_1, W_2, W_3, \ldots, W_n\} \subseteq D)$$
$$= P(D^{+}) \times P(\{W_1, W_2, W_3, \ldots, W_n\} \mid D^{+}) / P(\{W_1, W_2, W_3, \ldots, W_n\}$$

- $P(D^{+})$ is the independent probability of D being positive, given by $P(D^{+}) = t(T^{+}) / t(T)$
- $P(\{W_1, W_1, W_1, \ldots, W_n\})$ is the total probability of occurrence of the words W_1, W_1, W_1, …, W_n given by $P(\{W_1, W_2, W_3, \ldots, W_n\}) = \prod^{n}_{(i=1)} [P(W_i)] = \prod^{n}_{(i=1)} [t(W_i, T / t(T)]$
- $P(\{W_1, W_1, W_1, \ldots, W_n\} \mid D^{+})$ is the probability of occurrence of the words W_1, W_1, W_1, …, W_n in the positive data given by

$$P(\{W_1, W_2, W_3 \ldots W_n\} \mid D^{+}) = \prod_{i=1}^{n} [P(W_i \mid D^{+})] = \prod_{i=1}^{n} \left[\frac{t(W_i, T^{+})}{t(T^{+})}\right]$$

The text was classified as positive if the probability of the text being positive was more than the probability of it being negative, and vice versa.

Google Search Based Relative Mutual Information

Mutual information (MI) of significant words in the text with sentiment words was calculated using Google search results representing probability of occurrence (Lin, Wu, & Yu, 2012). Mutual information between 2 words A and B is defined as:

$$\text{MI (A, B)} = \frac{P\ (A\ and\ B)}{P\ (only\ A) \times P\ (only\ B)}$$

To calculate the sentiment of a word W, we compare its MI with the words *best** and *worst**. For a word *W* to be positive, MI (*W*, 'Best') > MI (*W*, 'Worst').

$$\Rightarrow \frac{P(W + Best)}{P(Best)} > \frac{P(W + Worst)}{P(Worst)}$$

The probability is calculated by the number of Google search results for the particular word(s). Hence, a word *W* is considered to be positive if

$$\frac{Google\ results\ (W + Best)}{Google\ results\ (Best)} > \frac{Google\ results\ (W + Worst)}{Google\ results\ (Worst)}$$

While searching, another level of complexity was added by removing search results containing 'worst' in the Left hand term and 'best' in the Right hand term. This was done using '–' feature in Google advanced search. Therefore, the word *W* is positive if

$$\frac{Google\ results\ (W + Best - Worst)}{Google\ results\ (Best - Worst)} > \frac{Google\ results\ (W + Worst - Best)}{Google\ results\ (Worst - Best)}$$

Once sentiments for all words in a given text were determined, a tweet with more positive words than negative was tagged as positive and vice versa.

Sentiment Dictionary

Sentiment scores for a word were calculated using the WordNet sentiment database, which is a freely available online lexicon resource. The dictionary originally contained a list of about 30,000 words and word forms along with a corresponding sentiment score. One word could be mapped to multiple scores depending upon the different uses/meanings of the word. All good words have a positive score and all bad words have a negative score. In our methodology, we have used one consistent score for a given word, which is selected as the score with the maximum magnitude from amongst all the scores corresponding to that word. The overall sentiment score of a given text was calculated as follows:

$$\text{Text Score} = \text{Max}(P_1, P_2, P_3, \ldots, P_n) - \text{Max}(N_1, N_2, N_3, \ldots, N_n)$$

where $P_1, P_2, P_3, \ldots, P_n$ are positive scores corresponding to good words in the text and $N_1, N_2, N_3, \ldots, N_n$ are magnitudes of the negative scores corresponding to bad words.

A common dataset consisting of about 72,000 tweets was used to compare the performance of the models. The models were used to categorize the tweets into positive/neutral/negative buckets, and sentiment score calculation was not included at this stage. The results from these were evaluated based on accuracy and time consumption.

Refining the Approach

The final approach was selected after trying multiple methodologies. Based on the results, the sentiment dictionary approach was observed to be the most accurate and fast, and was hence chosen for sentiment scoring.

The basic approach went through multiple iterations based on result feedback and SME inputs. This feedback was selectively used to refine the methodology to improve accuracy and efficiency. The key improvements include:

Emoticon Score

The emoticon score is a measure of the sentiment associated with the emoticons in the text. As all special characters and numbers are removed during the data cleaning stage, it is important to calculate this score before that stage. Once the URLs and website names are removed, the text is searched for any of the emoticons listed in a pre-defined emoticon dictionary. Score calculation follows the following logic:

- If the text has no emoticons, or the number of positive and negative emoticons is the same, the text has an emoticon score of 0, which means that the text is neutral.
- If there are more positive emoticons than negative ones and the difference in the counts is less than 4, the text is given a score of +1, which means that the text is positive. If the difference is equal to or more than 4, the text is given a score of +2, which means that the text is highly positive.
- If there are more negative emoticons than positive ones and the difference in the counts is less than 4, the text is given a score of –1, which means that the text is negative. If the difference is equal to or more than 4, the text is given a score of –2, which means that the text is highly negative.

The emoticon score is a better indicator than the text score to estimate sentiment as emoticons are independent of language biases and contextual ambiguities. Due to this reason, researchers have used emoticons to automatically tag Twitter data in order to create training data for classifiers: a tweet having ☺ in it is associated with a positive emotion whereas a tweet having ☹ is associated with a negative emotion.

However, the limited availability of emoticons across different datasets limits the application of emoticon scoring.

Sentiment Dictionary Revision

Unlike probabilistic methodologies, our lexicon based approach takes scores for different sentiment related words/phrases based on a pre-determined mapping which is compiled in the sentiment dictionary. It has two major sections: the positive dictionary and the negative dictionary. Each of these sections has sentiment scores for words, word phrases (bigrams, trigrams etc.), emoticons and some special symbols.

Starting with the publically available WordNet dictionary, our sentiment dictionary has been updated multiple times to make it more relevant and exhaustive. These updates included the following:

- Adding new terms to the list of positive/negative words/phrases. These include swear words, multiple verb forms of some existing terms, etc.
- Modifying the scores of existing terms for better accuracy.
- Adding emoticons and special symbols to the dictionaries. These are not associated with any score as such.

The following is the summary of the dictionary as used in the analysis. Although having a lexicon based approach has proven to be highly efficient and accurate for estimating sentiment, it has several limitations. These are listed below:

- Every word score is mapped to a constant score. Although this maintains consistency across datasets, it does not account for the dynamic nature in which the word can be used. This risk is mitigated to some extent by other parts of the algorithm (like negation and amplification) but there remain several instances where the allotted score does not represent the actual emotion. This issue is particularly significant in the instances when the sentiment polarity itself is reversed.
- As language is a dynamic and evolving phenomenon, the sentiment dictionary also needs timely revisions to keep it up to date with the latest and most frequently used sentiment terms.
- A finite dictionary limits the vocabulary of the algorithm and hence the accuracy of sentiment calculation. Manual effort is required to make the dictionary as exhaustive as possible for the text that is being analyzed. This process can include multiple iterations, but improves the performance of the scoring algorithm significantly.

Despite the above limitations, we have been able to leverage the sentiment dictionary across datasets and industries to score text with varying degrees of convolution.

Implementation

The algorithm was implemented using a Python code due to Python's flexible and easy coding nature. There are various Python libraries that cater to problems related to different areas of linguistics. For our purposes, the Python NLTK library was most relevant and was leveraged for various NLP related tasks.

The program takes 2 Excel files as input:

1. The data file containing raw text to be scored.
2. The sentiment dictionary containing words, emoticons and n-grams along with their respective scores.

The analysis is done roughly at the rate of 1000 texts per second (speed may vary depending on available RAM, and text size and complexity), and the output is generated in the form of an Excel file that gives every text an overall polarity, an overall sentiment score, an emoticon score and also lists the sentiment related words in the text that went into score calculation.

Once the results are generated, the performance of the algorithm is benchmarked against scoring done by a leading sentiment scoring service. The results are compiled to identify loopholes in the methodology which is given as feedback to the model.

RESULTS

Comparison of Sentiment Scoring Techniques

As discussed in section 3.2, in order to come up with the most efficient sentiment scoring algorithm, multiple scoring techniques were run on a set of about 72,000 tweets from the social networking site Twitter. The results were compared to those produced by a professional sentiment scoring tool that also scored raw text on a scale of -5 to +5. However, for comparison of these techniques, only the polarity of the scores was compared. The accuracy of any approach was hence defined as the percentage of tweets that were given same polarity as the scoring tool. Accuracy was calculated in two ways: *overall accuracy* and *accuracy excluding neutrals*. This was because of 2 reasons. Firstly, there was more ambiguity in scoring of the border line cases, i.e. tweets with slightly positive / slightly negative / neutral nature, and secondly because around 83% of the data consisted of neutral tweets (Go, Bhayani, & Huang,

2009) and hence the overall accuracy may not represent the actual efficiency of the methodology to predict correct polarity.

The first method was the popular machine learning based scoring using a Naïve Bayesian classifier. Unlike the other approaches, this approach does not have any external contingencies. Another important advantage of using this was the unsupervised nature of the classifier. However, a major drawback of using a probabilistic classifier is the huge training time. The total execution time for the program was 15 hours, out of which most time was used by the training process. Despite this huge time investment, the overall accuracy was 25% and the accuracy excluding neutrals was 52%. Though this could be improved by larger training datasets, the rise in accuracy would not be significant.

The mutual information approach was found to be better than the classifier because of various reasons. Because it used Google to analyze words, the vocabulary of the classifier was practically infinite and it could automatically take care of misspelled words as well. Also, the score of a word/phrase would change dynamically with its changing usage on the net thereby accounting for the variation of a word's sentiment over time. The downside is that this approach depends on an external search engine and its privacy policies. Also, as the scoring logic is dynamic, there would be minor variations in the results with every run. We achieved an overall accuracy of 31% with this approach whereas the accuracy excluding neutrals went up to 59%. The total execution time was about 4 hours and 40 minutes. Although this was better than the first method, there was still a large percentage of tweets that were inaccurately scored. A major reason for this was that the number of Google hits was not a true representative of the mutual information between words.

The sentiment dictionary approach was observed to be the most accurate method with 57% overall accuracy and 81% accuracy excluding neutrals. As there was no training time or net searches involved, the execution time was also the lowest: about 2 hours. Although the vocabulary of the dictionary was limited it proved to be more effective than the other approaches as a direct and precise word-score mapping was used. The approach is not completely unsupervised as the dictionary would need to be updated with the changing language and context. But despite these drawbacks, this approach was observed to be the fastest and most effective scoring technique.

Evaluation of Final Performance

After going through multiple iterations, the scoring algorithm was able to predict the polarity of 91% of the data correctly. This percentage varied across sources is described in Figure 1.

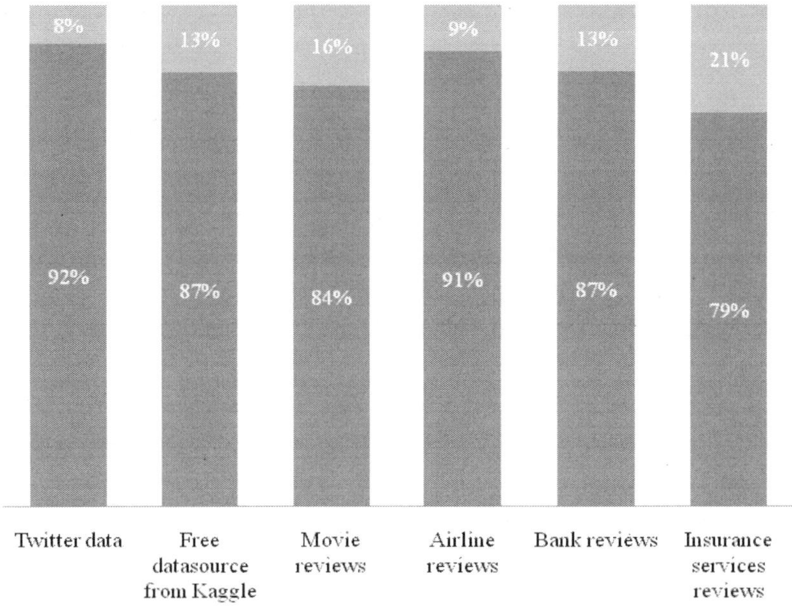

Fig. 1

As observed from the above, the algorithm performs better on small and simple data (like Twitter data which has an upper bound of 140 characters) as compared to large and complex paragraphs (like movie reviews).

A more detailed analysis of the individual score values (Figure 2) shows that across the range, the accuracy generally lies between 60% and 85%. The highly skewed numbers in the extremes are due to low total number of posts/reviews in

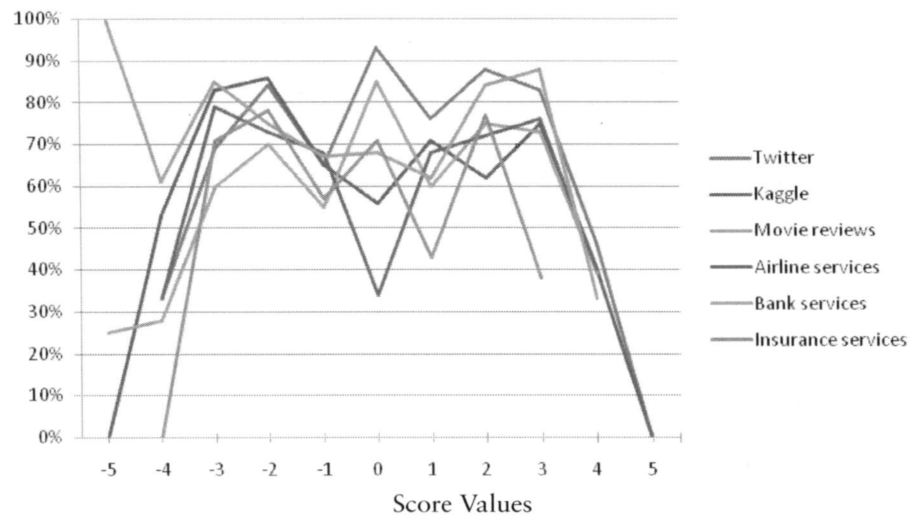

Fig. 2

those buckets. We also see that industries such as insurance services show low accuracy. This is because the terms and sentiments in such industries are not generic and hence require customization of the sentiment dictionary.

For the Twitter data, we further compared our complete distribution of sentiments scores with those produced by the industry scoring tool (Figure 3). The green regions represent the good/acceptable accuracy whereas red regions correspond to incorrect scoring. We observed that over 90% of the tweets were given the exact score by our algorithm as by the industry tool (Refer to the dark green regions in the following heat map). We observed that there is slight overestimation of the sentiment in case of ambiguous text. Also, the percentage of tweets given incorrect polarity is minimal.

		In-house Developed Tool		
		Negative	*Neutral*	*Positive*
Industry scoring tool	Negative	89%	9%	2%
	Neutral	1%	93%	6%
	Positive	2%	6%	92%

		In-house developed tool											
		-5	-4	-3	-2	-1	0	1	2	3	4	5	Total
Industry scoring tool	-5	0%	0%	0%	0%	0%	0%	N/A 0%	0%	0%	0%	0%	100%
	-4	0%	33%	53%	14%	0%	0%	0%	0%	0%	0%	0%	100%
	-3	0%	0%	69%	24%	3%	2%	0%	0%	2%	0%	0%	100%
	-2	0%	0%	2%	84%	3%	9%	1%	1%	0%	0%	0%	100%
	-1	0%	0%	1%	18%	65%	13%	2%	1%	0%	0%	0%	100%
	0	0%	0%	0%	1%	0%	93%	0%	5%	1%	0%	0%	100%
	1	0%	0%	0%	0%	2%	12%	76%	8%	1%	0%	0%	100%
	2	0%	0%	0%	1%	0%	6%	2%	88%	3%	0%	0%	100%
	3	0%	0%	1%	0%	1%	1%	1%	13%	83%	1%	0%	100%
	4	0%	0%	0%	0%	0%	4%	0%	8%	42%	46%	0%	100%
	5	0%	0%	0%	0%	0%	0%	0%	0%	83%	17%	0%	100%

Fig. 3

CONCLUSION

The paper demonstrates how simple algorithms can be used to effectively score open text, and have accuracy similar to machine learning or other complex approaches. Due to its simplicity, this algorithm becomes significantly advantageous in scenarios where Big Data is to be scored or where sentiment analysis is a part of a larger strategy model.

The approach has certain drawbacks that limit its application: The modification of the sentiment dictionary for a specific domain is still a manual task but can be automated using algorithms like Term Frequency–Inverse Document Frequency (TF-IDF) or nGram analysis which can identify top terms and phrases within the domain. Another constraint is the inability of the logic to understand contextual meanings or linguistic relations such as sarcasm, word sense ambiguity or use of puns in the text. Many of these issues can be mitigated by coupling the sentiment dictionary with machine learning algorithms. Such compound methodologies could remarkably expand the scope of sentiment analysis.

REFERENCES

Dhar, Vasant, & Chang, Elaine A. (2009). Does Chatter Matter? The Impact of User-Generated Content on Music Sales. *Journal of Interactive Marketing, 23,* 300–307.

Go, A., Bhayani, R., Huang, L. (2009). *Twitter Sentiment Classification using Distant Supervision.* CS224N Project Report, Stanford. Retrieved from http://cs.stanford.edu/people/alecmgo/papers/TwitterDistantSupervision09.pdf

Lin, Wei-Hsuan, Wu, Yi-Lun, & Yu, Liang-Chih (2012). Online Computation of Mutual Information and Word Context Entropy. *International Journal of Future Computer and Communication, 1*(2).

Mishne, G. (2005). Experiments with mood classification in blog posts. In *1st Workshop on Stylistic Analysis of Text for Information Access.* Heidelberg: Springer Verlag.

Ortony, Andrew, Clore, G, & Collins, A. (1988). *The Cognitive Structure of Emotions.* Cambridge Univ. Press.

Pang, B., Lee, L., & Vaithyanathan, S. (2002). Thumbs up? Sentiment classification using machine learning techniques. In *Proceedings of the Conference on Empirical Methods in Natural Language Processing (EMNLP),* pp. 79–86.

Snyder, Benjamin, & Barzilay, Regina (2007). Multiple Aspect Ranking using the Good Grief Algorithm. In *Proceedings of the Joint Human Language Technology/North American Chapter of the ACL Conference (HLT-NAACL).* pp. 300–307.

Su, Fangzhong, & Markert, Katja (2008). From Words to Senses: a Case Study in Subjectivity Recognition". In *Proceedings of Coling 2008,* Manchester, UK.

Turney, Peter (2002). Thumbs Up or Thumbs Down? Semantic Orientation Applied to Unsupervised Classification of Reviews. In *Proceedings of the Association for Computational Linguistics.* pp. 417–424. arXiv:cs.LG/0212032.

Wikipedia: http://en.wikipedia.org/wiki/Sentiment_analysis.

PART
ONE-D

PROMOTION

One of the challenges that many companies face is how to promote their products among target customer groups. In the era of information overload, customer attention span is low and they filter out messages from companies really fast. They are bombarded with promotions from different companies through varied sources. At one hand there are large companies using extensive mass media with big promotional budgets. On the other hand, there are smaller companies and start-ups with limited budgets that look for new age media channels for targeted promotions. Both traditional mass-media channels as well as new-age media channels have their separate positions and relevance in promotional strategies of companies. While effectiveness of mass media is well-established, new age media channels like internet marketing, mobile marketing and social media marketing are increasingly taking a prominent share of promotional budget of companies.

In this section, in the first paper Anjali Malik, Rajiv Kumar and Lalit Sharma use case study approach to understand implementation and effectiveness of mobile marketing campaign. They discuss case of Rocketalk's Global Social Application, an application with 8.2 million active users spread across small towns in different parts of India. Rocketalk allowed personalization of the content for marketing campaigns to a set of targeted consumers for their clients. This paper presents an evaluation of some successful campaigns for Rocketalk's clients Channel V, Tata Motors, Bausch & Lomb, Idea, and Mirinda. Major strategies used by Rocketalk for engaging consumers with high data consumption behaviour included content download, social interactions and contesting.

In the paper titled 'Coupon Redemption: Power to predict valued shoppers', Akshatha Krishna explores challenges faced by retailers to acquire and retain customers. Consumer response models are intended to help retailers understand how consumers individually and collectively respond to marketing activities. Coupon promotions are one of the major vehicles used for marketing a product especially in the retail world. However, effectiveness of coupons in increasing the sale and repurchase behaviour continues to be a challenge for most of the retailers. This study proposed a predictive modeling approach using factors such as brand loyalty, consumer purchase cycle, coupon attractiveness, etc., as determinants of redemption behavior. The model is aimed at providing distinct characteristics of one time and loyal customers that can be leveraged by the retailers for customized target marketing.

CHAPTER EIGHT

IMPLEMENTATION AND EFFECTIVENESS OF MOBILE MARKETING CAMPAIGNS: A CASE STUDY OF ROCKETALK

Anjali Malik, Rajiv Kumar and Lalit Sharma

ABSTRACT

As the uptake of mobile telephones has increased at a very fast pace in India, mobile marketing has offered marketers an extraordinary opportunity to explore new channels of advertising and promotion. This paper aims to offer new insights into the implementation and evaluation of effectiveness of mobile marketing campaigns. The present study followed a case study research method, with an aim to report specific comprehension and as detailed a description of the phenomena as possible. The paper discusses a case of Rocketalk's Global Social Application, for understanding the effectiveness of the usage of mobile phones as promotional media. Rocketalk had 8.2 million active users in India, with a very large base contributed by smaller towns of Punjab, Haryana, Andhra Pradesh, Tamil Nadu, Karnataka, Kerala, Gujarat and Maharashtra. Rocketalk allowed personalizing the content and distribution of their marketing campaign to the set of targeted consumers. Major strategies used for engaging consumers with high data consumption behaviour were, content download, social interactions and contesting. This paper further presents an evaluation of some successful campaigns for Channel V, Tata Motors, Bausch & Lomb, Idea, and Mirinda. The study contributes to the existing body of knowledge about mobile marketing campaign management and also provides suggestions for more effective management of mobile campaigns. Discussion, conclusion, and directions for future research are presented.

INTRODUCTION

The marketing communications environment is rapidly changing and companies are exploring ways to receive better value for their investments in marketing. Of late marketers have started questioning the effectiveness of traditional channels of marketing communication such as T.V., radio commercials, magazine advertisements, direct mail campaigns and so on. With more and more consumers spending significant amounts of online time accessing through their mobile devices, the mobile platform offers a perfect mechanism for reaching consumers. The mobile phone today, because of its interactive capabilities, presents extraordinary opportunities to marketers to engage the target customers. Mobile devices such as cell phones enhance consumers' ability to quickly, easily and electronically exchange information about products and to receive mobile advertisements immediately at any time and in any location (e.g., using mobile text message ads) (Drossos et al., 2007). Also, cell phones have the potential to reach most consumers due to their high penetration rate (EITO, 2012). The proliferation of smartphones has given marketers an opportunity to offer a rich mobile consumer experience to its users. There is substantial increase in the number of consumers visiting the internet from their mobile phones. Leading research agencies have projected high levels of growth both in mobile usage and spending. According to Morgan Stanley Report (2014), data subscribers in India are expected to grow at a 25 per cent Compound Annual Growth Rate (CAGR) from 210 million to 519 million in 2016 and 35 per cent CAGR in data usage to 750 MB per subscriber. As per TRAI (Telecom Regulatory Authority of India) the total number of internet subscribers at the end of 2013 stood at 210 million, out of which 90 per cent users (188 million) access it on mobile devices. Though the evidence of effectiveness of mobile marketing campaigns is scarce, still the total expenditure on mobile marketing campaigns by businesses has significantly increased. Global Internet advertising totaled $113 billion in 2013, up 16% from the year before. **Mobile** advertising accounted for 11% of that, up 47%. In 2014, mobile phones accounted for 25 per cent of global web usage which was up from 14 per cent in 2013 (Forbes, 2013). In order to fill this gap in the literature the objective of the study was to gain new insights into implementation and effectiveness of designing and executing mobile campaigns using Rocketalk, a social mobile application platform as an example.

FEATURES OF MOBILE MARKETING CAMPAIGNS

Mobile marketing is basically a set of practices that enables organisations to communicate and engage with their audience in an interactive and relevant manner through any mobile device or network (Mobile Marketing Association Inc, 2014). Mobile devices include all characteristics necessary to establish a direct dialogue between the marketer and the potential customer (Bauer et al, 2005). Mobile marketing campaigns are either push based or pull based. Push based mobile messaging means sending content to the mobile subscriber at a time other than when the subscriber requests for it e.g. Audio, SMSs, E-mails etc. Pull based messaging is defined as any content sent to the mobile subscriber upon request shortly thereafter on a one time basis (MMA, 2014). As per previous literature, mobile marketing campaign management can be divided into four phases: campaign design, campaign development, campaign execution, and tracking analysis and reporting. Execution of the mobile campaign in the mobile channel can be done in various ways such as SMSs, Multimedia messaging service (MMS), mobile e-mailing. Though SMS is still the most popular mode, a variety of other services based on the mobile internet are gradually gaining popularity (Haig, 2002). Among the other various mobile applications, mobile apps with social sharing capabilities are gaining fast popularity. One of such mobile apps with integrated social-networking capabilities was designed by Rocketalk, which is studied here as a case. Effectiveness of the marketing campaigns is measured with reference to the advertisement's potential effect on awareness, knowledge, preference or sales (Karjaluoto et al., 2007). Effectiveness of mobile campaigns is measured using metrics like number of banner clicks, number of banner views, and a metric named CTR (Click Through Rate). CTR measures the percentage (or rate) at which mobile users click an app's advertisement. For the advertiser it evaluates the efficacy of their campaign. CTR is calculated by dividing the total number of clicks on an ad by the total number of impressions.

METHODOLOGY OF STUDY

This study took place in India with the company Rocketalk, a social mobile application platform. It is basically an exploratory case study to understand designing, implementation and measuring effectiveness of mobile campaigns. This research has studied business-to-consumer applications of the mobile platform. The case study method was chosen for the study because little is known about this phenomenon and present theories seem inadequate. As a method face-to-face interviews were conducted with the practitioners and they were presented with the how-and-why type of questions to further explore and understand the phenomena (Yin, 2003). This research has used a single case study method with Rocketalk example for understanding the firm's experience of executing mobile marketing campaigns on their social network platform, as suggested by Kumar, Stern and Anderson (1993).

Interviews with the practitioners in the firm were directed towards understanding their knowledge and experience in designing and implementing mobile campaigns. Interviews were further supplemented with the secondary data available within the organisation for measuring the effectiveness of the mobile campaigns.

About Rocketalk

'RockeTalk, a mobile social networking app, has now become the most widely used mobile app in India overtaking both Orkut (a giant in India) and Facebook, according to a report by mobile analytics firm Informate."

– *Social Times*, February 2, 2011)

"RockeTalk is the top mobile social network in India."

– *Mobile Social Networking 2011-2015*, Visiongain

RockeTalk was founded in 2009 with a vision of taking social interaction, expression and entertainment to a new level for any mobile phone user. The company envisioned a social app that could serve as a bridge between consumers and marketers. Rocketalk's vision was to become a place of escape from daily life where subscribers can hang out with like-minded people, join in live conversations, express themselves or simply enjoy content posted by others. The aim was to enrich the lives of the billions of new Internet consumers for whom the mobile phone is a primary window to the online world. Their applications are compatible to full spectrum of devices, ranging from entry level feature phones to the very latest smart devices. For the wide variety of their users, it promises that everyone always has something to do. Social modules available on the application created user clusters for various activities such as contests & games; mobile talk shows; content M-store; people profile; UGC posting & sharing; Live multimedia communities; chat & social communication. Rocketalk has over 14 million registered users, out of which 8.2 million active users are from India,

Table 1: User Base Segmented by Geography

S. No.	*States of India*	*Percentage of Subscribers*
1	Punjab, HP, NCR, Haryana	23.00%
2	Tamil Nadu, AP, Karnataka, Kerala	26.00%
3	Gujarat, Maharashtra, Goa	21.00%
4	UP, Uttaranchal, Bihar, Jharkhand	12.00%
5	W. Bengal, Orissa, Assam	8.00%
6	MP, Rajasthan, Chhattisgarh	8.00%

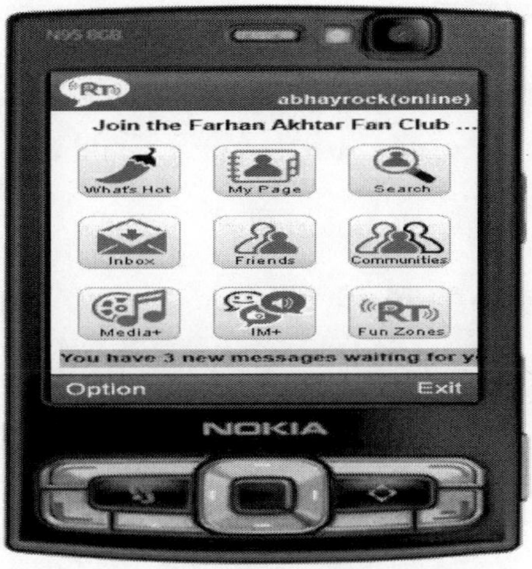

a. Home Screen

b. What's Hot Section

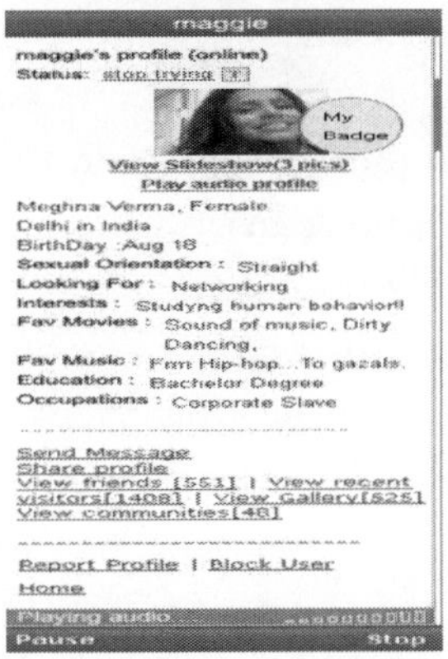

c. My Page Section

d. Friends Section

e. Inbox Section

f. Fun Zone

Exhibit 1: Product Details of Rocketalk

with a very large base contributed by smaller towns of Punjab, Haryana, Andhra Pradesh, Tamil Nadu, Karnataka, Kerala, Gujarat and Maharashtra. (Table1: User base segmentation). The rest, approximately 4 million users, are from other parts of the world. Rocketalk offers communication in around 100 languages and out of all, Hindi, English and Urdu are the most popular ones.

Mobile Campaign Management (Implementation and Effectiveness)

Rocketalk offers nine functions to its users namely, What's Hot, My Page, Friends, Inbox and Rich Messaging, Communities, Media, Instant Messaging, Search, and Fun Zone. (For Product Snapshot refer Exhibit 1). What's Hot is a high traffic section and serves as a gateway to whatever is new and user popular in the application. My Page is the user's dedicated space and consists of a snapshot of the user's activities, it also has a profile wall. Friends section constitutes a contact list of friends with online and offline markers. Inbox is Rocketalk's lifeline where all communication begins and ends. It receives and sends P2P messages, community messages, contest messages and supports all combinations of voice, video, picture and text. Fun Zone offers free and paid downloads for ringtones, wallpapers, greetings, music and video. 'Communities' is an interest based virtual hang-out zone. There are around 140,000 communities which host Live Shows, discussion and debates. Instant messaging section allows users to create their own chat rooms with multiple friends in real-time. Rocketalk allows personalizing the content and distribution of marketing campaigns to the set of targeted consumers. Major strategies used for engaging consumers with high data consumption behaviour were, content download, social interactions and contesting. Evaluations of some successful campaigns executed on the Social Mobile Application platform of Rocketalk are discussed in the following section:

OVERVIEW OF THE CAMPAIGNS

- **Channel V Exhausted:** The first campaign was executed for Channel V. The name of the campaign was Channel V Exhausted, which was a reality game show that required 8 finalists to stay awake for more than 48 hours, doing impossible tasks. Channel V wanted to popularize its show widely across various big and smaller cities and towns in India so as to maximize its reach hence chose to launch a mobile media campaign through Rocketalk. Rocketalk replicated the same on its social mobile environment, using a program called Wake-a-thon, where users participated and sent audio/video entries of the tasks they were asked to perform. The campaign was run for twenty – three days and the results of the campaign were phenomenal. Channel V/Wake-a-thon Videos were viewed by 2,54,431 people across various towns and Channel V contest questions were attempted by around 43,729 people. The Channel V/Wake-a-thon banner received 27,50,111 impressions. In additions to this, there were 1,98,466 unique users who saw the Login message about Channel V and 27,50,111 Impressions that were generated for System Buzz were sent for show introduction and TUNE IN. (For Campaign details refer Exhibit II)

- **Tata Maanza:** The second campaign was designed for Tata Motors for the launch of their new car Tata Manza. The objective of the campaign was not only to promote their new car, Tata Manza, but also to collect general user feedback about medium end cars. To achieve the objective, Rocketalk was used as a mobile platform for popularizing their mobile campaign which promoted the TATA Manza brand jingle to their users and along with the advertisement, a contest was also launched asking users to create their own song based on the Advertisement jingle and users were allowed to sing their jingle in their own style. The campaign was run for 30 days and the results obtained were quite impressive. The campaign was able to gain 15,802 entries during the period of campaign with 1,74,96,067 banner views and 1,81,745 banner clicks. (For Campaign details refer Exhibit II)
- **Bausch & Lomb:** The aim of the campaign of Bausch & Lomb was that it wanted to promote their Model Hunt Contest already running on Face Book on a mobile platform in order to drive more traffic to the contest. The campaign was promoted by Rocketalk through the Bausch & Lomb contest via promotional banners thus increasing the number of people voting and raised awareness among the targeted audience significantly. The results of the campaign were as follows: in the city of Jaipur, the campaign was run for 2 days and it was able to garner 1,74,300 banner views in such a short duration, with around 5969 banner clicks and CTR of 3.42% was achieved. The campaign was also launched in the city of Chandigarh, where it was run for 15 days. During this period 9,12,287 banner views were achieved and the total number of banner clicks was around 50,380. CTR of the campaign was 5.52%. (For Campaign details refer Exhibit II)
- **Idea:** Idea approached Rocketalk with an aim of promoting IDEA 3G to tier 2 and tier 3 city users in India. The goal was to increase the number of unique users, raise awareness and increase subscriptions to the mobile service provider. The solution offered to achieve the objective was in the form of Jingle based banners promoting the theme of IDEA 3G with lead capturing promotional themes of IDEA's TV commercial campaigns already running across electronic

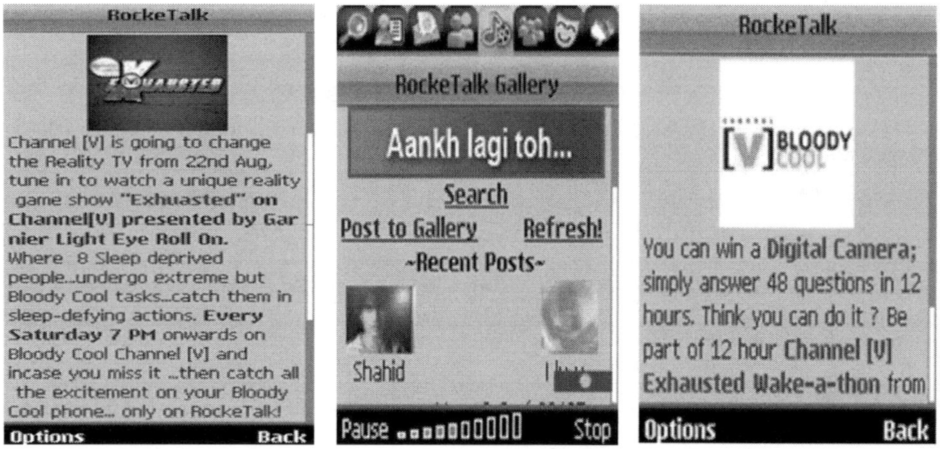

a. Channel V: Wake-a-Thon

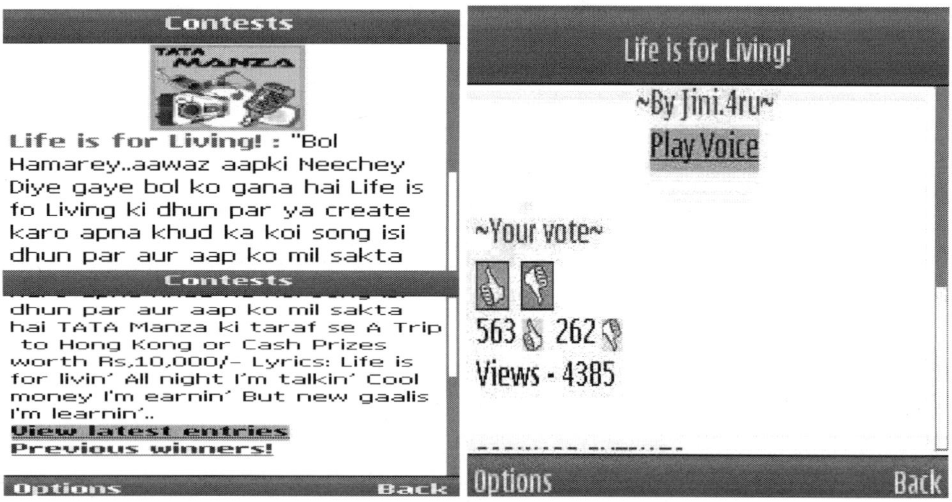

b. Tata Maanza Contest

c. Bausch and Lomb: Model Hunt Contest

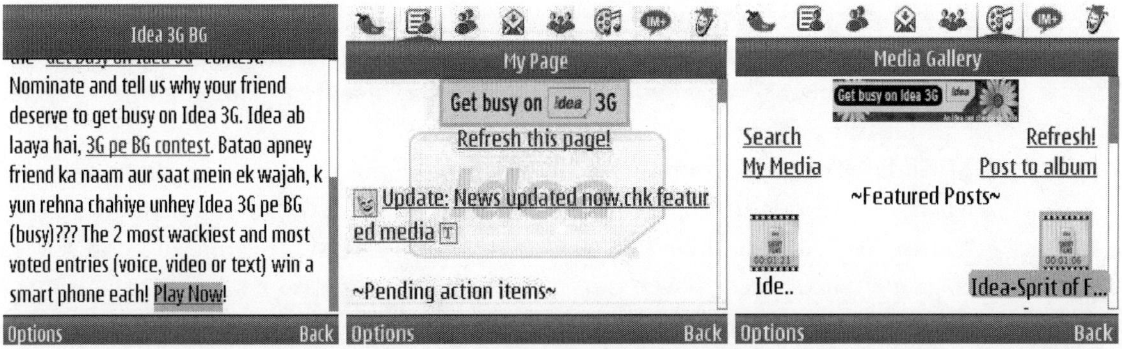

d. IDEA: Jingle Based Banners

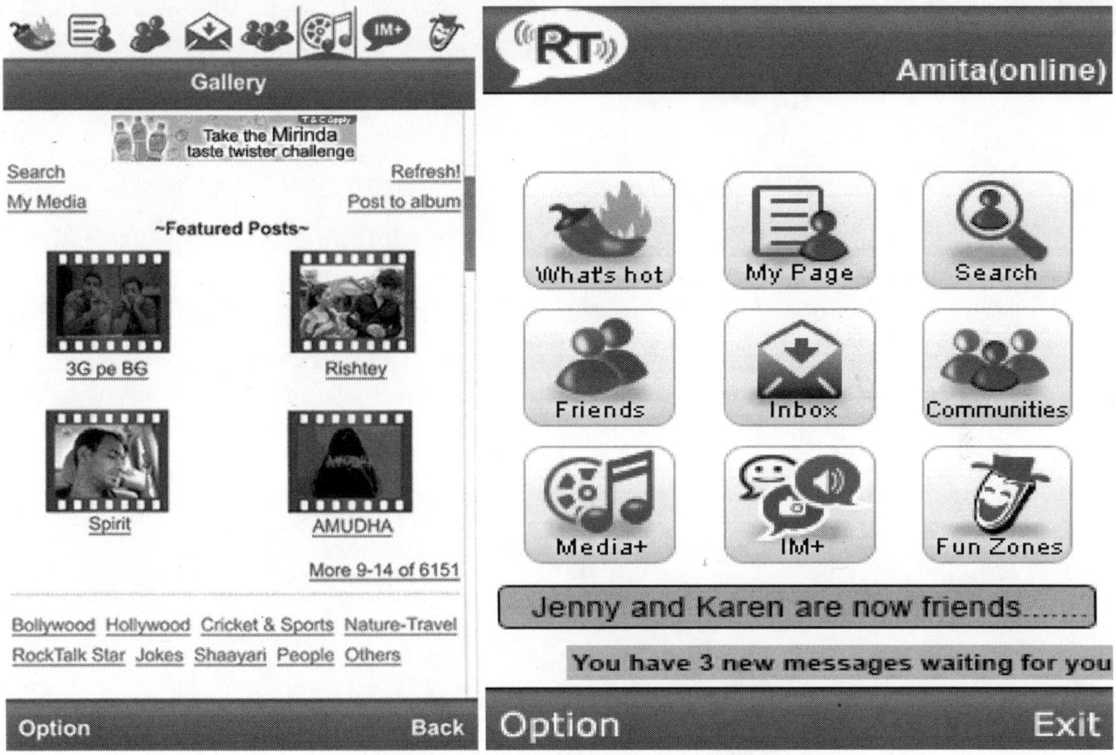

e. Mirinda : Taste Twister Challenge

Exhibit II: Rocketalk Campaign Details

and digital media. The duration of the campaign was 30 days, during this period the banner campaign with jingles received 36,62,161 banner views, and 65,097 banner clicks and CTR of 1.78%. The banner campaign was also run without jingles again for 30 days duration, the results of the campaign were as follows: the number of banner views received were 2,05,83,481, the number of banner clicks were 1,93,557, and the CTR was 0.94%. IDEA's TV commercial was also featured in Rocketalk's Media Gallery, total 6 videos were uploaded and the average number of views it received were 3,52,784. (For Campaign details refer Exhibit II)

- **Mirinda:** The last campaign studied for the purpose of our study was for Mirinda. Mirinda had launched a nationwide 'Taste Twister Challenge' and they wanted to promote their IVR (Interactive Voice Response) based contest to a large audience across India, directing the participants to be a part of Mirinda's breathless movement. As a solution to this objective more than twenty-six thousand calls were generated on the Mirinda IVR through various engagement methods. The campaign was run for 9 days and total calls generated were 26,406, with 7,351 brand profile views and 2,631 brand profile friends. (For Campaign details refer Exhibit II)

ANALYSIS AND DISCUSSION

"RockeTalk... a new form of self expression through the mobile phone that informs, entertains and connects people through the media they create."

– *WINNER, mBillionth Awards 2012*, Judge panel

"We (the Judges) have been astonished by the pace of innovation shown by the RockeTalk team this year in pioneering new digital formats for mobile and believe they are worthy recipients of this overall recognition."

– Rajiv Dhingra, *CEO WAT Consult, WAT Awards 2013*

Mobile platforms in India are offering a new way to forge brand-consumer connections, especially among teenagers and young adults of small towns in India. The results of the campaigns explain and highlight users' willingness to engage in mobile marketing activities such as accessing content, registering for contests and incentives and receiving advertisements via their mobile phones. Mobile messages may drive consumers to either make purchases through mobile apps, or have them interact with the brand digitally to drive them to physical stores to buy their products. Every marketing communications campaign needs to be evaluated in terms of efficiency and effectiveness, in case of mobile market campaigns one advantage is that we can monitor campaign actions in a very short time. Although reporting of data depends on the service provider and the nature of the messages, as we have also observed in case of different examples highlighted above including videos, banner, IVR calls, contests etc. There are a number of metrics available for measuring effectiveness of mobile marketing such as number of messages sent, number delivered, number bounced, number of stop messages, number of replies, number of downloads, etc. For the purpose of our study we have used the following metrics: number of banner views, number of banner clicks and Click Through Rate (CTR). According to Appflood (2013), the average CTR for banner ads on mobile phones is 0.23%. In comparison to the industry average, we found that Rocketalk achieved a very high CTR ranging from 7.20 per cent to 0.94 per cent for the various mobile campaigns it executed on its platform. (Refer Table 2)

Table 2: Promotional Banner Campaign Results

S. No.	*Name of Company*	*Campaign Details*	*Number of Banner Views/ Impressions*	*Number of Banner Clicks*	*Click Through Rate (CTR)*
1	Channel V	Banner, Wake-a-thon Videos	27,50,111	1,98,466	7.20%
2	Tata Motors (Tata Manza)	Banner, Jingles and contest	1,74,96,067	1,81,745	1.04%
3	Bausch & Lomb	Banner & Contest (City – Jaipur – 2 days)	174300	5969	3.42%
		Banner & Contest (City – Jaipur – 15 days)	912287	50380	5.52%
4	IDEA	Banner with Jingles	3662161	65097	1.78%
		Banner without Jingles	20583481	193557	0.94%

Rocketalk has won several awards for effectiveness in executing mobile campaigns. Rocketalk won Silver EMVIES of Advertising Clubs EMVIES (2013) for Best Media Innovation and a silver award also for Best Integrated Campaign for the IDEA campaign. They have also received Bronze Smarties Global for Best Use of Mobile Social Application awarded by MMA Global in 2013. They had also won Mobile Campaign of the year Award in 2012 from MMA. The awards were given to Rocketalk as a platform for all the mentioned Brands campaigns in the study.

CONCLUSION

The power of mobile technologies to overcome physical and time barriers and to provide connectivity from anywhere 24 × 7 is motivating marketers to focus on consumers who are not reachable with other media options. U.S. consumers spend

20% of their time on mobiles, which gets only 4% of ad spending. (They spend 5% of their time on print, which gets 19% of advertising.) Consumers in emerging markets like India are more willing to engage in mobile marketing and promotions because in these markets consumers' experience and exposure to mobile marketing and communications is less, unlike in the developed markets where mobile platforms are cluttered with advertisements. A growing number of people in India now have access to voice and mobile data communication services, and consumers also are more willing to engage and interact in mobile space. Hence, companies in India are emphasizing on the mobile platform for advertising and promotion efforts in order to capitalize on the favourable condition. The above case study has reiterated that the proliferation of smart phones with Internet and computing functions have given marketers an opportunity to offer a rich mobile consumer experience even in smaller towns in India. There was a substantial increase in the number of users from different parts of India participating in the various mobile campaigns run by Rocketalk. The analysis of the above data highlights that the projected level of growth in both mobile usage and spending is high. While planning and executing marketing communication campaigns on mobiles, the most important factor that needs to be taken care of is, how the promotion content of print or electronic campaign is changed for a mobile application.

As was shown in the above example, social networks are here to stay and best practices of designing mobile apps with social integration would keep on evolving. Rocketalk with the help of its application made sharing a truly one click effortless experience hence was subscribed by a very large base of users across various states of India including subscribers from Tier 2 and Tier 3 cities. This research has provided a very useful insight for marketers that if they learn to use the mobile channel efficiently, both the customers and the company will benefit. Mobile marketing can prove to be extremely efficient if it succeeds in generating viral effects. One of the important things to consider here is that though mobile phones fall under call-to-action media, if too many messages are received by users, it may cause message fatigue as well. Hence, we suggest that more insights into the emerging mobile marketing value system are desired in order to exploit its full potential in terms of offering marketing opportunities.

REFERENCES

Bauer, H.H., Reichardt, T., Barnes, S.J., & Neumann, M.N. (2005). Driving Consumer Acceptance of Mobile Marketing: A Theoretical Framework and Empirical Study. *Journal of Electronic Commerce Research*, 6 (3), 181 -92.

D'Vorkin, Lewis (30 June 2014). Being Everywhere All the Time. *Forbes, 193*, Issue 9, p.12

Drossos, Dimitris, Giaglis, George M., Lekakos, George, Kokkinaki, Flora, & Stavraki, Maria G. (2007). Determinants of Effective SMS Advertising: An Experimental Study. *Journal of Interactive Marketing,* 7(2), 16–27.

EITO. (Feb. 2012). More Than Five Billion Mobile Phone Users. http://www. eito.com/press/Press-Releases-2010/More-than-five-billion-mobile-phone-users. Accessed 13 Feb. 2012.

Forbes Fifty Essential Mobile Marketing Facts (2013). Retrieved from: www.forbes.com/sites/cherylsnappconner/2013/11/12/fifty-essential-mobile-marketing-facts.

Haig, M. (2002). *Mobile Marketing the Message Revolution.* Kogan Page Publishers.

Karjaluoto, H., et al. (2007). Insights into the Implementation of Mobile Marketing Campaigns. *International Journal of Mobile Marketing,* 2(2), 10 – 20.

Kumar, N., Stern, L.W. and Anderson, J.C. (1993). Conducting Interorganizational Research Using Key Informants. *Academy of Management Journal, 86*(6), 1651 – 1688.

Leppaniemi, M. & Karjaluoto, H. (2008). Mobile Marketing: From Marketing Strategy to Mobile Marketing Campaign Implementation. *International Journal of Mobile Marketing, 3*(1), 50 – 61.

Mobile Marketing Association Inc. (2014). *MMA Updates Definition of Mobile Marketing.* Retrieved from: mmaglobal.com/news/mma-updates-definition-mobile-marketing

Morgan Stanley Report (2014). Retrieved from: www.morganstanley.com/about/ir/shareholder/3q2014.pdf.

Yin, R.K. (2003) *Application of case study research* (Applied Social Research Method Series, Volume 34). London: Sage.

CHAPTER NINE

COUPON REDEMPTION: POWER TO PREDICT VALUED SHOPPERS

Akshatha Krishna

ABSTRACT

With different platforms like social media, advertisements, and word of mouth influencing customers' buying behavior, retailers are challenged with competitive and innovative strategies to acquire and retain customers. Understanding the buying behavior of customers is of utmost priority for the retailers for efficient marketing strategies. Retailers spend huge amount in promotion with the intention to draw more customers. Consumer response models are intended to help retailers understand how consumers individually and collectively respond to marketing activities. Appropriately estimated effects constitute a basis for improved decision making in marketing. Coupon promotions are one of the major vehicles used for marketing a product especially in the retail world. In seeking to enhance the effectiveness of coupon promotions researchers have long sought to identify 'coupon prone' consumers. The loyal customers would anyway purchase with or without any offer whereas one time customers would redeem the offer and might not return. In both the cases the retailer will have to bear huge losses. The objective of this study is to predict the likelihood of a customer to repeat the purchase which will help the retailer to segment the target market and to allocate the marketing expenditures effectively.

This study proposes a framework for measuring coupon proneness using predictive modeling approach. The methodology is based on a model of coupon redemption that accounts for factors such as brand loyalty, consumer purchase cycle, coupon attractiveness etc. as determinants of redemption behavior which will provide distinct characteristics of one time and loyal customers which can be leveraged by the retailers for customized target marketing.

Keywords: Predictive Modeling, Coupon Redemption, Loyalty, Consumer Purchase Cycle, Target Marketing.

INTRODUCTION

Coupons are an important promotional tool in many consumer product categories, with about 315 billion coupons distributed in the United States in 2013 with an average redemption rate of 2.8% (NCH Marketing Services). As manufacturers and retailers seek to enhance the effectiveness of coupon promotions, they have focused considerable attention on the identification of 'coupon prone' customers and on the measurement of the extent of coupon proneness.

Coupon proneness needs to be assessed across all product categories because a consumer who is prone to using coupons in general may choose to disregard coupons for his favorite brand in a category where he is highly brand loyal. In a different category, where he is less loyal to any particular brand, he may switch brands to take advantage of a coupon offer. This suggests that if we are to understand and predict consumer response to specific coupons, we need to measure coupon proneness at the level of the product category. Bawa and Shoemaker (1987a) found that while households' coupon usage across categories is correlated, there is substantial variation from one category to another. The major implication of their research is that households may differ in their propensity to redeem coupons across categories. Hence, we need to distinguish between the general coupon proneness of an individual and the propensity to redeem coupons in different categories.

Past research has identified a number of coupon characteristics that have an effect on redemption behavior. These researches suggests that coupon face value, distribution media, consumers' prior inclination of purchasing the couponed brand, past promotional pattern and consumer's expertise are all significant drivers of coupon redemption rates. Hence we need to conduct research on category-specific propensity to redeem coupons in order to formulate effective promotional strategies. In this paper we investigate how category specific factors such as purchase frequency, perceived coupon availability and brand loyalty vary with category-specific coupon proneness.

The purpose of this study is to determine factors that drive the consumer's propensity to redeem coupons. The paper seeks to contribute to the literature in two ways. First, it provides a framework for the measurement of coupon proneness at a brand category level. The proposed framework takes into account factors such as brand loyalty, consumer purchase cycle, coupon attractiveness etc. Second, it seeks to provide a better understanding of redemption behavior by segmenting the target market so that business managers can identify potential customers who have higher probability of making a re-purchase and optimize the marketing budget cost effectively.

MODELING COUPON REDEMPTION

Among the various forms of consumer promotions, coupon promotion continues to be popular among manufacturers. According to a leading media and marketing services organization in the US, Consumer Packaged Goods (CPG) manufacturers distributed 315 billion coupons in 2013, 3.3% more than the year prior and consumers' expectations for value and desire for coupons remained strong in 2014 indicating increasing coupon redemption trends in the US market.

The objective of this study is to be able to predict shoppers who are most likely to make repeat purchases when presented an offer/coupon. Uncovering the trend and patterns of the already existing customer and making appropriate strategic actions is an easily accomplishable task, whereas, prediction of a new customer's likelihood to purchase a product based on the offer provided is quite a challenging task. Without knowing in advance which new customers will turn out to be hit-and-run customers, a costly retention campaign sacrifices too much revenue on customers who would return anyway i.e. if every new customer is offered a rebate on their second purchase, those destined to come back will simply pay that much less when they do.

The predictive model plays a pivotal role in these situations. The model is created with data mining methods that understand the underlying behavioral patterns and learn from transactional information. The model then applies what has been learned to produce a predictive score for each new customer in real time which can provide insight to which new customers are likely to return and which are probably one-timers. In this way, new customers who would otherwise never return are targeted and enticed to stay. Since the retention offers on new customers are not wasted, they are likely to return and the overall growth rate increases substantially and immediate-term profits are not put at risk.

If it is predicted that first-time customers will not return, they can be targeted with an aggressive conversion campaign, enticing those that would otherwise leave with a heavy discount or free trial. In this way, they would be converted to have a long-term relationship with the brand or retailer. Predictive analytics enables retail organizations to gain more insight into what customers will buy, their needs, and shopper behavior which will empower them to target new and existing shoppers in a better manner. It will also help the retailers to take proactive decisions based on trends and patterns in the huge amount of historical data.

How can Existing Customer Profiles be Used for Prediction?

A lot of transactional behavior and product use history, and demographic information about the existing customer is available, which can be utilized to target for retention of the existing customers as well as building predictive models, the insights from which can be used to target prospective customers for acquisition. The final objective of targeting acquisition of new customers is conversion to long term repeatable, loyal customers in order to have higher profit margins, more frequent purchases and lower sensitivity to price changes.

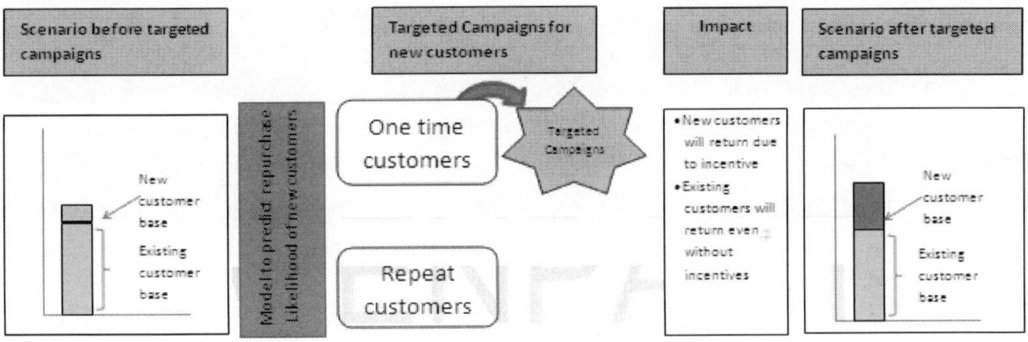

Fig. 1

TESTING THE MODEL

Data

We used panel data for approximately 1,60,000 customers in the United States. The data included ~130 stores and tracked panel purchases and coupon redemption by the store. Customers were given different coupon offers and their response to that offer was recorded. We also had information about the offers i.e. the category brand combination that the offer belonged to, the offer value as well as the store in which they were given the offer. Along with this, we also had daily transaction data for all these customers for about a year before the coupon offer was made. We did not have transaction data after the offer was made, instead we had an indicator indicating whether they came back to purchase the product on which they were given the offer and the number of repeat trips made after the offer. The idea was to use the transaction history to come up with predictors based on their transaction history and the offer, which could be used to predict the behavior of other customers who were given similar offers.

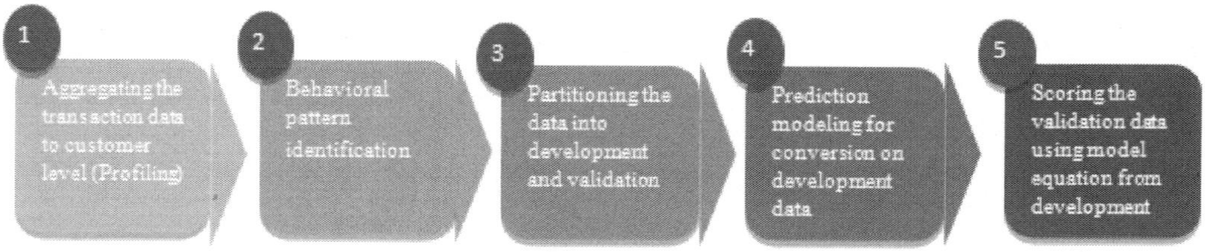

Fig. 2

Model

The study explores usage of predictive analytics to identify shopping patterns of existing customers, and using these patterns along with transactional metrics to predict likelihood of purchase for a new customer. The focus lies on establishing a mathematical equation as a model to represent the relationship between the different factors/variables in consideration in order to forecast the future outcomes. Transaction data was used wherein all the transactions of every individual customer were aggregated at customer level, since patterns cannot be derived from isolated transactions and also transaction behavior changes quickly over time making the handling of granular level of data difficult. For this reason data we rolled up the data at customer level, which is known as profiling. With profiling, models provide accurate and effective results in predictive modeling. The observed dependent variable assumed values of 'Y' – coupon redeemed or 'N' – coupon not redeemed. Using maximum likelihood estimation the model finds parameters that yield predicted probabilities of coupon redemption for a particular set of independent variables. The PROC LOGISTIC procedure in SAS was used for estimation. The significance of the overall regression was tested with a chi-square test using the log likelihood ratio. Each coefficient was tested with a t-test and each category analyzed in split-halves to test the reliability of the model.

$$Logit_i = \ln\left(\frac{prob_{event}}{1 - prob_{event}}\right) = b_0 + b_1x_1 + \ldots + b_nx_n$$

This model was cross-sectional as all purchases of potential coupon users were analyzed together. Based on the widespread nature of coupon use, the model makes the assumption that coupon redemption is a characteristic of purchase situations rather than solely a characteristic of individual consumers. The model also assumes that coupon redemption is a zero-order process. Any time series effects of sequential redemptions by individual consumers are not modelled. Each consumer's history is known to some extent and is used to calculate a brand loyalty variable, the time since last purchase and the average quantity purchased. The model also assumes that coupon distribution has reached the point where coupons are always available to consumers who wish to use them.

A number of predictor variables were constructed which would aid in predicting the likelihood of repurchase. Metrics like most frequently purchased brand, occasionally purchased brand, number of transactions, amount spent, number of brands purchased, number of categories transacted in the past one, two, four, six months and past one year were created. These metrics were created at each customer level (i.e. transactions were rolled up at customer level). The data was randomly sub-setted into development and validation sets. Predictive validity was tested by estimating the propensity on the development sample. The response probabilities were then compared with the individual's stated repurchase intentions for the product.

Hypotheses Used to Create Metrics

1. The higher the consumers' brand loyalty in a category, the lower their propensity to redeem coupons in that category.
2. The higher the consumers' usage rates of the category, the higher their propensity to redeem coupons in that category.
3. The higher the availability of coupons in a category perceived by consumers, the greater their propensity to redeem coupons in that category.
4. The higher the consumer's general coupon proneness, the greater his or her propensity to redeem coupons in different categories.

Modeling Variables

The variables used in the model are defined as follows:

- **No. of transactions for the category-brand-company** – A measure of loyalty for the particular brand for which the customer was offered the coupon. It measured the number of transactions that the customer had done for that brand in his purchase history. Frequency is the most powerful determinant of high volume consumers for retailers. Research shows that among the major grocery chains, frequency of trips contributed 1.5 times more than basket size in differentiating pivotal consumers from average brand buyers. For the average brand, frequency contributes 2.4 times as much as volume per purchase in separating high-volume consumers from average brand buyers.

- **No. of units purchased for the category** – A measure of loyalty at the category level. Gives information about whether the customer is a frequent buyer from the category. This is crucial for manufacturers who are looking to enter the market with a new product where they can target frequent buyers from the category and give coupons which could induce some of them to switch to their brand.
- **No. of units purchased for that company** – A measure of loyalty at the manufacturer level. Gives information about whether the customer is a frequent buyer from the manufacturer. This information is also important for manufacturers who are present in some categories but are looking to enter other categories. With the knowledge of their loyal customers who seem to trust their brand name, they can specifically target those customers who would have a higher propensity of buying their product.
- **No. of days since last purchase for that category-brand-company** – Recency, along with frequency and monetary value form the basis to predict the probability of a customer being active. We use the number of days since the customer last purchased the brand. More the number of days since the last purchase, the less likely he is to be an active buyer of the product, and consequently less likely to redeem a coupon for that brand.
- **Product Size assortment available for that category brand company** – The likelihood of redeeming a coupon for a brand also depends on the range of pack sizes available for the brand on discount. A brand with a wide range of pack sizes is more likely to be bought on a coupon redemption than a brand with fewer pack sizes.
- **No. of competitor brands for that category** – Consists of the number of brands in the category for which the coupon is offered.
- **No. of transactions in that store** – A measure of how frequently the customer has purchased from the store where he is offered the coupon. A more frequent customer of the store is more likely to visit the store and redeem the offered coupon.
- **Offer value** – A measure of coupon attractiveness. Offer value is the discount offered upon redeeming a coupon. A higher discount offer makes the coupon more attractive as against a lower discount. The attractiveness of the discount offer also depends on the list price of the product. A moderate discount on a highly priced product may not be as attractive as a moderate discount on a relatively low priced product.

- **Total sale of the category-brand-company** – Measures the success of the brand. A highly successful brand is more likely to be bought on a coupon redemption than a moderately or low successful one.
- **No. of transactions on discount** – Measures the extent to which a customer is prone to make a discounted purchase. We try to look at the customer's transaction history and determine the number of purchases made on discount. A high number indicates a high discount prone customer and is more likely to redeem a coupon offer.

RESULTS

Overall, the model provided a good prediction of coupon redemption. All predictors were statistically significant and the model fit was good. Loyalty as well as recency variables were negatively related to coupon redemption. This was in line with our expectation. Assortment was positively related as was offer value. The more attractive the offer the more likely was the customer to redeem that offer. Brand success was expectedly positively related with coupon redemption, so was discount proneness of a customer.

Analysis of Maximum Likelihood Estimates

Table 1

Parameter	*Estimate*	*Standard Error*	*Wald Chi-square*	*Pr > ChiSq*
Intercept	9.1979	10.995	0.6998	0.2028
No. of transactions for the category-brand-company	–0.2265	0.3219	0.495	0.2817
No. of units purchased for the category	–0.0516	0.0652	0.626	0.1288
No. of units purchased for the company	–0.114	0.0862	1.7495	0.1859
No. of days since last purchase for the category-brand-company	–0.019	0.0195	0.9475	0.1303
Product Size assortment available for the category brand company	5.3987	5.4241	0.9907	0.2196
No. of competitor brands for the category	–0.1724	0.1867	0.8526	0.3558
No. of transactions in the store	–0.019	0.0137	1.9338	0.1643
Offer value	18.0333	17.8658	1.0188	0.1128
Total sale of the category brand company	0.0001	0.000097	0.966	0.1257
No. of transactions on discount	9.1979	10.995	0.6998	0.2028

Table 2

Effect	*Point Estimate*	*95% Wald Confidence Limits*		*Probability*
No. of transactions for the category-brand-company	0.842	0.584	1.214	0.457112
No. of units purchased for the category	0.981	0.955	1.008	0.495204
No. of units purchased for the company	0.931	<0.001	1.243	0.482134
No. of days since last purchase for the category-brand-company	0.732	0.543	1.214	0.456728
Product Size assortment available for the category brand company	1.254	0.667	2.357	0.556344
No. of competitor brands for the category	0.842	0.584	1.214	0.457112
No. of transactions in the store	0.981	0.955	1.008	0.495204
Offer value	1.053	0.927	1.196	0.512908
Total sale of the category brand company	1.121	0.947	1.327	0.528524
No. of transactions on discount	1.254	0.667	2.357	0.556344

Odds Ratio Estimates

Table 3

Effect	*Point Estimate*	*95% Wald Confidence Limits*		*Probability*
No. of transactions for the category-brand-company	0.842	0.584	1.214	0.457112
No. of units purchased for the category	0.981	0.955	1.008	0.495204
No. of units purchased for the company	0.931	<0.001	1.243	0.482134
No. of days since last purchase for the category-brand-company	0.732	0.543	1.214	0.456728
Product Size assortment available for the category brand company	1.254	0.667	2.357	0.556344
No. of competitor brands for the category	0.842	0.584	1.214	0.457112
No. of transactions in the store	0.981	0.955	1.008	0.495204
Offer value	1.053	0.927	1.196	0.512908
Total sale of the category brand company	1.121	0.947	1.327	0.528524
No. of transactions on discount	1.254	0.667	2.357	0.556344

Association of Predicted Probabilities and Observed Responses

Table 4

Percent Concordant	77.3	Somers' D	0.682
Percent Discordant	9.1	Gamma	0.789
Percent Tied	13.6	Tau-a	0.328
Pairs	286	c	0.841

The Prediction Accuracy of the model was checked based on 2 criteria. First was the concordance rate which was at 77.3% well above the acceptable limit of 70% which implies that the levels (1 and 0) are well separated. This is also reflected in the C Statistic of 0.84 which indicates the Area under the ROC curve. The second criteria was the Hosmer Lemeshow classification test wherein the predicted dataset is divided into 10 classes and the number of actual and predicted events are compared in each class using the Chi Square test. The prediction is of good accuracy if a higher percentage of values occur in the top deciles and the percentage decreases gradually to the lower deciles, which is observed in the Gains chart below.

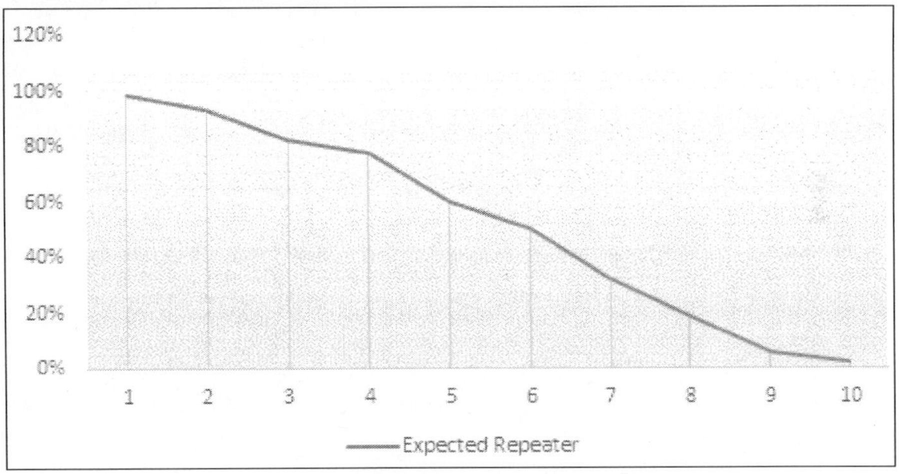

Fig. 3: Gains Cjart fpr Repeater

The separation power of the model was also checked using the KS statistic. A plot of the percentage predicted versus the deciles gives us the separation power. If we obtain the resultant graph as wide as possible, it indicates that the model is able to distinguish between the levels of the dependent variable well.

The parameters obtained from development set model were applied on the validation set where all the independent variables were created in the same manner as in the development set. The response probabilities were then compared with the individual's stated repurchase intentions for the product. Higher proximity of the predictions to the actual in the validation set as well as number of correct predictions in the validation set being closer to the number of correct predictions in the development set were considered to be indications of a good predictive model.

Table 5

Deciles	*Repeater*	*Non-Repeater*	*Difference*
0	0%	0%	0.00%
1	20%	1%	19.68%
2	39%	3%	35.28%
3	55%	8%	46.42%
4	68%	15%	53.53%
5	79%	24%	55.57%
6	87%	36%	51.56%
7	93%	49%	43.97%
8	98%	64%	33.12%
9	99%	82%	17.38%
10	100%	100%	0.00%

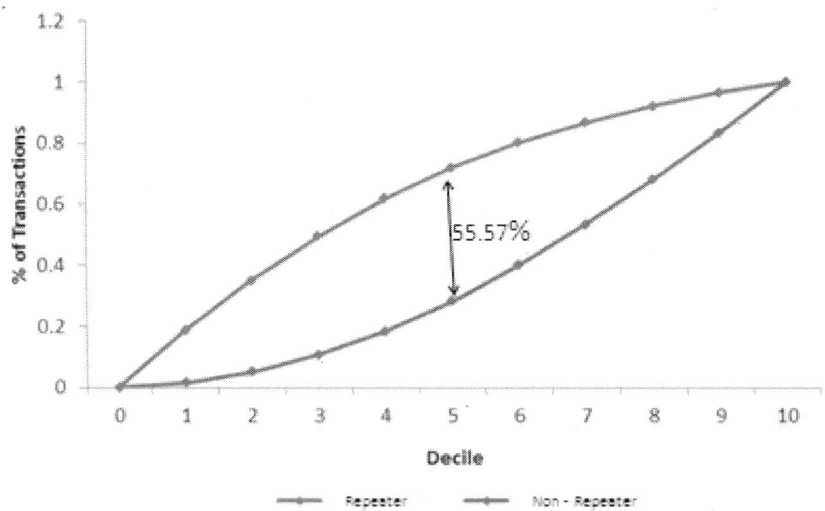

Fig. 4: Separation Power of the Model

CONCLUSION

Coupon redemption can be analyzed on the level of the individual purchase and involves a three stage process. This view can be valuable in designing coupon programs which have an impact on collection, intention and redemption through careful selection of distribution media, face values, and use of advertising or in-store promotion. While the empirical analysis has shown that the redemption stage is correlated with several variables which are under the manager's control, the degree to which redemption occasions are determined by time and effort minimization needs further analysis. This exploratory analysis needs to be extended with additional variables and with breaking the decision down into its three component parts. Future work might also contrast this approach with shopping strategy models derived from alternative views: for example, that consumers integrate coupons indiscriminately into their shopping patterns to derive satisfaction from being a "smart shopper" or as part of 3 scripted responses.

REFERENCES

Bawa, Kapil, & Shoemaker, Robert W. (1987). The Coupon-Prone Consumer: Some Findings Based on Purchase Behavior across Product Classes. *Journal of Marketing, 51* (4), 99-110.

Bawa, Kapil, Srinivasan, Srini S., & Srivastava, Rajendra (1997). Coupon Attractiveness and Coupon Proneness: A Framework for Modeling Coupon Redemption. *Journal of Marketing Research, 34*, 517-525.

Blattberg, Robert C., & Neslin, Scott A. (1990). *Sales Promotion.* Englewood Cliffs, NJ: Prentice Hall.

Lichtenstein, Donald R., Netemeyer, Richard G., & Burton, Scot (1990). Distinguishing Coupon Proneness from Value Consciousness: An Acquisition-Transaction Utility Theory Perspective. *Journal of Marketing, 54*(3), 54-67.

Narasimhan, Chakravarthi (1984). A Price Discrimination Theory of Coupon Usage. *Marketing Science, 3*(2), 128-46.

Raghubir, Priya and Corfman, Kim. (1999). When Do price Promotions Affect Pretrial Brand Evaluations? *Journal of Marketing Research, 36*, 211-222.

Reibstein, David J., & Traver, Phillis A. (1982). Factors Affecting Coupon Redemption Rates. *Journal of Marketing, 46*(4), 102-13.

Shoemaker, Robert W., & Tibrewala, Vikas. (1985). Relating Coupon Redemption Rates to Past Purchasing of the Brand. *Journal of Advertising Research, 25*(5), 40-47.

Ward, R.W., & Davis, J.E. (1978). A Pooled Cross-Section Time Series Model of Coupon Promotions. *American Journal of Agricultural Economics, 60*(3), 393-401.

Webster, Frederick E., Jr. (1965). The 'Deal-Prone' Consumer. *Journal of Marketing Research, 2*, 186-189.

PART
ONE-E

PRICING

According to a McKinsey report, a 1% price increase on an average translates into an 8.7% increase in operating profits (assuming no loss of volume). Yet, every year upto 30% of the innumerable pricing decisions organizations make do not deliver the best price. This number is particularly troubling because the sheer volume of data at the disposal of companies presents an opportunity to make significantly better pricing decisions. Price points need to stay abreast with the explosive growth of customer touchpoints and multichannel complexity that accompanies digitization. Not leveraging on the power of big data, many companies are leaving millions of dollars of profit on the table. They need to harness big data to determine the best price at the product – not category- level rather than being overwhelmed by the flood of data.

The steady growth of private labels, which often directly compete with national brands for market share, has presented retailers with a challenge of maintaining the right price gap between them and national brands. The paper, 'What Is the Right Price Gap for Private Label Brand with Its Key Competitors', proposes a regression-based methodology to identify the right price gap between a private label brand and national brand, during recession and post-recession, which will help private labels to achieve staying power with consumers and eventually build loyalty.

In a highly competitive, price-sensitive and dynamic product category such as consumer high tech products on a direct online channel such as dell.com, pricing managers are constantly challenged to make pricing decisions so as to increase the top line, margins and volumes. These decisions are driven by multiple information sources, intuition and experience and thus a predictive pricing framework is a necessity. The paper, 'Pricing It Right – A Scientific Approach to Consumer Product Pricing' lends a scientific angle in determining optimal pricing points using demand sensitivity and predictive modeling techniques. The analytical framework thus developed would help managers in making data-based pricing decisions across their product life cycles.

CHAPTER TEN

WHAT IS THE RIGHT PRICE GAP FOR PRIVATE LABEL BRAND WITH ITS KEY COMPETITORS

Ani Babu and S. Ravi Kumar

ABSTRACT

The Private label/Store brand remains a growth opportunity for many retailers and is of great importance to further developing loyalty and increasing margins. With an average 30% discount on national brands, private label goods provide shoppers with a strong value proposition. With many countries suffering recession, stagnant wage and inflation, the economic reason for choosing a Private Label is clear. Most shoppers are more price-driven than they have ever been in the recent past. Private labels should maintain the right Price Gap (difference between the prices of the Private Label product with its competitor branded product). Price Gaps thresholds are preconceived thresholds in the consumer's mind, which when breached have an impact on the volume sales. The behavior of customers towards the price gap is very different during recession and post-recession. Recession is hitting us more often than not in recent years.

This paper proposes a regression based methodology to identify the right price gap that a private label brand should maintain with its key competitors during recession and post-recession. The model being used to identify the right price gap also controls other variables, which can influence the consumer's behavior, other than the gap and identifies the right price that should be maintained with the key competitors.

Keywords: Retailers, Private Label, National Brands, Recession, Price Gap.

INTRODUCTION

Background of Research

Retailer-owned brands, often denoted by Private Labels (PLs) (or simply store brands) are uniformly less expensive than their National Brand (NB) substitutes and they allow retailers to differentiate themselves from one another in terms of product offerings. They also typically have higher margins than NB and the profits from the sale of PLs are not shared with NB manufacturers, and hence PLs increase the bargaining power of retailers relative to manufacturers in the food distribution channel.

Over the past two decades, private label food products have grown steadily in sales and often directly compete for market share with national brands. As consumers have been affected by the pressures of the economy and job market, they have become more price-sensitive these days. The struggling economy has given private label products a big boost on the store shelf and on consumers' shopping lists. According to Symphony IRI, the private label dollar share increased from 16.4 percent in 2007 to 18.5 percent in 2011 (Bowmer, 2011).

Retailers are increasingly using PLs as a means to differentiate themselves from competitors. In addition to standard flagship PLs that bear firm names, supermarkets are offering more premium and organic brands, such as Safeway's *SELECT* and *O Organics*, Kroger's *Private Selections* and *Naturally Preferred*, and Giant's *Nature's Promise* (Volpe, 2011). These premium PLs serve not only to distinguish supermarket chain product lines from one another but also to place NBs and PLs more directly in price and quality competition.

Problem Statement

The unrelenting growth of store brands presents retailers with a new challenge: managing the price gap between private label and national brands. Managing the right price gap between private brands and National brands provides opportunities for retailers to communicate value and quality information to the customers and helps alert retailers to capture more margin.

For example, by raising prices on slower moving items with weak consumer price memory, retailers can increase profit without sacrificing volume, inching closer to national brand levels. As usual, pricing is a category-dependent function, with differentials as narrow as 24 percent between national and store brands in the frozen food department and as wide as 73 percent in the non-food department (Nielsen, 2012).

Purpose

This paper proposes a methodology to identify the right price gap that a private label brand should maintain with its key competitor (say, Brand 1) during recession and post-recession. The ANCOVA model being used to identify the right price gap also controls for other variables, which can influence the consumer's behavior other than the gap and identifies the right price that should be maintained with the key competitor.

DATA AND METHODOLOGY

Data

The data used for analysis is the weekly sales data for category X from ABC store for 2 years. Category X is assumed to have 3 competing brands within the store in terms of price and quality namely, Private label, Brand 1 and Brand 2. Brand 1 gives very tight competition to PL, i.e. they compete directly for market share. ABC store has to be very cautious while pricing their product (private label). By maintaining the right price gap with Brand 1, PL can attain increased market share and thus ABC store in turn gets more revenue. We have 104 observations for each variable. The variables included in the study are Private label volume sales (Vol_PL), Price gap[1] between Private label and Brand 1 (Gap_Brand1) and Price gap between PL and Brand 2 (Gap_Brand2). Based on the range of values, Gap_Brand1 is categorized into different levels. This categorical variable (Group) is included in our analysis instead of Gap_Brand1.

Approach: ANCOVA Approach

Analysis of covariance (ANCOVA) is a general linear model which blends ANOVA and regression. ANCOVA evaluates whether population means of a dependent variable (DV) are equal across levels of a categorical independent variable (IV), while statistically controlling for the effects of other continuous variables that are not of primary interest, known as covariates (CV).

Using ANCOVA we can check if different levels of price gap with the key competitor (Brand1) have any effect on Private Label volume while statistically controlling for other competitor gap (Brand2) effects.

[1] Price gap is taken as the difference between Private Label Actual price and Competitor Actual price.

The model that we are fitting is:

Vol_PL = β0 + β1*Gap_Brand2 + β2*Group
+ β3*Interaction of (Gap_Brand2, Group) + Error term

where, Dependent Variable: Volume Sales of Private Label, **Vol_PL.**

Independent Variable (Categorical): Price gap between Private label and Brand 1, **Group**

Independent Variable (Continuous): Price gap between PL and other competitor brands, **Gap_Brand2**

Group is a categorical variable created based on the range of price gaps between PL and Brand1 (Gap_Brand1)

Group=1, if Gap_Brand1 <$ 0.5
2, if Gap_Brand1 is between $ 0.5 and $ 0.9
3, if Gap_Brand1 >$ 0.9

Here, we are testing

H0: Mean volume sales of PL do not differ across groups
Mean(Group1) = Mean(Group2) = Mean(Group3)

Against

H1: Means are different for at least one group

Assumptions of ANCOVA

- Normality of Residuals: The residuals (error terms) should be normally distributed.
- Homogeneity of Variances: The error variances should be equal for different treatment classes.
- Homogeneity of Regression Slopes: The slopes of the different regression lines should be equivalent, i.e. regression lines should be parallel among groups.
- Linearity of Regression: The regression relationship between the dependent variable and concomitant variables must be linear.
- Independence of Error terms: The error terms should be uncorrelated.

The third issue, concerning the homogeneity of different treatment regression slopes is particularly important in evaluating the appropriateness of ANCOVA model. Also note that we only need the error terms to be normally distributed.

The SAS code below is used to generate the results :

```
Title "ANCOVA model using GLM";
procglmdata=gap_data;
class Group;
```

```
modelVol_PL= Gap_Brand2 Group Gap_Brand2*Group;
means Group /BON;
run;
```

The ANCOVA *F* test evaluates whether the population means on the dependent variable, adjusted for differences on the covariate, differ across levels of a factor. If a factor has more than two levels and the *F* is significant, follow-up tests should be conducted to determine where there are differences on the adjusted means between groups. For example, if a factor has three levels, three pairwise comparisons among the adjusted means can be conducted: Group 1 versus Group 2, Group 1 versus Group 3, and Group 2 versus Group 3.

Some of the pairwise comparison tests that can be used are Tukey test and Bonferroni test. As a general rule, the Bonferroni test is used if there are unequal numbers of cases of each group. So we have used the Bonferroni test in our analysis. Here we are testing if the mean volume sales of one group are significantly different from the mean volume sales of another group. This comparison test will help us identify the right price gap that the PL should be maintaining with its key competitor. This test is performed by the BON option included in the GLM procedure of the SAS code above.

ANALYSIS

We interpret the overall significance by looking at the Analysis of Variance table given below (Table 1(a) and Table 1(b)). We see that the model has 5 degrees of freedom, corresponding to the 3 predictors included in the model. The overall model is significant, $F(5,98) = 21.60$, $p<0.001$. The R-square is 0.5242.

Table 1(a)[2]

Source	*DF*	*Sum of Squares*	*Mean Square*	*F Value*	*Pr > F*
Model	5	134436843779.00	26887368756	21.6	<.0001
Error	98	122016520958.00	1245066540		
Corrected Total	103	256453364736.00			

Table 1(b)

R-Square	*CoeffVar*	*Root MSE*	*Vol_PL Mean*
0.524216	48.00746	35285.5	73500.04

So Table 1 above tells us that the average volume sales of Private Label are significantly different across various levels of Private label_Brand1price gap.

[2] Output generated by SAS glm procedure.

In Table 2 below, the Type I SS shows the effect of each predictor in the model, sequentially. That is, the effect of Gap_Brand2 is evaluated without controlling for the other predictors. The effect of Group is evaluated with only Gap_Brand2 in the model, and the effect of interaction between Gap_Brand2 and Group is evaluated, after adjusting for both main effects. The total of the Type I SS is equal to the total model SS.

Table 2

Source	*DF*	*Type I SS*	*Mean Square*	*F Value*	*Pr > F*
Gap_Brand2	1	57134108520	57134108520	45.89	<.0001
Group	2	72459601527	36229800763	29.1	<.0001
Gap_Brand2*Group	2	4843133732	2421566866	1.94	0.1485

The Type III SS (Table 3) below shows the effect of each predictor in the model, controlling for all other effects. The Type III SS is sometimes called the regression sum of squares or partial sum of squares. In this case, the total of the Type III SS does not equal the total model SS.

Table 3

Source	*DF*	*Type III SS*	*Mean Square*	*F Value*	*Pr > F*
Gap_Brand2	1	3054654328	3054654328	2.45	0.1205
Group	2	74600617	37300308	0.03	0.9705
Gap_Brand2*Group	2	4843133732	2421566866	1.94	0.1485

The insignificance of the interaction term indicates that the ANCOVA model is appropriate. It supports the homogeneity of slopes assumption of ANCOVA. This indicates that depending on the level of Group variable, the relationship between the covariate and the dependent variable is not changing.

The results of the Bonferroni comparison test are shown in Table 4(a) and Table 4(b) below:

Table 4(a)[3]

Alpha	0.05
Error Degrees of Freedom	98
Error Mean Square	1.25E+09
Critical Value of t	2.43577

[3] Output generated by BON option in SAS glm procedure.

Table 4(b)

Comparisons significant at the 0.05 level are indicated by ***				
Group Comparison	*Difference Between Means*	*Simultaneous 95% Confidence Limits*		
1-3	114793	77993	151594	***
1-2	119182	90393	147970	***
3-1	–114793	–151594	–77993	***
3-2	4388	–22176	30953	
2-1	–119182	–147970	–90393	***
2-3	–4388	–30953	22176	

The '***' indicates the significant group pairs. From the above table, it is clear that average PL Volume sales of Group 1 are significantly different from those of Group 2 and Group 3. However, Group 2 and Group 3 have insignificant difference in average volume sales of Private label.

RESULTS AND CONCLUSION

Managing the right price gap with the competitor National Brands will help Private Label brands achieve staying power with consumers, and in turn, build loyalty to the retailer.

The Bonferroni test results shown in Table 4(b) tell us that, when the price gap between Private Label and Brand 1 is increased above 0.5, there is significant difference in mean volume sales of Private Label. This happens because Consumers have a preconceived gap threshold in their mind (0.5). When this threshold is breached there is a steep decline in Private label volume sales.

But there is no significant difference in mean volume sales of Private Label between group 2 and group 3.

From Table 4(b) it is evident that by decreasing the PL and Brand 1 price gap from 0.9 towards 0.5, there is no significant difference in average volume sales of PL. In this scenario, ABC store can increase the PL price, without losing its customers. By selling the same product at an increased price, ABC store can attain greater profits. We can also see that average volume sales of PL are highest in the case of group 1 (i.e. when the gap between PL and Brand 1 is less than 0.5). This is the most ideal price gap between PL and Brand 1 for category X in ABC store.

REFERENCES

Bowmer, Robin (2011). *The Effects of Recession on Brand Loyalty and Buy Down Behavior 2011 Update* (ComScore) Retrieved from: http://www.comScore.com/BuyDown2011

Nielsen (2012). *Private Brands U.S. Outlook: Flash in the Pan or the Real Deal?* Retrieved from: http://www.nielsen.com/us/en/insights/webinars/2012/private-brands-outlook-flash-in-the-pan-or-the-real-deal.html)

Volpe, Richard James. (2010). *National Brand and Private Label Pricing and Promotional Strategy.* Selected Paper prepared for presentation at AAEA, CAES, & WAEA Joint Annual Meeting, Denver, Colorado, July 2010. Davis: University of California. Retrieved from: http://ageconsearch.umn.edu/bitstream/60986/2/10181.pdf

Volpe, Richard. (2011). *The Relationship between National Brand and Private Label Food Products – Prices, Promotions, Recessions, and Recoveries.* USDA Economic Research Service, Economic Research Report Number 129. Retrieved from: http://www.ers.usda.gov/media/187072/err129_1_.pdf

Understanding Analysis of Covariance (ANCOVA) (n.d.). Retrieved from: http://oak.ucc.nau.edu/rh232/courses/eps625/handouts/ancova/understanding%20ancova.pdf

CHAPTER ELEVEN

PRICING IT RIGHT – A SCIENTIFIC APPROACH TO CONSUMER PRODUCT PRICING

Rajkumar Dan and Dinesh RC

ABSTRACT

The paper presents the technique and concepts behind predictive modelling for price determination using demand sensitivity, specifically in the highly price sensitive, competitive and dynamic consumer high tech products category. It also addresses the other non-price drivers that affect sensitivity of a product.

Keywords: Predictive Modelling, Price Sensitivity, Product Pricing.

PURPOSE

Strategic Pricing decisions, price positioning of products across the product life cycle, promotional and discount pricing decisions are complex issues in a highly competitive market, especially when it is on a direct online channel such as Dell.com. The Pricing Managers are regularly faced with challenges in making price changes in this turbulent market so as to **maximize margins, revenues and units** and mostly rely on multiple information inputs, intuition and experience. A predictive pricing framework for price recommendations hence plays a critical role in decision making.

The Dell analytics team works with the pricing managers across markets in multiple geographies and is working towards lending a scientific angle in determining the optimal prices using predictive modelling techniques and analysis. **This is aimed at delivering incremental revenue and margins by identifying optimal prices in a market with high price volatility.** According to Gartner analyst Steve Prentice, innovation is now coming from customers and their favourite technologies. **"Consumers are increasingly in charge. They are driving the specifications of technology. They are driving disruption and changing the balance of power."** The Internet strongly empowers consumers, letting them compare deals with the click of a mouse. The key lies in figuring out what pricing and promotion related factors drive sales and identifying the products and segments that are sensitive to changes in these factors.

The steps involved in building an analytical framework to enable Pricing are

- **Identify Key Factors (Pricing and Promotions)** that affect sales for different products
- **Quantify Elasticity** (Price and Promotion) across all price ranges and product categories
- **Product Categorization** into various elasticity bands using a Profit-Elasticity Matrix
- **Building Demand Simulator** based on demand models built with historical data

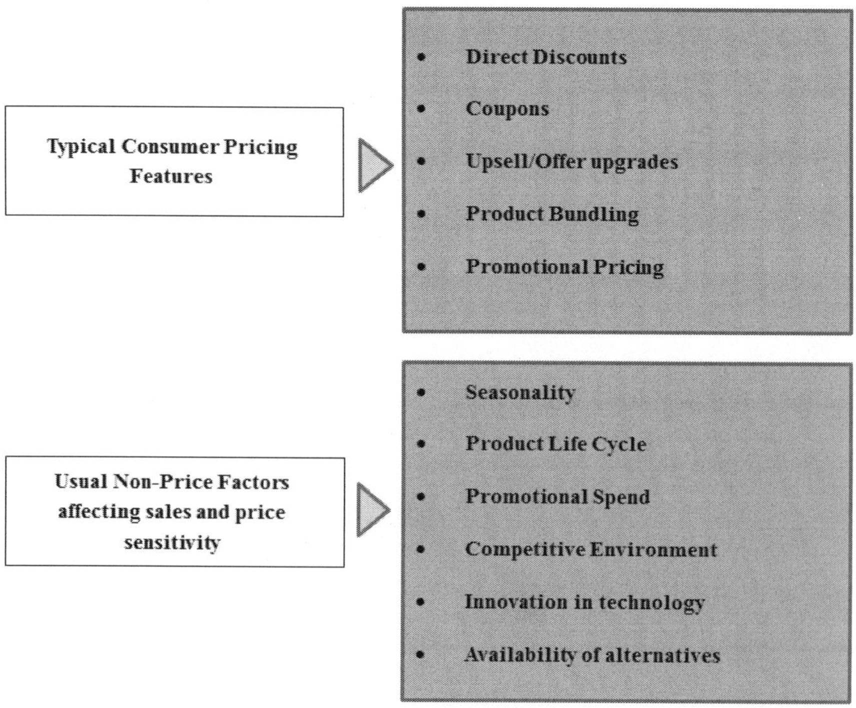

Fig. 1: Factors impacting Consumer Pricing Strategy

- Further use the **Predicted Vs. Actual** sales to fine-tune the analytical demand model

This information is critical in an environment where change in sales with optimized price changes may result in a positive trade off with respect to added revenues and profit margins.

LITERATURE REVIEW

Which products should I target for aggressive pricing?
Are we leaving too much money on the table?
Which promotions have worked well?
Which competitor prices/promotions are hurting our sales?
Are retail channel prices affecting our direct channel sales?

These are the most frequently confronted questions while dealing with problems related to price optimization and the answer to these questions can only be given by a good understanding of product level elasticity measures related to prices and promotions. Elasticity in general measures the sensitivity or responsiveness of one variable w.r.t. another variable. Price elasticity of demand is a term in economics often used when discussing price sensitivity. It is defined as the percentage change in the quantity demanded to a one percentage change in the price.

Own Price Elasticity

Own price elasticity is a measure used to capture the sensitivity of consumers' demand for a good or service in response to changes in the price of that particular good or service. If the price elasticity of demand is equal to 0, demand is perfectly inelastic (i.e., demand does not change when price changes). Values between zero and one indicate that demand is inelastic (this occurs when the percent change in demand is less than the percent change in price). When price elasticity of demand equals one, demand is unit elastic (the percent change in demand is equal to the percent change in price). Finally, if the value is greater than one, demand is perfectly elastic (demand is affected to a greater degree by changes in price).

Cross Price Elasticity

Cross price elasticity measures the interaction or the sensitivity of demand for a particular good to changes in the price of another good. When the cross price elasticity is positive, the two goods are substitutes, when it is negative the goods are complementary.

If we look at the current literature, price elasticity is estimated using a variety of models and with seemingly large differences in results. Reasons for this variation include differences in functional form, model assumptions, selection of control variables and the estimation techniques. So, we can discuss the existing literature on elasticity along the various streams mentioned above.

Functional Form

Most of the studies assume a log-log (log-linear) relationship to calculate elasticity for the purpose of simplicity and ease of interpretation. In our case, we will also use a log linear relationship between sales and price, not because it is a popular specification but also because it fits our data reasonably well.

Estimation Technique

Mulugeta et al (2013) in their paper titled "Price and Cross Price elasticity estimation using SAS" measured own elasticity using mid-point elasticity estimation method as shown in the following equation:

EA = %ΔQA / %ΔPA

where EA = Own price elasticity

(%ΔQA)) = Percent change in quantity (Q) of product A computed as [(QA(w) – QA(w–1)) / (QA(w–1) + QA(w)) / 2]

(%ΔPA) = Percent change in price (P) of product A computed as [(PA(w) – PA(w–1)) / (PA(w–1) + PA(w)) / 2]

w and (w–1) refer to current and previous weeks, respectively. This method is more useful only when we are dealing with small data. Other researchers have unambiguously used regression analysis to derive elasticity but even with the same estimation technique, there is a lot of variation in their models evidently due to the selection of variables, the topic which is being looked at in the next section. Since we will be compiling time series data for our analysis, multiple regression is more appropriate and hence will be made use of throughout.

Variable Specification

There are practically two ways to see the impact of price change on sales in isolation. In principle, they are quite identical, the difference being in the way of calculation and interpretation. The traditional method suggests taking a set of control variables. Several papers on demand modelling have considered different independent variables as regressors on the right side of the demand equation.

A new approach to see the impact of price change on sales independently of other factors suggests taking the route of reference value analysis. Yanagisawa (2011) in her paper on energy consumption adopted the same method. She described the method in two stages.

1. Quantifying a 'reference value', an imaginary energy consumption which includes continuous change factors.
2. Estimating price elasticity using ratio of actual energy consumption to the reference energy consumption.

This practical method enables one to avoid infiltration of structure change factors into price elasticity. Although this method is quite an improvement over earlier methods, identifying the reference value is a mammoth task specifically for our analysis since historical data is not of much help.

In our case, the traditional approach is used because the objective of the study is not just to estimate own price elasticity, but also quantify and communicate measures on Cross Price Elasticity and other market related factors.

METHODOLOGY AND DATA SOURCES

In this project we have implemented the construct of optimal price determination to simulate the various pricing scenarios that have the maximum impact on the unit sales and margins.

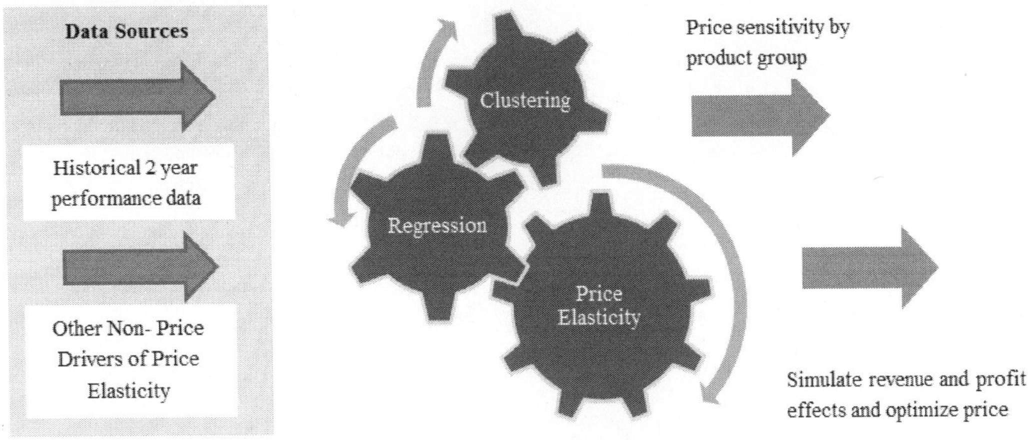

Fig. 2: Model Architecture

Price elasticity (ε) is defined as percentage change in Quantity (Q) due to percentage change in price (P), i.e.

$$\varepsilon = \frac{\partial Q / Q}{\partial P / P}$$

Price elasticity (ε) = (% Change in Quantity) / (% Change in price)

There are practical challenges in implementing insights from these models. Even though the relationship between price and quantity and cost are broadly understood, it is difficult to estimate the exact relationship. **The assumption of linear, non-linear constant elasticity and other demand functions have their own limitations.**

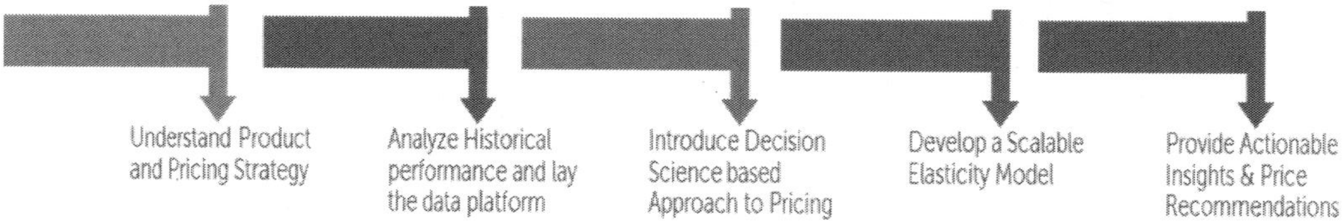

Fig. 3: Implementation

The following three major steps are involved in the project:

Statistical Modelling

As indicated earlier, we use a multiple linear regression model with log transformed sales in the 'Direct' consumer channel as the dependent variable and log transformed pricing and promotion related factors as predictor variables (continuous/dummy values). The multiple regression method allows for controlling all non-price factors and hence isolates the impact of only prices on sales and hence provides an accurate

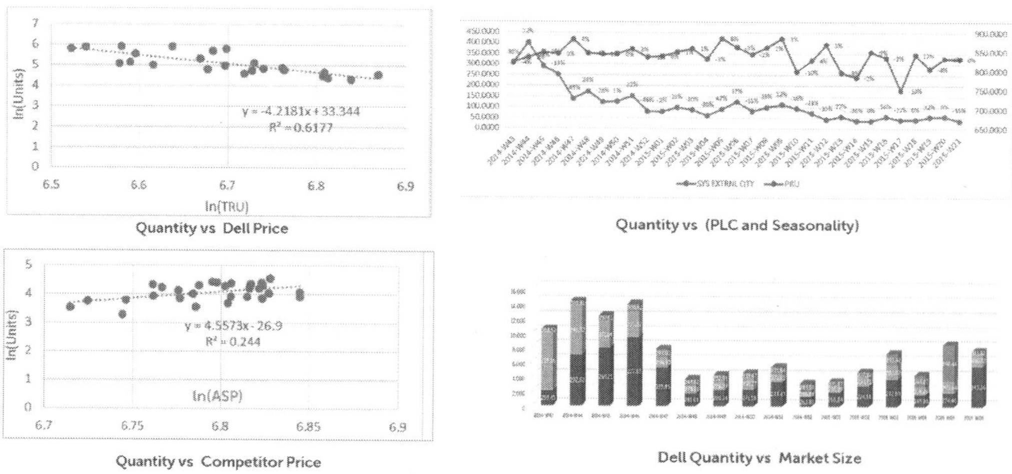

Fig. 4: Impact of Prices, Lifecycle and Market Performance on Sales

estimate of elasticity. This also allows us to quantify the effect or market variables, competitors and promotions on product sales. The interactions between price and other factor variables are also considered to estimate how sensitivity changes with changes in other factors.

The multivariate demand equation is modelled as below,

Quantity Sold = F (rice, product life cycle, seasonality, competitor price(s), other channel price(s), market demand, promotions, product launches)

$$\ln(Y) = \underbrace{C0 + C1\ln(X1) + C2X2}_{\text{Predictor Value}} + \underbrace{C3X3 + \ldots C4(\ln(X1) * X3)}_{\text{Interaction Terms}} + \ldots$$

Y = Qty Sold, X1 = Unit Price, X2 = Competitor_1_Unit_Price, X3 = PLC_Introduction_Dummy…etc.

C1 – Price elasticity (% Change in Quantity /% Change in price),

C2 – Cross Price Elasticity

C4 – Price/PLC Interaction Coeff

Data Considered: (12- Months of weekly data from internal and external sources)

1. Sales Data – Dell Unit Sales, Price, Revenue and Profit
2. Promotion Data – Dell Discounts, Offers, Coupons, Ad-spends
3. Product Attributes – Product type, Line of Business, Form Factor, Product Life Cycle (PLC)
4. Competitive Data – Sales, Prices, Discounts, Offers, Ad-spends across channels
5. Channel Data – Dell Prices, Promotions across partner channels

Model Details

Factor	*Model Values*
Quantity (Output)	Ln (Qty)
Price	Ln (PRU)
PLC	PLC – 1% to 100% (Dummy for Intro, Growth, Maturity, Decline)
High-Seasonality	Dummy Variable
Low-Seasonality	Dummy Variable
Competitor Prices	Simple/Weighted Average of ASP
Dell Retail Price	Ln(ASP) of Dell at Reseller
Market Size	Ln (Overall Market Units in the segment)
Offer Type	Dummy Variable
Competitor Product Launches	Dummy Variable

We consider all major factors affecting sales to build a multiple regression model to estimate their effect on sales.

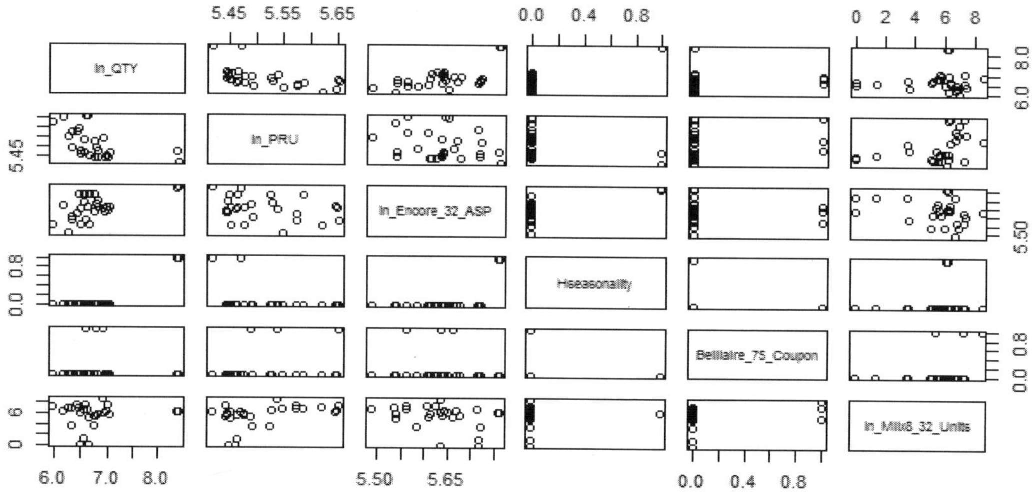

Fig. 5. Pairwise Scatterplot of Qty vs Predictor Variables
(Some variable names are masked)

Dummy variables are used to define weeks seasonality based on historical data. For considering competitor prices, the following approach was used,

1. **Determine Closest Compare:** For every Dell product we are building these models for, we find the closest matching competitor products. This is done using a combination of business understanding and product features. For instance, for a product X in Dell's product family D-A, we consider products in a competitor's products in family C-A. We then use "close-match" algorithm to rank the competitor products by their order of similarity to product X. This is done by comparing product prices and feature sets to quantitatively determine how close they are.
2. **Determine ASP:** For all competitor products considered to be the closest to Dell's product X, we determine their average price weighed by the number of units they sold. This approach helps us consider the prices of the top selling competitor products into the model to determine cross price elasticity. Alternatively, we also use each competitor product price as a different variable in the regression model in cases where averaging of prices was not found to be statistically significant.

We use dummy variables to mark new product launches, inventory stockouts, and promotion type in the historical sales data. For market size, we consider the total units sold in the market of all comparable products actively selling in the market.

Interaction Terms

The model uses interaction terms between price and other factors to determine if there is change in price elasticity between different levels of these factors. For instance, for Product Life Cycle, we use 4 different dummy variables that are mutually exclusive – Intro, Growth, Maturity, Decline. The model coefficients of these variables can be used to quantify the % change in units when their values change (for instance, when product moves from introduction to growth stage). The interaction terms bring out the change in elasticity when model values change from 0 to 1.

For example, consider the following instance,

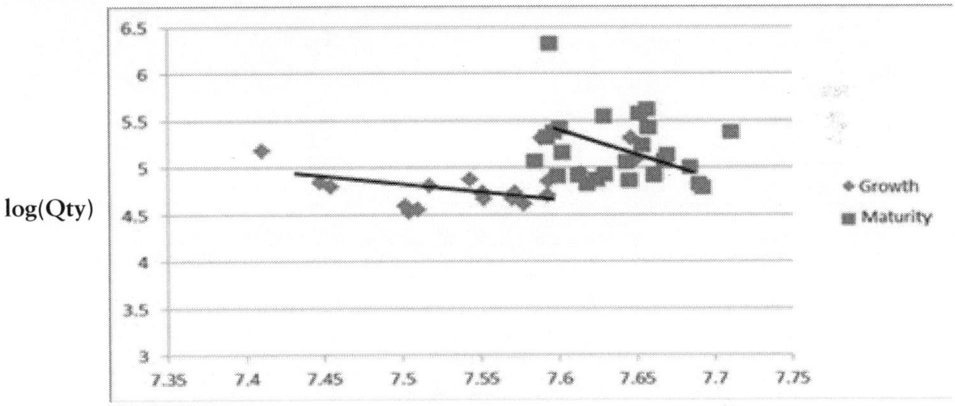

Fig. 6: Price Elasticity as Product Life Cycle

In this Price vs Quantity plot, we could clearly see that the product exhibits different sales behaviour in the two different life cycle stages. On an average, Maturity stage sells more units and it is a coefficient of the dummy variable for Maturity. However, the difference in elasticity (slope of the lines) between these two stages can only be quantified through the interaction terms. Hence the interaction terms play a crucial role in converting price elasticity from a single average to a value that interacts with other factors thus providing us with a much more realistic estimate for each product.

Model Output

The multiple regression demand models are built for each product in a family and the following equation is derived for each of them. Only statistically significant variables are considered for the final model and ANOVA is used to compare different models and their significance levels. The final output of the regression model typically consists of the following coefficients,

Log(Qty) = 24.2 -3.2* log(Price) + 1.04 * Seasonality+2.67 * PLC + 0.92 * log(CompPrice) + 1.23 * Promo_Type1

Price Elasticity	Seasonality Uplift	Cross Price Elasticity	Uplift for Promo_1

A sample output from the Regression Model in R (Statistical Software) is given below,

```
Call:
lm(formula = ln_QTY ~ ln_PRU + Hseasonality + Lseasonality +
                                                              _Price,
                                                              ==
         "      "))

Residuals:
    Min       1Q   Median       3Q      Max
-0.6327 -0.1641   0.0018   0.1898   0.4506

Coefficients:
                                  Estimate Std. Error t value Pr(>|t|)
(Intercept)                       33.28369    3.79303   8.775 1.17e-09 ***
ln_PRU                            -4.85163    0.68959  -7.036 9.74e-08 ***
Hseasonality                       1.50495    0.20352   7.394 3.79e-08 ***
Lseasonality                       0.47836    0.19154   2.497   0.0184 *
ln_                       _Price   0.06702    0.02509   2.671   0.0123 *
                  Coupon           0.29806    0.17192   1.734   0.0936 .
ln_                    Price       0.07594    0.01394   5.446 7.34e-06 ***
---
Signif. codes:  0 '***' 0.001 '**' 0.01 '*' 0.05 '.' 0.1 ' ' 1

Residual standard error: 0.2701 on 29 degrees of freedom
Multiple R-squared:  0.8381, Adjusted R-squared:  0.8046
F-statistic: 25.02 on 6 and 29 DF,  p-value: 3.155e-10
```

Fig. 7: Multiple Regression Model Example
(Product names are masked for confidentiality reasons)

Deep-Dive Analysis

Once the model values are obtained, the next step is to do deep-dive analysis on the model output. We examine the relative elasticity between different products, look at the most significant competitor products, promotions to understand more on why they impact Dell's sales.

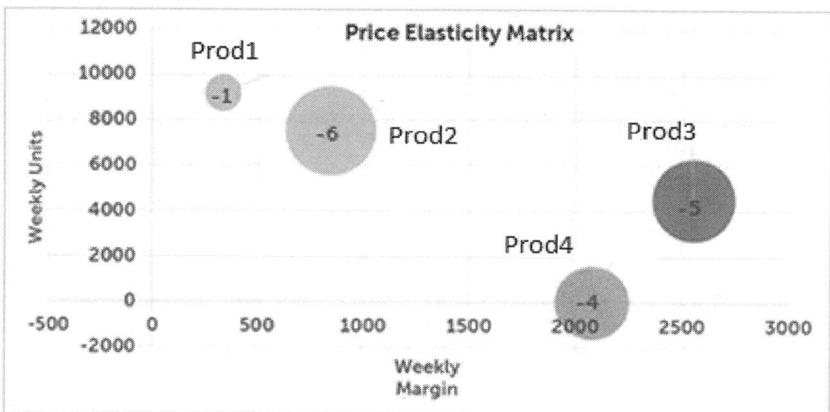

Fig. 8: Price Elasticity Matrix

The Price Elasticity Matrix in the chart above helps Pricing Managers get a relative view of elasticity between different products in the portfolio. The size of the bubble in the chart is relative to the elasticity and position in the matrix determines whether the product is a candidate for unit extraction or margin maximization when price changes are made. Besides this, we also analyse the historical data on how products have responded to price decreases and price increases from the average life cycle price. This analysis helps understand the sensitivity at different levels of price changes.

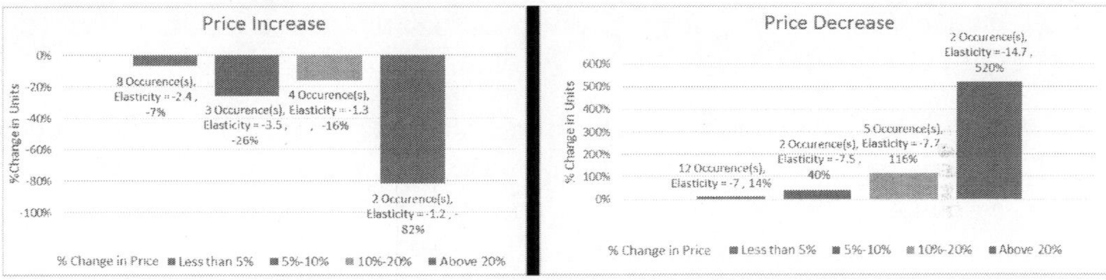

Fig. 9: Price Elasticity at Various Price Levels

Model Based Scenario Analyser

For the Pricing Managers to use the model output on an ongoing basis, a scenario analyser is built based on the model outputs such that we can estimate the expected unit sales, revenue and profit margins based on the control factors input by the user. This allows the business to use the model as a **multiple price scenario simulator** to predict the impact of a particular price change on the sales and profit margins. Also,

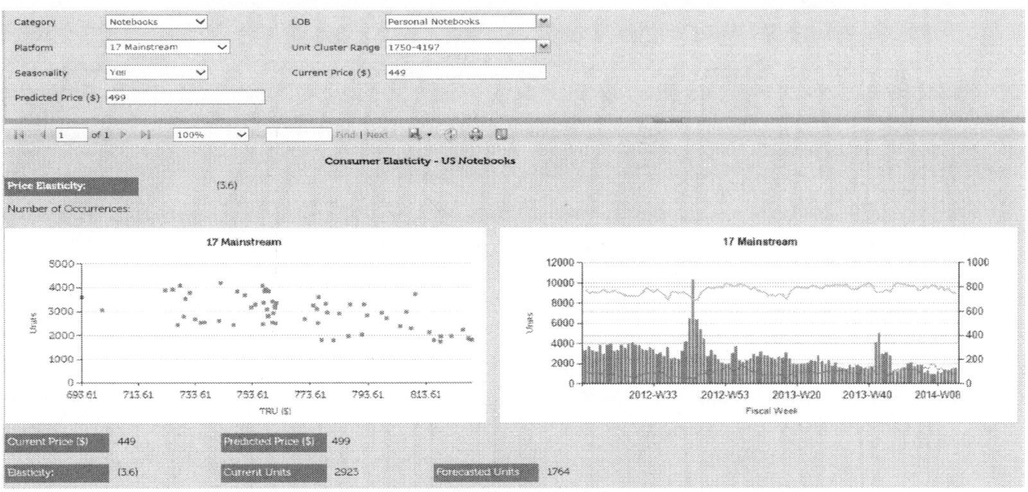

Fig. 10: Model based Scenario Analyser
(Product Names are masked for confidentiality)

it allows a Pricing Manager to take a call with respect to optimal pricing, so as to not leave out money on the table in case of an inelastic product and gain unit share in a relatively elastic product. The bottom-line is to have a good unit share in the market while maintaining overall profit margins in a product portfolio.

CONCLUSION

The outcome of the project is an analytical framework that helps in data-based decision making in pricing products across their product life cycle. The derived results thus aim at achieving the following:

- Identify the most impactful price changes and promotions from both Dell and competitors and their effect on unit sales, revenue and profit margin
- Understand the effect of one channel's prices on the other channel's sales to derive a holistic omni-channel pricing strategy
- Enable data driven decisions by the Pricing Managers through simulation of multiple price-demand scenarios derived from the statistical pricing models.

BIBLIOGRAPHY

Feldman, David and Wurst, John. (2001). Optimal Pricing through Value Modeling. *The Journal of Professional Pricing,* 2nd quarter 2001. Retrieved from: http://www.sdr-consulting.com/article7.html

Gjaja, Marin, Hulings, Sims, and Stanger, Peter. (2003). *Profit Parabolas: Bringing Science to the Art of Pricing*, The Boston Consulting Group. Retrieved from: http://www.bcgindia.com/documents/file14225.pdf

Knowledge@ Wharton. (2008). *The Blurring line between Consumer and Corporate Technologies* . Retrieved from: http://knowledge.wharton.upenn.edu/article/gadgets-at-work-the-blurring-boundary-between-consumer-and-corporate-technologies/

Magin, Vera and Jesse, Hanna. (2001). *Confronting the challenge of Pricing Hundreds of products*, The Pricing Advisor, Mar 2001. Retrieved from: http://media.pricingsociety.com/publications/Confronting_the_Challenge_of_Pricing_Hundreds_of_Products.pdf

Mulugeta, Dawit, Jason Greenfield, Tison Bolen and Lisa Colley. (2013). Price and cross price elasticity estimation using SAS. *SAS Global Forum 2013*, Paper 425-2013 Retrieved from: http://support.sas.com/resources/papers/proceedings13/425-2013.pdf

Schmidt, Fabian (2013). *Smart Profit Growth through Consumer Pricing Tactics.* Pricing Advisor (April 2013). Retrieved from: http://media.pricingsociety.com/publications/Smart_Profit_Growth_Through_Consumer_Pricing_Tactics.pdf?elq=f54ec0b6af6949658f671d5c56c494e1&elqCampaignId=161

Smith, Tim J. (2013). *Who Should Control Pricing? Sales, Marketing, or Finance?* The

Pricing Society (Sep 2013) Retrieved from: http://www.pricingsociety.com/news-details/2014/03/18/who-should-control-pricing-sales-marketing-or-finance-

Yanagisawa, Akira (2011). *Estimation of Price Elasticity of Energy Demand in Japan Considering Socio–economic Structure Changes*. Retrieved from: https://eneken.ieej.or.jp/data/4160.pdf

APPENDIX

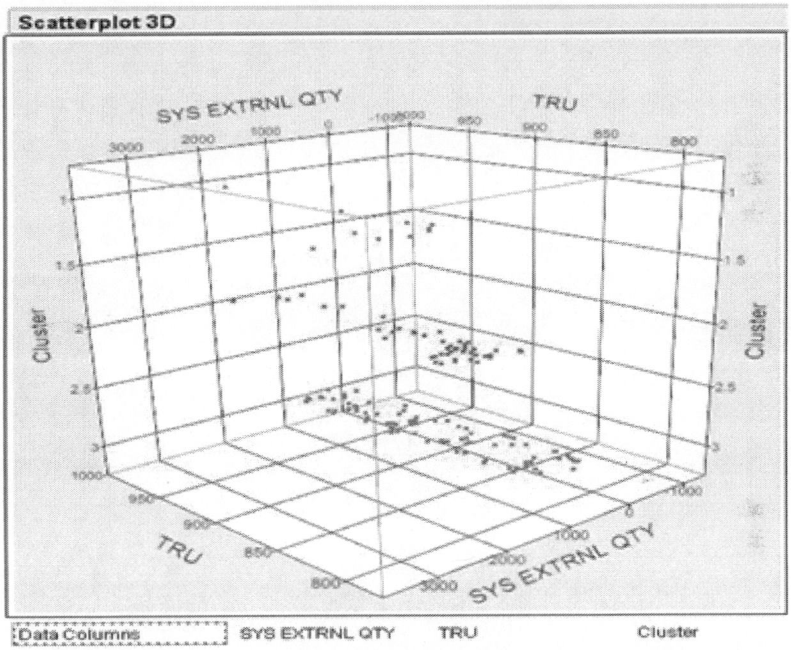

Fig. 11. Cluster Analysis – For Unit Clustering across product families

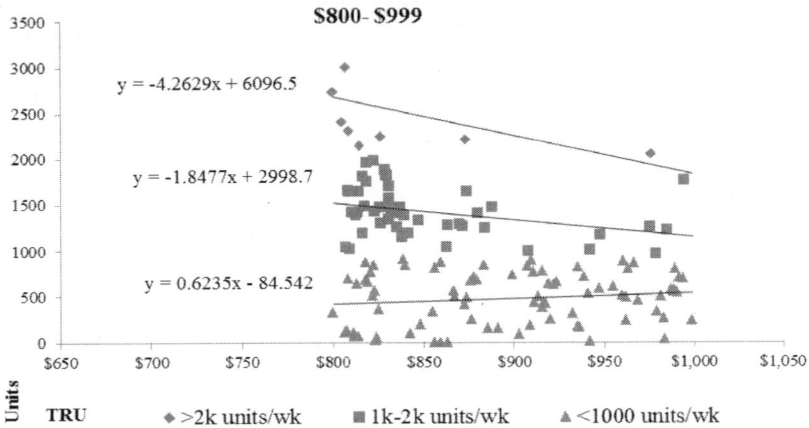

Fig. 12. Need for Clustering–Varied slope with different Elasticity for each Unit Cluster

PART

ONE-F

ONLINE MARKETING

Thanks to the proliferation of social media tools, consumers have gone from plain message receivers to message generators and propagators, and those who exert the most influence over consumer-generated word-of-mouth—i.e. market mavens. These particularly market-motivated customers are more important than ever to marketers. Social media networks such as Twitter are rife with opportunities for creating more effective online marketing campaigns but one of the most pressing problems confronting online marketers is identifying market mavens and gathering and analyzing the data created on these networks.

The paper, 'Lost In Translation? Identification of Online Market Mavens Using Big Social Media Data' proposes the use of publicly available social media metrics to identify market mavens who can be used strategically for marketing purposes. Four main dimensions of market mavenism are identified: user network, user behaviour, message readability and message structure. These dimensions are illustrated through Twitter by means of a self-report survey and social media data-scraping.

The paper 'Evaluating Success of New Design of Web Page Using Fractional Factorial Framework' behaviourally segments online users and tests multiple website designs simultaneously on them through a Fractional Factorial framework Using Fractional factorial framework, a list of possible factors that would influence the consumer purchase journey for each segment is identified and a set of treatments with different levels of those factors is rolled out in testing for that segment. Each target group is monitored for their engagement and conversion rates in order to decide which designs are effective in driving traffic.

CHAPTER TWELVE

LOST IN TRANSLATION? IDENTIFICATION OF ONLINE MARKET MAVENS USING BIG SOCIAL MEDIA DATA

Kristof Coussement, Paul Harrigan, Tim Daly, Julie Lee and Geoff Soutar

ABSTRACT

The proliferation of social media tools has led to a substantive blurring of the boundaries between organization and consumer. To illustrate, 92 of the top 100 global brands tweet more than once per day while around 20 per cent of all users' tweets contain brand mentions. Consumers can no longer be considered simply as message receivers, but also as important message generators and propagators. In this study we use a two-phase methodology, including survey and social media data scraping, to illustrate that market mavens can be identified on Twitter through the following dimensions: user network, user behaviour, message readability and message structure.

Keywords: Market Mavens, Social Media, Twitter, Customer Engagement.

INTRODUCTION

The proliferation of social media tools (such as Twitter, Facebook, YouTube, Pinterest, Reddit, and Tumblr) has led to a substantive blurring of the boundaries between organization and consumer (Aral, Dellarocas, & Godes, 2013).

To illustrate, 92 of the top 100 global brands tweet more than once per day (Shively, 2014), while around 20 per cent of all users' tweets contain brand mentions (Smith, Fischer, & Chen, 2012). These bi-directional marketing activities build interactive relationships between organizations and consumers. Consumers can no longer be considered simply as message receivers, but also as important message generators and propagators. Our objective in this study is to examine particularly market-motivated consumers (i.e. market mavens) and propose publicly available social media metrics to constitute a decision support system that can be used to identify and target market mavens for marketing purposes.

Introduced by Feick and Price (1987), market mavens are individuals who act as hubs, gatherers and disseminators of general market information, and who have a perceived high level of credibility and expertise. Mavens are knowledgeable about many products, and about the place, promotion and pricing aspects of the marketing mix (Brancaleone & Gountas, 2007). Mavenism has taken on an even more important role since the advent of social media, which has dramatically increased the visibility of consumer-generated word-of-mouth. Ho and Dempsey (2010) and Phelps, Lewis, Mobilio, Perry, and Raman (2004) describe 'e-mavens' as a particular group of people who acquire and spread information via electronic platforms. Throughout marketing history, endorsement marketing has always involved engaging with people with expertise or a good reputation to recommend products or services more widely (Li, Lee, & Lien, 2012). Market mavens are such a group, and one with whom marketers seek to engage on social media.

The challenge facing marketers is being able to identify market mavens on social media. If marketers are able to identify and target influential consumers like mavens, they would be able to disseminate marketing messages more efficiently and effectively via social media and also gather reliable feedback on trends in the marketplace. In this paper, we propose that marketers can use publicly available social media data to do just that. Specifically, we outline four main dimensions of market mavenism: user network, user behaviour, message readability and message structure. We then propose metrics, relevant to a major micro-blogging site, for each of these dimensions.

The following sections of the paper describe our focus on Twitter and present a range of hypotheses around the use of social media data to identify market mavens. We utilise a two-phase methodology, including a self-report survey and social media data-scraping approach. We report findings of theoretical and managerial significance to the marketing and social media domains.

TWITTER

One of the most favoured approaches for consumer engagement on social media is micro-blogging, and Twitter is the dominant micro-blogging platform. Twitter was launched in 2006 and now has more than 250 million active users generating an average of 500 million tweets per day (Twitter, 2014a). Research shows that a significant number of tweets mention a brand (Smith et al., 2012). From a market research perspective, Twitter is particularly open and amenable to public mining of 'big data' and thus analysis of consumer behaviour (Mostafa, 2013). This is possible through its application programming interface (API). Due to the sheer numbers of consumers on Twitter, identifying influencers is paramount for marketers (Pagani & Mirabello, 2011; Rishika, Kumar, Janakiraman, & Bezawada, 2013). However, this is difficult due to the aforementioned number of users, the volume of data they create, the real-time and high-velocity nature of the data, and the variety of the data where textual data is difficult to analyse (Mostafa, 2013).

As a brief introduction to the process and nomenclature of Twitter, messages sent through the services are called tweets. Tweets can contain text, images, videos, links and hashtags within a limit of 140 characters. By default, these tweets are publicly available. However, in a practical sense, users only are aware of the tweets from the other users that they choose to follow. Thus each user will have a list of followers (users who follow them) and following (users who they follow). Users are identified through Twitter handles, such as @ANZMAC. Thus, even public tweets can be directed at other users, enabling a level of interaction.

A very common behaviour, besides posting original tweets, is retweeting other users' tweets. For example, if a user follows @ANZMAC and ANZMAC tweets about an upcoming conference deadline, it would be simple for that user to retweet that message so that all of his/her followers would also see it. This propagates messages across user networks creating a wider sphere of influence. Another function that is relevant to this study is the list function. Users are able to create separate lists within the users they are following. In this way, a user can create a list of the sports organisations he/she follows, which will display only their tweets. Likewise, a user could create a list of the market mavens he/she is following, which will display only their tweets. This is separate from the main timeline, which displays all the tweets of all the users being followed. Finally, there is the hashtag function. Hashtags allow for information classification. Thus, running a search on the hashtag, #AFL, will display a list of all the tweets on this subject from users followed and not followed. The hashtag function allows for trends to quickly develop and be tracked on Twitter, and has now also been introduced as a function on Facebook.

CONCEPTUAL DEVELOPMENT

Based on a review of the market mavenism literature, we propose a classification of four dimensions, that relates to mavens' network characteristics, mavens' behaviours, the readability levels of their messages and the structure of their messages. Appendix A provides an overview of these market maven dimensions, the related Twitter variables and descriptions, and units of analysis.

User Network

Market mavens will exhibit higher levels of specific information provisions to other consumers across a range of product categories e.g. (Abratt, Nel, & Nezer, 1995; Barnes & Pressey, 2012; Feick & Price, 1987). Due to both market mavens' efforts to share information to help others and the need from others for information, we propose that they are likely to be situated within a substantial network (Laughlin & MacDonald, 2010; Phang, Zhang, & Sutanto, 2013; van der Merwe & van Heerden, 2009). Thus we hypothesize that;

H1a: Market mavens have a significantly higher number of Twitter followers compared to non-mavens

Moreover, being seen as a source of expertise or a central actor within a network could lead to a classification by others of market mavens (Feick & Price, 1987; van der Merwe & van Heerden, 2009). Mavens tend to display a level of self-efficacy that provides them with the confidence to stand out from the crowd to assist others (Abratt et al., 1995; Geissler & Edison, 2005). In this way, consumers will likely be able to recognise mavens and identify them as valuable sources of expertise. Thus we hypothesize that;

H1b: Market mavens have a significantly higher number of Twitter listings compared to non-mavens

User Behaviour

Market mavens are more likely to generate information in their chosen channels of communication (Abratt et al., 1995; Barnes & Pressey, 2012; Feick & Price, 1987). It follows that mavens' usage of social media platforms such as Twitter is likely to be greater than that of non-mavens (Ho & Dempsey, 2010). Thus we hypothesize that;

H2a: Market mavens have a significantly higher number of tweets compared to non-mavens

As previously discussed, social media platforms like Twitter also facilitate information sharing, as well as information generation, by providing mavens with access to large amounts of information as well as the means to share it (via retweets). Previous research has found that market mavens collect, retain and share information (Brancaleone & Gountas, 2007; Higie, Feick, & Price, 1987). Thus, we hypothesize that;

H2b: Market mavens have a significantly higher percentage of retweets compared to non-mavens

Finally, with regard to user behaviour, we posit a positive relationship between market mavenism and information interactions. Twitter easily facilitates direct public interactions between users. Previous research has found that mavens' altruistic behaviours around information sharing are actually driven by an interpersonal need for inclusion or belongingness (Price, Feick, & Guskey, 1995). It follows that mavens both initiate discussions about marketplace information *and* respond to requests from others for such information (Feick & Price, 1987; Walsh, Gwinner, & Swanson, 2004). In this way, mavens are able to achieve one-to-one social gratification for their information generating or sharing behaviour (Slama & Williams, 1990). Thus we hypothesize that;

H2c: Market mavens have a significantly higher percentage of interactions compared to non-mavens

Message Readability

Market mavens tend to seek to influence their wider social network (Goldsmith, Clark, & Goldsmith, 2006; Ho & Dempsey, 2010). With this aim in mind, the style of their messages becomes important. Therefore, writing in a manner that is readable may be an important trait of mavens. The Automated Readability Index (ARI) is one approach to measuring readability of pieces of text (Smith & Senter, 1967). It produces an approximate representation of the US grade level needed to comprehend the text. We hypothesize that;

H3: Market mavens have significantly more readable tweets compared to non-mavens

Message Structure

Market mavens are said to place some emphasis on self-esteem; that is the extent to which a person has a positive attitude about him- or herself. More than this, mavenism has been shown to be positively related to the personality trait of extraversion. Through extraversion, mavens may be able to distinguish themselves and maintain their social position (Goldsmith et al., 2006; Ho & Dempsey, 2010). Goldsmith, Flynn, and Goldsmith (2003) also found that mavens are more assertive than other consumers. There is a generally accepted etiquette online that the use of upper case is akin to shouting, or attention seeking. Thus we hypothesize that;

H4a: Market mavens have a significantly higher percentage of uppercase letters per tweet compared to non-mavens

Linked to this, we are also interested in the percentage of distinct words in mavens' tweets. Due to the 'noise' on social media, it is difficult for individuals and brands to make their message stand out. With regard to Twitter, the official Twitter business website makes recommendations around the best tweet length for audience engagement. It is reported that tweets with less than 100 characters average 17 per cent higher levels of engagement (Twitter, 2014b). Engagement in this case is defined as retweets, replies or favourites. With this prior research in mind, it is highly likely that mavens will seek to keep their tweets shorter with fewer distinct words. Thus, we hypothesize that;

H4b: Market mavens have a significantly lower percentage of distinct words per tweet compared to non-mavens

Information classification via hashtags is a prominent function on Twitter, and one that market mavens may make significant use of. The hashtag function would allow for clear information classification and searching by both mavens and general consumers. Mavens do exhibit higher levels of specific information provisions to other consumers across product categories (Abratt et al., 1995). Mavens are also more likely to be comfortable with technology and display self-efficacy (Geissler & Edison, 2005; Ho & Dempsey, 2010; Ruvio & Shoham, 2007). Therefore, based on mavens' needs to disseminate information in crowded online environments (Geissler & Edison, 2005), they may be more likely to utilise the hashtag function on Twitter. Thus we hypothesize that;

H4c: Market mavens have a significantly higher percentage of hashtags per tweet compared to non-mavens

METHODOLOGY

We collected the data for this study from members of the Amazon Mechanical Turk (MTurk) marketplace. Participants were required to be located in the United States and be 'active' Twitter users. We defined 'active' as having operated a public and personal Twitter account for at least six months, and having sent at least 100 tweets prior to the study being launched. Participants were asked to complete a questionnaire and agreed to provide their Twitter handle and consent for the researchers to follow their Twitter account. Of the 459 users who completed the initial survey, 36 were disqualified due to not satisfying the Twitter account requirements, leaving 423 usable responses.

In order to obtain the focal Twitter metrics, we used the Twitter application programming interface (API) to scrape the Tweets and download the basic Twitter profile variables on the collection date. Out of the 423 completed surveys, we were able to match and scrape the Tweets from 370 respondents, a matching rate of 87 per cent. The dropout is caused by spelling mistakes of Twitter profiles by the respondents, which makes it impossible to match it with a valid twitter account. This resulted in a total of 520,700 Tweets.

Self-reported market mavenism on Twitter was operationalized using three items adapted for the Twitter context from the original market mavenism scale developed by Feick and Price (1987). Table 1 shows the three adapted scale items, measured on a 7-point Likert scale. A median split on the market mavenism construct is used to create a high and low level group. In the remainder of the paper, the high scoring respondents ($M_{\text{Market Mavenism}}$ = 5.07, M_{Age} = 29.19, $\text{Ratio}_{\text{Men/Women}}$ = 1.26, n = 172) are called market mavens, and the low scoring group are called non-market mavens ($M_{\text{MarketMavenism}}$ = 2.33, M_{Age} = 28.86, $\text{Ratio}_{\text{Men/Women}}$ = 0.74, n = 198).

Table 1: Description of Market Mavenism Construct Adapted for Twitter

Market Mavenism (Cronbach's alpha = .91)
I like introducing new brands and products to my followers.
I like helping my followers by providing them with information about many kinds of products.
My followers think of me as a good source of information when it comes down to new products or sales

RESULTS

Appendix B provides the results of the hypothesis testing process using independent sample t-tests.

In support of H1a, market mavens have a significantly higher number of other Twitter users that are following them compared to non-mavens (M_{high} = 784.97; M_{low} = 174.61; t (175.98) = -2.17; p = .03). However H1b was not supported; the degree of market mavenism does not play a significant role in the number of listings Tweeters have (M_{high} = 8.44; M_{low} = 5.25; t (279) = -1.40; p = .16).

The hypotheses related to information generation on Twitter, H2a and H2c are supported. More specifically, market mavens generate significantly more messages on Twitter compared to their counterparts (M_{high} = 1608.18; M_{low} = 1232.79; t (368) = –3.10; p < .01), and they also have more personal interactions with other Twitter users (M_{high} = 22.62; M_{low} = 18.95; t (335.48) = -2.02; p = .04). However, in terms of information sharing, i.e. retweeting posts from other Twitter users, the market mavenism dimension does not play a significant role (M_{high} = 22.62; M_{low} = 18.95; t (368) = .46; p = .65). Thus, H2b is not supported.

Contrary to H3, market mavens write significantly less readably than non-mavens, i.e. the latter group has a significantly lower US grade level than the market mavens (M_{high} = 8.01; M_{low} = 7.04; t (368) = -3.59; p < .01). In support of H4a market mavens use significantly more capitals than the non-market mavens (M_{high} = 8.51; M_{low} = 7.47; t (368) = -3.59; p< .01). There is marginal support for H4c, as the use of hashtags in the Tweets is higher for mavens (M_{high} = 29.31 vs M_{low} = 24.44; t (332.81) = -1.86; p = .06). Moreover, in support of H4b the results show that the non-mavens rely on a significant larger variety of words compared to market mavens when writing their Tweets (M_{high} = 27.92 vs M_{low} = 30.16; t (368) = 2.05; p = .04).

DISCUSSION

This study sought to illustrate that market mavens can be identified based on their user network, behaviour and message characteristics. Results indeed demonstrate that this is the case. Specifically, around the hypotheses on *User network*, we find that mavens do tend to have a greater number of followers on Twitter than non-mavens (H1a). This confirms previous research around the network size of mavens in an offline setting (Laughlin & MacDonald, 2010; van der Merwe & van Heerden, 2009), and also some conceptual research around mavens' networks online (Phang et al., 2013; Phelps et al., 2004; Walsh et al., 2004).

Unexpectedly, we find that mavens tend not be listed more on Twitter than non-mavens (H1b). Where being listed denotes a level of expertise and an interest in this expertise among the user's followers, we would have expected the likelihood of market mavens being listed as high. This in a way disconfirms previous research, which has indicated that mavens would be particularly capable and central actors within their network, which would easily enable others to identify and classify them (Feick & Price, 1987; van der Merwe & van Heerden, 2009). Our finding infers that, on Twitter, it may be more difficult for mavens' influence and expertise to stand out. A contrasting explanation is that the general nature of the maven's expertise does not lend itself to narrow categorizations that generally make up these lists.

A practical explanation may be the practical limitations of the listing function on Twitter. The social media blogger, Dave Delaney, recently stated that less than a quarter of his social media savvy audience at an event utilised Twitter lists. The function is not immediately obvious in the Twitter interface, which could perhaps lead to under-use.

Regarding *User behaviour*, we find that mavens do tend to post more tweets (H2a) and interact directly more with other users than non-mavens (H2c). This supports our hypotheses and confirms previous research on mavens generally, in that mavens are more likely to generate information in their chosen channels of communication (Abratt et al., 1995; Barnes & Pressey, 2012; Feick & Price, 1987). Previous research has also found that they value interpersonal interaction, often responding to requests from others for market information (Feick & Price, 1987; Price et al., 1995; Walsh et al., 2004).

We do find, however, that mavens tend not to retweet more than non-mavens (H2b). We had hypothesized a positive relationship between mavenism and retweeting behaviour, which represents information sharing. This hypothesis was based on prior research that emphasized the role of mavens in seeking out and disseminating information among their network (Goldsmith et al., 2003; Higie et al., 1987; Walsh et al., 2004). Perhaps this finding can be explained in that market mavens on social media tend to be content creators, more than content sharers. Pagani and Mirabello (2011) have characterised different levels of behaviour and influence on social media. Where so much content is user-generated on platforms such as Twitter, it may be that mavens are more likely to create and disseminate their own content.

We find results around *Message readability* surprising, where mavens' messages are actually less readable, that is more complex, than non-mavens (H3). We had hypothesized that readability would be higher for mavens, where they seek to communicate to and engage with wider groups of consumers (Goldsmith et al., 2006; Ho & Dempsey, 2010). In an attempt to explain the lower readability/higher complexity of market mavens' messages, we return to literature that alludes to the importance of social position (Feick & Price, 1987; Walsh et al., 2004). Perhaps mavens try to achieve a higher position by communicating their expertise through the complexity of language in their messages. This is the opposite approach to communicating to the wider consumer group by creating easily readable messages, and is certainly an interesting finding regarding mavens on social media.

Our results around *Message structure* could also follow this line of argument, where we find that mavens tend to use more uppercase letters (H4a) and hashtags (H4c) in their tweets. The use of uppercase letters may confirm previous literature around extraversion as a personality trait, or a general need to attract attention through assertiveness (Goldsmith et al., 2003; Ho & Dempsey, 2010). The high use of hashtags, which represents information classification, confirms that mavens' information provision is high on social media (Abratt et al., 1995), and that they are relatively comfortable with the norms around Twitter use (Geissler & Edison, 2005; Ho & Dempsey, 2010).

Finally, we find that mavens tend to use fewer words in their tweets (H4b). This supports our rationale that mavens will tend to keep their tweets shorter, as this increases the likelihood of garnering attention and engagement from their followers. Previous research focused on Twitter has shown that shorter tweets tend to lead to higher follower engagement, and research on online advertising generally shows that message length is negatively related to audience engagement (Baltas, 2003).

CONCLUSION AND IMPLICATIONS

The research into market mavens in the online context is an important area for marketing and business research in general. This research demonstrates how market mavens on Twitter can be identified using freely accessible data via the Twitter API. This is a valuable contribution to the marketing and general business knowledge as social media usage and consumer communications are at the forefront of current business practices. Marketers will still need to make decisions about what mavens can do for their campaigns, and how they will engage with them, but having built a first step in identifying mavens we believe the way forward is bright with possibilities.

REFERENCES

Abratt, R., Nel, D., & Nezer, C. (1995). Role of the market maven in retailing - a general marketplace influencer. *Journal of Business and Psychology, 10*(1), 31-55. doi: 10.1007/bf02249268

Aral, Sinan, Dellarocas, Chrysanthos, & Godes, David. (2013). Social Media and Business Transformation: A Framework for Research. *Information Systems Research, 24*(1), 3-13. doi: 10.1287/isre.1120.0470

Baltas, G. (2003). Determinants of Internet advertising effectiveness: an empirical study. *International Journal of Market Research, 45*(4), 505-513.

Barnes, Stuart J., & Pressey, Andrew D. (2012). In Search of the "Meta-Maven": An Examination of Market Maven Behavior across Real-Life, Web, and Virtual World Marketing Channels. *Psychology & Marketing, 29*(3), 167-185. doi: 10.1002/mar.20513

Brancaleone, Vito, & Gountas, John. (2007). Personality Characteristics of Market Mavens. In Gavan Fitzsimons and Vicki Morwitz, Duluth, MN (Eds.) *Advances in Consumer*

Research Volume 34, Association for Consumer Research, Pages: 522-527. Retrieved from http://acrwebsite.org/volumes/12859/volumes/v34/NA-34

Delaney, Dave. (2013). How to use Twitter like a pro. Retrieved from: http://daveadelaney.com/how-to-use-twitter-lists-like-a-pro/

Feick, L. F., & Price, L. L. (1987). The market maven - A diffuser of marketplace information. *Journal of Marketing, 51*(1), 83-97. doi: 10.2307/1251146

Geissler, G. L., & Edison, S. W. (2005). Market mavens' attitudes towards general technology: Implications for marketing communications. *Journal of Marketing Communications, 11*(2), 73-94. doi: 10.1080/1352726042000286499

Goldsmith, Ronald E., Clark, Ronald A., & Goldsmith, Elizabeth B. (2006). Extending the psychological profile of market mavenism. *Journal of Consumer Behaviour, 5*(5), 411-419. doi: 10.1002/cb.189

Goldsmith, Ronald E., Flynn, Leisa R., & Goldsmith, Elizabeth B. (2003). Innovative Consumers and Market Mavens. *Journal of Marketing Theory and Practice, 11*(4), 54-65. doi: 10.2307/40470118

Higie, R. A., Feick, L. F., & Price, L. L. (1987). Types and amount of word-of-mouth communications about retailers. *Journal of Retailing, 63*(3), 260-278.

Ho, Jason Y. C., & Dempsey, Melanie. (2010). Viral marketing: Motivations to forward online content. *Journal of Business Research, 63*(9–10), 1000-1006. doi: http://dx.doi.org/10.1016/j.jbusres.2008.08.010

Laughlin, John D., & MacDonald, Jason B. (2010). Identifying market mavens online by their social behaviors in community-generated media. *Academy of Marketing Studies Journal, 14*(1), 55-70.

Li, Yung-Ming, Lee, Yi-Lin, & Lien, Nine-Jun. (2012). Online Social Advertising via Influential Endorsers. *International Journal of Electronic Commerce, 16*(3), 119-153. doi: 10.2753/jec1086-4415160305

Mostafa, Mohamed M. (2013). More than words: Social networks' text mining for consumer brand sentiments. *Expert Systems with Applications, 40*(10), 4241-4251. doi: http://dx.doi.org/10.1016/j.eswa.2013.01.019

Pagani, Margherita, & Mirabello, Alessandra. (2011). The Influence of Personal and Social-Interactive Engagement in Social TV Web Sites. *International Journal of Electronic Commerce, 16*(2), 41-67. doi: 10.2753/jec1086-4415160203

Phang, Chee Wei, Zhang, Chenghong, & Sutanto, Juliana. (2013). The influence of user interaction and participation in social media on the consumption intention of niche products. *Information & Management, 50*(8), 661-672. doi: http://dx.doi.org/10.1016/j.im.2013.07.001

Phelps, J. E., Lewis, R., Mobilio, L., Perry, D., & Raman, N. (2004). Viral marketing or electronic word-of-mouth advertising: Examining consumer responses and motivations to pass along email. *Journal of Advertising Research, 44*(4), 333-348. doi: 10.1017/s0021849904040371

Price, L. L., Feick, L. F., & Guskey, A. (1995). Everyday market helping-behavior. *Journal of Public Policy & Marketing, 14*(2), 255-266.

Rishika, Rishika, Kumar, Ashish, Janakiraman, Ramkumar, & Bezawada, Ram. (2013). The Effect of Customers' Social Media Participation on Customer Visit Frequency and Profitability: An Empirical Investigation. *Information Systems Research, 24*(1), 108-127. doi: 10.1287/isre.1120.0460

Ruvio, Ayalla, & Shoham, Aviv. (2007). Innovativeness, exploratory behavior, market mavenship, and opinion leadership: An empirical examination in the Asian context. *Psychology and Marketing, 24*(8), 703-722. doi: 10.1002/mar.20180

Shively, J. (2014). How Top Brand Marketers Used Twitter During Q4 of 2013. Retrieved 6 May, 2014, from http://simplymeasured.com/blog/2014/01/20/twitter-study/

Slama, Mark E., & Williams, Terrell G. (1990). Generalization of the Market Maven's Information Provision Tendency Across Product Categories. *Advances in Consumer Research, 17*(1), 48-52.

Smith, Andrew N., Fischer, Eileen, & Chen, Yongjian. (2012). How Does Brand-related User-generated Content Differ across YouTube, Facebook, and Twitter? *Journal of Interactive Marketing, 26*(2), 102-113. doi: 10.1016/j.intmar.2012.01.002

Smith, E. A., & Senter, R. J. (1967). Automated readability index. *AMRL-TR. Aerospace Medical Research Laboratories (6570th)*, 1-14.

Twitter. (2014a). About Company. Retrieved 18 June, 2014, from https://about.twitter.com/company

Twitter. (2014b). Business Best practices. Retrieved 18 June, 2014, from https://business.twitter.com/best-practices

van der Merwe, R., & van Heerden, G. (2009). Finding and utilizing opinion leaders: Social networks and the power of relationships. *South African Journal of Business Management, 40*(3), 65-76.

Walsh, Gianfranco, Gwinner, Kevin P., & Swanson, Scott R. (2004). What makes mavens tick? Exploring the motives of market mavens' initiation of information diffusion. *The Journal of Consumer Marketing, 21*(2/3), 109-122.

APPENDICES

APPENDIX A

Overview of Market Maven Dimensions and Twitter Terminology

Market Mavenism Dimension	*Twitter Variable*	*Description*	*Unit of Analysis*
User network	Number of followers	The number of people that have agreed to receive your messages (or Tweets) through Twitter. If someone adds you to their 'followers', they 'follow' you.	#
	Number of listings	The number of people that have added you to their own curated group or list of Twitter users. Lists are a way of categorising users posting ('tweeting') on certain topics.	#
User behaviour	Number of tweets	The number of times the user posts a new Tweet.	#
	Percentage of retweets	The number of times the user shares a Tweet from someone else divided by his/her total number of Tweets.	%
	Percentage of interactions	The number of times the user interacts with another Twitter user divided by his/her total number of Tweets.	%
Message readability	Automated Readability Index	The user's average readability measure that gauges the understandability of the Tweet, while approximating the representation of the US Grade level needed to comprehend the text. The formula is given below: $4.71\left(\frac{characters}{words}\right)+0.5\left(\frac{words}{sentences}\right)-21.43$	US grade level
Message structure	Average percentage of uppercase letters	The user's average of the Levenshtein edit distance between the original Tweet and the lower case converted Tweet divided by the total Tweet length. The Levenshtein edit distance represents the number of single characters that need to be capitalized to obtain the original Tweet.	%
	Average percentage of distinct words	The user's average of the sum of distinct words in the Tweets divided by the total Tweet lengths.	%
	Average percentage of hashtags	The user's average of the sum of the hashtags (#) used in the Tweet portfolio.	%

APPENDIX B

Summary of Results

Market Mavenism Dimension	*Twitter Variable*	*Unit of Analysis*	*Market Mavenism*		*t-Value (df)*	
			High level Mean (Std)	*Low level Mean (Std)*		
User network	Number of followers	#	784.98 (3667.40)	174.61 (474.61)	–2.17 (175.98)	**
	Number of listings	#	8.44 (25.93)	5.25 (16.22)	–1.40 (279)	
User behaviour	Number of tweets	#	1608.18 (1205.49)	1232.79 (1120.53)	–3.10 (368)	**
	Percentage of retweets	%	13.50 (13.88)	14.08 (13.86)	.46 (368)	
	Percentage of interactions	%	22.62 (18.78)	18.95 (15.78)	–2.02 (335.48)	**
Message readability	Automated Readability Index	US grade level	8.01 (2.76)	7.04 (2.43)	–3.59 (368)	***
Message structure	Average percentage of uppercase letters	%	8.51 (2.78)	7.47 (2.32)	–3.87 (334.23)	***
	Average percentage of distinct words	%	27.92 (10.85)	30.16 (10.16)	2.05 (368)	**
	Average percentage of hashtags	%	29.31 (27.18)	24.44 (22.50)	–1.86 (332.81)	*

*p < .10; **p <. 05; ***p < .01

CHAPTER THIRTEEN

EVALUATING SUCCESS OF NEW DESIGN OF WEB PAGE USING FRACTIONAL FACTORIAL FRAMEWORK

Nitin Kumar

ABSTRACT

In today's world, one cannot deny the rising significance of e-commerce and its impact on the purchase process of a customer. With the growing share of customers, e-commerce retailers have a big challenge in hand – whether a new design of the web page will be successful or not? There are chances to incur potential loss if the new design is not successful in driving traffic. The objective of this study is to identify the right set of customers who can be used for preview testing of the new design and to evaluate the success of the new design based on their web behavior. The conversion and engagement metrics on the target group would be monitored and if there is a dip in sales, the experiment would be rolled back and a smaller percentage (say <10%) of customer traffic would be impacted.

This study proposes a framework to predict the success of a new design using segmentation and fractional factorial experiment methodology. It essentially means creating segments of customers and then focusing on one of the segments which would be subjected to different types of web layout. For that segment, a list of factors which would influence the purchase decision making process of a visiting customer would be prepared. Using Fractional Factorial framework, the factors and their respective levels would form a set of treatments which would be rolled out to the test groups of customers belonging to that particular segment. Subsequently, the traffic behavior and conversion rate would be analyzed after the test period is complete and the results would be assessed to check the significant treatments which actually drive the traffic or the conversion rate. The new design which is a combination of a profitable set of treatments would be launched for all the customers. If none of the treatments yield significant sales improvement, then the new design would be rolled back and a small percentage of traffic and sales would be impacted. This study can help retailers identify profitable marketing strategies as per the customer's requirement and also optimize the marketing budget allocations.

Keywords: Segmentation, Fractional Factorial Experiment, Marketing Budget Allocation, Customer Purchase Behavior.

INTRODUCTION

Typically, the e-commerce marketing team, as part of their campaigns, sends emails to all customers informing them about the products and offers available. Mass mailing is used to reach out to all customers. This many a times leads to customer dissatisfaction and low conversion rate over a period of time.

A web user usually shows behavior relating to one of the following:

1. Content (he browses through product categories)
2. Intent (he collects information about the product categories he is interested in)
3. Action (he buys the product)

Since we know the behavioral changes in a web user, we can differentially target them with relevant promotions after creating appropriate segments. In a typical e-commerce scenario, it becomes difficult to measure the impact of multiple factors

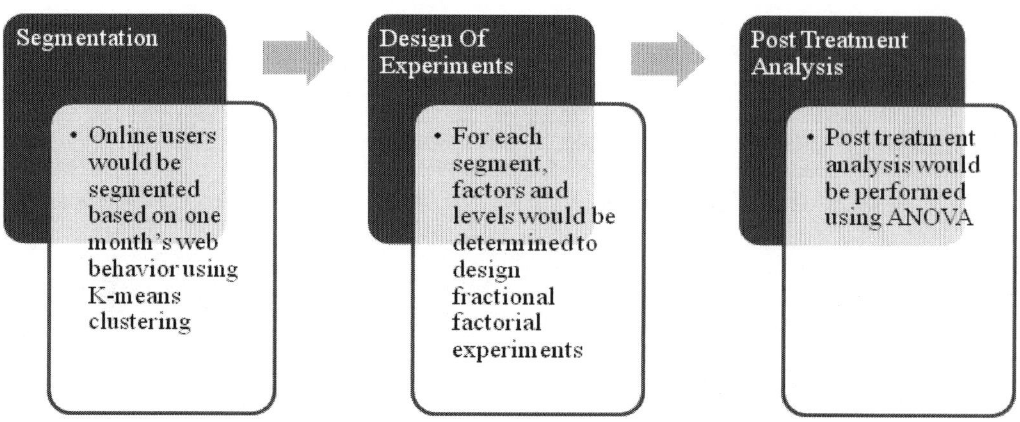

in a web portal using standard A/B testing technique as it would require more time and resources. Therefore, we would look into another alternative technique i.e. "Fractional Factorial design" to see how we can test multiple treatments together at the same time. Overall, the paper is broadly divided into 3 components as shown in diagram.

SEGMENTATION

For such an efficient targeting, the users would have to be segmented into groups as targeting each user individually is a difficult and expensive process. Hence users with similar behaviors need to be grouped together for easier targeting. This requires monitoring changes in customer behavior over time (1 month of web activity considered in this case). This is explained by the diagram below.

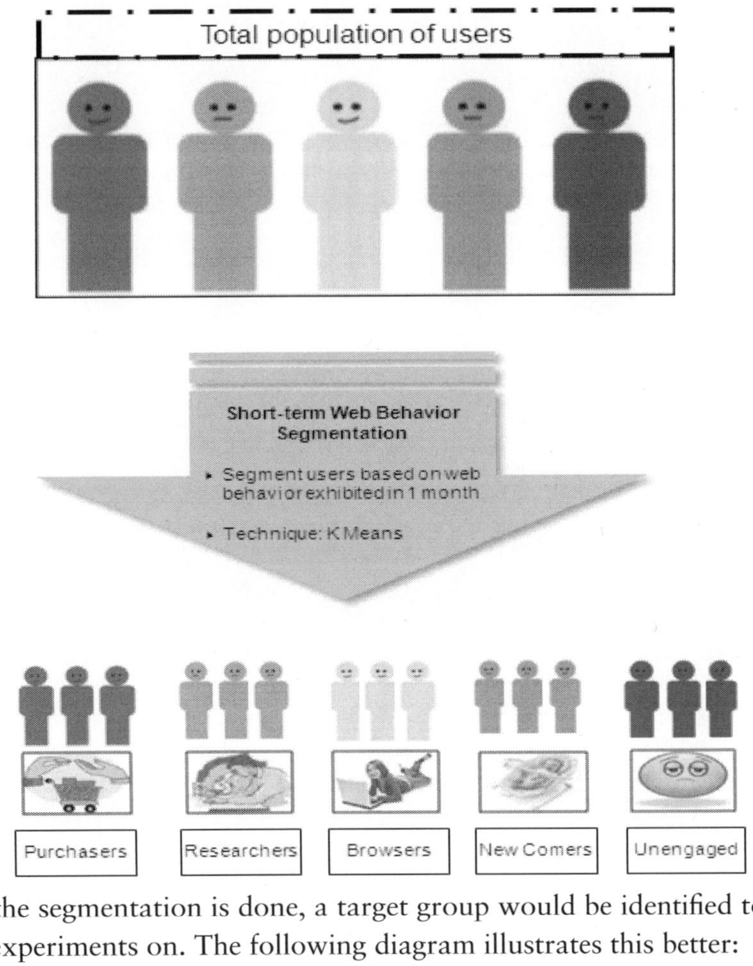

Once the segmentation is done, a target group would be identified to create the design of experiments on. The following diagram illustrates this better:

- **Web Behavioral Segments:** The web users would be divided into five segments based on web behavior exhibited in a month. The five segments are Purchasers, Researchers, Browsers, New Comers and Unengaged. Kindly note that the segmentation was performed on the actual data from one of the e-commerce portals.
- **Target Identification:** Target user groups would be identified based on the recent web behavior. These groups when appropriately targeted will lead to increase in purchase and site engagement rates.

Process Details

Clustering would be done using K-means technique on 1 month of weblogs data.

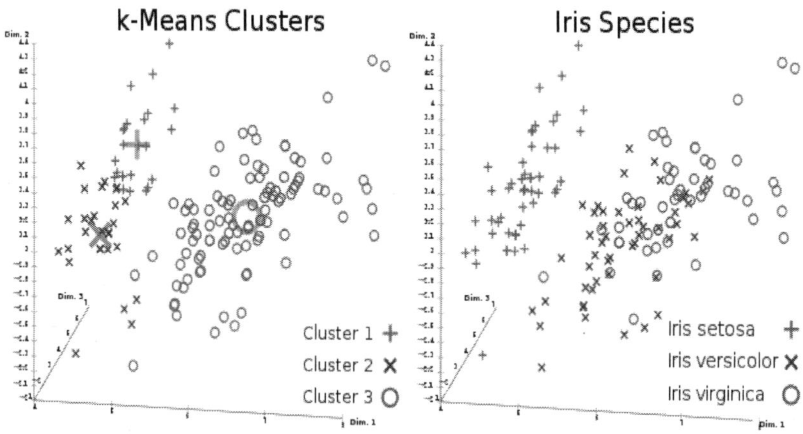

K-means clustering is a technique which groups the points in such a way that the distance between the points within the same cluster is as low as possible and the distance between points of 2 different clusters is high.

- The 1st step was to create and select relevant metrics and variables
- The variables were treated for missing values and outliers
  – The distribution of each variable has to be looked at for removing outliers
- The variables are then standardized
- The variables selected represent certain specific user characteristics/dimensions. If any of these dimensions are over represented, it may lead to skewness in segmentation
- Clustering was done based on these and iterations were done for each of the schemes in order to arrive at the best possible segmentation scheme
- The results of final segmentation are highlighted below.
- Stability of the segmentation needs to be checked for the subsequent months to observe if the segments are stable in terms of the proportion of users.

Metrics Used for Segmenting Customers and the Distribution of the Segments

Behavioral segments	Distribution of users	Segmentation Variables					
		Purchase	# of brands visited per session	# of categories visited per session	Total # of pages visited	Session duration	Tenure
Purchasers	8%	More than average	Average	Average	More than average	Average	Average
Researchers	8%	Less than average	More than average	More than average	More than average	More than average	Average
Browsers	15%	Less than average	More than average	More than average	More than average	Average	Average
New Comers	35%	Less than average	Less than average	Less than average	Less than average	Average	Less than average
Unengaged	33%	Less than average	Less than average	Less than average	Less than average	Less than average	More than average

Legend: ● Less than average ● Average ● More than average

Definition/Interpretation of Segments

	Purchaser	I engage well with the site with long lasting sessions. I made a purchase this month.
	Researcher	I visit high # of pages and spend substantial time in each session. I am more category specific than the Browsers.
	Browser	I visit high # of pages across brands and categories. However, I do not make any purchase.
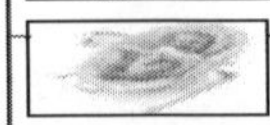	New Comer	I am a relatively new user. My engagement with the site is low and I do not make any purchase.
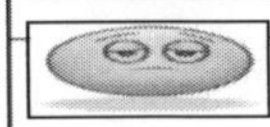	Unengaged	I have been in the system for long but my engagement with the site is low.

Note: The Web Behavioral Segmentation is based on a rolling 1 month period

A few scenarios are illustrated below where the intent to increase the purchase rate and site engagement is highlighted.

Behavior of Users is Analyzed and Appropriate Triggers are Sent to Increase Purchase Rate

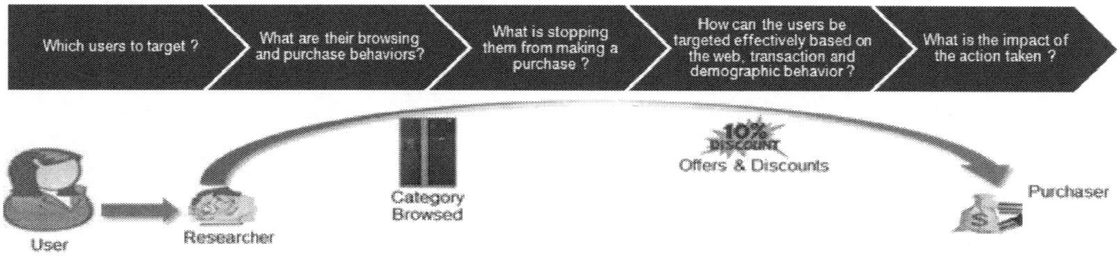

- Consider a user who is 'Researcher'. This indicates that the user has an intent of buying but has historically purchased less number of items
- Based on recent purchase behavior of the user, a deep dive is done to identify the categories he has researched. For example : A product comparison page of refrigerator category shows his intent of buying a refrigerator and hence it can be hypothesized that the user might not have made a purchase because of high price (price can be one of the deterrent)
- Therefore an offer or a discount on refrigerator category can drive the user to make purchase and hence increase the purchase rate.

Behavior of Users is Analyzed and Appropriate Triggers are Sent to Increase Site Engagement

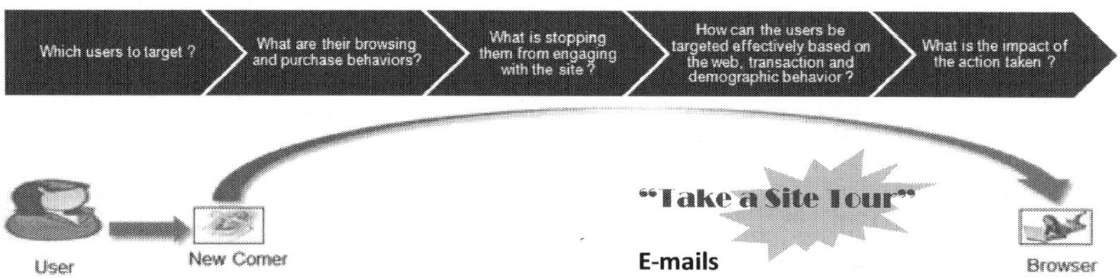

- Consider a user who is a 'New Comer' and 'Non Purchaser'
- This user is relatively new and his site engagement is very low and he needs to get familiarized with the website before making purchase
- Sending him a 'take a site tour' mailer would help him increase his site-engagement.

Overall, the segments could be targeted for site familiarity, site association and conversion. **In this paper, we would focus on Researcher and Browser segments due to their inherent similarities in web behavior.** A design of experiments framework would be created to target these 2 segments together.

DESIGN OF EXPERIMENTS

Factors and levels would be determined to develop treatments for Researcher and Browser segments

- An exhaustive list of factors and levels would be listed as a precursor to determining the factors and levels for the first design of experiment for the Researcher and Browser segments
- The top 4 factors (most suited) would be considered with 2 levels each. For our Researcher and Browser segments, the factors and their corresponding levels can be highlighted as below:

S. No.	*Test Factors*	*Level 1*	*Level 2*
1	Discount ($ off)	$X off	$Y off
2	Shipping	No Free Shipping	Free Shipping
3	Policy Information	Information on Return (Buy with confidence)	Information on Delivery and Installation (Buy with confidence)
4	Site Engagement	Information about categories and existing promotions	Advertising successful customer experiences

Methodology Brief

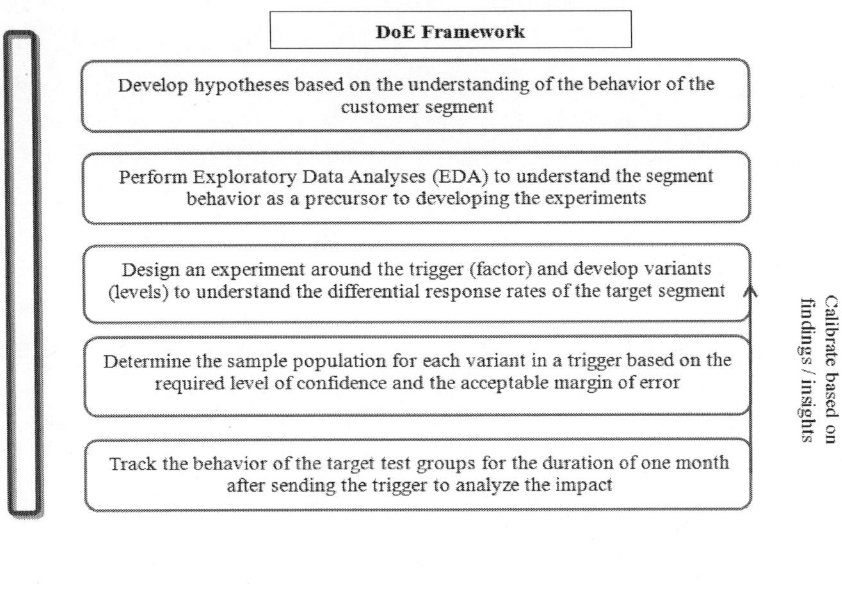

- The Design of Experiment (DoE) will be an iterative process based on the web behavioral segments of online users
- The number of test groups of users for each experiment will depend on the number of treatments generated from the fractional factorial design.
- One control group of users will be determined for each experiment. The split of test and control groups is shown in the diagram below. As we are considering both Researcher and Browser segments, we need to split them into 8 test groups and 1 control group respectively and then combine the population from both the segments before performing the post trigger analysis.

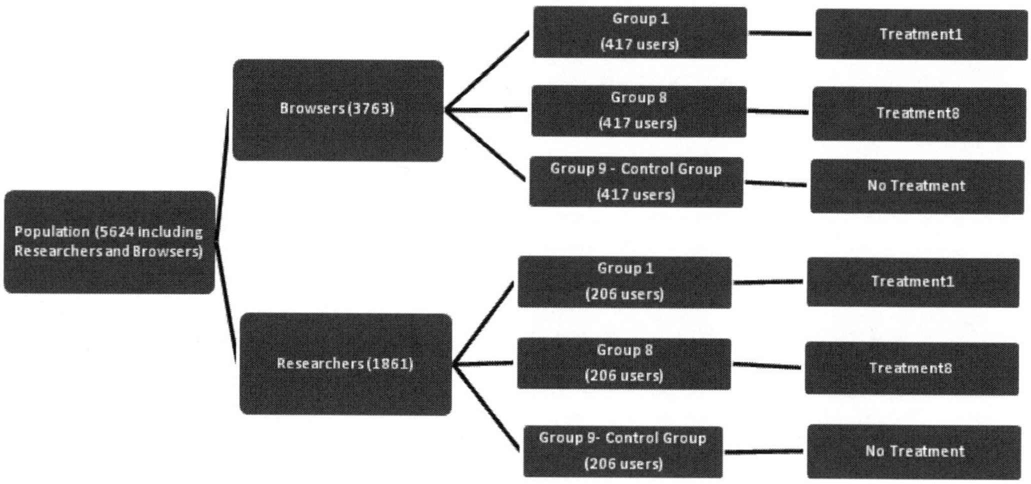

- Impact will be measured based on difference in behavior of test and control groups in pre and post trigger period
- Using fractional factorial design, we would generate 8 treatments, i.e. $2^{(4-1)}$, which basically means there are 4 factors with 2 levels each. Full factorial design would generate $2^4 = 16$ treatments while a fractional factorial would generate $16/2 = 8$ treatments.
- All the 8 types of treatments created would then be targeted to the customers belonging to each of the 8 test groups while one control group would not receive any treatment. The list of treatments (shown below) is generated from the fractional factorial design, which is explained below.

Fractional Factorial Design

The goal is to create designs that allow us to screen a large number of factors but without having a very large experiment. In the context where we are screening a large number of factors, we are operating under the assumption that only a few are very important. This is called sparsity of effects. Let us use the concept of the generator and construct a design for the 2^{4-1} fractional factorial. This gives us a one half fraction of the 2^4 design. Here, we would like to pick a high order interaction. Let us select ABCD as the generator (I = ABCD) and by hand we can construct the design. I = ABCD implies that D = ABC. As, $2^{4-1} = 2^3 = 8$, we will have eight observations in our design. Here is a basic 2^3 design in standard Yates notation defined by the levels of A, B, and C:

trt	*A*	*B*	C	*D = ABC*
(1)	-	-	-	-
a	+	-	-	+
b	-	+	-	+
ab	+	+	-	-
c	-	-	+	+
ac	+	-	+	-
bc	-	+	+	-
abc	+	+	+	+

We can then construct the levels of D by using the relationship where D = ABC. Therefore, in the first row where all the treatments are minus, D = –1 * –1 * –1 = –1. In the second row, D = +1, and so forth. Also, kindly note that, – and + are used as a shorthand for –1 and +1 respectively.

This is a one half fraction of the 2^4 design. A full 2^4 design would have 16 factors. This 2^{4-1} design is a **Resolution IV** design. The resolution of the design is based on the number of the letters in the generator. If the generator is a four letter word, the design is Resolution IV. The number of letters in the generator determines the confounding or aliasing properties in the resulting design.

We can see this best by looking at the expression I = ABCD. We obtain the alias structure by multiplying A × I = A × ABCD = A^2BCD which implies A = BCD. If we look at the aliasing that occurs we would see that A is aliased with BCD, and similarly all of the main effects are aliased with a three-way interaction:

B = ACD

C = ABD

D = ABC

The main effects are aliased with three-way interactions. Using the same process, we see that two-way interactions are aliased with other two-way interactions:

AB = CD

AC = BD

AD = BC

In total, we have seven effects, the number of degrees of freedom in this design. The only effects that are estimable from this design are the four main effects assuming the 3-way interactions are zero and the three 2-way interactions that are confounded with other 2-way interactions. All 16 effects are accounted for with these seven contrasts plus the overall mean.

Applying the concept above to the given set of factors and levels, we would get the following set of 8 treatments which would best reflect the effects of all the 4 factors and 2 levels, i.e. 16 treatments:

S. No.	*Discount ($ off)*	*Shipping*	*Policy Information*	*Site Engagement*
1	$ X Discount	No Free shipping	Information on Return Policy	Information on Categories & Promotions
2	$ X Discount	Free shipping	Information on Delivery & Installation	Information on Categories & Promotions
3	$ Y Discount	Free shipping	Information on Return Policy	Information on Categories & Promotions
4	$ Y Discount	Free shipping	Information on Delivery & Installation	Advertizing successful customer experience
5	$ X Discount	No Free shipping	Information on Delivery & Installation	Advertizing successful customer experience
6	$ Y Discount	No Free shipping	Information on Delivery & Installation	Information on Categories & Promotions
7	$ Y Discount	No Free shipping	Information on Return Policy	Advertizing successful customer experience
8	$ X Discount	Free shipping	Information on Return Policy	Advertizing successful customer experience

POST-TRIGGER ANALYSIS METHODOLOGY AND FRAMEWORK

- The total population from the Browser and Researcher segment would be divided into 9 groups where 8 out of 9 groups will be test groups for each treatment while one group will be kept for control (customers of this group will not be sent any emails)
- The response would be analyzed for these 9 groups after a month's time since the treatments were sent out to the users.
- Using ANOVA we would calculate the responses of main effects as well as first order interactions and determine the significant factors and levels.

The Post trigger analysis dataset should be as below:

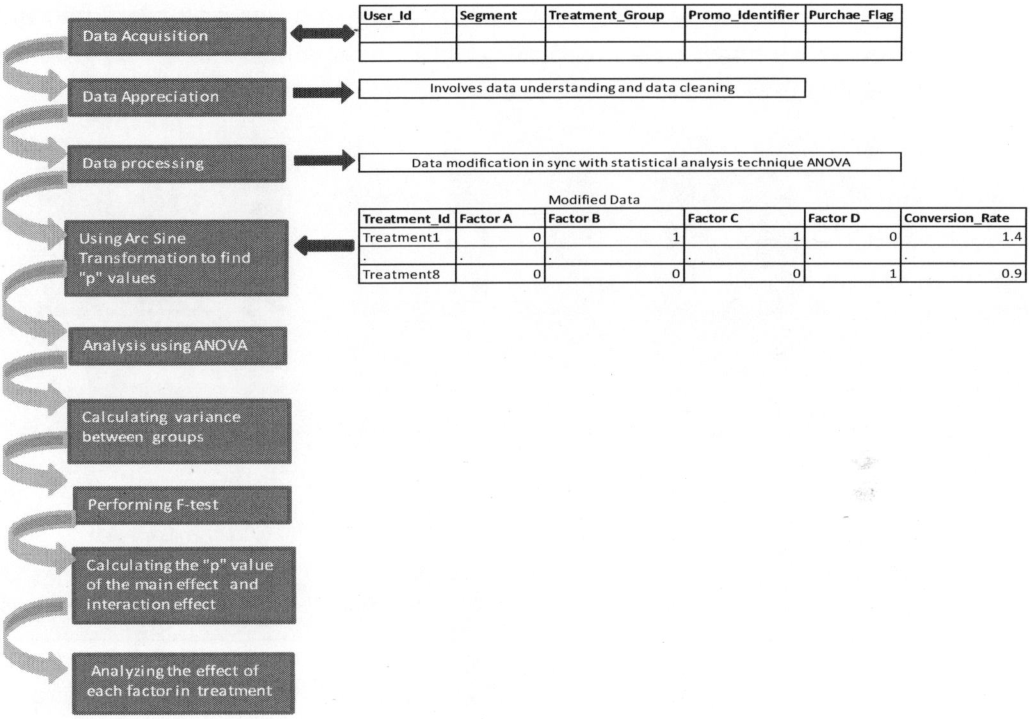

User_Id	Segment	Treatment_Group	Promo_Identifier	Purchae_Flag

Modified Data

Treatment_Id	Factor A	Factor B	Factor C	Factor D	Conversion_Rate
Treatment1	0	1	1	0	1.4
.	.	.	.	.	.
Treatment8	0	0	0	1	0.9

RESULTS AND INSIGHTS

Some of the post-trigger analysis results are captured in the following charts for illustration:

There are 8 test groups and one control group as shown in the chart below for which the following observations were captured:

- The e-mails had an impact on the purchase and login behavior of the test groups
- The average conversion rate for test groups was 1.71%, against 0.47% for control group as shown below

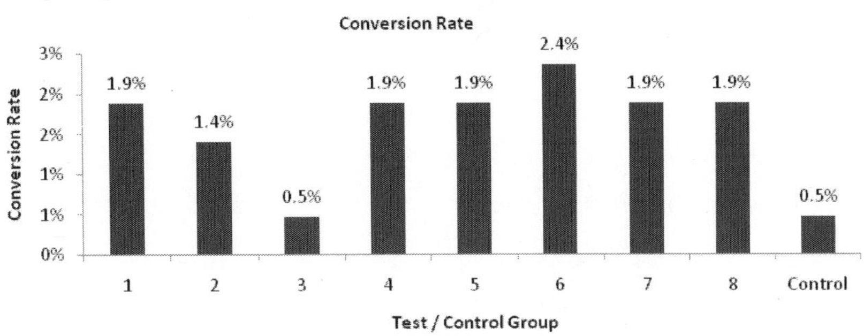

- The average login rate for test groups was 19.69%, against 12.74% for control group as shown below

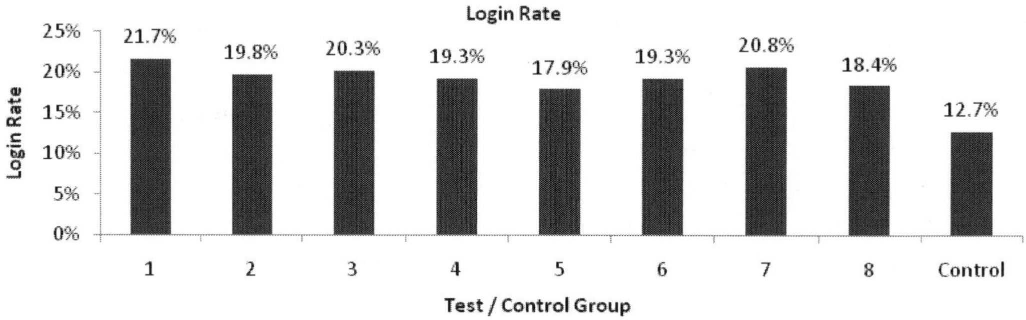

- The average number of orders placed by test groups was also higher as compared to the control group.

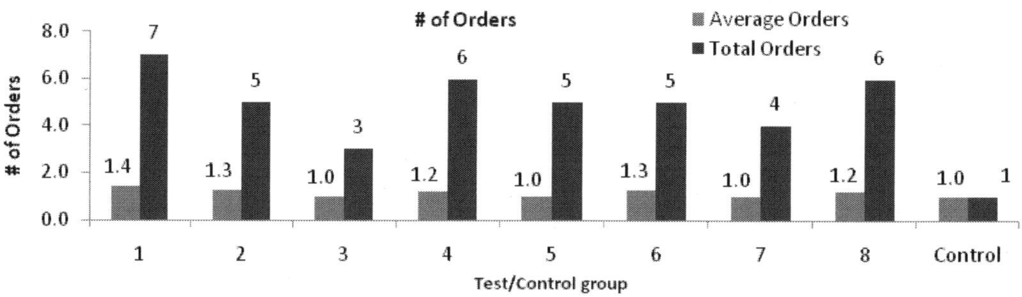

The summary of the metrics captured from post-trigger analysis are as follows:

Treatment	*Conversion Rate*	*Average Orders*	*Average Dollar Value*	*Total Categories Browsed*	*Total Orders*	*Average Time Spent_ Min*	*Active Conversion*
1	1.9 %	1.4	$2,302	231	7	45.39	9.43%
2	1.4 %	1.25	$2,321	241	5	43.77	7.84%
3	0.5 %	1	$567	228	3	42.75	6.25%
4	1.9 %	1.2	$1,411	228	6	39.88	10.20%
5	1.9 %	1	$1,187	219	5	41.91	11.36%
6	2.4 %	1.25	$2,529	181	5	42.66	9.30%
7	1.9 %	1	$1,568	254	4	34.16	7.41%
8	1.9 %	1.2	$1,812	234	6	42.88	10.64%
Control	0.5 %	1	$753	164	1	53.97	3.23%

Legend: Conversion_Rate = total_purchasers / sample_size; Average_Orders = no_of_orders / total_purchasers; Average_dollar_Value = total_price / total_purchasers; Average_Time_Spent = total_time_spent_min / active_users; Average_Categories_Browsed = total_categories / active_users

Observations and Recommendations for Researcher and Browser Segment

1. All the treatments, except #3 have higher conversion rate as compared to the control group, with treatment 6 having the highest conversion rate (2.4%)
2. Total number of orders as well as average number of orders is the highest for users who were given Treatment 1
3. All the treatments have higher average dollar value as compared to the control group with Treatment 6 having the highest dollar value ($2529)
4. The total number of categories browsed by users is higher for all the treatments as compared to control group with Treatment 7 being the highest (254)
5. The average time spent by user is highest in control group as compared to any of the treatment groups.

BIBLIOGRAPHY

Box, G.E., Hunter, J.S., & Hunter,W.G. (2005). *Statistics for Experimenters: Design, Innovation, and Discovery,* 2nd Ed. Hoboken, NJ: John Wiley & Sons.

Eberly College of Science (n.d.). *Stat 503 – Design of Experiments.*

Forgy, E.W. (1965). Cluster analysis of multivariate data: efficiency versus interpretability of classifications . *Biometrics, 21,* 768-769.

Fractional Factorial Designs: A Tutorial (PPT) (2014). dept.stat.lsa.umich.edu. Retrieved from: dept.stat.lsa.umich.edu/~samurphy/nida/seminars/ffd-tutorial.ppt

Hartigan, J.A. (1975). *Clustering algorithms.* New York: John Wiley & Sons.

Montgomery, Douglas (2013). *Design and analysis of experiments* (8th ed.). Hoboken, NJ: John Wiley & Sons.

Mostad, Petter (n.d.). *Chapter 6: Fractional Factorial Designs.* Retrieved from: www.math.chalmers.se/Stat/Grundutb/GU/MSA830/V08/Chapter6.pdf

Wikipedia. *Fractional Factorial Design.* http://en.wikipedia.org/wiki/Fractional_factorial_design

Wikipedia. *K-means Clustering.* http://en.wikipedia.org/wiki/K-means_clustering

PART
ONE-G

CUSTOMER RELATIONSHIP MANAGEMENT

It is an exciting time in the world of CRM wherein immense developments have taken place the way businesses are aligned and focussed at customer.CRM has evolved very fast and beyond its traditional self from being a technology solution to an over-arching business strategy that reached every part of the business. As a result of which businesses have responded very fast and evolved itself from a reactive product-driven eco-system to a real-time proactive customer eco-system (Michael Maoz, Gartner Group Guru). Simultaneously transformation of CRM has also taken place, from being data-centred to process centred along with evolution of business processes from a corporate to a customer eco-system.

Various extant researches have proved that CRM has enabled organisations to drive the return on investment of marketing programs and to increase efficiency of customer service. The increased popularity of CRM definitely makes sense but key essential in the development of these key offerings has been the power of internet. The amount of data available through internet and other sources such as video content, customer feedback can be integrated with the existing CRM solution of the organisation for optimal solutions. The focus is how to analyse the data and convert it into insights, innovation and business value.

So how can companies know what the right things on which to focus attention are? The papers in this section have attempted to present some tools and techniques to show how to analyse the customer related metrics and guide business decision making towards the right decisions. These tools are based on facts, on data and on analysis. Finally, it looks at implementation and achieving great financial benefit by applying these principles.Paper 1 delves into the hands on fundamentals of data-mining and evolving the essentials of highly profitable marketing and service programs using customer data.The paper has shown the value of big data and its business implication with implementation of marketing program as an example. The paper focusses on using customer life cycle value and power of appropriate recommendations of probable next best products for the customer. The research highlights how referrals can be exploited for generating new accounts through referrals as well as enhancing frequency of purchase by existing customers. The technique used in the research includes similarity analysis and propensity calculation using collaborative filtering technique.

Major organisations across industries are joining the movement of data analytic based decision making using big data. It's clear that the primary value from big data does not come from the data in its raw form (no matter how big it is), but from the processing and analysis of it and the insights, products and services that emerge from analysis. Second paper focusses on role of big data analytics in customer relationship management. Research highlights how big data analytics has changed the way in which organisations are maintaining customer relationships for creating competitive advantage. The paper has used in-depth interviewing technique to obtain views of key decision-makers within the organisation to explore opportunities available and highlight major challenges in implementing and integrating big-data analytics with CRM. The findings present attractive opportunities in form of development of new product and service offerings, personalized communication to customers and accurate forecasting and prediction methods by integrating big data analytics with customer relationship management. At the same time, it offers some major challenges that organisations are facing in form of the quality of data available, access to the data and information sharing, organisational commitment to the strategy and availability of required skills and lack of intent to collaborate to name a few. The environment today itself is quite complex as compared to what prevailed in the past. And it is probably going to become more complex before it gets simplified.

CHAPTER FOURTEEN

USE OF BIG DATA ANALYTICS FOR SEGMENTATION, EMAIL MARKETING AND BUILDING LOYALTY

Deepali Nair

INTRODUCTION

When you think of a 'Vacation', which destination comes to your mind? Sandy beaches of Goa, snowcapped Manali or plantations at Coorg? You are not alone. Everyone would want to holiday in exactly these locations. The popularity of these locations poses a serious problem to resorts and other hospitality brands. How do you satisfy the demand of thousands with only 100 rooms?

On the other hand, the beauty of certain locations like Naukuchiatal, Kanatal, Poovar would go unknown if everyone went to only the 'popular' locations. And let us not forget that the cost of running these empty resorts could possibly bankrupt the company.

This situation does not bode well with most hospitality brands. But Club Mahindra has found a unique way to solve it.

THE 'VACATION OWNERSHIP' PRODUCT

Mahindra Holidays & Resorts is India's leading vacation ownership company with a network of 40 resorts. It offers 25 year holiday memberships and has over 1,71,000 members. There are 4 tiers of membership, and the time of the year when a member can holiday depends on the tier a member holds.

Each member is credited with 7 nights of holidays in a year, for utilization at any of the resorts in accordance with the product they own. The resorts are spread across the country and offer a diverse mix like beaches, hill stations etc.

'The Big Fat Problem'

Members have their own preferences when it comes to where and when to holiday. This leads to a typical slack and peak demand situation. During peak seasons, most of the resorts operate at full capacity and on the other hand during slack season many resorts have unutilized inventory. Both situations are not ideal for Club Mahindra; resorts operating at low level of occupancy means huge unutilized inventory across resorts, not forgetting the operating costs. This results in huge revenue opportunity loss for Club Mahindra. On an average at a resort a member would spend 4 times more than the amount it costs to carry an empty room. On the other hand, a resort operating at its peak capacity means any more holiday requests from more members will be rejected.

Imagine you had planned the perfect holiday and at the time of booking, the resort was completely booked. As a member, rejection leads to dissatisfaction. This puts at stake the Customer Life Cycle Value of a Club Mahindra member which can be pegged at approximately Rs. 5 Lakhs per member per year.

Another reason why Club Mahindra has to ensure that members holiday is **Referral**. Referral is an important source for Club Mahindra for new member acquisition. Between one third and one fourth of the current member base has been acquired through referral. And most of the referrals come from holidaying members. Hence, it is essential to ensure every member gets a chance to experience Club Mahindra resorts.

Considering this context, the business challenge was to come up with a solution that met these strategic objectives.

- Ensure each member holidays and thereby maximize member satisfaction by providing the 'Right' recommendation to each member based on his preference
- Maximize Resort Occupancy

'Thinking through to the Solution'

The solution was required to address two key business problems, A) Recommend the next best resort to members to ensure they holiday and B) improve the occupancy at various low occupancy resorts.

The solution framework had 3 important components with each one flowing into the next one. The 3 components were as follows:

- Identification
- Analysis
- Implementation

Identification

The first step was to identify the resorts which would need marketing push to meet the desired level of occupancy. The last 3 years' monthly occupancy was studied to estimate the current year's monthly occupancy. This gave us a list of resorts which would have low occupancy problem.

Once low occupancy resorts were identified, the next step was to determine room night targets across these problem resorts. In order to determine the room night targets the following key variables were used:

- **Average Occupancy for the Last 3 Years**
- **Target Occupancy this Year** – This was calculated based on a rule. The average occupancy for 3 years was analyzed. The target was set such that occupancy at all resorts should be a minimum amount (say x). If average occupancy was more than x, then the target was set 10% higher than the last 3 years' average occupancy. (We determined 10% as historically our campaign contribution to overall occupancy was 5%. We decided to increase it to 10%)
- **Total Inventory Allocated this Year** – This figure indicates total available inventory at the resort for members
- **Campaign Contribution Last Year** – Room night contribution through campaigns last year

Illustration (Figures are indicative)

Average occupancy for last 3 years	35%	
Target Occupancy this year	45%	
Total inventory allocated this year	2315	
Incremental Room Nights	232	Calculated as (45% - 635%) * Total Inventory
Campaign contribution last year	444	
Campaign Target	676	Campaign Target = Incremental room nights + campaign contribution last year

Analysis

The Analysis component had the following steps:

- Similarity analysis
- Propensity Calculation
- Superimposing business rules

Similarity Analysis

The first step was to identify similar resorts. This was based on the rationale that members visiting similar resorts will have similar holiday preferences. Therefore, the recommendations made to a member were based on the holiday trend of members visiting similar resorts.

In order to find the similarity between two resorts we used **cosine similarity function.** Cosine similarity is extensively used for similarity searches.

Past members' visits were used to calculate the cosine similarity. We looked at all the historical reservations of members across all resorts to arrive at the number of times they have visited a particular resort, which was the input to find out similarity.

Propensity Calculation

On the basis of the output of similarity analysis next step was to find out the propensity of members to travel to each resort. In order to calculate the propensity we used **Collaborative Filtering.**

Collaborative Filtering is technique used to arrive at the product the customer is likely to buy and thereby driving higher relevance in product offering. **Collaborative Filtering** has two methods to arrive at a recommendation, Item-based collaborative technique and User-based collaborative technique. An item-based technique computes similarity between two items to arrive at the recommendation whereas user-based technique computes similarity between two users to arrive at the recommendation. This technique is predominantly used on e-commerce websites to suggest the most suitable product for each user.

In our case we used item-based collaborative filtering to recommend resorts that a member is likely to travel to in his/her next visit.

Collaborative Filtering is a computationally intensive technique. Since the computation was required to be done for every combination of Resort and Member, the processing for ~ 25,000 members and 40 resorts was over **38 Million computations.**These members were selected on their past holidaying behavior and the members who holiday regularly were selected.

Executing computations of this volume in absence of big data platform would have been practically impossible as platforms like SQL server would perform these 38 million computations one after another which would take an inordinately long time to execute.

We used Hadoop which facilitated Map Reduce technique allowing simultaneous processing. This resulted in completion of the activity in less than an hour.

MAP reduce is at the heart of big data platform Hadoop. This is a programming model used for processing large data sets. Map reduce facilitates simultaneous processing of non-related computation which reduces the time taken for processing. In our case say, for example, calculating similarity between Coorg and Goa Varca is independent of that of calculating similarity between Virajpet and Ooty and therefore these computations can happen simultaneously.

Implementation

'Putting it across'

Email communication is the most effective proven medium of reaching out to Club Mahindra members for occupancy campaigns. Therefore, highly customized emails were sent out to micro customer segments on the basis of the propensity score. Each member received a mail with most recommended resorts for him/her as a customized image. The time and day of sending the emails was determined on the basis of our historical analysis of ideal day and time of sending the communication in order to maximize the open rates.

'The Final Say'

As a result of the identified base and customized communication alone, 30% of the overall room nights achieved during the first round were through 15% of the overall member universe.

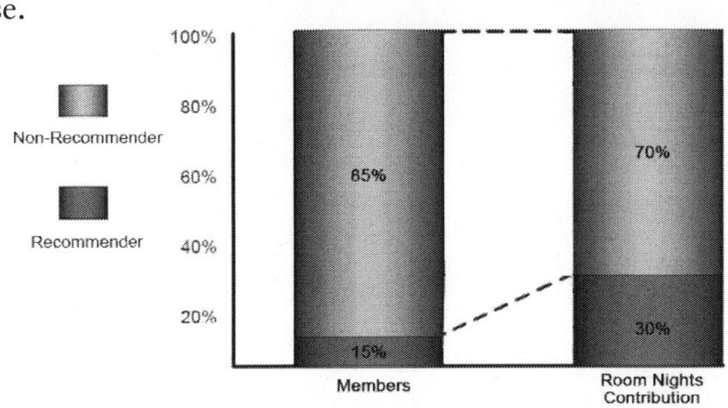

Fig. 1

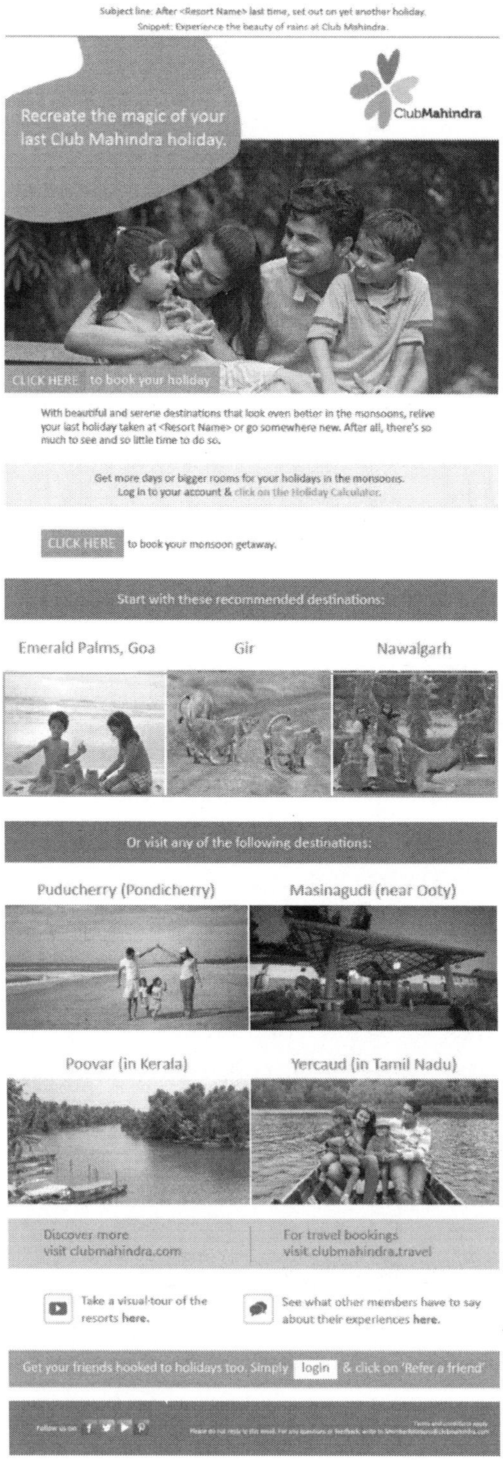

Recommended destinations customized for each member

Double the response rate was achieved from the recommender base as compared to the remaining 85% of the member universe. Targeted room nights were achieved with fewer rounds of communication.

As compared to 2013, this year the same set of members booked 52% more room nights. In 2013, we sent out three rounds of communication to the same set of members to achieve the same number of room nights as compared to a single round of communication this year.

Apart from the meeting the occupancy targets with fewer communications we were also able contribute to resort revenue through these members. Members spent 18% more than the other members who travelled during the same period at these resorts.

CHAPTER FIFTEEN

CUSTOMER RELATION MANAGEMENT IN THE ERA OF BIG DATA ANALYTICS

Surabhi Verma and Som Sekhar Bhattacharyya

ABSTRACT

Big Data Analytics (BDA) refers to the (almost) real time analytics of a vast volume of data that has been generated and captured in a variety of formats and from a number of distinct sources. BDA has changed the way organizations are doing business, discovering insights and interacting with customers. To obtain value from BDA, firms need a cohesive set of solutions for collecting, processing and analyzing data. The output from the analyzed data could be used for discovering new insights to make repeatable decisions and scale the associated information systems (IS). The corporate organization must manage its businesses in a systematic way to bring the customer's perspective from outside in decision making. BDA has the potential to change the way in which organizations are managing customer relationships. This could be achieved by offering new business tools which could combine the internal data with external data like social media data, which could be used in identifying sales opportunities and analyzing customers' responses to the product. Integrating BDA in business processes for customer relationship management (CRM) could benefit organizations and create competitive advantages. It could also enable organizations to better predict customers' buying patterns, improve customer products and services delivery. It would benefit ROI. The analysis of large volumes of data in real or almost real time has potential for improving front office and back office operations for many organizations in marketing. Despite all huge possibilities available with integrating BDA with CRM, there are several obstacles in implementation in organizations. This paper will help in identifying the opportunities that could be provided by BDA in CRM. It will also fill the gap of understanding the actual obstacles and challenges organizations are facing while implementing BDA with CRM. Following the literature review, an exploratory study of 10 experts from a variety of industries was undertaken using in-depth semi-structured interviews with respondents. The results provided a better understanding of opportunities like 360° view of customers, attribution modelling, personalized offerings, benchmarking, new products and services development and forecasting and predictions created by BDA when integrated with CRM. The findings also suggested that data quality, data access and information sharing, organizational commitment, availability of skills, organizational culture and lack of collaboration were major challenges and obstacles in integrating BDA with CRM in organizations.

Keywords: Big Data (BD), Big Data Analytics (BDA), Customer Relationship Management (CRM).

INTRODUCTION

The proliferation of digital devices, and the applications and extensive usage of internet by social networks have been generating huge amounts of new data every second (The Economist, 27th Feb, 2010). Sources for this data could be mobile, sensors and GPS devices, social networking sites, company websites, transactional data sources and more (Lavelle et al., 2011). Moreover, user activities could also generate data about their needs, preferences, as well the quality of their experiences (Ericsson, 2013). Even when devices are in offline mode, the associated networks are generating data with their location and other types of data which could be used for different purposes. All this unstructured information such as social media, blogs, email, video, call center conversations and more represents about 80 percent of data generated today (Savvas, 2011), while 20 percent of the total data is structured information generated by traditional legacy systems stored in relational databases.

The explosion of new digital and mobile devices, applications (internet-based or legacy) and cloud computing have led to the era of big data. According to Katal et al. (2013) this new change brings new challenges to organizations such as:

- What to do with this vast amount of data?
- How to exploit it and extract insights to improve business?

Nowadays the decision-making process in organizations has been based on the ability to analyze huge amounts of data and combine this data from various sources to obtain a more holistic and comprehensive view of business (Kiron et al., 2013). This new paradigm arose to solve the problem of analyzing data from different sources, exploiting it and making decisions on real time to fulfill the customer needs and expectations. Big data has changed the way firms and people do business, discover insights and interact with customers. This paper addresses the opportunities and challenges of CRM in the era of big data.

LITERATURE REVIEW

Big Data Analytics (BDA)

BDA has its roots in a fundamental shift in the data environment, that is, it reflected the increased digitization of business and society, the decreased cost of data storage and the increased availability of third party data (Manyika et al., 2011). Digital data is now everywhere, in every use of digital technology, in every economic sector and organization. Organizations could create value from analytics by transforming huge volumes of complex and high-velocity data into business insights to improve existing processes and drive better managerial decision making (Lavelle et al., 2011). To achieve this purpose, firms should know what data to use, how to process and correlate data and how to interpret and apply the resulting insights to different business processes (Hopkins et al., 2010). Since this complex data is difficult to process with traditional database management tools, a need was felt for a cohesive set of solutions to capture, process, analyze data and discover new insights to make repeatable decisions and scale the associated IS (Ferguson, 2013). So, BDA refers to the vast amount of data that has been generated and captured in a variety of formats and from a number of disparate sources and analyzed in (almost) real time to extract business insights (Kwon et al., 2014).

In 2012, Gartner described big data as high volume, high velocity and/or high variety information assets which required cost effective, innovative forms of information processing for enhanced insight, decision making, and process optimization. The main characteristics of big data were defined "the V's of big data" (Buhl et al., 2013):

1. **Volume:** It is related with the significant increase amount of data and its granular characteristics (Ularu et al., 2012). Organizations have been overflowing with the ever-growing data of different types generated from social media, digital devices and transactions.
2. **Velocity:** This characteristic meant that big data arrives more rapidly, often in real-time, and needs to be used more rapidly. Real-time data only adds

value if turned into real-time insights, for example fraud detection, customer churn and more (Chen and Zhan, 2014).

3. **Variety:** It consists of all the data – structured, semi-structured and unstructured – which have been difficult to be handled by the existing traditional analytic systems (Katal et al., 2013). BDA relied on new types of data, from social network sites, company websites, call centers conversations and more.
4. **Veracity:** It refers to the degree of trustworthiness of the used information in order to take decisions (Buhl et al., 2013). The uncertainty about the consistency and completeness of data and other ambiguities grows as the variety and number of sources grows.

BDA offers many business opportunities to organizations including the optimization of operations, better decision making tools, the management and mitigation of financial and other risks, and the development of new business models which led to increase in productivity and innovation. The data-driven firms collect data for new analytical insights about their customers. BDA gives insights into the problem areas of a business such as change in customer behavioral trends, competition and more (McAfee and Brynjolfsson, 2012). It also helps to discover new facts about a business operation (new customer segments) and helps firms to understand the highly volatile nature of the market and gives the power to change business tactics for survival as well for growth (Kabir and Carayannis, 2013). A survey undertaken by MIT Sloan Management Review and IBM concluded that top-performing companies used analytics five times more than lower performers (Lavelle et al, 2011). In the same survey half of the respondents felt that improvement of information and analytics was a top priority in their organizations and more than one in five were under intense or significant pressure to adopt advanced information and analytics approaches. Besides the increased opportunities available to businesses, BDA also created more challenges to organizations.

Customer Relationship Management (CRM)

According to Buttle (2009), CRM has been considered as one of the fastest growing management approaches adopted by many firms. From the marketing perspective, customers have always been the cornerstone for business activities. Therefore to gain comparative advantage, business organizations need to build relationships with their customers more effectively by integrating customers' knowledge (Parvatiyar & Sheth, 2002). An enriched relationship with customers could ultimately lead to greater customer satisfaction, retention and profitability (Ngai et al., 2009). In addition, the rapid growth of the internet, mobile devices and their associated technologies have increased the opportunities of marketing and also transformed the way relationships between organizations and customers have been managed (Bauer, 2002).

CRM has been a technology-based solution that extended transactions, databases and automation tools which linked marketing and transactions to a focused targeted effort. CRM applications connect front office operations such as transactions, customer service and marketing with back office operations such as operations, logistics and financial functions with the firm's customers touch points (Fickel, 1999). CRM has been defined as a business strategy that has a goal to develop value-creating relationships with customers based on knowledge by using information technology (IT) as an enabler (Garrido & Padilla, 2011). It has emerged as an effective and extremely important strategy to manage interactions with customers by combining the latest technology with existing business processes (Chen and Popovich, 2003). CRM has been more than the automation of supply-chain, traditional transactions, and back-office or service functions using technology (Xu et al., 2002). According to Goldenberg (2000), CRM has also been a cross functional, customer driven, and technology integrated business process management strategy which increases relationships with customers and covers the whole organization. The benefits offered by CRM included (Jutla, et al., 2001):

- Value creation for the customer.
- Customization of products and services
- Lower prices and higher quality products and services
- Increased customer retention and loyalty
- Higher customer profitability

As stated earlier, CRM has included all activities organizations carried out to develop as well as retain customers through increased loyalty and satisfaction (Zineldin, 2006). It dynamically integrates transactions, customer care service and marketing in order to create and add value for organizations and their customers (Chen and Popovich, 2003). CRM has been expanded to include an integrated perspective on customer service, sales, marketing, logistics, channel management and technology to ensure customer satisfaction (Nguyen & Mutum, 2012). The right CRM deals with customers using more than one media channel and yet has customers' up-to-date views with no gaps in information.

METHODOLOGY

The main research objective of this paper was to study the opportunities and challenges of BDA in CRM. An exploratory research method has been used to identify the opportunities and challenges of BDA in CRM. A thorough literature review of research studies has been conducted for investigating factors. After the literature review qualitative interviews were conducted with the experts of BDA in firms across sectors (see Table 1). These experts of BDA have minimum 10 years of analytics experience. A one-to-one personally administered interview with open ended semi-structured questions was conducted with each respondent. Telephonic interview was also used as a data collection instrument. The questions included the firm's background, opportunities and challenges of BDA in CRM. Interviews were recorded with the participants' permission and the recorded data was transcribed into text after the interview session. The data obtained from interviews was condensed by summarizing and simplifying it (Saunders et al., 2007). Further information was derived from the condensed data which finally lead to the conclusion of this research (Miles and Huberman, 1994).

Table 1: Summary of Respondents

Serial No.	*Industries*	*Expertise*
C1	IT	BDA Strategist
C2	IT	BDA consultant
C3	Online payment gateway	Senior BDA Analyst
C4	Telecommunication	Practice head of BDA
C5	Telecommunication	Senior BDA Analyst
C6	Banking	Vice-president
C7	Banking	Vice-president
C8	Banking	Senior manager
C9	Retail	Senior manager
C10	Retail	Senior BDA analyst

RESULTS, FINDINGS AND DISCUSSION

Opportunities with Big Data Analytics in CRM

This section identifies and discusses some of the opportunities the business managers dealing with BDA technologies in CRM face for gaining competitive advantages for their businesses (see Table 2).

Thematic Findings

1. **360° view of customer profile:** BDA drives the organization's ability to understand

customers better by providing a high resolution view of customers' preferences, values, activities and behaviors. Through the accumulation of data, firms could deliver relevance to markets (Chen et al., 2012). The view of customers to firms becomes clearer as more data are infused into the customer profile (Davenport, 2006). BDA drives value by providing enriched data sets that include social behavior, call center activities, in-store purchase, and loyalty program buying behaviors.

Table 2: Opportunities Created when BDA is Integrated with CRM

Opportunities	*Respondents*
360° view of customers profile	C6-C10
Attribution Modelling	C1,C2, C9,C10
Personalized offerings	C1,C2, C4-C10
Benchmarking	C1-C10
New products and services development	C1, C2, C6-C10
Forecasting and predictions	C3-C10

2. **Attribution modelling:** Whether it is a time decay, linear or last interaction model, BDA always drives the attribution model. Each touch point along the customer's path provided value (Malthouse et al., 2013). The analysis of customers' touch points, including internet, email, social media and call center, allow CRM and BDA to segment customers according to actions. Customer trends could be mined from BDA and used to predict needs, directing product development and promotional efforts. Also, organizations could increase marketing efficiency by connecting sales to engagement points.
3. **Personalized offerings:** Leveraging BDA with personalized messaging resonates because of its focused appeal. BDA provides a high-resolution view of customers, which could be used by the organization to create the most personalized, relevant engagements possible. The high-resolution view to customers enable firms to craft personalized campaigns (Chen et al., 2012).
4. **Benchmarking:** BDA has the ability to implement comprehensive benchmarking over time. This powerful ability of BDA enables the organization to define vital indicators such as customer retention, sentiment, and cost/revenue per call (Malthouse et al., 2013). Once the areas which need improvement are emphasized, organizations have the tools necessary to rise above industry standards.
5. **New products and services development:** BDA helps organizations to deliver personalized products and services that deliver the exact customers' needs across multiple segments in any industry (Manyika et al., 2011). Consumer

preferences, latent opportunities and geographic disparity are all embedded with BDA. Customer sentiment can be easily captured through web, search, email and social engagements. Marketers could leverage BDA for product development by analyzing these customers' data in real time.

6. Forecasting and predictions: BDA increases the predictive capabilities of the organization across business functions (Kwon et al., 2014). The forecasting by organizations becomes clearer because of the ability of BDA to segment data sets and analyze end user behavior. Accumulation of data provides real-time updates of consumers and enabled sharper decision making. For example, organizations using agile management techniques could adapt to market changes on real time basis.

Challenges with Big Data Analytics in CRM

While the promise of BDA with CRM, both for cost reduction and revenue increase has been significant, this could not be achieved unless its usage were successful in organizations. CRM is a combination of people, processes and technologies that seeks to understand firms' customers. Managing a successful integration of BDA with CRM requires an integrated and balanced approach of technology, people and process. Different industries could harness technology, people, and processes to manage resilient customer relationships. Some of the key challenges encountered in successful implementation of BDA with CRM were identified and summarized below (see Table 3).

Table 3: Challenges for Integrating BDA with CRM

	Factors	*Respondents*
Technology	Data quality	C3, C6, C7
	Data access and information sharing	C3, C6, C7
People	Organizational commitment	C1-C10
	Availability of skills	C1-C10
Process	Organizational culture	C3-C7
	Lack of collaboration	C4, C5, C9, C10

Technology

BDA could enable CRM to take full advantages of technology innovations with their ability to collect and analyze data to interpret customer behavior, customer patterns and develop predictive models in real time. BDA with CRM could also help to improve customized communications and deliver products and services to individual customers. However, many organizations tend to overspend on tools and technology, paying insufficient attention to data quality and data access and data sharing in organizations.

1. **Data quality:** Usage of huge amounts of data for decision-making or for predictive analysis in business could definitely lead to better results (Chen and Zhang, 2014). But collecting and storing such huge amounts of data could cost heavily to organizations (Katal et al., 2013). Therefore, for better results and conclusions BDA should focus more on storing quality of data rather than storing very large irrelevant data. This further leads to various other questions like: how much data would be enough for decision-making, whether the stored data of organizations was accurate for drawing conclusions, which data would be relevant, does all data needed to be stored and analyzed.
2. **Data access and information sharing:** For getting accurate decisions in time, availability of accurate, complete data in timely manner becomes the necessity of organizations (Katal et al., 2013). This makes the data management and governance process more complex by adding the necessity to make data open and available to different organizations. Better decision-making and productivity improvements need data availability in standardized manner with standard Application Programming Interface (APIs), metadata and formats. Sharing of data between organizations about clients and operations threatens the culture of secrecy and competitiveness. Therefore, data sharing between organizations would be difficult because of the need to get an edge in business.

People

CRM involves a wide variety of people – marketing, frontline sales, business analysts, service providers, IT professionals and managers (Nguyen and Mutum, 2012). These people must collaborate to ensure that BDA integrated with CRM strategies has been well defined, delivered and deployed. This diversity in people creates accountability issues and complicates the challenges of persuading employees to embrace BDA with CRM. To overcome these challenges organizations should have organizational commitment and people who technically and strategically understand BDA with CRM.

1. **Organizational commitment:** It has been identified as a key element for the success of an innovation (Alshamaila, 2012; Hwang et al., 2002). Organizational commitment encompasses aspects like senior management's support, participation, involvement and support of stakeholders for innovation (Ramamurthy et al., 2008). Organizations could succeed in the era of BDA if

their business leaders spot the opportunities, understand the developing market, articulate a compelling vision, and persuade employees to embrace it and work hard to realize it.

2. **Availability of skills:** It has been identified as a leading barrier to BDA (Wielki, 2013; Hopkins et al., 2013). Most of organizations have skills available to exploit data warehouse and business intelligence (Katal et al., 2013). The skill set required for using BDA is not the same as that for data warehouse and business intelligence. It includes skills to architecture a BDA system and make big data usable for end users. The skills required for BDA are not limited to technical ones only but they also need to extend to research, analytical and interpretive ones.

Process

CRM has changed the business process from product focused to customer centric in the organization. CRM strategy was to identify profitable customers and make them more profitable (Hawkes, 2000). It has been a continuous effort that required redesigning of core business processes started from the customer perspective and customer feedback involvement (Chen and Popovich, 2003). BDA integration with CRM could help in redesigning front office functions and could also help in improving the flow of information between front and back office operations. But organizational culture and lack of collaboration have been identified in this study as the barrier in this process change.

1. **Organizational culture:** Culture is an intangible set of convictions, conducts and postulations which steer an individual's day to day activities (Alatawi et al., 2012). Organizational culture is the consequence of the shared value and experience which cumulated individual experiences into the organizational consciousness (Ryan et al., 2000). Instead of taking decisions based on the manager's hunches and instinct, organizations should be more inclined toward data-driven decision making. Firms need to develop an analytical mindset that supports the usage of data and analytics across a wide range of corporate activities.
2. **Lack of collaboration:** The silos of information in organizations whether built from data store or management protectionism act as a major impediment to the effective usage of BDA (Kiron et al., 2013). This enterprise-wide change needs a substantial information infrastructure investment as well as a dramatic culture shift. Increased agility of BDA also increases the integrated possibilities for users to collaborate. A lack of collaboration could cause transparency issues and avoid reuse of reports.

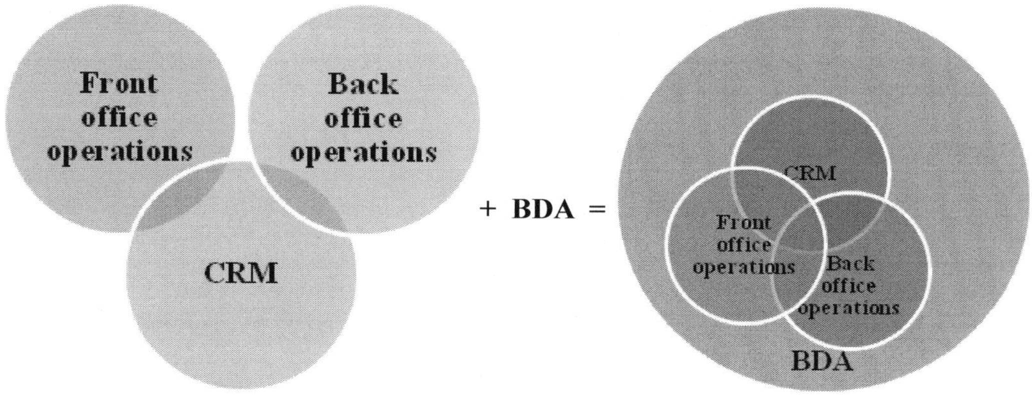

Fig. 1: Integration of CRM with BDA

CONCLUSION

Organizations in every industry are trying to make sense of massive data. They are also trying to develop analytic platforms that have the capability to synthesize traditional structured data with semi-structured and unstructured data. When properly captured and analyzed, BDA could provide unique insights into customers' behavior and enable more targeted business decisions. To obtain value from BDA, organizations need a cohesive set of solutions to capture, process, and analyze data, to discover new insights for repeatable decisions and scale the associated information systems.

BDA had changed the way organizations do businesses, discover insights and interact with one another. Organizations that successfully adapted their data architecture and processes to address the attributes of BDA – volume, variety, velocity and veracity – improved operational efficiency, increased revenues and empowered new business models. Organizations struggled to make sense and create opportunities from structured, unstructured, and semi-structured data, yet BDA also represented an expanding set of powerful new opportunities.

BDA when integrated with CRM in organizations has the potential to create value in the front office including attribution modelling, personalized offerings, and new products and services development, as well as in the back office, like 360^0 view of customer information, benchmarking, and forecasting and predictions. BDA with CRM helps in integrating front office functions with back office functions in organizations (see Figure 1). It will also enable organizations for "one-to-one marketing" with customers. Despite all the opportunities provided by BDA, it is facing many challenges for integration with CRM in organizations. The success of BDA has been affected by technology, people and process in organizations. The technological challenges in organization are data quality and data access and information sharing, while the organizational commitment and availability of skills are challenges of people in organizations. The challenges created by the process in organizations were organizational culture and lack of collaboration. By controlling these challenges organizations could extract maximum value from BDA, by integrating it with CRM.

IMPLICATIONS

This research paper is the first known empirical paper to study the integration of BDA with CRM. In organizations deploying BDA with CRM, to improve front office operations or back office operations or both, BDA would give managers a common platform to manage their customers on real time basis. This paper will also give a clear view to managers about the context in which BDA could be used for relationship marketing. It also suggests the dimensions (technology, people and process) which need to be considered before implementing BDA with CRM.

REFERENCES

Alatawi, F.M.H., Dwivedi Y.K., Williams M.D., & Rana N.P. (2012). *Conceptual Model for Examining Knowledge Management System (KMS) Adoption in Public Sector Organizations in Saudi Arabia. tGov Workshop '12 (tGOV12)*, Brunel University, West London, UB8 3PH.

Alshamaila, Y., & Papagiannidis, S. (2012). Cloud computing adoption by SMEs in the north east of England. *Journal of Enterprise Information Management, 26*(3), 250-275.

Buhl, H.U., Röglinger, M., Moser, F., & Heidemann, J. (2013). Big Data – A Fashionable Topic with(out) Sustainable Relevance for Research and Practice?. *Business & Information Systems Engineering, 5*(2), 65–69.

Buttle, F. (2009). *Customer relationship management: concepts and technologies.* 2nd ed., Oxford: Butterworth-Heinemann.

Chen, H., Chiang, R.H.L., & Storey, V.C. (2012). Business Intelligence and Analytics: From Big Data to big impact, *MIS Quarterly*, 36(4), 1165-1188.

Chen, I. J., & Popovich, K. (2003). Understanding customer relationship management (CRM): People processes and technology. *Business Process Management Journal, 9* (5), 672 – 688.

Davenport, T.H. (2006). Competing on Analytics. *Harvard Business School January 2006,* 84(1), 98-107. Retrieved from http://www.insightdata.com.au/mirror/hbr/CompetingOnAnalyticsHBR2006.pdf.

Ericsson, A. B. (2013). *Big Data Analytics.* (Online document). Available: http://www.ericsson.com/res/docs/whitepapers/wp-bigdata.pdf.

Ferguson, R.B. (June 2013). How eBay Uses Data and Analytics to get Closer to its (Massive) Customer Base. *MIT Sloan Management Review.*

Garrido, M.A., & Melendez, P. (2011). Analyzing the impact of knowledge management on CRM success: The mediating effects of organizational factors. *Journal of Information Management, 31*, 437-444.

Goldenberg, B. (2000). What is CRM? What is an e-customer? Why you need them now. *Proceedings of DCI Customer Relationship Management Conference, Boston, MA*, pp. 27-29.

Hawkes, V. A. (2000). The heart of the matter: The challenge of customer lifetime value. *CRM Forum Resources*, pp. 1–10.

Hopkins, M.S., LaValle, Balboni F., Kruschwitz, N., & Shockley, R. (Fall 2010). 10 Insights: A First Look at the New Intelligent Enterprise Survey on Winning With Data. *MIT Sloan Management Review.*

Hwang H., Ku, C., Yen, D., and Cheng, C. (2004). Critical Factors Influencing the Adoption of Data Warehouse Technology: A study of the Banking Industry in Taiwan. *Decision Support Systems, 37*, 1-21.

Jutla, D., Craig, J., & Bodorik, P. (2001). Enabling and measuring electronic customer relationship management readiness., *Proceedings of the 34th annual Hawaii international conference on system sciences organizational systems and technologies track*, pp. 1–10.

Kabir, N., & Carayannis, E. (2013). Big Data, Tacit Knowledge and Organizational Competitiveness. *Journal of Intelligence Studies in Business, 3*(3).

Katal, A., Wazid, M., & Goudar, R.H. (2013). Big data: Issues, challenges, tools and Good practices. *Sixth International Conference on Contemporary Computing (IC3)*, pp. 404-409.

Kiron, D., Ferguson, R.B., & Prentice, P.K. (Spring 2013). From Value to Vision: Reimaging the Possible with Data Analytics. *MIT Sloan Management Review.*

Kwon, O., Lee, N., & Shin, B. (2014). Data quality management, data usage experience and acquisition intention of big data analytics. *International Journal of Information Management, 34*, 387-394.

LaValle, S., Lesser, E., Rebecca, S., Hopkins, M.S., & Kruschwitz, N. (2011). Big Data, Analytics and the Path from Insights to Value. *MIT Sloan Management Review*, 21-31.

Malthouse, E. C., Michael, H., Bernd, S., Egbert, W., & Michael, Z. (2013). Managing Customer Relationships in the Social Media Era: Introducing the Social CRM House. *Journal of Interactive Marketing, 27*(4).

Manyika, J., Chui, M., Brown, B., Bughin, J., Dobbs, R., Roxburgh, C., & Byers, A. H. (2011). Big data: The next frontier for innovation, competition, and productivity. Retrieved from: https://www.mckinsey.com/.../Technology%20and%20Innovation/Big%...

McAfee, A., & Brynjolfsson, E. (2012). Big data: the management revolution. *Harvard Business Review, 90*(10), 60-66.

Miles, M.B., & Huberman, A.M. (1994). *Qualitative Data Analysis*. London: Sage.

Ngai, E. W. T, Xiu L., & Chau, D. C. K. (2009). Application of data mining techniques in customer relationship management: A literature review and classification. *Expert Systems with Applications*, 36(2), 2592–2602.

Nguyen, B. & Mutum, D. (2012). A Review of Customer Relationship Management:

Successes, Advance, Pitfalls and Futures. *Journal of Business process Management, 18*(3), 2-4.

Parvatiyar, Atul, and Sheth, Jagdish. (2002). Customer Relationship Management: Emerging Practice, Process, and Discipline. *Journal of Economic and Social Research, 3*(2), 1-34.

Pettey, C., & Goasduff, L. (2011). Gartner Says Solving "Big Data" Challenge Involves more than just Managing Volumes of Data", *Gartner*. Retrieved March 31, 2014, from http://www.gartner.com/newsroom/id/1731916.

Ryan, S.D., Abitia, G.R., & Windsor, J.C. (2000). Factors Affecting the Adoption of Knowledge Management Technologies: An International Perspective. *Americas Conference on Information Systems:* pp. 1291-1294.

Saunders, M., Lewis, P. & Thornhill, A. (2007). *Research Methods for Business Students.* Essex: Financial Times/Prentice Hall.

Savvas, A. (2011, October 25). *IBM: Businesses unable to analyse 90 percent of their data. Computerworld UK*. Retrieved March 31, 2014, from http://www.computerworlduk.com/ news /it-business/3313304/ibm-businesses-unableto-analyse-90-percent-of-their-data/.

The Economist. (Feb 2010). *Data, data everywhere.* Retrieved on 5 May 2014 from: http://www.economist.com/node/15557443

Ularu, E.G., Puican, F.C., Apostu, A., & Velicanu, M. (2012). Perspective on Big Data and Big Data Analytics. *Database Systems Journal, III*(4).

Xu, Y., Yen, D., Lin, B., & Chou, D. (2002). Adopting customer relationship management technology. *Industrial Management and Data Systems, 102*(8).

Zineldin, M. (2006). The royalty of loyalty: CRM, quality, and retention. *Journal of Consumer Marketing*, 23(7), 430–437.

PART TWO

METHODS

PART
TWO-A

MODELING TECHNIQUES

The paper, 'Modeling the Spread of Product Related Rumors in the Marketplace – An Agent Based Simulation' discusses the importance of marketers understanding rumors and factors causing their spread as rumors can influence product and brand image. The paper identifies the motivating factors behind the spread of product-related rumors and the relationship between each factor and the consumer's intention to share the rumor.. It then simulates the aggregate market level rumor spreading behavior using a powerful simulation technique, Agent Based Simulation in NetLogo 5.1, thus helping to visualize the rumor propagation in the marketplace.

Measuring the ROI in digital marketing spends is a challenge that plagues CMOs across the globe. In light of complex patterns of consumer behaviour and an increased number of customer touchpoints, traditional ROI attribution methods like first touch, last touch, linear fail to attirbute investments accurately. The paper, "Integrated Media Mix Model and Online Fractional Attribution for Digital Marketing Investment Optimization and Holistic Decision Making' discusses Media Mix Model (MMM) and Online Fractional Attribution (OFA) Model, and their integration with big data in order to optimize media spends.

CHAPTER ONE

MODELING THE SPREAD OF PRODUCT RELATED RUMORS IN THE MARKETPLACE – AN AGENT BASED SIMULATION

Subin Sudhir and Anandakuttan B. Unnithan

ABSTRACT

Rumors are often shared in the marketplace about products, services, brands or organizations; both in online and offline scenarios. With the advancements in technology, rumors get communicated between consumers in the form of Word of Mouth (WOM). Rumors can affect perceptions about the product and brand images, and they cause changes to the credibility of brands and affect consumer loyalty. Hence, it is extremely important for marketing scholarship to study rumors and understand their spread.

The objectives of the paper are (1) to try and identify the factors influencing the spread of product related rumors in the market, (2) develop a mathematical model to predict the probability of a customer sharing the rumor and (3) simulate the aggregate market level rumor spreading behavior by Agent Based Simulation. The paper comprises of two studies. The first study uses directions provided in earlier research to identify and measure motivation of consumers to share rumors. Data is collected from 438 respondents on these factors and the consumer's intention to share rumors.

The second study uses the data collected from the first study to simulate an agent based environment of the market; NetLogo is used as the simulation platform. The simulation uses suitable assumptions to model the marketing environment and the behavior of agents. Rumors are planted in the simulated environment and the spread of these rumors is studied in detail. The role of credibility, novelty and valence of the rumors (as moderators) is studied.

The major contributions of the paper are that (1) it identifies and models the four major motivations that consumers have in rumor sharing and (2) it helps us observe rumor propagation in a simulated environment and thereby understand the key drivers of rumor transmission in the market at an aggregate level. Together the paper builds a unique view of combining the individual consumer's predispositions to aggregate market level spread of rumors. Learnings from this paper will provide useful aid to marketing managers in developing rumor combating strategies.

Keywords: Details about Data, Analysis, Results and the References are available upon request.

INTRODUCTION

Word of Mouth (WOM) communication has been an integral part of marketing scholarship. 'WOM is a consumer-dominated channel of communication where the sender is independent of the market.' (Brown, Broderick and Lee, 2007). The initial work in the field of WOM started in the early 1950s, ever since then the field has seen a flurry of research interests, including the recent developments into e-WOM (e.g. Arndt, 1967; Sheth, 1971; Day, 1971; Stock and Zinsner, 1987; Engel et al., 1969; Richins, 1983; Mangold, 1987; Bolfing, 1989; Murray, 1991; Herr et al., 1991; Woodside et al., 1992; Webster, 1991; Zeithaml et al., 1993; Buttle, 1998).

Koenig (1985) suggests that rumors are the dominant form of WOM in circulation. A rumor is defined as "*an unverified and instrumentally relevant information statement in circulation that arises in contexts of ambiguity, danger, or potential threat and that functions to help people make sense and manage risk*" (DiFonzo and Bordia, 2007). Rumors can potentially affect perceptions about the product and brand images, cause changes to the credibility of the brands and affect consumer loyalty (Kimmel, 2004; Kapferer, 1990; Koenig, 1985). The overload of commercially generated marketing communication confuses the consumer and guides the consumer to explore non-commercial forms of information; like WOM (Meiners et al., 2010). Marketplace rumors are fast propagated especially through social networks (Kostka et al., 2008). In the recent years there have been many rumors that have emerged in the marketplace and have created drastic effects on the marketing scenario (Kimmel, 2004). But, despite the importance of rumors, there has been little attention paid to rumor research in the marketing context (Kimmel and Audrain-Pontevia, 2010), although this stream of research is not totally new (e.g. Kamins et al., 1997; Kimmel, 2004; Kimmel and Audrain-Pontevia, 2010).

Despite the importance of rumors in the marketing context, little is known about the psychological factors driving rumor propagation (Dubois et al., 2011). Although there have been a few studies focusing on the motivations to share WOM (e.g. Dichter, 1966; Engel et al., 1993; Sundaram, Mitra and Webster, 1998; Hennig-Thurau et al., 2004), sparse attention has been given to the motivations to share rumors in the marketplace and correspondingly there are inadequacies in the instruments to measure these motivations. The objective of this paper is to identify the consumer motivations to share rumors in the marketplace and to simulate the market level rumor spreading behavior.

LITERATURE REVIEW

Word of Mouth (WOM)

WOM has been defined as '*an oral, person-to-person communication between a perceived non-commercial communicator and a receiver concerning a brand, a product, or a service offered for sale*' (Arndt, 1967). There have been further definitions in the literature (e.g. Westbrook, 1987; Stern, 1994; Hennig-Thurau et al., 2004). WOM has been identified to be more persuasive on consumer behavior than other sources of information that are marketer controlled (Buttle, 1998), neutral sources of information like market reports (Herr et al., 1991) and advertising (Sheth, 1971; Meiners et al., 2010). WOM is found to be effective on changing negative or neutral attitudes into positive attitudes (Day, 1971). It has been suggested that WOM will influence the expectations and the perceptions of consumers (Lynn, 1987; Stock and Zinsner, 1987; Woodside et al., 1992; Webster, 1991; Zeithaml et al., 1993). WOM has also been mentioned to be one of the most influential methods to manage the expectations of consumers (Engel et al., 1969; Richins, 1983; Tybout et al., 1981; Bolfing, 1989; Mangold, 1987; Berger and Heath, 2007; Basuroy, Chatterjee, and Ravid, 2003; Chevalier and Mayzlin, 2006). WOM increases sales and helps in the diffusion of new products (Chevalier and Mayzlin, 2006; Moe and Trusov, 2011; Godes and Mayzlin, 2009; Iyengar et al., 2010).

Motivation to Share WOM

Research in WOM has looked at the motivation for people to engage in WOM. The research on this stream can be categorized into three domains (i) Self Enhancement Motivation, (ii) Emotion Motivation and (c) Information Exchange Motivation.

The Self Enhancement motivation to engage in WOM suggests the motivations of a consumer to engage in WOM for enhancing his/her self-image and thereby self enhancement. The self enhancement motivation of engaging in WOM includes (i) self-disclosure (Berger and Milkman, 2013), (ii) sharing interesting products and messages; which deals with sharing interesting, original, funny or controversial messages (Moldovan, Goldenberg, and Chattopadhyay, 2011; Heath, Bell, and Sternberg, 2001) and (c) impression management (Sengupta, Dahl, and Gorn, 2002; Argo, White, and Dahl, 2006).

The Emotional motivation to share WOM suggests that people communicate to manage emotions. The emotional motivations include (i) anxiety reduction (Sundaram et al., 1998), (ii) arousal (Berger and Milkman, 2013; Heath et al., 2001; Moldovan et al., 2011), (c) need for vengeance (Richins, 1983; Sundaram et al., 1998) and (d) dissonance reduction (Engel et al., 1993).

Information exchange motivation has been looked at in three different sub-themes; which include (i) sharing information useful to others (Chiu et al., 2007; Berger and Milkman, 2013), (ii) Altruism (Dichter, 1966; Engel et al., 1993; Hennig-Thurau et al., 2004) and (c) seeking information to make and validate decisions (Engel et al., 1993; Gatignon and Robertson, 1986).

WOM and Rumors

WOM and rumors are not different; rather one must consider rumors as a form of WOM. Marketers term the communication between consumers as WOM (Kamins et al. 1987); and rumor is a form of communication that occurs between consumers. We could not identify any single source where different forms of WOM have been illustrated in literature; rather there have been studies that have reported different forms of WOM.

Kimmel (2004) has looked at rumor, news and gossip as different forms of WOM and classified them based on their significance, evidence and orientation. Dunn and Allen (2005) have reported rumors, urban legends and internet hoaxes as the different forms of WOM. DiFonzo and Bordia (2007) report the forms of WOM as rumor, gossip and urban legends. Guerin and Miyazaki (2006) suggest that WOM would include rumors, gossip, urban legends and hybrid forms. Hence, in the context of this study, rumors are viewed as a form of WOM.

Rumor Research

The initial studies on rumor had been in the context of both the World Wars. Allport (1919) was the first to mention and study the construct of rumor in the World

War I context. Prasad (1935) had reviewed close to 30 rumors in the context of an earthquake and then provided his early conclusions about rumor propagation. Later during the World War II, there was a greater interest in the field, including seminal contributions by Allport and Postman (1947), who focused on the spread of rumors among soldiers in the war (Rosnow and Foster; 2005).

Rumor has been formally defined in many studies (e.g. Knapp, 1944; Allport and Postman, 1947; Peterson and Gist, 1951; Rosnow and Fine, 1976; Kapferer, 1990; DiFonzo and Bordia, 2007). For the purpose of this study, we define a rumor as "an unverified and instrumentally relevant information statement in circulation that arises in contexts of ambiguity, danger, or potential threat and that functions to help people make sense and manage risk" (DiFonzo and Bordia, 2007).

Rumor research has mostly looked at the role of isolated variables or their combinations in rumor propagation. Studies have focused on uncertainty, involvement, credulity and anxiety as the factors affecting rumor spread (e.g. Prasad, 1935; Allport and Postman, 1947; Rosnow, 1991; Bordia and DiFonzo, 2004). Studies have partly mentioned a few other variables like ambiguity (uncertainty) (e.g. Allport and Postman, 1947), importance (Prasad, 1935), anxiety (Rosnow, 2001), credulity (belief) (Brodin and Roux, 1990; as cited Kimmel, 2004), fantasies (Jung, 1917; as cited Kimmel, 2004), rumors in consumer environments (Kimmel, 2004), source credibility (Kimmel, 2004), psychological control (DiFonzo and Bordia, 2002), valence (Kamins, Folkes, and Perner, 1997; Weenig, Groenenboom, and Wilke, 2001), belief (Rosnow et al., 1988), social acceptance (Allport and Postman, 1947; DiFonzo and Bordia, 2007), conscious spread (Kapferer, 1990), propaganda (Rosnow, 1991) and self-esteem/self-confidence (DiFonzo and Bordia, 2007). Though there has been a considerable amount of research in the field of rumors, there have hardly been any studies that identify the motivations that bind these variables together.

MOTIVATION FOR RUMOR SHARING

The review of literature from the context of rumor research shows four major motivational themes. These themes have been identified based on the motivations for people to engage in rumor sharing. These motivations become the foundation for this study. Literature suggests that the major themes under rumor studies are (1) Relationship Development, (2) Anxiety Management, (3) Information Sharing and (4) Self Enhancement.

Relationship Management Motivation

Relationship management motivation of rumor sharing in the marketplace refers to the motivation of a consumer to communicate a rumor to another consumer with a desire to manage their relationship. Rumor has been viewed in literature as a mechanism for social transaction and relationship management (Kamins, Folkes, and Perner, 1997; Weenig, Groenenboom, and Wilke, 2001). DiFonzo and Bordia (2007) mention that the motivation to share a rumor will be based on the effect it would have on the relationship goals. People will share rumors to enhance the chances of a long-term relation. A negative rumor will be shared with a friend if considered useful to the friend – in averting bad outcomes (Weenig et al., 2001). In conditions of low information availability, people would share rumors with an objective to be socially accepted for possessing this information (Allport and Postman, 1947; DiFonzo and Bordia, 2007). People will share credible rumors to be considered as a valuable source of information and gain acceptance through the same (Guerin, 2003). Rumors are shared as they provoke anxiety and interest and hence become good conversation topics; which will in turn help in building better relationships (Guerin and Miyazaki, 2006). Relationship management motivation is one of the key drivers to sharing rumors in the marketplace. Consumers will share rumors about products, services, brands or organizations in the market with other consumers; as an act to maintain and manage their relationships.

Anxiety Management Motivation

The anxiety management motivation suggests that the people share a rumor as a mechanism to manage their anxiety and to have a better control over the situation (Bordia and DiFonzo, 2004). In conditions of uncertainty and lack of formal information, people engage in informal information sharing and collective problem solving. In conditions with high uncertainty and involvement, it is suggested that people will have high anxieties and they will thus use rumor sharing as a mechanism to reduce this anxiety (Allport and Postman, 1947; Rosnow, Esposito and Gibney, 1988; Rosnow, 1991). When there is a lack of psychological control, anxiety levels are raised which also leads to rumor sharing (DiFonzo and Bordia, 1998; Bordia and DiFonzo, 2002). In a marketplace context rumors are shared with a desire to reduce anxieties about a product, service, brand or organization.

Information Sharing Motivation

People often share rumors to engage in a process on sense making and finding explanations (Bordia and Rosnow, 1998; DiFonzo and Bordia, 1997). It is suggested that in situations where there is no formal explanation, people will share rumors to make sense of the situation, in many cases rumors act as a readymade explanation to the situation (Allport and Postman, 1947; Bordia et al., 1999; Bordia and Rosnow, 1998). Often rumors are used by small groups to share information and develop explanations of the uncertain situations (Bordia et al., 1999; Bordia, 1996; Bordia and Rosnow, 1998). Rumor transmission is also a process to share valued information (Allport and Postman, 1947; Rosnow, 1980 and Rosnow and Fine, 1976). Information sharing motivation of rumor sharing in the marketplace thus refers to the motivation of a consumer to communicate a rumor with another consumer to share valued information.

Self Enhancement Motivation

Self enhancement motivation of rumor sharing refers to the motivation of a consumer to communicate a rumor with another consumer to enhance his own self-image and thereby his self-esteem. The self-enhancement motivation refers to the need to feel good about oneself (DiFonzo and Bordia, 2007). The self enhancement motivation has been underemphasized in literature (DiFonzo and Bordia, 2007), but a few studies have highlighted this aspect. Kapferer (1990) and Rosnow (1991) have highlighted the role of conscious spread of rumors as well as rumor spread for propaganda. Many studies have highlighted the role of propaganda at times of elections or war (DiFonzo and Bordia, 2007). Propaganda rumors are used to attain the goal of the person engaged in rumor sharing; which accentuates self enhancement. Rumor sharing has also been established to be enhancing self-esteem or self-confidence. DiFonzo and Bordia (2007) suggest that sharing a rumor in many instances is viewed to improve self esteem and self confidence. Consider for example the case of a consumer propagating a rumor in favor of his preferred brand, which will help boost his self-image and self-esteem. Research has indicated that sometimes rumors are generated and transmitted to achieve some propaganda related to political agenda, sales targets, to demoralize opponents etc. (Airport and Postman, 1947; DiFonzo and Bordia, 2004; Kapferer, 1990; Rosnow, 2001). Studies have also focused on rumors being consciously spread to mislead or misguide someone (Kapferer, 1990) and the fact that sometimes people fantasize and share such fantasies as rumors (Brodin and Roux, 1990; as cited Kimmel, 2004).

STUDY 1

Continuing the discussion from the literature review and the identification of the motivations for consumers to share rumors; we study the role of these four motivations, and their influence on the consumer's intention to share the rumor. The section will highlight the methodology and findings of this study.

Intention to Share the Rumor

The model is being developed in order to explain a customer's intention to share a product-related rumor. Intention to share a product-related rumor is the dependent measure in the model and in the proposed study. Many previous studies have looked at rumor activity. But, most of these studies have looked at the rumor activity after the rumor has been propagated. Anthony (1973) had studied the rumor sharing that had happened in a school; Jaeger et al. (1980) looked at a classroom scenario and how many people had heard the rumor; Rosnow, Esposito, and Gibney (1988) had studied the rumors arising after the death of a college student; there are many other similar studies. A major challenge in the marketing context is the fact that it is difficult to identify an unbiased sample of consumers who have engaged in rumor sharing. Hence, intentions to share the product-related rumor are one of the best measures available. Kamins et al. (1997) have used "willingness to tell others" as a dependent variable. Willingness to tell others is similar to the intention to share product related rumor in the case of this study. It is not new to study intentions in place of actual outputs in the marketing context. Hence, we use intention to share product-related rumor as the dependent variable in the study. The intention to share product related rumor is considered at five different levels. These levels include (1) Communicating the Rumor Face-to-face to a family member, (2) Communicating the Rumor Face-to-face to a friend, (3) Communicating the Rumor Face-to-face to a stranger, (4) Communicating the Rumor on online social media like Facebook/ Twitter and (5) Communicating the Rumor on online websites anonymously. Intention to Share product related rumor is defined as the intent and the likelihood of the consumer to share a product related rumor at a future instance.

Design of Stimulus

The design of the stimuli for testing the relationships was done in an orthogonal fashion. Eight rumor messages were developed based on the three moderating variables that are being considered in the study – credibility, novelty and valence. (Please refer to Appendix 2 for the stimuli used in the study.) The rumor messages were developed in four different product categories. The choice of categories was done by consultation among experts. The main assumption for the selection of the product categories was to ensure that the sample (students) would be aware about and would be using these products/services. A pre-test was conducted with a total of 181 respondents who participated in the pre-testing of the stimuli. The results of the pre-test indicated a good fit with the design of stimuli. The Believability of Information scale reported by Gurhan and Maheswaran (2000) was used to measure the consumer's perception of credibility of the message. The scale had five items that were originally from a seven point semantic scale. After a few pilot tests we modified the scale to a four point Likert scale. The Novelty (General) scale reported by Cox and Cox (2002) was used to measure perceived novelty. The original scale had five bi-polar adjectives that were measured in a seven point scale. The scale was modified after a few pilot tests to a more convenient format having five items in a four point Likert scale. Appendix 1 provides details of all the scales used in the study. Table 1 provides the summary of the orthogonal design.

Table 1: Orthogonal Design of Stimuli

Code	*Credibility*	*Novelty*	*Valence*	*Product Category*
1N	Low	High	Negative	Soft Drink
1P	High	Low	Positive	Soft Drink
2N	High	High	Negative	Shampoo
2P	Low	Low	Positive	Shampoo
3N	Low	Low	Negative	Mobile Phone
3P	High	High	Positive	Mobile Phone
4N	High	Low	Negative	Social Media
4P	Low	High	Positive	Social Media

Measures

The study uses established scales from literature to capture the four motivations for consumers to engage in rumor transmission. These motivations are measured using the Sudhir and Unnithan (2014) scale for measuring consumer motivations to share rumors in the marketplace. The scale is a 21 item four point Likert scale that measures all the four motivations. Intention to share rumors scale was adopted from single item intention scales used by Kamins et al. (1997) and DiFonzo and Bordia (2007). The scale used in these studies only had a single item that asked the respondents about their intention to share the rumor with others. We modified the scale to capture the same question in five different contexts. These contexts included sharing the rumor with (1) family, (2) friends, (3) strangers, (4) on social media and (5) on product review websites. We believe that such a contextual approach can provide a better insight into the consumer's sharing intentions. Appendix 1 provides details of all the scales used in the study.

Method

In all 438 questionnaires were collected from the respondents. Each of these respondents used between 6 minutes and 13 minutes to complete the survey. The respondents were briefed at the beginning of the survey about the purpose of the study and later de-briefed about the fact that these rumor messages are untrue. This was done to ensure that no negative effects are created in the minds of the respondents about the brands used in the study. Responses that had more than 10% missing values were removed and not used in the analysis.

Results

A linear regression analysis was performed on the data collected to analyze the effect of each of the motivations on the consumer's intention to share the rumor. The below Table 2 provides the summary of the linear regression analysis. The results are shown for the linear regression analysis for each message and the regression analysis for the total data collected.

Table 2: Results of Regression Analysis

				Path coefficients with Intention to Share [INT]			
	N	R^2	*Constant*	*Information Sharing Motivation [INF]*	*Relationship Management Motivation [REL]*	*Anxiety Management Motivation [ANX]*	*Self Enhancement Motivation [SELF]*
1N	44	0.421	–0.275**	0.534**	0.059	0.448**	0.038
1P	54	0.485	0.384	0.391**	0.348*	0.326	–0.267**
2N	56	0.352	0.725**	0.449**	–0.005	0.224	–0.053
2P	52	0.603	–0.053	0.404***	0.143	0.411**	–0.034
3N	56	0.592	0.381	0.591***	–0.041	0.144	0.085
3P	57	0.506	0.341	0.437***	–0.220*	0.294**	0.211*
4N	40	0.539	0.230	0.663***	–0.167	0.359**	–0.007
4P	67	0.550	–0.335	0.638***	0.165	0.269*	0.006
Total	438	0.504	0.240**	0.525***	0.020	0.348***	–0.072

*** p-value < 0.000, ** p-value < 0.05 and *p-value < 0.1

The results of the linear regression analysis are reported above in Table 2. The results show that three out of the four motivations have significant effects on the last model which used all the 438 surveys that were collected. But, when we compare the significance of the motivations and their effect on the consumer's intention to share the rumor for each of the eight messages that were provided to the respondents; we observe that there are only a few of the motivations that have a significant effect for each rumor message. Below, we have represented the various linear regression models for each message type separately.

$$INT_{TOTAL} = 0.240 + 0.525*INF + 0.348*ANX - 0.072*SELF + \quad \ldots[1]$$
$$INT_{1N} = 0.534*INF + 0.448*ANX + \quad \ldots[2]$$
$$INT_{IP} = 0.391*INF + 0.348*REL - 0.267*SELF + \quad \ldots[3]$$
$$INT_{2N} = 0.725 + 0.449*INF + \quad \ldots[4]$$
$$INT_{2P} = 0.404*INF + 0.411*ANX + \quad \ldots[5]$$
$$INT_{3N} = 0.591*INF + \quad \ldots[6]$$
$$INT_{3P} = 0.437*INF - 0.220*REL + 0.294*ANX + 0.211*SELF + \quad \ldots[7]$$
$$INT_{4N} = 0.663*INF + 0.359*ANX + \quad \ldots[8]$$
$$INT_{4P} = 0.638*INF + 0.269*ANX + \quad \ldots[9]$$

Discussion

The result of the linear regression analysis shows that for the total model that uses all data from all the 438 respondents, three out of the four motivations have a significant correlation. On the other hand when we compare the effects on each message type; there is significant effect only from a few of the motivations. Overall it can be understood that all the four motivations have a significant relationship with the consumer's intention to share the rumor. The non-significance of some of the motivations could be explained by the moderating effect of credibility, novelty and valence. The significance values are considered at a 90% confidence interval for better interpretation of the simulation in Study 2.

STUDY 2

In the study 2 we simulated the aggregate market level behavior for all the regression models identified in study 1. The objective of the study was to understand the aggregate rumor sharing behavior among consumers in the marketplace. The simulation was conducted using NetLogo 5.1. Agent-based modeling (ABM) is a powerful simulation technique. A system can be modeled using ABM as a group of autonomous entities called agents. Each agent individually assesses its situation and makes decisions on the basis of a set of rules. Agents may execute various behaviors appropriate for the system they represent. For example if we consider the ABM of a retail store; we can model each customer and his decision making heuristics and understand the aggregate results. Epstein and Axtell (1996) and Axelrod (1997) have suggested that repetitive competitive interactions between agents are a feature of agent-based modeling, which relies on the power of computers to explore dynamics out of the reach of pure mathematical methods. An ABM is a simulated multi-agent system constructed with a particular goal: to capture key theoretical elements of some social or psychological process (Smith and Conrey; 2007).

ABM is used in this study for two reasons; (1) the inherent need in understanding the dynamics of rumor sharing at an aggregate level and (2) the inherent nature of people (agents) to having different motivations. Since customers have different motivations to share product-related rumors, we identified ABM as the most influential method in this scenario. Railsback, Lytinen and Jackson (2006) have reviewed the tools available for conducting ABM. Their findings had helped us to streamline the use of NetLogo as the most useful tool for ABM in this case. NetLogo is a programmable modeling environment for simulating natural and social phenomena. It was authored by Uri Wilensky (1999) and has been in continuous development ever since at the Centre for Connected Learning and Computer-Based Modeling at Northwestern University. NetLogo is open source and has extensive documentation. It also comes with the Models Library, a large collection of pre-written simulations that can be used and modified. These simulations address content areas in the natural and social sciences including biology and medicine, physics and chemistry, mathematics and computer science, and economics and social psychology. These were again strong reasons for the adoption of this tool for this study.

The simulation was conducted based on the *Rumour-Mill* model developed by Dr. Helen M. Doerr and is part of the NetLogo library. The basic code available in the NetLogo library was modified to suit the purpose of the study. Appendix 3 provides the complete code that was used in the study. The code was altered for each of the models that were identified from the Study 1.

Method

Each regression model identified from Study 1 was simulated one after the other. During each simulation each '*patch*' was randomly assigned a value for each of the four motivations. Each *patch* could assume a value between 0 and 4 for each motivation. At the beginning of the simulation a rumor is planted with one patch – each patch plays the role of an agent. Figure 1 provides a diagrammatic description of the simulated market with one patch having heard the rumor. Patches that are displayed in white have heard the rumor and those in blue have not heard the rumor. Then the rumor sharing is started by using a button in the interface, the graphical interface gives a good indication of the rumor spreading in the network; figure 2 shows the rumor spreading in the market. All the white area in the figure is patches (agents) who have heard and spread the rumor forward. Each time an agent hears the rumor; he assumes a random value for each of the four motivations and then runs the regression model. If the value of intention to share is greater than 2; the agent decides to share the rumor. The rumor sharing happens randomly to one of the eight agents who are adjacent to the agent making the sharing decision. There are eight adjacent agents as each patch is a square surrounded by eight squares. This process is allowed to continue until everybody in the market has heard the rumor. Figure 3 shows the final stage; where everyone has heard the rumor and there are no patches left in blue.

Fig. 1

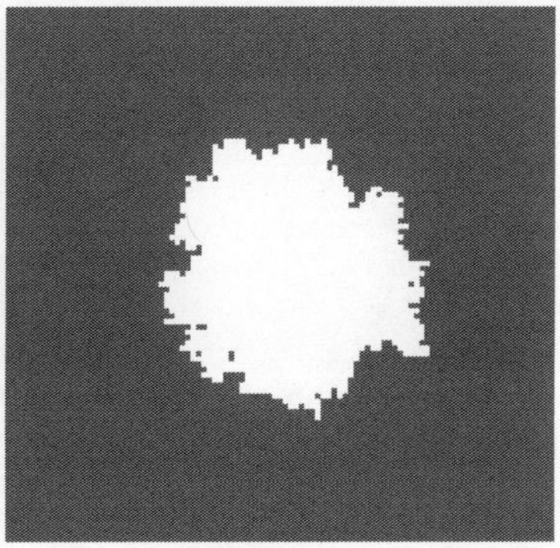

Fig. 2

Fig. 3

Results

The results of the simulation provided some interesting insights. Firstly, we were able to study the aggregate market level spreading of the rumor. The simulation was mapped to a real-time and the analysis was conducted on the basis of the time required to achieve 100% rumor spread. Figure 4 provides a summary of the rumor spreading characteristics for each of the nine models identified from Study 1.

We can clearly see that rumor sharing in the marketplace is an 'S'-shaped curve. There is a slow rate of spread in the initial stages and there is a similar slow rate of spread in the final stages of the rumor spread. Rumor spreading is most dangerous for the marketer in the middle portion; where there are enough agents who are trying to spread the rumor. The Figure 4 is not very insightful in understanding the role of each message type and the differences among them. To better understand these, we studied two rumor messages at a time and the results were quite interesting.

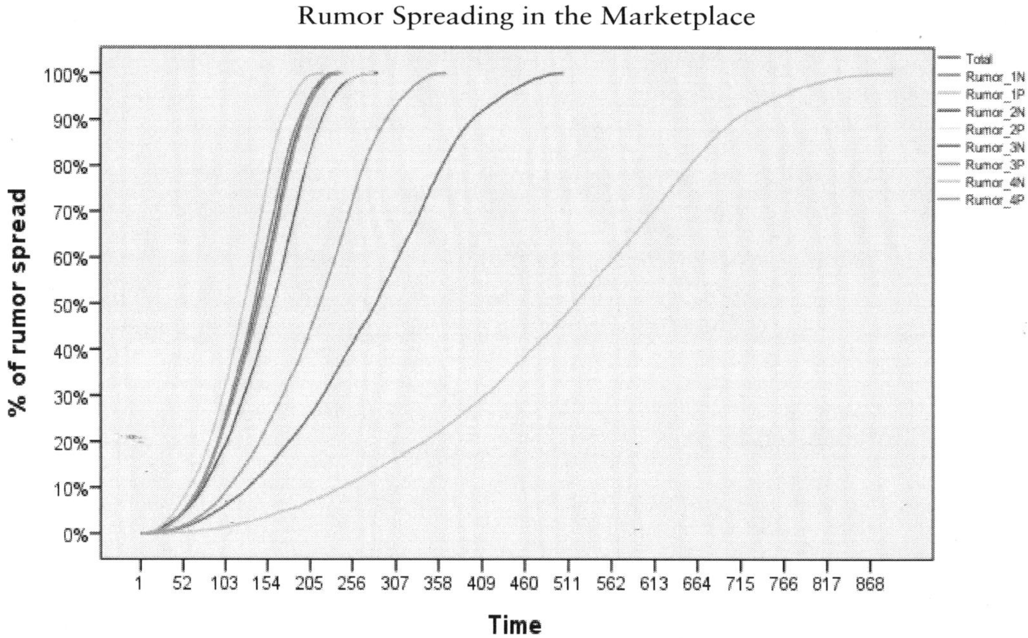

Fig. 4: Simulation Results

Credibility

Literature has proposed this construct in multiple terms; credulity (Allport and Postman, 1947; Rosnow, 1991), belief (Prasad, 1935; DiFonzo and Bordia, 2002) and credibility (Kimmel, 2004). For the purpose of this study we call the construct as credibility. The theoretical orientations of the functional approach of rumor sharing (Kimmel, 2004), the fact-finding motivation of rumor sharing (DiFonzo and Bordia, 2007) and the relationship-enhancement motivation of rumor sharing (DiFonzo and Bordia, 2007) are all implied in the role of credibility in the rumor sharing process; where credibility is shown to positively affect the rumor spreading activity. In order to study the role of credibility alone, we looked at two messages that were high and low on credibility; but both were low novelty and negative valence. We looked at the rumor messages 3N (Low Credibility, Low Novelty and Negative Valence) and rumor 4N (High Credibility, Low Novelty and Negative Valence). Results of the analysis are shown in Figure 5.

From the graph it can be clearly visualized that high credibility (4N) rumor spreads much faster as compared to a low credibility (3N) rumor. This is under the conditions where the other factors are kept constantly at a low condition.

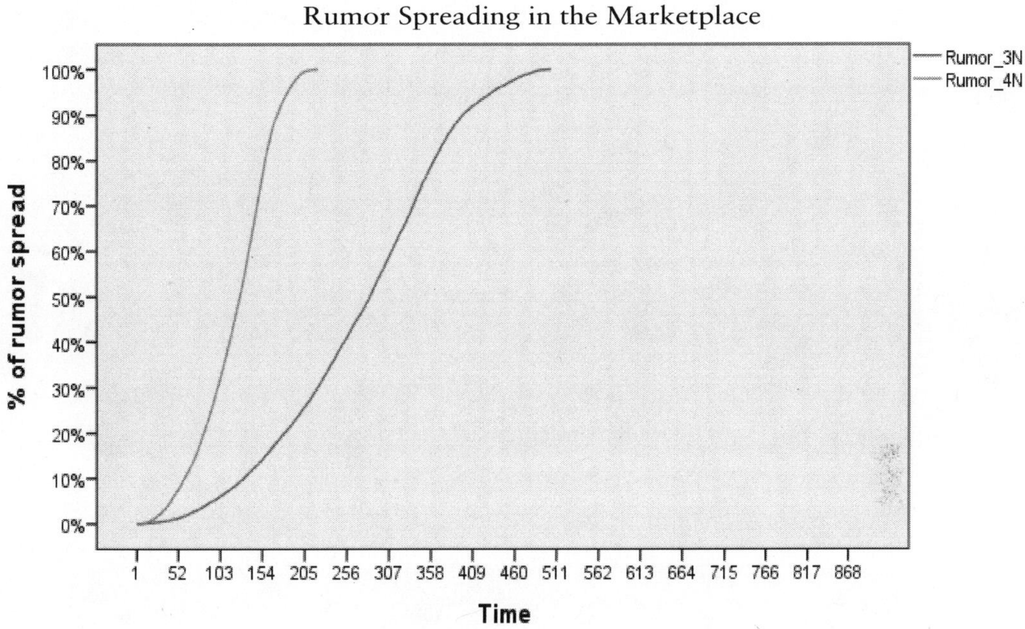

Fig. 5: Role of Credibility

Valence

Rumor Valence has been studied and mentioned in quite a few recent studies. Kimmel (2004) suggests that consumers tend to convey negative information to more people than positive information. Kamins, Folkes, and Perner (1997) have suggested from their study that people will refrain from passing negative rumors (compared with positive rumors), fearing that these rumors might generate negative effect in the recipient—a relationship-enhancing goal (DiFonzo and Bordia, 2007). Studies have also suggested that in conditions where the negative rumor is viewed as a source of helping people cope with negative events, a negative rumor would be shared more (Weenig, Groenenboom, and Wilke, 2001). To understand the role of rumor valence, we use two rumor messages and then compare their spread. Rumor message 3N (Low credibility, Low Novelty and Negative Valence) and rumor 2P (Low credibility, Low Novelty and Positive Valence) are studied. As in the previous case of credibility, it is important to eliminate the effects of all other factors; thus we take two messages that are low on credibility and novelty. Figure 6 provides the summary of the rumor spread characteristics. It is quite evident that a positive rumor takes less time to spread than a negative rumor. This reiterates the findings of Kamins et al. (1997) that consumers share positive rumors more often than negative rumors.

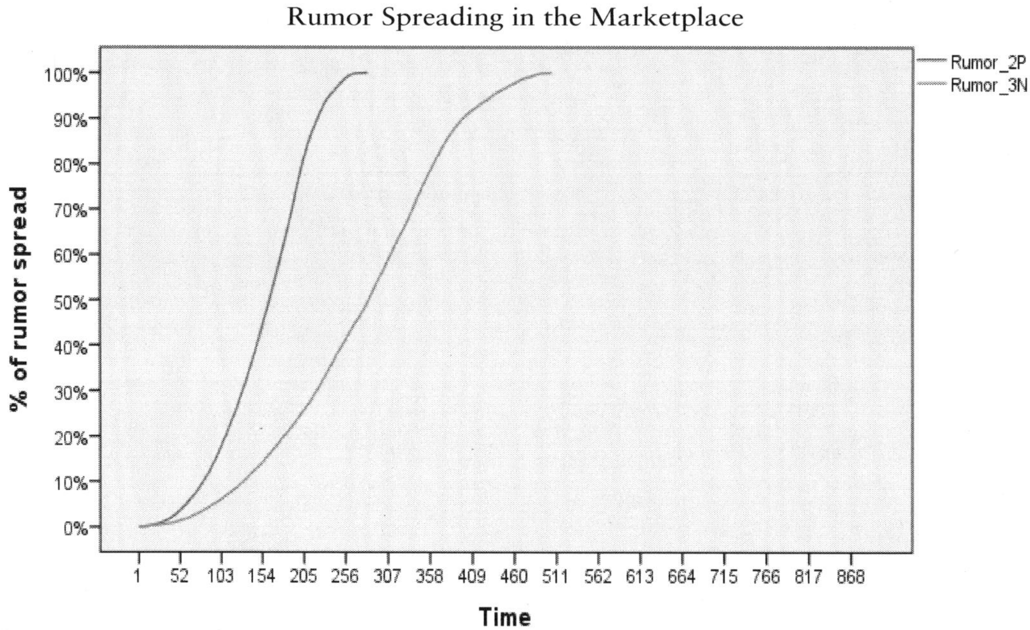

Fig. 6: Role of Valence

Novelty

Novelty has generally not been studied as a separate component in rumor transmission, perhaps because it is obvious that rumors about new topics are spread more than rumors about old topics (Brooks, DiFonzo and Ross; In press) Novelty is a foundational aspect of rumor transmission (Allport & Postman, 1947). But, in a marketing context rumors can originate and then be away for some time and then re-originate after a certain period of time (Kimmel, 2004). This would indicate the role of novelty in rumor transmission. We suggest that novel rumors will be transmitted more frequently than old and heard about rumors. To study this, we look at the rumor spreading characteristics of two rumors. We compare the rumor spreading characteristics of rumor message 3N (Low Credibility, Low Novelty and Negative Valence) and 1N (Low Credibility, High Novelty and Negative Valence). The results of the simulation are shown in Figure 7 below. Again, like in the cases of credibility and Valence, there is a very strong reason to believe that Novelty of the rumor helps in rumor propagation. This is clearly seen in Figure 7, where the High Novelty rumor spread much faster than a Low Novelty Rumor.

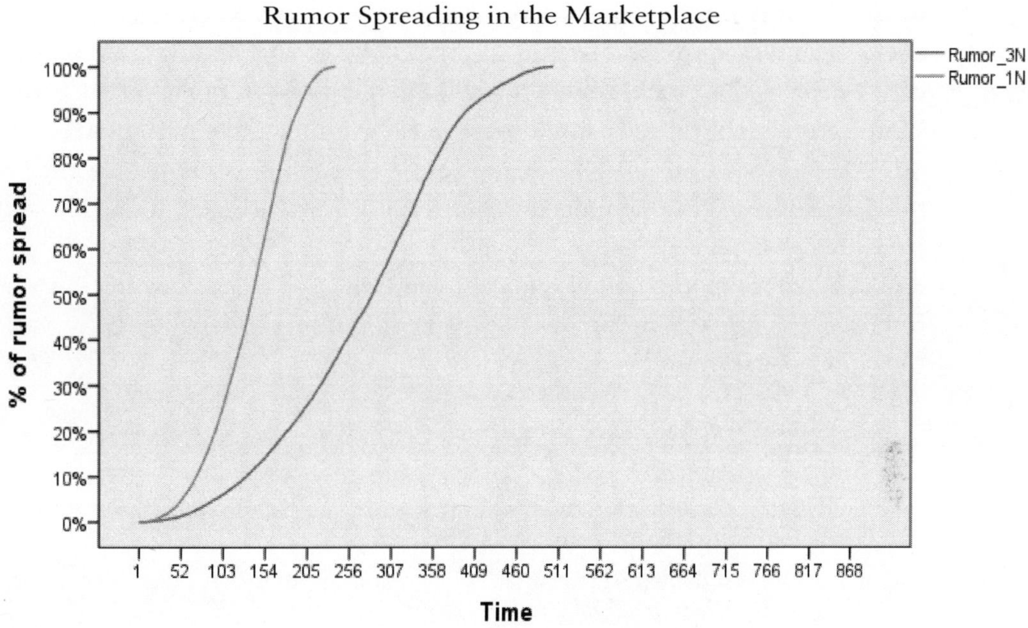

Fig. 7: Role of Novelty

DISCUSSION AND CONCLUSION

The paper basically tries to understand the motivations behind a consumer's motivation to share a rumor in the marketing context. The paper also tries to simulate the rumor spreading in the marketplace using Agent Based Simulation in NetLogo 5.1. Firstly, the paper illustrates the role of the four motivations identified from literature and the study 1 signifies the relationships between each of these motivations and the consumer's intention to share the rumor. The results of the regression analysis show significant relationships for three out of the four motivations and the consumer's intention to share the rumor. This finding gives us the foundation to move on to the simulation.

In study 2 we simulated the rumor spreading of each rumor message using the regression models identified in Study 1; further we also simulated the overall regression model to identify the rumor spreading characteristics of rumor messages. It is clearly understood from the study that rumor spreading in the marketplace follows an S-shaped curve with respect to time. This finding is true for all the rumor messages. Further study 2 looked at the role of credibility, novelty and valence of the rumor message and their effect on rumor sharing. It was found that credibility, novelty and valence; all affect the rate of rumor spreading in a positive manner.

Higher credibility, higher novelty and positive valence; are characteristics which enable a rumor to spread faster in the marketplace. The findings of this paper can be used by marketing practitioners to device better strategies in combating rumor. This is only a preliminary study into the spread of rumors in the marketplace and the use of ABM to study consumer behavior. Marketing scholarship can use the findings of this paper to further the understanding we have with respect to WOM and Rumor spreading in greater detail.

In conclusion, this study explores the motivations of consumers to engage in rumor spreading and by simulating the rumor spread this study helps visualize the rumor propagation in the marketplace.

REFERENCES

Allport, F. H. (1919). Behavior and experiment in social psychology. *The Journal of Abnormal Psychology*, *14*, 297–306.

Allport, G. W., & Postman, L. (1947). *The psychology of rumor*. New York: Holt, Rinehart & Winston.

Anthony, S. (1973). Anxiety and rumor. *The Journal of Social Psychology*, *89*(1), 91-98.

Argo, J. J., White, K., & Dahl, D. W. (2006). Social comparison theory and deception in the interpersonal exchange of consumption information. *Journal of Consumer Research*, *33*, 99–108.

Arndt, J. (1967). Role of product-related conversations in the diffusion of a new product. *Journal of Marketing Research*, *4*, 291–296.

Basuroy, S., Chatterjee, S., & Ravid, S. A. (2003). How critical are critical reviews? The box office effects of film critics, star power, and budgets. *Journal of Marketing*, *67*, 103–117.

Bentler, P. M. (2007). On tests and indices for evaluating structural models. *Personality and Individual Differences*, *42*, 825–829.

Berger, J., & Heath, C. (2007). Where consumers diverge from others: identity signaling and product domains. *Journal of Consumer Research*, *34*, 121–134.

Berger, J., & Milkman, K. L. (2012). What makes online content viral? *Journal of Marketing Research*, *49*, 192–205.

Bolfing, C. P. (1989). How do customers express dissatisfaction and what can service marketers do about it? *Journal of Services Marketing*, *3*, 5–23.

Bordia, P. (1996). Studying verbal interaction on the Internet: The case of rumor transmission research. *Behavior Research Methods, Instruments, & Computers*, *28*, 148-151.

Bordia, P., & Difonzo, N. (2004). Problem solving in social interactions on the internet: rumor as social cognition. *Social Psychology Quarterly*, *67*, 33–49.

Bordia, P., DiFonzo, N., & Chang, A. (1999). Rumor as group problem-solving: Development patterns in informal computer-mediated groups. *Small Group Research*, *30*, 8-28.

Bordia, P., Jones, E., Gallois, C., Callan, V. J., & DiFonzo, N. (2006). Management are aliens! Rumors and stress during organizational change. *Group & Organization Management, 31*(5), 601-621.

Bordia, P., & Rosnow, R. L. (1998). Rumor Rest Stops on the Information Highway Transmission Patterns in a Computer Mediated Rumor Chain. *Human Communication Research, 25*(2), 163-179.

Brown, J., Broderick, A. J., & Lee, N. (2007). Word of mouth communication within online communities: Conceptualing the online social network. *Journal of Interactive Marketing, 21*, 2–20.

Buhrmester, M., Kwang, T., & Gosling, S. D. (2011). Amazon's mechanical Turk: a new source of inexpensive, yet high-quality, data? *Perspectives on Psychological Science*, 6, 3–5.

Buttle, F. A. (1998). Word of mouth: understanding and managing referral marketing. *Journal of Strategic Marketing*, 6, 241–254.

Chevalier, J. A., & Mayzlin, D. (2006). The Effect of Word of Mouth on Sales: Online Book Reviews. *Journal of Marketing Research, 43*, 345–354.

Chiu, H.-C., Hsieh, Y.-C., Kao, Y.-H., & Lee, M. (2007). The determinants of email receivers' disseminating behaviors on the internet. *Journal of Advertising Research, 47*, 524.

Churchill, G. A. (1979). A paradigm for developing better measures of marketing constructs. *Journal of Marketing Research, 16*, 64.

DiFonzo, N., & Bordia, P. (1997). Rumor and prediction: Making sense (but losing dollars) in the stock market. *Organizational Behavior and Human Decision Processes, 71*, 329-353.

DiFonzo, N., & Bordia, P. (2002). Rumor and stable-cause attribution in prediction and behavior. *Organizational Behavior and Human Decision Processes, 88*, 329-353.

DiFonzo, N., & Bordia, P. (2007). *Rumor Psychology: Social and Organizational Approaches*. Washington, DC: American Psychological Association.

Dubois, D., Rucker, D. D., & Tormala, Z. L. (2011). From rumors to facts, and facts to rumors: the role of certainty decay in consumer communications. *Journal of Marketing Research, 48*, 1020–1032.

Dunn, Henry B., and Charlotte A. Allen. (2005). Rumors, urban legends and internet hoaxes. *Proceedings of the Annual Meeting of the Association of Collegiate Marketing Educators*.

Engel, J. F., Blackwell, R. D., & Miniard, P. W. (1995). Consumer behavior. *Chicago: Dry Den, 12*, 251–264.

Engel, J. F., Kegerreis, R. J., & Blackwell, R. D. (1969). Word-of-mouth Communication by the Innovator. *Journal of Marketing, 33*, 15–19.

Epstein J. M. & Axtell, R. L., (1996) *Growing Artificial Societies: Social Science from the Bottom Up*. Cambridge, MA: MIT Press.

Gatignon, H., & Robertson, T. S. (1986). Competitive Effects on Technology Diffusion. *Journal of Marketing*, *50*, 1-12.

Godes, D., & Mayzlin, D. (2009). Firm-created word-of-mouth communication: evidence from a field test. *Marketing Science*, *28*, 721–739.

Goyette, I., Ricard, L., Bergeron, J., & Marticotte, F. (2010). e-WOM Scale: word-of-mouth measurement scale for e-services context. *Canadian Journal of Administrative Sciences*, *27*, 5–23.

Guerin, B. (2003). Language use as social strategy: A review and an analytic framework for the social sciences. *Review of General Psychology*, *7*(3), 251.

Guerin, B., & Miyazaki, Y. (2006). Analyzing Rumors, Gossip, and Urban Legends through Their Conversational Properties. *Psychological Record*, *56*(1).

Heath, C., Bell, C., & Sternberg, E. (2001). Emotional selection in memes: the case of urban legends. *Journal of Personality and Social Psychology*, *81*, 1028–1041.

Hennig-Thurau, T., Gwinner, K. P., Walsh, G., & Gremler, D. D. (2004). Electronic word-of-mouth via consumer-opinion platforms: What motivates consumers to articulate themselves on the Internet? *Journal of Interactive Marketing*, *18*, 38–52.

Herr, P. M., Kardes, F. R., & Kim, J. (1991). Effects of word-of-mouth and product-attribute information on persuasion: an accessibility-diagnosticity perspective. *Journal of Consumer Research*, *17*, 454.

Iyengar, R., Bulte, C. Van den, & Valente, T. W. (2010). Opinion leadership & social contagion in new product diffusion. *Marketing Science*, *30*(2), 195–212.

Jaeger, M. E., Anthony, S., & Rosnow, R. L. (1980). Who Hears What from Whom and with What Effect: A Study of Rumor. *Personality and Social Psychology Bulletin*, *6*(3), 473-478.

Kamins, M. A., Folkes, V. S., & Perner, L. (1997). Consumer responses to rumors: good news, bad news. *Journal of Consumer Psychology*, *6*, 165–187.

Kapferer, J.-N. (1990). *Rumors: Uses, interpretations, & images*. New Brunswick, NJ: Transaction Publishers.

Kimmel, A. J. (2004). *Rumors & rumor control: A manager's guide to understanding & combatting rumors*. Mahwah, NJ: Erlbaum.

Kimmel, A. J., & Audrain-Pontevia, A.-F. (2010). Analysis of commercial rumors from the perspective of marketing managers: Rumor prevalence, effects, and control tactics. *Journal of Marketing Communications*, *16*, 239–253.

Knapp, R. H. (1944). A psychology of rumor. *Public Opinion Quarterly*, *8*, 22–37.

Koenig, F. (1985). *Rumor in the marketplace: The social psychology of commercial hearsay*. Dover, MA: Auburn House Pub. Co.

Kostka, J., Oswald, Y. A., & Wattenhofer, R. (2008). Word of mouth: rumor dissemination in social networks. *Structural Information and Communication Complexity*, 185–196.

Lynn, S. A. (1987). Identifying buying influences for a professional service: Implications for marketing efforts. *Industrial Marketing Management*, *16*, 119–130.

Mangold, W. G. (1987). Use of commercial sources of information in the purchase of professional services: What the literature tells us. *Services Marketing Quarterly*, *3*, 5–17.

Meiners, N. H., Schwarting, U., & Seeberger, B. (2010). The renaissance of word-of-mouth marketing: a 'new' standard in twenty-first century marketing management?! *International Journal of Economic Sciences and Applied Research*, *3*, 79.

Moe, W. W., & Trusov, M. (2011). The value of social dynamics in online product ratings forums. *Journal of Marketing Research*, *48*, 444–456.

Moldovan, S., Goldenberg, J., & Chattopadhyay, A. (2011). The different roles of product originality and usefulness in generating word-of-mouth. *International Journal of Research in Marketing*, *28*, 109–119.

Murray, K. B. (1991). A Test of services marketing theory: consumer information acquisition activities. *Journal of Marketing*, *55*, 10–25.

Peterson, W. A., & Gist, N. P. (1951). Rumor and public opinion. *American Journal of Sociology*, *57*, 159.

Prasad, J. (1935). The psychology of rumour: A study relating to the great Indian earthquake of 1934. *British Journal of Psychology*, *26*, 1–15.

Rapopaport, A. & Rebhun, L.I. (1952). *On the mathematical theory of rumor spread. Bulletin of Mathematical Biology, 14,* 375-383.

Richins, M. L. (1983). Negative word- of-mouth by dissatisfied consumers: pilot study. *Journal of Marketing*, *47*, 68–78.

Rosnow, R. (2001). Rumor and gossip in interpersonal interaction and beyond: A social exchange perspective. In R.M. Kowalski (Ed.), *Behaving badly: Aversive behaviors in interpersonal relationships* (pp. 203–232).

Rosnow, R. L. (1980). Psychology of rumor reconsidered. *Psychological Bulletin*, *87*, 578–591.

Rosnow, R. L. (1991). Inside rumor: A personal journey. *American Psychologist*, *46*, 484–496.

Rosnow, R. L., & Fine, G. A. (1976). *Rumor and gossip: The social psychology of hearsay*. New York: Elsevier.

Rosnow, R. L., Esposito, J. L., & Gibney, L. (1988). Factors influencing rumor spreading: Replication and extension. *Language & Communication*, *8*(1), 29-42.

Rosnow, R. L., & Foster, E. K. (2005). Rumor and Gossip Research. *APA - Psychological Science Agenda*. Retrieved from http://www.apa.org/science/about/psa/2005/04/gossip.aspx

Rothbaum, F., Weisz, J. R., & Snyder, S. S. (1982). Changing the world and changing the self: A two-process model of perceived control. *Journal of personality and social psychology*, *42*(1), 5.

Sengupta, J., Dahl, D. W., & Gorn, G. J. (2002). Misrepresentation in the consumer context. *Journal of Consumer Psychology*, *12*, 69–79.

Sheth, J. N. (1971). Word-of-mouth in low-risk innovations. *Journal of Advertising Research*, *11*, 15–18.

Shibutani, T. (1966). *Improvised news: A sociological study of rumor*. Indianapolis, IN: Bobbs-Merrill.

Stern, B. B. (1994). A revised communication model for advertising: multiple dimensions of the source, the message, and the recipient. *Journal of Advertising*, *23*, 5–15.

Stevens, L. E., & Fiske, S. T. (1995). Motivation and cognition in social life: A social survival perspective. *Social cognition*, *13*(3), 189-214.

Stock, J. R., & Zinszer, P. H. (1987). The industrial purchase decision for professional services. *Journal of Business Research*, *15*, 1–16.

Sudhir, S., & Unnithan, A. B. (2014). Measuring Consumer Motivations to Share Rumors: Scale Development. *International Journal of Online Marketing (IJOM)*, *4*(3), 51-67.

Sundaram, D. S., Mitra, K., & Webster, C. (1998). Word-of-mouth communications: a motivational analysis. *Advances in Consumer Research*, *25*, 527–531.

Tybout, A.M., Calder, B.J. and Sternthal, B. (1981) Using information processing theory to design marketing strategies. *Journal of Marketing Research 23*, 73–79.

Webster, C. (1991). Influences upon consumer expectations of services. *Journal of Services Marketing*, *5*(1), 5–17.

Weenig, M. W., Groenenboom, A. C., & Wilke, H. A. (2001). Bad news transmission as a function of the definitiveness of consequences and the relationship between communicator and recipient. *Journal of personality and social psychology*, *80*(3), 449.

Westbrook, R. A. (1987). Product/consumption-based affective responses and postpurchase processes. *Journal of Marketing Research*, 258-270.

Wilensky, U. (1997). *NetLogo Rumor Mill model*. Center for Connected Learning and Computer-Based Modeling, Northwestern University, Evanston, IL.

Wilensky, U. (1999). *NetLogo*. *http://ccl.northwestern.edu/netlogo/*. Center for Connected Learning and Computer-Based Modeling, Northwestern University, Evanston

Woodside, A. G., Wilson, E. J., & Milner, P. (1992). Buying & marketing CPA services. *Industrial Marketing Management*, *21*(3), 265–273.

Zeithaml, V. A., Berry, L. L., & Parasuraman, A. (1993). The nature and determinants of customer expectations of service. *Journal of the Academy of Marketing Science*, *21*, 1–12.

APPENDICES

APPENDIX 1 – SCALES USED IN THE STUDY

1. Motivations to Share product related Rumor (Sudhir and Unnithan, 2014)

	Strongly Disagree	*Dis-agree*	*Agree*	*Strongly Agree*
Anxiety Management Motivation				
I will feel relaxed after sharing this message				
I am worried about others and sharing this message will help keep them safe				
Sharing this message will make me feel in control of the situation				
Sharing this message will create a pleasant mood in me				
Sharing this message will make me feel confident				
I am motivated to share this message and reduce my anxiety regarding the product				
Information Sharing Motivation				
I will share this message to inform others				
I will share this message as it will be useful to others				
By sharing the above message I will be able to help others make wise choices				
I am motivated to find out if this message is true or not				
I will share this message to get feedback on the message				
I will be able to help others by sharing this message				
Relationship Management Motivation				
I will share this message to be in touch with others				
Sharing this message will make others want to talk to me more often				
Sharing this message will help me communicate with others				
Others will consider me an expert if I share this message				
Others will respect me more if I share this message				
Self Enhancement Motivation				
I will share this message to pass time				
I will share this message to let others know about my activities				
Sharing this message will help others know about my interests				
I will share this message because it's enjoyable to me				

2. Intention to Share (Kamins et al., 1997; DiFonzo and Bordia, 2007)

Having read the above message regarding 'Soft Drink', will you share this message with others?

		Strongly Disagree	*Dis-agree*	*Agree*	*Strongly Agree*
I will share the above message	With my immediate family members.				
	With my friends.				
	With strangers.				
	On Facebook/Twitter/etc., to people on social media.				
	On public review websites				

3. Credibility

Original scale by Gurhan and Maheswaran (2000)

Please describe your perceptions of the information provided to you by answering each of the following questions. For each question please circle one number on each scale that best describes your perception.

In your opinion the claim made was:	*1*	*2*	*3*	*4*	*5*	*6*	*7*	
Not al all believable								Highly believable
Not at all true								Absolutely true
Not at all acceptable								Totally acceptable
Not at all credible								Very credible
Not at all trustworthy								Completely trustworthy

Modified scale

What do you feel about the above message? Please answer by ü the appropriate box.

	Strongly Disagree	*Dis-agree*	*Agree*	*Strongly Agree*
I think that the above message is highly believable				
To me, the above message is completely true				
The above message is totally acceptable to me				
I believe the message is credible				
The above message is completely trustworthy				

4. Novelty

	In your opinion the object is 1 2 3 4 5 6 7				
Original scale Cox and Cox (2002)	New				Old
	Original				Unoriginal
	Unusual				Common
	Familiar				Novel
	Typical				Atypical
Modified scale	*What do you feel about the above message? Please answer by ü the appropriate box.*				
		Strongly Disagree	*Dis-agree*	*Agree*	*Strongly Agree*
	I have come across the above message earlier				
	The above message is new				
	I have commonly heard messages similar to the above message				
	It is the first time that I am reading the above message				
	I think the above message is very familiar				

APPENDIX 2 – DESIGN OF STIMULUS

Code	*Credi-bility*	*Novelty*	*Valence*	*Product Category*	*Message*
1N	Low	High	Negative	Soft Drink	Think before you drink Coke or Pepsi or any another soft drink. Have you ever thought what you drink when you drink an aerated drink? You gulp down carbon dioxide, something that nobody in the world would advise you to do. Two months ago, there was a competition in Delhi University 'Who can drink the most Coke?' The winner drank 8 bottles and died on the spot because too much carbon dioxide in the blood and not enough oxygen. From then on, all soft drinks have been banned from the university.
1P	High	Low	Positive	Soft Drink	Diet cola is the best soft drink that you can consume. Rumors suggest that the new diet soda available in the market is claimed to have 0 calories and 99% water in its ingredients. The diet soda is considered to be safer than all other packaged beverages. The rumor suggests that the diet soda has artificial sweeteners and is sugar free, making it safe on the health requirements of the urban youth.
2N	High	High	Negative	Shampoo	Rumors suggest that shampoo can cause cancer. The word goes around says that substance by the name of Sodium Laureth Sulfate or simply SLS; found in most shampoo can cause cancer. Most of the manufactures use it because it produces a lot of foam and it is cheap. This substance (SLS) is what makes the shampoo foamy, hence most manufacturers use it in their products. Another possible carcinogen is the dandruff prevention medication in shampoo called Ketoconazole. This substance is used in all anti-dandruff shampoo; but new rumors suggest that this too can be dangerous and lead to cancer in regular use.
2P	Low	Low	Positive	Shampoo	The word is going around in the market that shampoo can actually help you to have better hair. Shampoo provides you better hair growth and healthier hair. The use of shampoo regularly can reduce hair fall and increase the longevity of beautiful hair. Rumors even suggest that the more frequently one uses shampoo, the better it is for better hair.

Code	*Credibility*	*Novelty*	*Valence*	*Product Category*	*Message*
3N	Low	Low	Negative	Mobile Phone	'I felt headaches all the time so I went to see a doctor; I suspected that it might have to do with my exposure to mobile phones' said a rumor spreading on social media. In 2011 rumors suggested that radio frequency electromagnetic fields are possibly carcinogenic to humans, based on an increased risk for glioma, a malignant kind of brain cancer, related to the use of wireless phones. The rumor suggests that the use of mobile phones and being in a place with mobile phone towers can both be dangerous.
3P	High	High	Positive	Mobile Phone	There are unconfirmed reports doing rounds on the internet that a new smart phone will be launched in Dec, 2013. Rumors indicate that this flagship device will be priced around Rs. 25,000; and will be called 'Mighty'. It is rumored that the device will have a 'floating touch' feature, which will allow users to navigate their phones without ever touching the display. Samsung is rumored to be provided the phone with a quad core processor and a 50mp resolution camera; this makes it the best camera for any smart phone till now and surely very advanced technology for cheap prices.
4N	High	Low	Negative	Social Media	Rumors have erupted suggesting that major social media websites are providing access to user content for third party advertisements. These rumors suggested that social media websites like Facebook and Google+ have started providing access to advertisers to use your pictures in their ads on the social media. This rumor goes on to say that if you don't explicitly secure your photos with the privacy settings, advertisers will be using your pictures to lure your friends into their ads by using your photos in these ads.
4P	Low	High	Positive	Social Media	Rumors suggest that social media firms like Facebook, Twitter, etc., have partnered with NGOs and charitable organizations to help in social causes. The rumor suggests that when members forward or like a social cause in the social media, the system tracks the popularity of such issues and the partnering NGOs and charitable organizations take up the most popular issues and help them. This is after a lot of scams about 'Facebook donating money for each share, etc.', that this rumor has originated asking people to share and like the social cause that they think needs to be addressed.

APPENDIX 3 – NETLOGO CODE

```
globals [
  color-mode      ;; 0 = normal, 1 = when heard, 2 = times heard
  clique           ;; how many patches have heard the rumor
  previous-clique  ;; value of clique from last tick, for use in the "successive"
plots
]
patches-own [
  times-heard    ;; tracks times the rumor has been heard
  first-heard    ;; clock tick when first heard the rumor
  just-heard?    ;; tracks whether rumor was heard this round -- resets each round
  RELT         ;; Relationship management motivation
  INFO         ;; information sharing motivation
  ANXT         ;; anxiety management motivation
  SELFE        ;; self enhancement motivation
  INTENTIONN   ;; Intention to share the rumor
]
;;; setup procedures
to setup [seed-one?]
  clear-all
  set color-mode 0
  set clique 0
  ask patches
    [ set first-heard -1
      set times-heard 0
      set just-heard? false
      recolor ]
  ifelse seed-one?
    [ seed-one ]
    [ seed-random ]
  reset-ticks
end
to seed-one
  ;; tell the center patch the rumor
  ask patch 0 0
    [ hear-rumor 0 ]
end
to seed-random
  ;; seed with random number of rumor sources governed by init-clique slider
  ask patches with [times-heard = 0]
    [ if (random-float 100.0) < init-clique
```

```
        [ hear-rumor 0 ] ]
end

to go
  if all? patches [times-heard > 0]
    [ stop ]
  ask patches
    [ if times-heard > 0
        [ spread-rumor ] ]
  update
  tick
end
to spread-rumor  ;; patch procedure
  set RELT random 5
  set INFO random 5
  set ANXT random 5
  set SELFE random 5
  let neighbor nobody
  ifelse eight-mode?
    [ set neighbor one-of neighbors ]
    [ set neighbor one-of neighbors4 ]
  set INTENTIONN = (-0.181 + 0.37*RELT + 0.335*INFO + 0.264*ANXT + 0.134*SELFE) ;;
CHANGE THIS EQUATION FOR OTHER MODELS
  if (INTENTIONN >= 2)
  [ask neighbor [ set just-heard? true ]]
end
to hear-rumor [when]  ;; patch procedure
  if first-heard = -1
    [ set first-heard when
      set just-heard? true ]
  set times-heard times-heard + 1
  recolor
end
to update
  ask patches with [just-heard?]
    [ set just-heard? false
      hear-rumor ticks ]
  set previous-clique clique
  set clique count patches with [times-heard > 0]
end
;;; coloring procedures
to recolor  ;; patch procedure
```

```
  ifelse color-mode = 0
    [ recolor-normal ]
    [ ifelse color-mode = 1
      [ recolor-by-when-heard ]
      [ recolor-by-times-heard ] ]
end
to recolor-normal  ;; patch procedure
  ifelse first-heard >= 0
    [ set pcolor white ]
    [ set pcolor blue ]
end
to recolor-by-when-heard  ;; patch procedure
  ifelse first-heard = -1
    [ set pcolor black ]
    [ set pcolor scale-color yellow first-heard world-width 0 ]
end
to recolor-by-times-heard   ;; patch procedure
  set pcolor scale-color green times-heard 0 world-width
end
;;; mouse handling
to spread-rumor-with-mouse
  if mouse-down?
    [ ask patch mouse-xcor mouse-ycor
        [ hear-rumor ticks ]
        display ]
end
; Copyright 1997 Uri Wilensky.
; See Info tab for full copyright and license.
```

CHAPTER TWO

INTEGRATED MEDIA MIX MODEL AND ONLINE FRACTIONAL ATTRIBUTION FOR DIGITAL MARKETING INVESTMENT OPTIMIZATION AND 'HOLISTIC DECISION MAKING'

Veena Ranjeeth and Dinesh R.C.

ABSTRACT

When marketers run a campaign it is common for them to utilize multiple media such as social media, display, flyers. Each media has a publisher, campaign, and so on. Measuring Digital Marketing ROI and shrinking media budgets are the biggest challenges for the CMOs across the globe. There is a need to use scientific methods to more accurately attribute the impact each media has on purchase, in order to optimise investment. About 65% of Dell.com visitors touch more than one digital media before a purchase. Traditional ROI attribution methods such as last touch, first touch, linear, U shaped, etc., are biased and lack the "intelligence" required to make right sense of the large and complicated patterns of consumer behaviour. Media Mix Model (MMM) has been used by some of the organisations to assess brand level ROI. Integrating Online Fractional Attribution (OFA) model, that uses micro factors and consumes touch point level data providing visibility into true media performance at the most granular level, was the key for decision making.

MMM helps assess the impact of offline channels on online and vice versa to help incorporate the halo effect. The unique points of the project are 1. Big data with MMM and OFA integration; 2. Real time planning at granular level; 3. Reallocation of budget depending on cases; and 4. Cross channel mix, frequency, funnel analysis for budget optimisation. The challenge was also in integrating cost, taxonomy, revenue, and touch point data from many vendors. About 25-30% efficiency impact has been assessed from the POC. The implication it has on marketers is that on the average organisations spend about 2.5% of their revenue on marketing spend (Gartner study) and the impact can be extrapolated. Dell has invested in the above and is also integrating visitor demographics for customer segmentation and targeting.

Keywords: Marketing Investment Optimization, Media Mix Model, Online Fractional Attribution, Media Management, Cross channel marketing, Multi-channel attribution, Cross Channel Attribution.

BACKGROUND

CMOs and Media partners need to rethink marketing attribution in order to resolve multi touch point challenge in Media Management

These have been exciting years! Dell went private to focus long term without having to channelize energy on Wall Street and quarterly results. From the year 2006-07 onwards, as a result of increase in competition, inflation and economic downturn, sales margins have taken a hit across the industry. It is understood that CMOs change their marketing strategy in order to improve or maintain Return On Investment (ROI) and accommodate for the shrinking margins. Dell also needs to be proactively optimizing media budgets in such a way that the most effective media gets the highest focus even in terms of investment. Also, it is important to target customers with the right mix of vehicles, with the right message at the right time in order to be efficient and effective.

Dell spends over $100m on marketing. This calls for measuring the effectiveness of different marketing media, campaigns and so on. Dell focuses on its home and work segments. This includes the consumer segment that targets household customer buying, laptops, Desktops etc., Small Business selling precision workstations, Vostro, latitude and so on, apart from Medium business, Public and Large Enterprises targeting Government and Large corporations respectively selling private cloud computing, servers, storage consolidation, solutions and business consulting. The scope of the current work is limited to Consumer and Small Business.

WHY SHOULD WE INTEGRATE ONLINE AND OFFLINE

- All of the media touch points of a visitor to Dell.com share a part of the purchase funnel, viz., awareness, consideration and purchase

- Both online and offline channels influence the purchase
- There are deeper insights generated in using the wholeness of both

SWOT ANALYSIS

Based on SWOT analysis it is understood that it is important to have a method to integrate both online and offline data and derive insights at the deepest level possible in order to find solutions to media management problems and reallocate the budget between online and offline as also within vehicles at the most granular level for ROI impact. This understanding resulted in the project detailed in the following pages. Like many other organizations we were one of the early adopters of the Media Mix Model (MMM) for brand, country and segment level insights for online and offline.

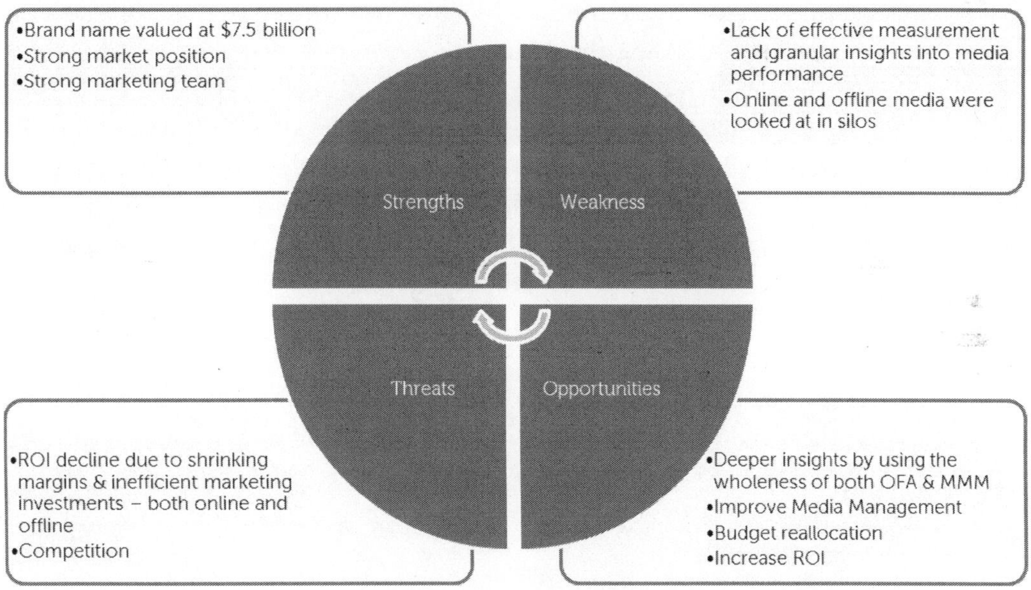

Fig. 1: Swot Analysis

The above mentioned MMM project gave us the top level story, and nothing granular for granular optimization, scenario planning etc. Hence the Online Fractional Attribution model was used for online data and to get deeper insights. As mentioned before, since cookie level tracking means the ability to track the entire path of the customer, we could apply all innovative analytics for insights. Given that MMM is existing in several organizations including Dell, we have detailed steps for OFA, then followed by integration methodology. We have used DMAI framework to explain the steps.

DEFINE PHASE

In this phase it is important to identify what the goal is and translate the business goal into metrics. For example, if the goal is to improve ROI, the metric would be Revenue or Conversions and Spend which may be used to calculate ROI, depending on the organizational focus metrics.

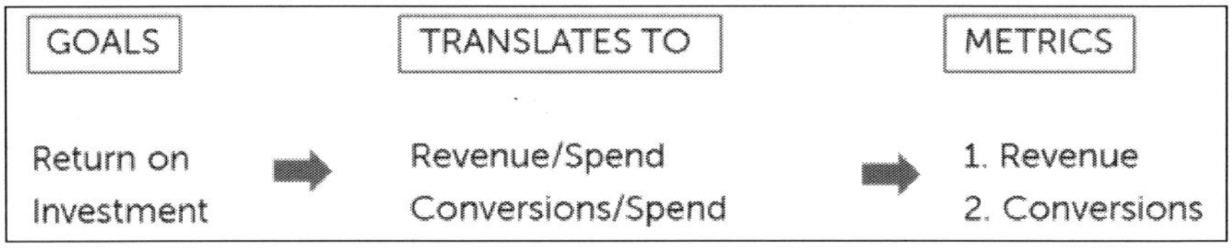

Fig. 2: Translating Goals into Metrics

(a) The next step is to define the path leading to revenue or conversion; this would give us the picture of which online vehicles were involved in the path to conversion, including those that were merely exposed to a visitor (impressions) and those which the visitor to Dell.com had clicked upon (clicks). The purchase funnel consists of the first exposure which creates "awareness" of the brand, mid exposure where the visitor is familiarized with the product and competition options and alternatives, and is called "consideration", and the last exposure during purchase which is called the "Action". Both clicks and impressions influence the customer into making the purchase on Dell.com. Needless to mention, looking at the time lag to conversion would be the first step. Time lag to conversion defines the longest time it took historically for a purchase to happen overall from the visitor's first touch (click/impression). This time would be the window for data extraction of every purchase going backwards till the first touch, so we do not miss any exposure to the brand or product.

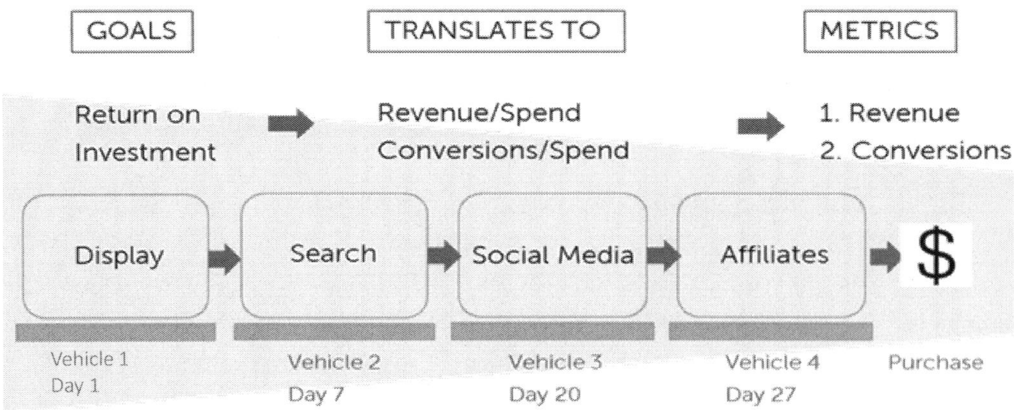

Fig. 3: Media Purchase Funnel

(b) *The Second step is to identify the drivers of the goals from the purchase path*
In this step, goals that are translated into metrics are hence translated into drivers of that metric in the given context. Drivers are attributes of the vehicle that impact the purchase influencing characteristic of the vehicle. They also determine granularity of the Online Fractional Attribution Model. It includes the Ad campaign of the vehicle, the publisher who publishes it such as Data Xu, Placement of the campaign, Creative, keywords if it is search vehicle and other variables such as frequency of that ad exposure on that day, time taken from that ad exposure to purchase and so on.

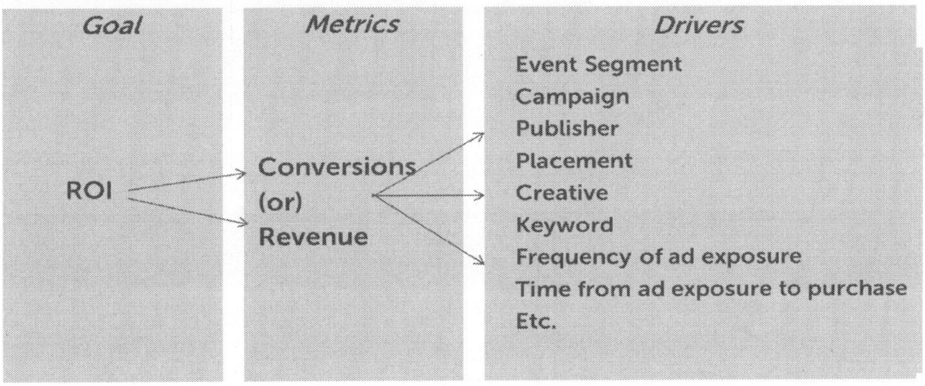

Fig. 4: Translating Metrics into Drivers

MEASURE PHASE

The Measure phase is a three-step process, and the first step involves arriving at the attribution at the highest level selected, let us say vehicle is at the highest level. We use algorithms to calculate the impact of each vehicle in the sequence on the final purchase. We should look at sequences that converted and that did not convert and use a method to calculate the likelihood of conversion given a vehicle. The values are normalized if required. This is followed by splitting the purchase revenue ($) in the ratio of normalized probability between vehicles.

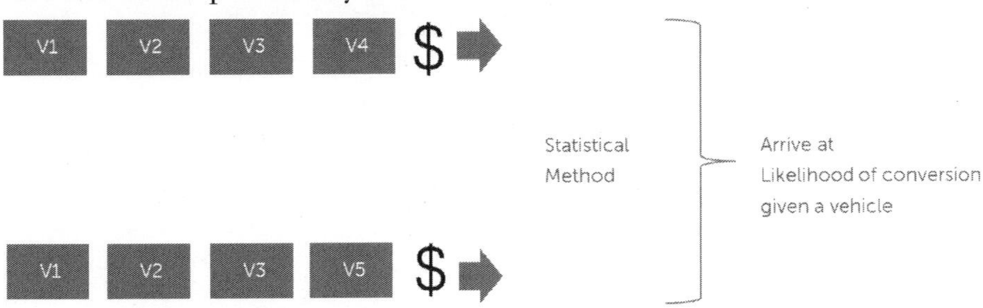

Fig. 5: Likelihood Lift Calculation for Attribution Assessment

The second stage in the attribution step is to apply a statistical technique to arrive at the impact of each of the variables identified in step 2 of the define phase. The coefficients arrived at for attributes should be used to split the attribution revenue of the vehicle arrived at from the previous stage into the impact from campaign, publisher, creative and so on. To go down below at a campaign or publisher level step 1 of Measure phase has to be repeated and incremented likelihood calculated in a similar manner for each campaign, publisher etc. Now that OFA output is ready, the third stage in the process is MMM-OFA integration.

Table 1: Illustration of MMM Output

Vehicle	*Share of Attributed Rev from MMM (%)*
Affiliates	10
Catalog	2
DM	4
Email	10
Insert	5
Magazine	3
Newspaper	20
Online Display	14
Social Media	5
Paid Search	7
TV	20

Using the numbers above, the chart below is shown to pictorially represent the values chosen for illustration purpose.

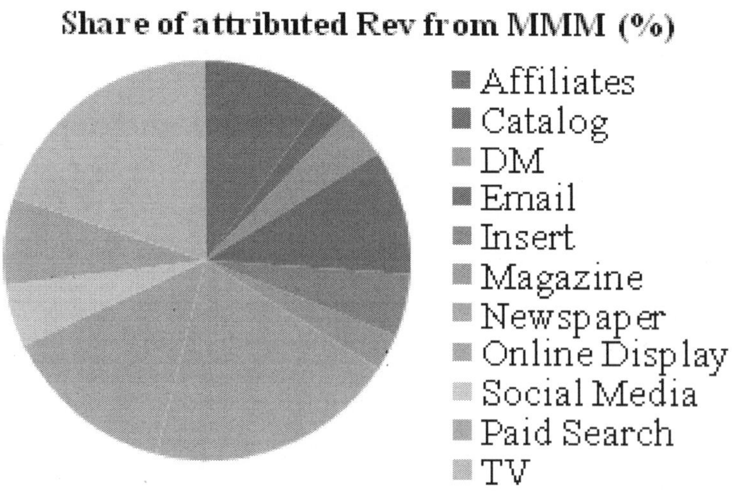

Fig. 6: Illustration of MMM Output

Table 2: Illustration of MMM-OFA Difference

	Affiliates	*Email*	*Display*	*Social Media*	*Paid Search*
	MMM – Considers both online and offline at high level – Top down				
Rev % from MMM	10	10	14	5	7
Rev % from OFA	20	12	30	20	18
Diff	10	2	16	15	11
	OFA – Considers purely online – Bottom up →				

Net effect of Impact of offline marketing on online purchase & impact of online marketing on offline

Needs to be knocked off from OFA

As shown above, in order to integrate MMM and OFA, it is important to compare the ratio of attributed revenue or conversions at vehicle level for all online vehicles between MMM and OFA and knock off the difference seen, to ensure that OFA uses MMM attribution of conversions in order to account for the impact of offline vehicles on online and online vehicles on offline and so on.

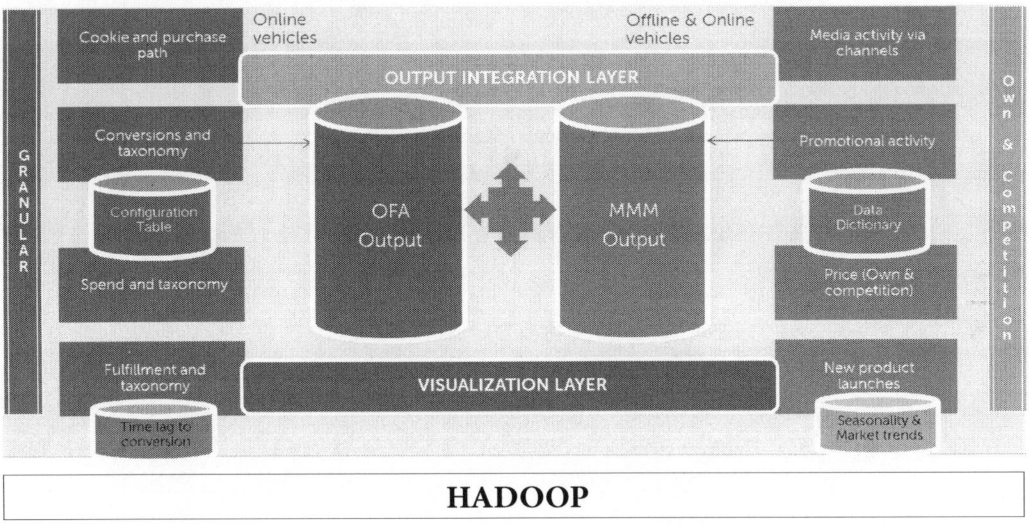

Fig. 7: Architecture of Integration

TOP THREE ASSUMPTIONS IN MMM-OFA INTEGRATION

1. Conversion segment definitions match between the two
2. Time window should match
3. Online media vehicles considered should be the same

CHALLENGES IN CROSS MEDIA ATTRIBUTION IF DONE AS A WHOLE

Cross media attribution poses multiple challenges such as tracking, linking online and offline media, changing customer behavior, and so on.

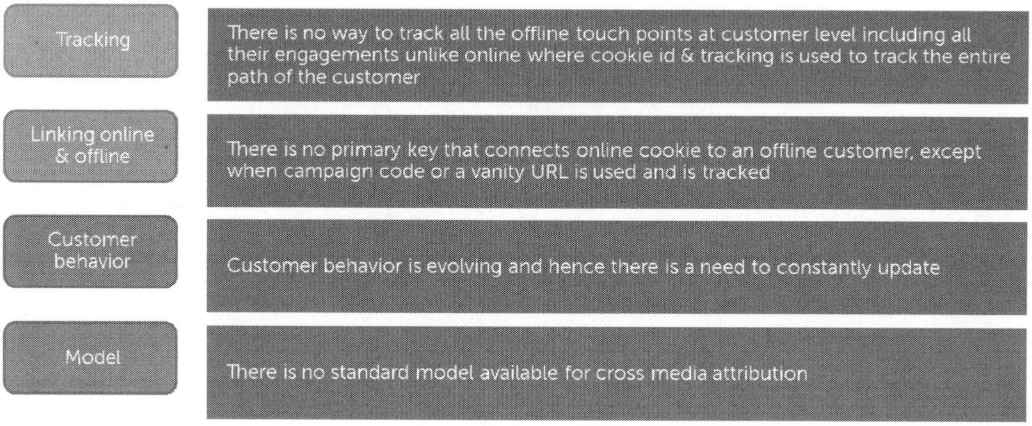

Fig. 8: Challenges

ANALYZE PHASE

In the Analyze phase, attribution output is used for deeper analysis for marketing insights and optimization.

In the short term, we measure the performance of vehicles, campaigns, publishers, placements, creative etc with revenue arrived at using attribution and actual spend on these. ROI is calculated as Revenue by Spend.

(a) *Frequency Capping Analysis*: Frequency is the number of times a visitor is exposed to an ad in a day. The assumption is that the higher the frequency higher the returns or conversions. This is not always true, in fact there is a point of diminishing returns. A plot of cumulative reach vs. frequency would give a picture of the point of saturating or diminishing returns. This could be used for frequency capping and the spend saved could be used to expand a publisher who is performing well.

(b) *Cross media synergy*: A plot of media mix and conversion rate would show that conversion rate is better when there is a mix of vehicles rather than one vehicle. Also mix of certain specific vehicles would show higher impact on the returns than others. This could be used for customizing messages to use the right combination of vehicles for ad messages.

(c) *Vehicle purchase funnel analysis*: Vehicles that are first touch points in the purchase path create awareness about the brand to the visitor. E.g. Social media could expose a person to a new brand. It is called the opener. Vehicles that are the last touch-points before a purchase assist in conversion. E.g.

Bookmarks (Referred) are called closers. Vehicle touch-points in between assist in consideration and are called advancers. E.g. search. Analysis of the share of reach and vehicle position would indicate the effectiveness of each vehicle as an opener, advancer and closer, with which we could customize the vehicle and mix depending on the intent for maximum impact.

(d) *Halo effect*: Halo effect is the psychological effect that something has, based on past experience with something related to it. E.g. we might buy a product of a brand due to the positive experience or exposure we have had from another product of the same brand in the past. Similarly we might get influenced to buy a product from a different segment due to our experience or exposure with another segment. This could be applied to search. There are search terms with high traffic and low revenue which search teams typically ignore as they are looked at as giving low returns. But a halo analysis of keywords used by a visitor before making a purchase would show that although the last search term resulted in the purchase, the rest of the keywords or search terms were assist keywords. They are high on traffic but would not show any revenue impact based on last touch attribution.

With the right mix of vehicles and having the right message at the right place at the right time would ensure that we improve time to convert and returns.

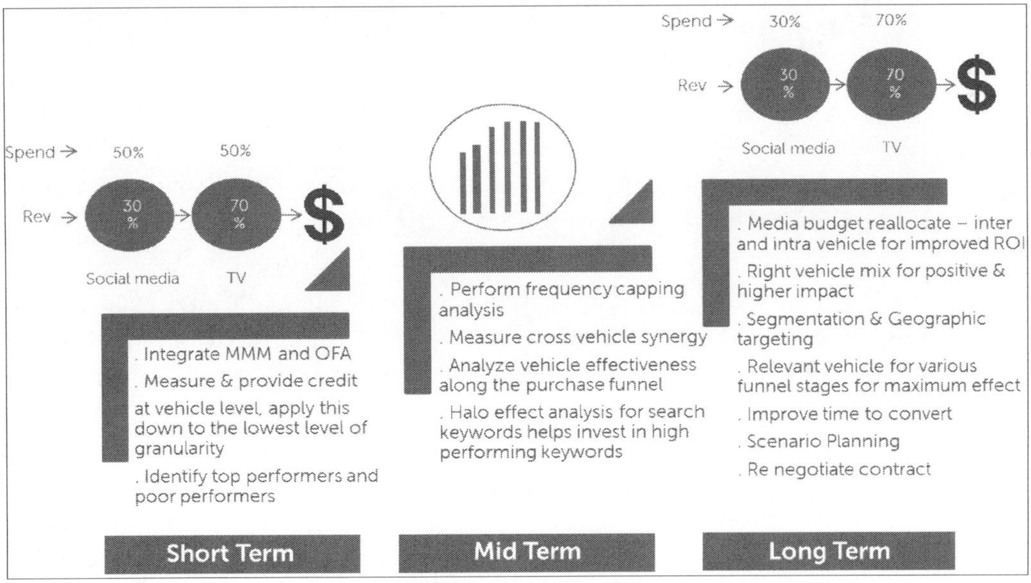

Fig. 9: End to End Media Management Using MMM-OFA Integration

IMPROVE PHASE

In the improve phase, the above insights are used for marketing implementation, including spend optimization based on performance and impact measured. This is a continuous process. We could also do customer geographic and demographic segmentation and measure performance and have targeted messages.

IMPORTANT THINGS TO BE KEPT IN MIND

- Adoption can be very challenging if not managed well. Change management by involving stakeholders in all stages of the project is crucial.
- It is important to have leadership involvement and goal revision as the next step to the MEASURE phase in order to ensure that business stakeholders are aligned and get started through a smooth transition.
- Revenue and spend reconciliation should be a step that should not be kept for last. As and when data feeds are set, it is important to ensure that total values match across different internal/external sources of data and historical reports (or) the reason for difference is known and noted.

CONCLUSION

Attribution modelling is very challenging and does not provide any value unless it is put to use in the right place at the right time. Also if we understand the nuances well we can avoid various roadblocks it poses. With more than 65-70% of the visitors touching more than one medium, taking Dell.com as an example, there is an attribution problem. Last touch revenue would not solve the complex marketing problems in the current environment with highly evolved customer behaviour. Application of these techniques and insights have given benefits to many organisations, although integration of MMM and OFA is an innovation and has added benefit. Attribution is getting even more complex with ever changing consumer behavior and advancements in mobility since it is not easy to track the same customer who switched devices. If sponsorship can be made available one should apply the right attribution methodology and benefit, 15% to 20% ROAS impact can be expected from applying this.

REFERENCES

Analyticbridge. (2013). *Attribution Modeling vs Market Mix Modeling. Data intelligence, Business analytics forum discussions*. Retrieved from: http://www.analyticbridge.com/forum/topics/attribution-modeling-vs-market-mix-modeling

Bayesia (2012). *Tutorial: Marketing Mix Optimization with Bayesian Networks and BayesiaLab* Retrieved from: http://www.youtube.com/watch?v=TThR-xqcdeo

Gartner (2013). *Key Findings From U.S. Digital Marketing Spending Survey, 2013.* Retrieved from: http://www.gartner.com/technology/research/digital-marketing/digital-marketing-spend-report.jsp

GfK MRI Market Solutions (2011). *Marketing Mix Modeling and Media Inputs.* Retrieved from: http://www.magazine.org/sites/default/files/Marketing-Mix-Modeling.pdf

Goldenberg, Georgiy, Jung, Dz-Mou, Lin, Long-Ji, & Natkovich, Olga L. (2005). Patent No. WO 2005006140 A2, Jan 20, 2005. *Methods to attribute conversions for online advertisement campaigns.*

Karel, David (2013). *Marketing Daily. Demystifying the marketing funnel: Lexicon.* Retrieved from: http://www.mediapost.com/publications/article/194256/demystifying-the-marketing-funnel-lexicon.html

Sequent Partners (2013). *Current state of marketing Mix models, A report for the Council for Research Excellence.* Retrieved from: http://www.researchexcellence.com/documents/misc/Sequent_Partners_Modeling_White_Paper_CRE_Branded.pdf

Visual IQ (n.d.). *IQ Envoy*, IQ Sage. http://www.visualiq.com/products/iq-intelligence-suite

Willcocks, Roger (2013). *E-commerce marketing: where your website traffic will come from & how.* Screen Pages. Retrieved from: http://www.screenpages.com/about/articles/ecommerce-traffic

PART TWO-B

PREDICTIVE MODELLING

Predictive modeling refers to a collection of statistical techniques having the common goal to find a mathematical relationship between the "dependent" variable and the 'independent' or 'predictor' variables. It is a general term for using models to support decision making. The goal may be to identify the target group for a marketing campaign, the product assortment that needs to be stocked or the possibility of fraud/default. Predictive modeling is undoubtedly the most exciting aspect in the emerging and highly sought after field of data analytics. Nearly every business in competitive markets has realized the need to use predictive modeling to remain ahead of the curve. Managers in FMCG, retail, banking and healthcare industries are the most active users of predictive analytics. The availability of a huge repository of data and emergence of improved software has enabled the managers in identifying real-time insights.

In their paper, Praveen Srinivasan and Ramya Chittigalan discuss the use of Artificial Neural Networks technique in risk prediction of the customer. Both the internal data of the Insurance Company (from claims, underwriting and marketing functions) and data from external sources like Social Media; Advisory Organizations etc. are used for the analysis. Finally, they discuss the opportunity for better sales conversion, hit ratio and resource utilization by the sales force using the combination of the list of profitable prospective customers with location data.

Retail chains have been known to run loyalty programs with the aim to gain bigger wallet share of the customers. These loyalty cards are the source of a wide range of information pertaining to card holders and their purchase behavior. In her paper, Aparna Mukherjee, explores the use of Quantile Regression in identifying the ideal profile of customers who would generate profit for the company through loyalty card usage. She also establishes its advantage over OLS, which cannot examine the differences of various customer groups or account for customer heterogeneity.

Multicollinearity is a common problem when developing predictive models. It occurs when there are high correlations among predictor variables, leading to unreliable and unstable estimates of regression coefficients. In their paper, Snigdha Pain and Vinayak Deshpande, discuss the performance of Principle Component Regression (PCR) in presence of multicollinearity. Under this method, the principal components of the explanatory variables are used as predictors instead of regressing the dependent variable on the explanatory variables directly.

CHAPTER THREE

APPLICATION OF ARTIFICIAL NEURAL NETWORKS FOR ENHANCED UNDERWRITING RISK PREDICTION AND PRICING IN INSURANCE

Praveen Srinivasan and Ramya Chittigala

ABSTRACT

One of the major goals of any Insurance company is to increase its profitability. One way of doing this is to help the underwriters predict the risk of customer prospects better by pricing the products accordingly. For targeting the right prospects at the right time and rating them accurately, we need advanced predictive models to give more accurate predictions regarding the risk of insuring the customers, and thus be profitable. Further, the location information of the expected profitable customer prospects could be used as input to the company's sales force for better sales.

To build a better predictive model, we capitalize on the internal data of the Insurance Company (from claims, underwriting and marketing functions) and capture relevant data about existing customers from various external sources like Social Media, Advisory Organizations and others. We use this as training data to perform data mining using the Artificial Neural Networks technique. Now we use the prospective customers' data obtained through several sources as test data on the predictive model designed to predict the risk of insuring the customer and divide them into various classes of risk.

Based on the risk-class predicted, underwriters will be able to better predict whether to insure the risk or not and price their products accordingly. After generating the list of profitable prospective customers by using the predictive model, we combine this information with location data of the prospects obtained through various external sources, which in turn will be used by the appropriate sales force. This will help them in better sales conversion, hit ratio and resource utilization by targeting the right customers with the right knowledge at the right time and improving CRM.

INTRODUCTION

In the insurance industry, statistical techniques have been used across functions like claims, underwriting, product development etc. Techniques like Regression, Anova, T-models, etc. have been used by underwriters for designing various models that improve decision-making capabilities. Artificial Neural Networks is one of the recent techniques that has permeated into the world of insurance underwriting and shows a lot of promise in this sector. In this paper, we will mainly concentrate on the artificial neural networks technique and how it can be widely used by the underwriter to predict the risk of the customer.

Artificial Neural Networks

Artificial Neural Networks are nothing but crude electronic models of the human brain's neural structure. In simple terms, an Artificial Neural Network is defined as a computing system which is made up of a number of highly interconnected processing elements. Most artificial neural networks are used to approximate functions that are generally complicated or unknown.

Every neural network has 3 layers: Input Layer, Hidden Layer and Output Layer. The number of nodes or neurons in the Input, Hidden and the Output layers will change depending on the problem in hand. The following diagram shows a simple artificial neural network with a single node in the hidden layer:

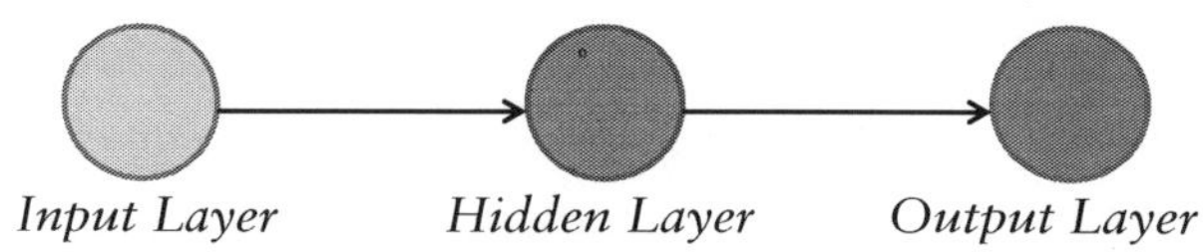

Fig.1: A Simple Artificial Neural Network

In an Artificial Neural Network, every node or neuron in the hidden node will have 2 parameters associated with it:

1. Weights and
2. Activation Function

The output of the neurons or nodes in the hidden layer is totally dependent on the inputs, their respective weights and the corresponding activation function. The activation function is used to transform the activation level of the node or neuron into an output signal. The output signal strength will be determined by the weight associated with the input signal of the node.

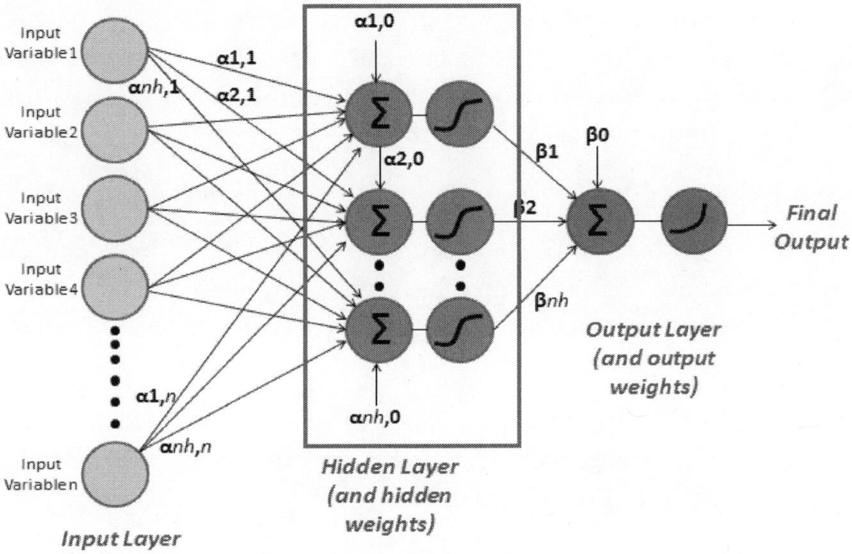

Fig. 2: The Different Layers of an Artificial Neural Network

Neural networks support a wide range of activation functions. Some of the commonly used functions are – Identity, Sigmoid, Logistic, Ramp, Hyperbolic and Exponential functions.

Function	Definition	Range
Identity	x	(-inf,+inf)
Logistic	$\frac{1}{1-e^{-1}}$	(0,+1)
Hyperbolic	$\frac{e^{x}-e^{-x}}{e^{x}+e^{-x}}$	(-1,+1)
-Exponential	e^{-x}	(0, +inf)
Softmax	$\frac{e^{x}}{\sum_i e^{x_i}}$	(0,+1)
Unit sum	$\frac{x}{\sum_i x_i}$	(0,+1)
Square root	$\sqrt{x}$	(0, +inf)
Sine	$\sin(x)$	[0,+1]
Ramp	$\begin{Bmatrix} -1 & x \leq -1 \\ x & -1 < x < +1 \\ +1 & x \geq +1 \end{Bmatrix}$	[-1,+1]
Step	$\begin{Bmatrix} 0 & x < 0 \\ +1 & x \geq 0 \end{Bmatrix}$	[0,+1]
Sigmoid	$1 \div (1+e^{-x})$	[0,+1]

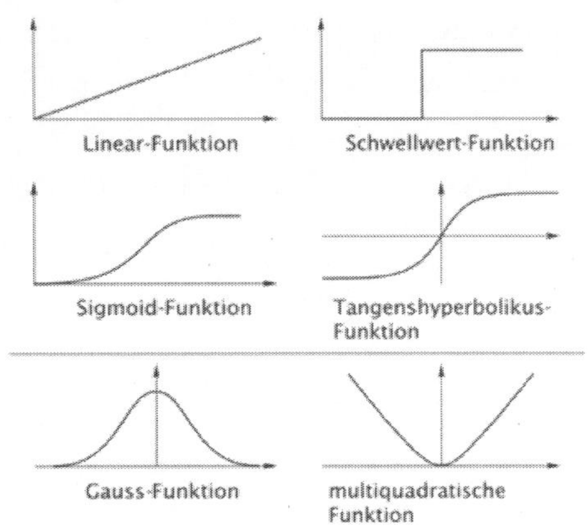

Fig. 3: Commonly Used Activation Functions

Types of Artificial Neural Networks

There are 2 types of artificial neural networks:

1. **The Feed-Forward (FF) ANN:** The Feed-Forward neural network is considered the simplest form of artificial neural network. Here, the information moves in only one direction, i.e. forward (from the input nodes through the hidden nodes to the output node). In this type of neural network, there are no feedback connections, that is, there are no connections from the output of one layer to the input of the same layer or the previous layers.
2. **Recurrent Network:** The Recurrent networks are those that contain feedback connections. In short, they have bi-directional data flow and propagate data from the later processing stages to the previous stages as feedback.

The Feed-Forward (FF) neural network is a Multi-Layer Perceptron (MLP), which uses supervised learning. Here the neural network is provided with a target variable (either single or categorical) and the network fits an appropriate function that can be used to predict the target variable.

In our analysis, we use the "Back-Propagation" algorithm for our layered feed-forward network. The back-propagation algorithm uses "supervised" learning. Here, we provide the algorithms of the inputs and the output we want our artificial neural network to compute. Then, the actual and the expected results are noted and the error is calculated.

Using this error, the scaling factor is calculated. The scaling factor is nothing but how much higher or lower the output should have been to match the desired output. Thus, the "Scaling Factor" is back-propagated as feedback to the previous layers to allow the system to "learn" the training data. The weights of the nodes are adjusted accordingly to minimize the errors in the output.

Predictive Modeling through Data Mining

Data Mining is one of the inherent techniques used to build any predictive model. Insurers have been employing data mining techniques across functions by harvesting information from the existing datasets from their data-warehouses.

The Data Mining process comprises of three main stages –

1. Data Acquisition
2. Pre-processing data
3. Data Exploration.

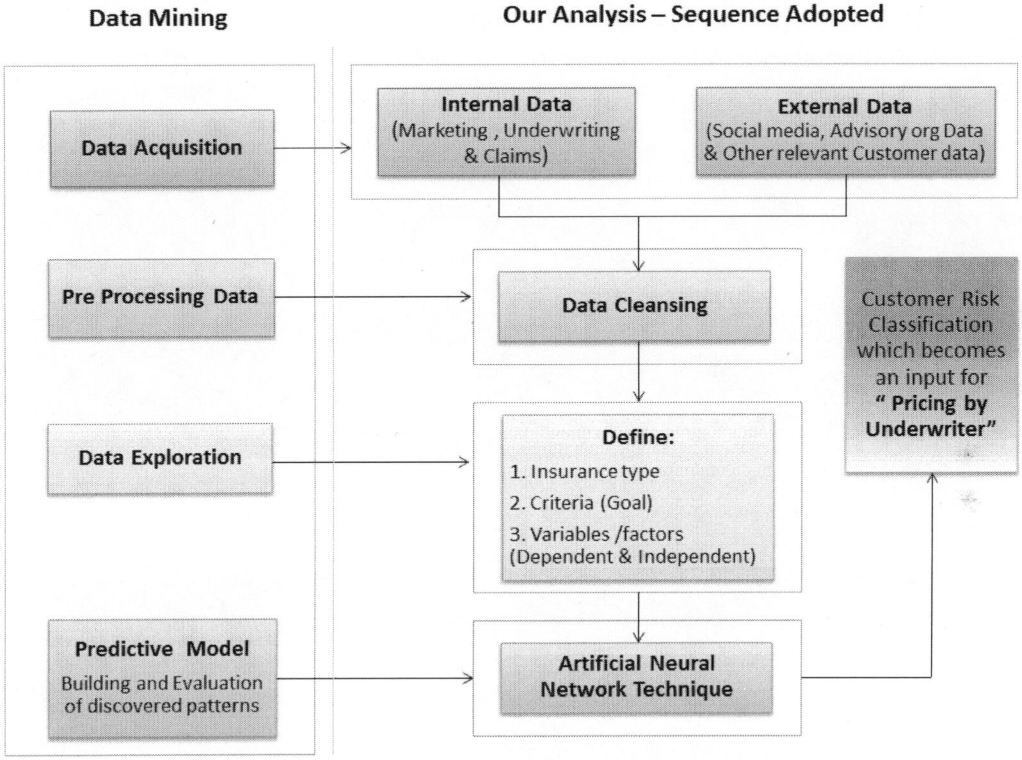

Fig. 4: Predictive Analytics through Data Mining using Artificial Neural Networks

Data Acquisition

During Data Acquisition, the data for each customer is gathered from both internal and external sources accordingly.

1. **Internal Sources** – Data from various teams inside the Insurance company like Sales, marketing, Underwriting and Claims will be utilized
2. **External Sources** – Social media (Facebook, PInterest, Instagram and Twitter) and other sources like blogs, personal WebPages, etc.

Pre-Processing Data

There are two stages during pre-processing of Data:

1. **Data Selection** – This involves choosing the types of data that are to be used for our analysis. This may include both internal and external data

2. **Data Transformation** – Once the data has been selected, the data has to be cleaned up and has to be transformed into a format that can be used for data mining

In our analysis, we classify customers based on the type of insurance purchased.

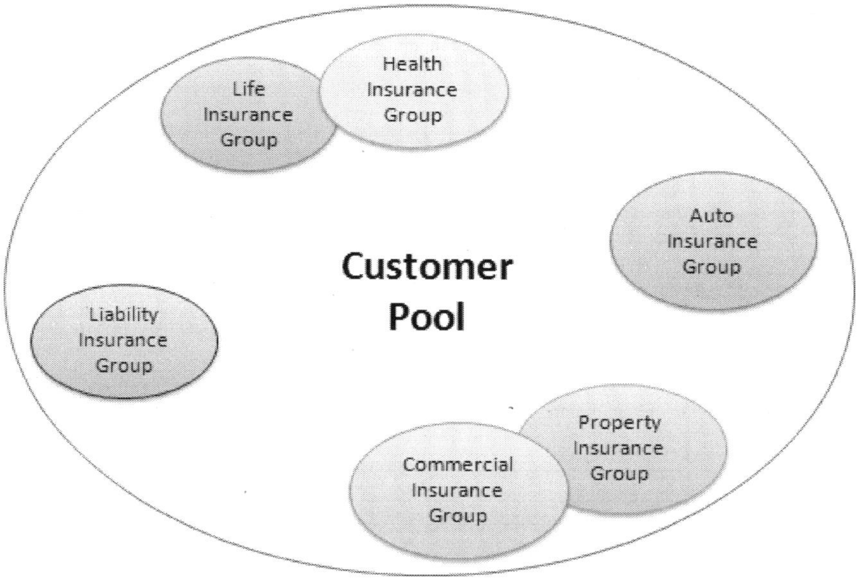

Fig. 5: Classification of the Customer Pool into Various Insurance Groups

Data Exploration

Under data exploration, a particular insurance class is chosen and the variables which are significant for underwriting decisions are defined for that respective class. Variables can be of two types – Dependent and Independent. In our analysis, the underwriter designates the various independent and dependent variables. The output variable, which is usually a dependent variable (in this case, the Customer Risk Classification), will be dependent on a number of input variables, which are independent.

BUILDING THE PREDICTIVE MODEL – METHODOLOGY

Classification of Existing Data for defined Insurance Classes

Each customer with all the relevant details for all the required variables is called an 'Observation'. The entire observation list is divided into three non-overlapping subsets – Training data, Validation Data and Test Data.

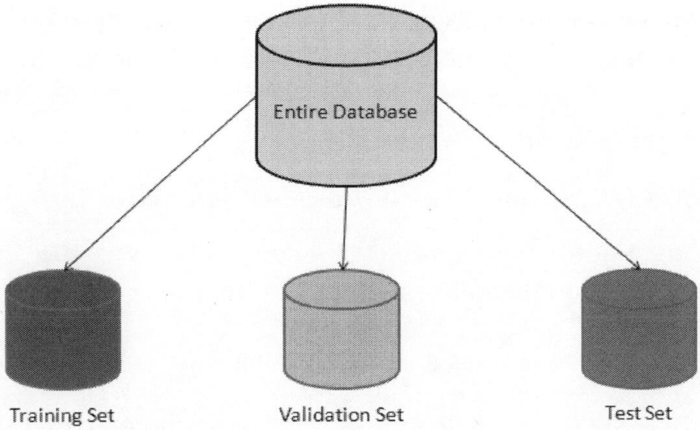

Fig. 6: Classification of Existing Data into sub-sets

Training Set

This data set is used to fit the model based on pre-determined input-output combinations.

Validation Set

To evaluate the performance of the fitted function on data points different from those used for fitting the model, i.e. the cases or scenarios that were not considered during the training set. This would give a hint on whether the function was over-fitted or not. An over-fitted function will exhibit a poor performance when tested on the validation set. So, basically the validation set will help affirm whether the model has cracked the underlying structure of the problem, in our case, the risk of the customer.

Based on the performance of the model with the validation set as the input, the performance of the model is improved by adjusting the number of neurons or nodes in the hidden layer. And the entire training – validation cycle is repeated multiple times with different number of nodes and the number of nodes that gives the best validation data set performance is retained.

Test Set

The performance of the model is finally evaluated by using the data points that were never used previously, i.e. the test data set, to give a completely unbiased measure of the performance that can be expected when we test the model on prospective customers' data.

We will now explore more about the various phases (Input layer, Hidden nodes and Output layer) of an Artificial Neural Network.

Artificial Neural Network Components

Output (Dependent) Variable – Customer Risk Categorization

The output dependent variable in our analysis is the Customer Risk which is categorized into the following four risk buckets:

Preferred Risk

Customers with lower than average risk when compared to the peers in the same homogenous group.

Standard Risk

Customers with more or less the same or average risk when compared to the peers in the same homogenous group.

Substandard Risk

Customers with higher than average risk, but still insurable for a slightly higher premium when compared to the peers in the same homogenous group.

Declined Risk

Customers with very high risk which the company cannot afford to insure (or insure profitably).

In our analysis, even though the output variable is standard (Risk of the Customer divided into 4 categories), the following can change:

Input Variables

The underwriter, through historical experience and various statistical analyses like regression, determines the important variables that determine the risk of the customer for each and every type of insurance. So every insurance type will have different variables or characteristics of the customer that determine the risk of the customer.

Note: Before using the predictive model, the underwriter has to ensure that there is no 'Multi-Collinearity' problem, i.e. the independent input variables are not correlated to each other. If the variables are highly correlated, collinearity has to be handled through techniques like increasing the sample size, removing the most inter-correlated variables from the analysis etc.

Hidden Nodes

The number of nodes in the hidden layer can also vary depending on the complexity of the insurance type. The neural network model represents the input – output relationship through the usage of mathematical functions. Simple mathematical functions can be expressed with a lesser number of nodes whereas complex functions need multiple nodes. The number of nodes will be finalized during the "machine – learning" stage of our analysis.

Statistical Techniques Employed

The following flow diagram shows the various techniques that are performed at various stages of the predictive modeling process:

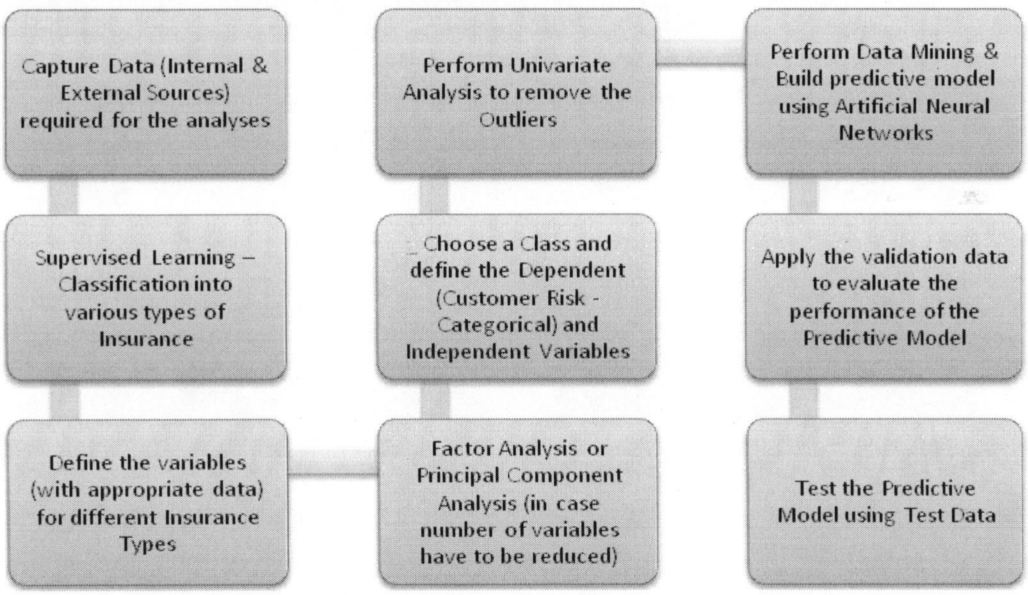

Fig. 7: Techniques Employed at Various Stages of Predictive Modeling Process

We make use of the following statistical techniques depending on the need or appropriateness:

1. **Classification/Discriminant Analysis** – This is used to identify to which cluster or pool a new observation belongs to, depending on the existing training data

2. **Univariate Analysis** – this is mostly done to remove the outliers
3. **Factor Analysis or Principal Component Analysis** – When the underwriter feels that he can categorize a large number of interrelated variables using their common aspects, he uses factor analysis
4. **Artificial Neural Network** – Artificial neural network can be used to build the predictive model by forecasting the behavior of the dependent output variable (Risk Classification in our analysis) based on the various independent input variables.

Training and Testing the Predictive Model

After finalizing the variables that are considered to be significant by the underwriter, the artificial neural network model is trained using the training data. Each observation's values for the corresponding variables are given as the input to the ANN. The model sends a particular output. This output is compared with the actual output and the model learns and adjusts the 'weights' of the corresponding inputs to the 'activation nodes' of the hidden nodes. When the accuracy of the model does not increase beyond a certain point, the number of nodes in the hidden layer is increased. This will help the ANN to generate more complicated functions that might increase the accuracy of the output.

After training the predictive model (ANN) with the training data and validating with the Validation Data, now the test data is used to check the accuracy of the predictive model. The obtained output from the predictive model is compared with the already available actual output of the test data. This gives the accuracy, or in statistical terms, 'confidence' with which we can predict the risk of the customer.

Risk Classification and Pricing for the Future Prospective Customers

By just capturing the relevant data for the future customers and feeding the data as input to the Predictive ANN Model, the underwriter can directly predict (at a certain confidence level) under which risk class the prospective customer falls into thus saving him precious time to concentrate on other more complex insurance deals. Based on the risk category into which the prospective customer falls, the underwriter can price the premium accordingly.

In a nut-shell, the following diagram summarizes the process flow of the entire predictive modeling used in our analysis:

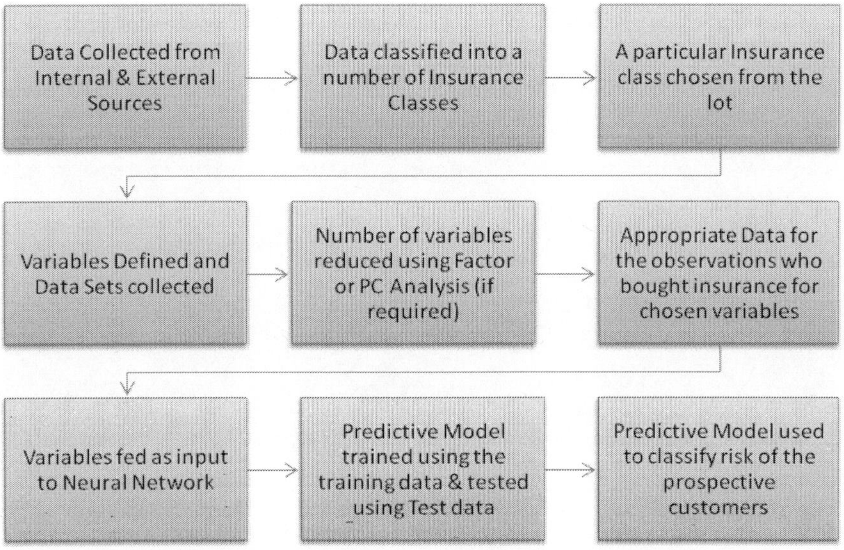

Fig. 8: Predictive Modeling Flow Summarized

Application of Predictive Model in Life and Auto Insurance – A Real Life Scenario

In our analysis below, we are considering 2 basic types of Insurance – one from the Life Insurance side and the other from the P&C Insurance side. Though the concept and its application remains the same for both, the significant factors that determine the risk of the customer will differ depending on the type of insurance that the customer is applying for (even for the same customer).

Here, we are considering two basic insurance policy types – a traditional life insurance policy and an auto insurance policy. We have a customer A, who is looking for a typical life insurance and an auto insurance policy. The following discussion helps us understand the various details that are sought:

The most essential information required by the underwriter to determine whether customer A is insurable or not is typically collected by an insurance company during the initial application processing stage itself. And the type of information collected also depends on the type of insurance that the customer is looking for.

For example, if the customer is looking for a life insurance, the type of information needed to determine the risk of the customer will depend on the type of life insurance policy (for example, term life insurance, whole life insurance, universal life insurance etc.), the coverage needed ($1 million, $10 million, $20000 etc) and other endorsements (accidental death benefit, disability benefits etc). For instance, if a customer needs a health insurance with a very high coverage amount, the insurance company might ask the customer to undergo various medical tests as apt (which might not be required for a simple term life insurance policy with a low face amount).

Similarly in the case of auto insurance, the amount of information required to issue an auto insurance policy depends on the type of coverage (e.g. Bodily Injury Liability, Comprehensive Coverage, Personal Injury Protection etc.), coverage and riders/endorsements.

In our analysis, we consider some of the following important variables:

1. Demographic Risk
2. Customer Behavioral Risk
3. Financial Risk
4. Occupational Risk
5. Life style/Hereditary Diseases Risk
6. Information from external sources
7. Additional Coverage/Endorsements
8. Family Risk Influence and
9. Residential/Locality Safety/Risk Standards
10. Family Risk Influence
11. Vehicle Risk

The above list is only a sample list of variables and not all encompassing. The underwriter can decide which variables are significant and will be appropriate to determine the risk. The variables are chosen by the underwriter only when they are both relevant and significant for a particular type of insurance.

The Tables 1 capture information about the different factors/variables that were considered important by the underwriter in predicting the risk and used in the analysis.

The Network Diagrams (Fig. 9) show a sample snapshot of the Predictive Model built for both a Traditional Life Insurance and an Auto Insurance using Artificial Neural Networks.

Traditional Life Insurance

Table 1: Independent Input Variables for the ANN – Traditional Life Insurance

Input Variables Considered Important by Underwriter	*Factors Affecting the Input Variable*	*Factor Analysis Required – Yes/No?*
Life Style & Hereditary Diseases Risk	Age, Gender, Type of Occupation, Habits, History of family illness, Current and past medical status, Master health check-up parameters, Past Health history	Yes

Input Variables Considered Important by Underwriter	*Factors Affecting the Input Variable*	*Factor Analysis Required – Yes/No?*
Customer Behavioral Risk	Past Insurance details (including type of insurance taken, frequency and severity of claims, record of insurance fraud, in-time premium payment, etc.), Current Insurance details	Yes
Family Risk Influence	Marital Status, Number of children, Beneficiary's dependency on the Insurance Claim Amount	Yes
Occupational Risk	Occupation, Type of Occupation, Regular Mode of Travel, Travel to foreign locations	Yes
Residential & Locality Safety/Risk Standards (Demographic factors)	Current and Permanent address details	No
Additional Coverage/ Endorsements	Personal interests & avocations, endorsements applied and additional coverage	Yes
Financial Risk	Income, Credit Rating score, Past insurance details	Yes
Information from External Sources	Input from advisory organizations, social media – Facebook, LinkedIn, Twitter, etc.	Yes

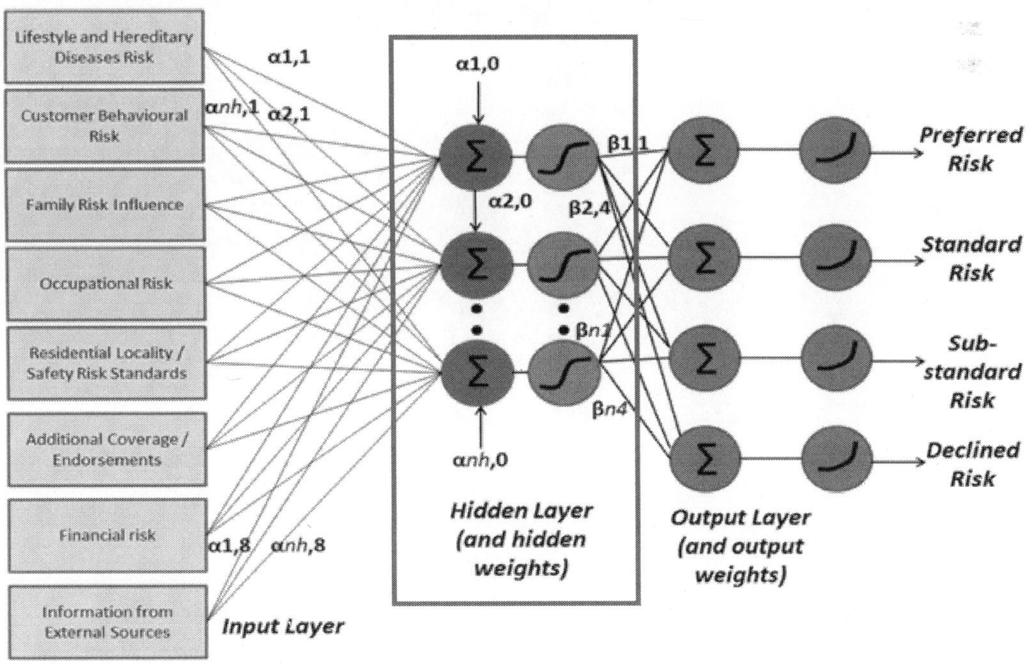

Fig. 9: Traditional Life Insurance – Predictive Model using Artificial Neural Networks

Auto Insurance

Table 2: Input Variables for the ANN – Auto Insurance

Input Variables considered important by Underwriter	*Factors affecting the Input Variable*	*Factor Analysis Required – Yes/No?*
Demographic Risk	Age, Gender, Marital status, number of children, Current and permanent locations of stay	Yes
Attitude/purpose of applying for an auto insurance policy	Past auto insurance details (including type of insurance taken, frequency and severity of claims, record of insurance fraud, in-time premium payment, etc.), Current auto insurance details	Yes
Occupational Risk	Occupation, type of occupation, average distance covered as part of occupation, regular mode of transport, frequency of travelling by auto-insured vehicle, place of travel	Yes
Driving risk	Driving license details, Years of driving experience, Input from Transport & Legal authorities (Past records of – Speeding tickets, drunken driving cases, accidents on record, etc.)	Yes
Habits & Hobbies	Details of hobbies and everyday activities (late-night partying, social drinking, racing enthusiasts, etc.), Personal Interest and Avocations	Yes
Vehicle Risk	Vehicle model, Features, Year of Purchase, Place of purchase, Year of Manufacture, Present condition, Past/known issues, Manufacturer safety records, Maintenance records	Yes
Financial risk	Income, Credit Rating score, Past auto-insurance details	Yes
Data from External Sources	Input from advisory organizations, social media – Facebook (Social posts and statuses – New baby in family, wedding, purchase/interest in new vehicles, etc.), LinkedIn, Twitter – input from in-built auto sensors and Telematics, input from drive-monitoring apps	Yes

Thus from the predictive model (Fig. 10), the risk of the customer is predicted by inputting the values for the various input variables. The model will help to speed up the underwriting decisions and insure the customers faster and appropriately (premium based on the risk class).

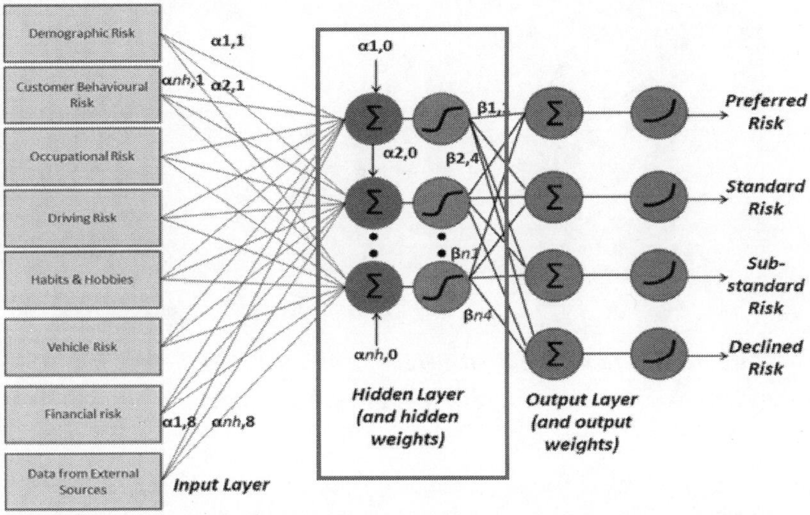

Fig. 10: Auto Insurance – Predictive Model using Artificial Neural Networks

Predictive Model using ANN – Advantages

The main advantages of Artificial Neural Networks over other techniques are as follows:

1. Highly accurate as they can even approximate non-linear, complex mappings
2. In Artificial neural networks we do not make any apriori assumptions about the form of interactions between the various factors (variables) or the distribution of data
3. Useful for dynamic environments as they can freshly be updated with new data
4. Noise tolerance and flexibility with respect to incomplete, missing or noise data
5. Neural networks can be implemented in parallel hardware

Note: The Appendix gives information about why artificial neural networks are gaining more popularity when compared to other techniques like regression.

Predictive Model using ANN– Limitations

1. One of the major limitations of using Artificial Neural Networks is there is no standard method to determine the optimal number of nodes or neurons to solve the problem in hand. So even in our analysis, the underwriter should be careful about the problem of "Overfitting" the data which is explained in Fig. 11.

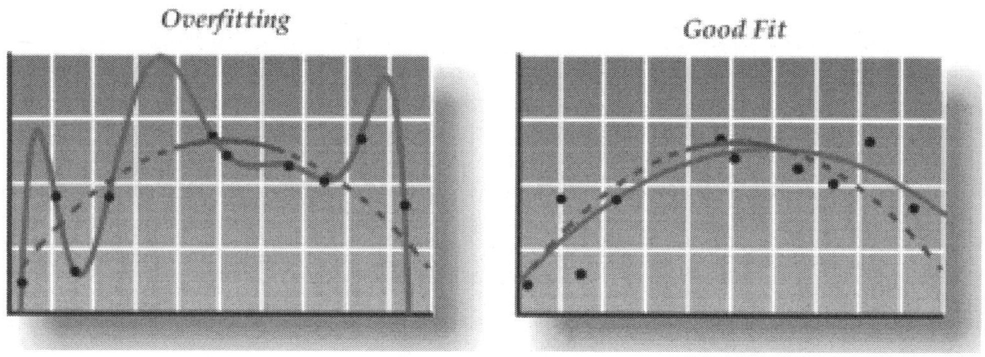

Fig. 11: Overfitting Problem

The more the number of nodes or neurons, the harder the neural network will try to over-fit the data. So, it is important that the data is not over-fit or under-fit to predict the output.

2. It is also difficult to select a set of observations for training data that fully describes the problem in hand to be solved. So, the underwriter has to tactfully select the training data that would depict all the possible scenarios that are possible (at least to the maximum possible extent).

Managerial Implications

1. Saves the precious time of the underwriter and allow him focus on underwriting more complex products or engaging in more strategic work
2. Better risk predictions by the underwriter boils down to better Organizational Net Profit
3. Gives opportunity to mould business decisions based on their existing market segments for future products
4. Understanding customers better to serve them beyond expectations (Improve CRM)
5. Engage the sales force more efficiently by referring them to more promising customers that will increase the hit ratio and better sales conversion
6. The same approach could be applied across products which will lead to better efficiencies across business units.

CONCLUSION

Statistical analyses have been used for years across functions in the insurance industry. Because of the ever increasing demands and needs of the customer, insurers try to develop customized and complex products. Artificial Neural Networks technique has been adopted across various industries over the past few years and has been becoming increasingly popular in insurance industry too. Though alternative techniques like regression also yield good results, artificial neural network is gaining increasing acceptance because of its flexibility and the ever increasing complexity of the insurance products due to customization at the individual level. ANNs finds its application not just in underwriting, as was discussed in this paper, but also across insurance functions like product development by actuaries, claims management, etc.

REFERENCES

Annotated SPSS Output Factor Analysis. Retrieved from: http://www.ats.ucla.edu/stat/spss/output/factor1.htm

Backprop Feedforward Neural Network. From Syncleus Wiki. Retrieved from: http://wiki.syncleus.com/index.php/dANN:Backprop_Feedforward_Neural_Network

Cluster Analysis. Retrieved from: http://www.norusis.com/pdf/SPC_v13.pdf

Cluster analysis with SPSS: K-Means Cluster Analysis. Retrieved from: http://www.fmi-plovdiv.org/evlm/DBbg/database/studentbook/SPSS_CA_2_EN.pdf

Curve Fitting with Linear and Nonlinear Regression. Retrieved from: http://blog.minitab.com/blog/adventures-in-statistics/curve-fitting-with-linear-and-nonlinear-regression

Database Marketing, Part II: Data Mining For Hidden Treasures—7 Steps of Knowledge Discovery in Databases. Retrieved from: http://kernagency.com/database-marketing/part-2-data-mining-for-hidden-treasures/

Francis, Louise. Neural Networks Demystified. Retrieved from: http://www.casact.org/pubs/forum/01wforum/01wf253.pdf

Multiple Regression Analysis. Retrieved from: https://explorable.com/multiple-regression-analysis

Neural Networks for Automobile Insurance Pricing (information science). Retrieved from: http://what-when-how.com/information-science-and-technology/neural-networks-for-automobile-insurance-pricing-information-science/

Neural Networks for Automobile Insurance Pricing. Retrieved from: http://www.irma-international.org/viewtitle/13984/

Neural networks in data mining. Retrieved from: http://www.jatit.org/volumes/research-papers/Vol5No1/1Vol5No6.pdf

Radboud University, Netherlands. Course RT2: Image Processing, Chapter 10 Neural Networks. Retrieved from: http://www.cs.ru.nl/~ths/rt2/col/h10/10neurENG.html

Statistical Learning Algorithms Applied to Automobile Insurance Ratemaking. Retrieved from: http://www.iro.umontreal.ca/~vincentp/Publications/itii.pdf

The steps involved in data mining. Retrieved from: http://www.tgc.com/dsstar/99/1102/101108.html

Utrecht University. Chapter 7 – Factor Analysis – SPSS. Retrieved from: http://www.cs.uu.nl/docs/vakken/arm/SPSS/spss7.pdf

Utrecht University. Chapter 8 Cluster Analysis. Retrieved from: http://www.cs.uu.nl/docs/vakken/arm/SPSS/spss8.pdf

APPENDIX

Regression is one of the commonly used techniques in insurance by the underwriters to determine which factors have strong influence in predicting the risk of the customer. Though regression is widely used currently, Artificial Neural Networks show a lot of promise and accuracy in various areas in the insurance life cycle, especially for more complicated products. In our analysis, we are using artificial neural networks. Even though each of the techniques has its own advantages, increasingly "Artificial Neural networks" has been proving to be more accurate, efficient, flexible and used for non-linear generalizations.

CHAPTER FOUR

PREDICTING REWARD POINTS ON LOYALTY CARDS USING QUANTILE REGRESSION APPROACH: A CASE STUDY

Aparna Mukherjee

ABSTRACT

Marketing activities, where the objective is to target consumers who are most likely to respond, assume that consumer behavior is homogenous across customers. Hence, traditional analytical techniques based on ordinary least squares (OLS) regression, which focus on the average customer, are employed. Ordinary least-squares regression models the relationship between one or more independent variables (Xi) and the average response variable Y. OLS cannot examine the differences of various customer groups or account for customer heterogeneity. This paper focuses on the use of quantile regression which, unlike OLS, models the relationship between X and the various quantiles of Y. It is especially useful in applications like Loyalty Cards where extreme values of Y, i.e. customers with high card usage and hence profitability, are important.

This paper also describes the QUANTREG procedure in SAS 9.1 which computes estimates for quantile regression.

Keywords: Prediction, Quantile, OLS, Regression, Marketing.

Paper Type: Predictive Modeling; Quantile Regression; Reward Points; Loyalty Cards.

INTRODUCTION

Retail chains or groups of stores run loyalty programs to gain a bigger share of a customer's wallet. Customers are rewarded for shopping and the reward is directly proportional to the amount of spending. This induces the shoppers to spend more in future. The loyalty programs are sometimes run by the retailers and in many cases they are operated by independent loyalty program management companies. Such programs are called coalition programs where independent companies partner with various retailers and manage their Loyalty programs. The program management company issues Loyalty Cards to customers. These cards capture all information pertaining to transactions that are made by them. Against all transactions, points can be accumulated which get recorded in the Loyalty Card and these can be redeemed against future transactions.

Loyalty cards over a time capture various types of information pertaining to the card holders and their purchase behavior. Demographic information thus can be overlaid with purchase information like price, place, and promotion and valuable analysis on customers can be done. Companies which run such programs find these analyses very helpful in generating insights pertaining to consumer behaviors. Through such analyses, profitable customer segments are identified and are targeted for more business.

The focus of this paper is to analyze the data collected through the use of a Loyalty Card which is operated by an independent company. This company has different types of retailers as its members and thus a single Loyalty Card can be used by its holder across various sectors or segments. Each time a card holder buys an everyday item like grocery or hardware the corresponding transaction generates reward points and is recorded in the Loyalty Card. The card holder can redeem these points for items sold by other retailers for types of items ranging from furniture to an aeroplane ticket. The study focuses on understanding the past customer behaviors and predicting the number of reward points to be earned over the next 12 months. This would help in identifying the loyalty card holders who are likely to generate higher reward points and thus higher profits.

DATA ANALYSIS

The data used in our paper comes from a retailer that sells hardware and allows accumulating reward points to all Loyalty Card holders whenever they make a purchase. Information of only those customers, also called collectors, who have earned at least 1 reward point over 1 year are considered as valid data points. There are 170,000 such customers in the data to be analysed.

Since these are permanent collectors, the database contains not only demographic details but also information on their long term behavior (36 months). Below is a snapshot of the different data tables available (Table 1). Within each table, the initial list of variables was quite exhaustive and contained all the demographic details of the customers, their behavior on the retailer's websites, transaction/redemption history, purchase patterns, etc.

Table 1

Description of Data Table	*Type of Data*
Reward Points collected in 2011	
Profile information captured in Loyalty Card database	
Call centre activities (3 years)	
Web Activities	
Card transaction history (3 years)	Behavioral details
Card redemption history (3 years)	
Marketing activities (contacts & responses)	
Activities at different retailers	
Travel related details	
Demographic details from census	Demographic details
Family expenditure history from census	

Since the objective of the study was to predict the number of reward points each customer would collect in future, the dependent variable is the '**Total Reward Points**' collected by each in the current year.

Before statistical analysis of our data, it is important to look at the distribution of the dependent variable, i.e. reward points through a histogram (Figure 1). It was seen that the distribution is skewed and not normal, proving that the data do not conform to the normality assumption. A frequency analysis shows that the mean (38) is larger than median (9).

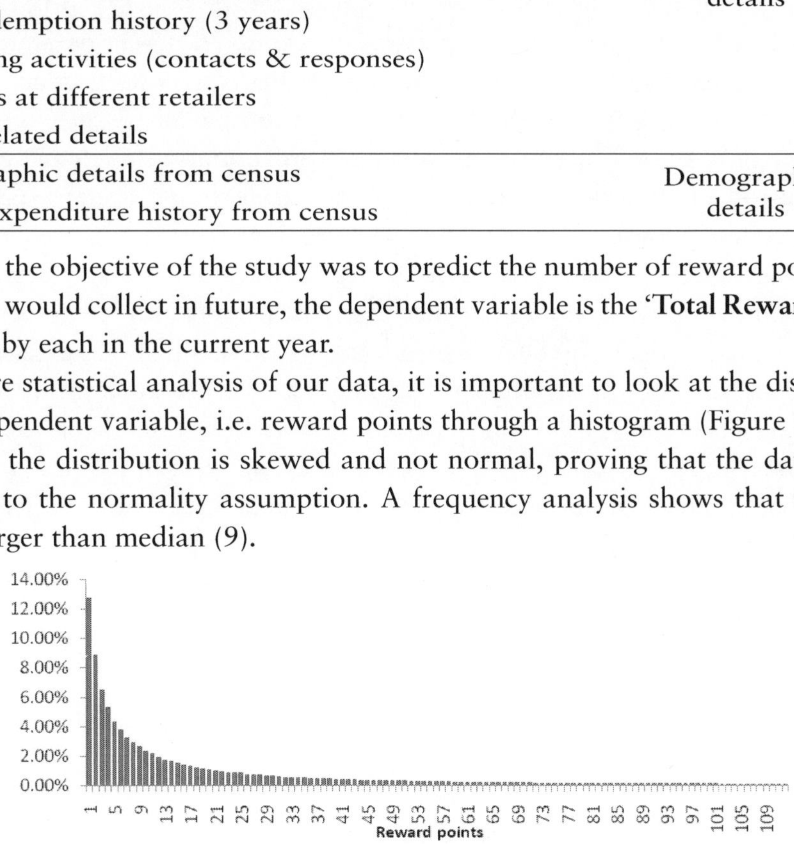

Fig. 1: Histogram of Reward points

Choice of Statistical Model

The traditional OLS regression would require identifying outliers and eliminating them. However, this analysis is about predicting behavior of especially those customers who generate very high reward points and hence more profit for the company. So, eliminating this group, no matter how small they could be, and using only the average customers for prediction will not be as helpful. Presence of outliers and their relative positions to the general customers are important here. However, by keeping them we would not be conforming to the basic requirements of using an OLS regression. OLS does not simultaneously model the average population and the outlier cases. Thus, OLS regression is inefficient to accomplish the goal of this analysis.

It is common to have a heterogeneous set of consumers and a statistical model should be such that is represents these different segments. It is difficult for a single model to represent multiple distinct consumer segments. So this study proposes to use a more direct approach namely, **quantile regression.** Quantile regression provides a different model for different segments through different parameter estimates.

It had been observed by the retailer that the collectors at the 75th percentile with average reward points of 29 are the most realistic set of customers to target for promotion. To generate higher reward points through these customers, these customers and their purchase behavior have to be understood fully. Thus, the business question was: "What influences reward points for collectors at the 75th percentile?" Hence, through our study we will use a quantile regression to generate a model for all quantiles but specifically focus only on the 75th percentile.

To build the model, we proposed a two-step sampling scheme in which the analysis is separated into a modeling phase and a validation phase. The modeling dataset contains 70% of the records of the whole dataset, while the validation dataset contains the remaining 30%. All the cases in both samples are drawn randomly so that the distribution of the dependant variable, i.e. reward points, is similar in both datasets (Table 2).

Table 2

	N	*N Miss*	*Mean*	*1st Pctl*	*10th Pctl*	*25th Pctl*	*50th Pctl*	*75th Pctl*	*90th Pctl*	*95th Pctl*	*99th Pctl*	*Maxi-mum*
Modeling Sample	118,749	0	38.16	1	1	3	9	29	77	136	393	47,684
Validation Sample	50,893	0	38.44	1	1	3	9	29	77	134	412	70,139

USE OF QUANTREG PROCEDURE IN SAS

Quantile regression can be implemented in various statistical software packages including SAS, using Proc Quantreg, and STATA, using Qreg. The following statements use the QUANTREG procedure to fit a simple linear model. The "quantile" option in the statement below allows the user to choose various percentiles for which the parameter estimate in the regression model has to be generated. Since our focus is on the collectors at the 75th percentile, in terms of the reward points that they have collected, the SAS statement, specified below, to build the model reflects the same.

```
proc quantreg data = in.all_merged1 algorithm=interior pp;
model Target = AGE_NEW LATEST_TRS WEB_AM_ACCOUNTMG_
DAYS_12M WALMART_DISTANCE POINTS_PB_12M TREND_POINTS_
BASE CONTACTS_DM_EMAIL_WEB_12M BBM_HIEXP_9999_2YR
/quantile = .75 ;
output out = scored(keep=target pred) p = pred;
```

The MODEL statement specifies a simple linear regression model with "Target" as the response variable Y and all variables defined subsequently on the right hand side of the equation as covariates X.

Target (dependent variable) in this case is the total reward points collected by each customer.

The option QUANTILE = 0.75 models the relation between the set of predictor variables and 75th percentile (or quantile) of the response variable.

MODEL BUILDING AND INTERPRETATION

Since we had data for hundreds of variables, we started off with different groups of variables that represented various behavioral and other aspects of the consumer. Ultimately, we decided to include 4 groups of variables to analyze collector behavior. These 4 classes were: 1) RFM factors, 2) transaction patterns, 3) marketing intensity, and 4) consumer demographic and other background factors. Using different variable combinations, the model that was obtained had 8 key variables which are described in Table 3.

The model form after multiple iterations was:

*TARGET = 19.9412 + (−0.1784) ∗ AGE_NEW + (-0.0234) * LATEST_TRS + 0.0393 * CONTACTS_DM_EMAIL_WEB_12M + 0.0202 * WALMART_DISTANCE + 0.0033* POINTS_PB_12M + 8.1378 * TREND_POINTS_BASE + 78.1889* bbm_hiexp_9999_2yr + 0.2531* WEB_AM_ACCOUNTMG_DAYS_12M*

Table 3

Variable Type	*Label*	*Variable Description*
Demographic	AGE_NEW	Age of customer (includes all imputed values)
RFM	LATEST_TRS (Recency)	Days since last transaction
Transaction	WEB_AM_ACCOUNTMG_ DAYS_12M	Number of views of account management pages
Demographic	WALMART_DISTANCE	Distance from Wal-Mart
RFM	POINTS_PB_12M (Monetary)	Number of product or bonus points earned during the last 12 months
RFM	TREND_POINT_BASE (Monetary Trend)	Ratio of Number of base points earned in last 12 vs. last 36 months
Marketing	CONTACTS_DM_EMAIL_ WEB_12M	Number of email and web contacts during the last 12 months
Demographic	BBM_HIEXP_9999_2YR	Percent spent $5,000-$9,999 on Home Improvement in past 2 years

The above model holds true for the collectors at 75th Percentile. Now, OLS assumes that estimates for the entire group of collectors would be same. To make sure that the assumption is not true and that the estimates are different for different segments of collectors, we also ran an OLS and the regression for other quantiles. As is evident from Table 4, the impact of the independent variable is different for different quantiles of customers. Not only that, these estimates are quite different from the OLS estimates thus validating our assumption that within a group of customers, each segment behaves or reacts differently to several independent factors.

Table 4

Predictors	*OLS*	*Quantiles*						
		10th	*25th*	*40th*	*50th*	*60th*	*75th*	*90th*
Intercept	19.930	1.000	2.535	4.160	6.160	9.706	19.941	52.464
Age	–0.255	0.000	–0.006	–0.029	–0.048	–0.081	–0.178	–0.558
Days since last transaction	–0.027	0.000	–0.003	–0.006	–0.009	–0.013	–0.023	–0.047
Number of email and web contacts during the last 12 months	0.105	0.000	0.002	0.007	0.013	0.020	0.039	0.115
Distance to Wal-Mart	0.069	0.000	0.002	0.007	0.009	0.013	0.020	0.182
Number of product or bonus points earned during the last 12 months	0.024	0.000	0.000	0.001	0.001	0.002	0.003	0.014

Predictors	*OLS*	*Quantiles*						
		10th	*25th*	*40th*	*50th*	*60th*	*75th*	*90th*
Trend Base points Earned (12M vs. 36M)	24.331	0.000	0.006	0.360	0.972	2.398	8.138	39.340
Percent spent \$5,000-\$9,999 on Home Improvement in past 2 years	38.879	0.000	4.445	18.390	28.394	41.231	78.189	158.651
Number of views of account management pages	-0.032	0.000	0.007	0.033	0.053	0.085	0.253	-0.128

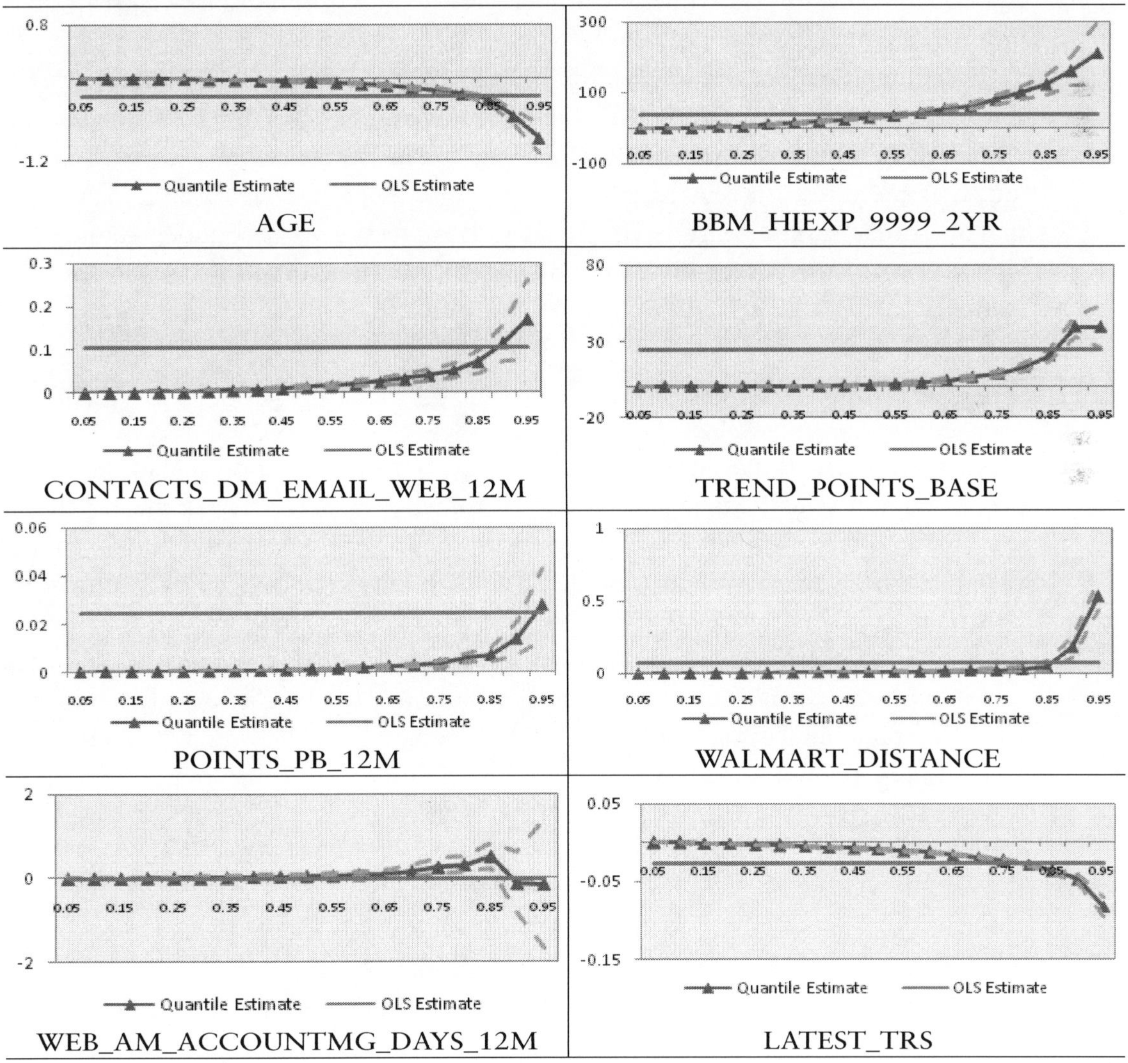

Fig. 2: Quantile Plots

OLS may have led us to conclude that the predictor "Number of views of account management pages" has negative impact on reward points collected, while it is actually influencing the collectors at 75th quantile in a positive way. Quantile regression estimated coefficients for "Trend Base points Earned" show that it has a small effect on low and middle quantile reward points (10th to 60th) but a significantly large effect on high quantile reward points (75th to 90th). Similarly, the magnitude of the effects is increasing for most variables as quantile increases. For example, one unit increase in the variable "Percent spent $5,000-$9,999 on Home Improvement in past 2 years" would increase the reward points by 4.445 units for 25th quantile customers while it will increase the points collected by 78.189 units for 75th quantile customers.

The quantile plots will explain the impact of the independent variable on total reward points for different quantiles better. Below are the plots for the 8 independent variables, in Figure 2. In each plot, the regression coefficient at a given quantile indicates the effect on reward points of a unit change in that variable, assuming that the other variables are fixed. The bands represent 95% confidence intervals. The fitted quantile curves reveal important information for the 75th percentile in comparison to lower percentiles.

PREDICTIVE RESULTS

Having established that use of Quantile Regression is important for accurate prediction for a heterogeneous mix of customers, let us focus on the predictive results. Now that we have informative estimation on the effects of the independent variables, using it we will predict the reward points collected by each customer. Using the estimated model from the modeling sample, we can extrapolate it onto the validation sample. Since the Loyalty Program Operator assumes that the 75th quantile of the client's reward points distribution is the realistic wallet they can hope for targeting, using the model for 75th quantile we calculate the predicted reward points for each customer in the validation dataset. To do that, we multiply the modeling dataset coefficients with the validation dataset independent variables.

Once each customer is assigned a predicted reward point, we rank the validation data sets by the predicted points in descending order and create deciles. We calculate total and percent actual reward points for each decile. Table 5 gives the results of 10-fold cross-validation. It is seen that the top 30% of the population will generate 40.57% of reward-points based on the ranking derived from the prediction. The top decile gives 1.65 times lift over the average of 38 Points and the second decile gives 1.34 times lift over the average.

In the absence of a model, one would choose collectors randomly and a random selection would have generated only 10% reward points at each decile. Using this model, the Program Operator can predict, identify and target customers who will generate higher reward points (Table 5).

Table 5

Rank by Predicted	*%age Observed Points*	*Avg Predicted Points*	*%age Points without Model*	*Cumulative %age Points without Model*	*Cumulative %age Observed Points*	*Lift*	*Cumulative %age Lift*
1	16.53%	56.79	10.00%	10.00%	16.53%	1.65	1.65
2	13.41%	43.13	10.00%	20.00%	29.94%	1.34	1.50
3	10.63%	37.5	10.00%	30.00%	40.57%	1.06	1.35
4	10.39%	33.54	10.00%	40.00%	50.97%	1.04	1.27
5	11.67%	30.33	10.00%	50.00%	62.64%	1.17	1.25
6	8.28%	27.4	10.00%	60.00%	70.92%	0.83	1.18
7	8.80%	24.54	10.00%	70.00%	79.71%	0.88	1.14
8	7.92%	21.67	10.00%	80.00%	87.64%	0.79	1.10
9	7.31%	18.37	10.00%	90.00%	94.94%	0.73	1.05
10	5.06%	12.53	10.00%	100.00%	100.00%	0.51	1.00

The lift chart below (Figure 3) proves that the validation holds well with the existing model. The two lines do not cross each other and the gain is significant from the use of a model.

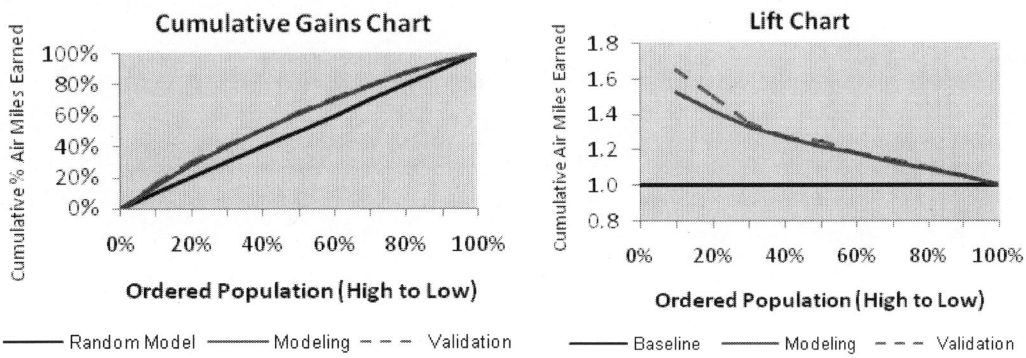

Fig. 3: Lift Charts

IMPLICATIONS

The analysis has several implications on the ideal profile of customers who would generate profit for the company through loyalty card usage. Summarizing the key lessons for the management:

- **Target customers within the age group of 37–44 years** – Among the high collectors, propensity to earn reward decreases exponentially with age. Card holders between 37 and 44 years are likely to spend more and earn more reward points.
- **Target people living in localities with significant spending ($4,999 and above) on home improvement items** – Neighborhoods where 15%-16% of the people spend on home improvement is a potential neighborhood for targeting. The top 5 deciles have similar expenditure pattern and spend being the strongest driver, marginal increase in spending profile delivers big bump in reward points.
- **Target collectors who are far from Wal-Mart** – Collectors belonging to neighborhoods with no Wal-Mart store in the vicinity tend to collect more points at this Retailer's. Wal-Mart may have a slight advantage as people located closer to Wal-Mart buy less at alternate retailers. This advantage is offset if the Wal-Mart store is beyond a 15 Mile radius from the collector's residence. Most collectors are not price sensitive so they might possibly be attracted to value-add offers.
- **Continue frequent touch points through web and email** – Email or web contacting has a positive impact amongst other marketing activities. Even more, the impact is high amongst the high collectors. With the average annual touch point @ 112, it indicates it is not a targeted marketing.
- **Leverage collectors showing higher base points in the last 12 months as compared to last 36 months as they are more active** – Collectors who have earned proportionately higher base points in the last 12 months as compared to last 36 months, are more likely to earn more reward points. The focus should be on people who have earned proportionately more (40%–50%) in recent months even if their overall earnings might be lower.
- **Reward loyal customers with greater bonus points to strengthen engagement** – Collectors who have earned more product/bonus points in the last 12 months are more likely to earn more points in a store. This is more of a positive reinforcement of loyal behavior as the impact is significant but small. The proportion of bonus to base in top decile is 77% which is significantly higher than the next decile with 39%.
- **It is important to have an account management page but the present content does not drive high traffic to the page** – High reward point collectors tend to visit their account pages more often. However, extremely high collectors (above the 90th percentile) visit them less often. The negative relationship with the top 10 percentile, coupled with an overall low average page view across deciles, suggest absence of compelling features on the pages.

- **Recency of transaction implies engagement and is hence a significant predictor** – Using the above model based recommendations, the management can decide the future course of action on a narrowed set of customers who have a high probability to generate reward points.

CONCLUSION

In this study, we investigated whether there was a predictive ability of various variables on reward points. We developed a modeling approach that was based on the quantile predictive regression technique and produced robust and accurate forecasts of the reward points at the 75th quantile. The proposed modeling approach is useful as consumer behavior with respect to usage of loyalty cards is very complex and the dynamic aspect cannot be captured through an OLS regression. Our model form was the most apt one given non-normal data which was highly skewed. Using this approach we could identify 8 potential differences in predictors across quantiles. For example, our analysis suggested that each predictor has a different impact on the various groups of customers. Thus, using quantile regression model a Card Operator can form a perspective on who the most profitable customers are and what business or demographic conditions affect them and in what way. This would further help in taking important business decisions.

BIBLIOGRAPHY

Abreveya, J. (2001). The Effects of Demographics and Maternal Behavior on the Distribution of Birth Outcomes. *Journal of Economics, 26*, 247–257.

Blattberg, R. and Sen, S.K. (1976). Alternative Procedures for Modeling Buyer Behavior Using Consumer Panels. *Proceedings of the American Statistical Association.*

Buchinsky, M. (1994). Changes in U.S. Wage Structure 1963-1987: An application of Quantile Regression. *Econometrica, 62*, 405-458.

Buchinsky, M. (1998). Recent Advances in Quantile Regression Models. *Journal of Human Resources, 33*(1), 88-126.

Chen, C. (2004). *Growth Charts of Body Mass Index (BMI) with Quantile Regression*. MS. available from the author.

Dotson, J. P., Retzer, J., & Allenby G.M. (2007). *A Simultaneous Quantile Regression Model for Customer Linkage Analysis*. Working paper, Ohio State University.

Koenker, R. and Bassett, G.W. (1978). Regression Quantiles. *Econometrica, 46*, 33–50.

Koenker, R. and Bassett, G.W. (1982). Robust Tests for Heteroscedasticity Based on Regression Quantiles. *Econometrica, 50*, 43–61.

Koenker, R. and d'Orey, V. (1993). Computing Regression Quantiles. *Applied Statistics, 43,* 410–414.

Koenker, R. and Hallock, K. (2001). Quantile Regression: An Introduction. *Journal of Economic Perspectives, 15,* 143–156.

Worthington, Steve, & Fear, Josh (2009). *The Hidden Side of Loyalty Cards program* Caulfield East, (Australia): The Australian Centre for Retail Studies, Monash University

Zhang, Xi (2009). *Improving the profitability of direct marketing: a quantile regression approach* M.Phil Thesis. Lingnan University, Hong Kong. Retrieved from http://commons.ln.edu.hk/mkt_etd/5

CHAPTER FIVE

DIRECT MARKETING: PREDICTIVE MODELLING IN THE PRESENCE OF 'MULTICOLLINEARITY' USING PRINCIPLE COMPONENT REGRESSION

Snigdha Pain and Vinayak Deshpande

ABSTRACT

Predictive modeling in direct marketing is a growing area. Direct marketing function uses predictive models as a vital tool to answer the question: Which customers are more likely to respond to promotional offers?

Historical data based on past campaigns are used to develop predictive models. Predictive models can help to manage the resources in a more efficient manner for direct marketing. One of the problems in predictive models is their instability due to 'Multicollinearity'. The multicollinearity problem exists when independent variables or predictors in the model are linearly related. In the presence of 'Multicollinearity', standard errors of regression coefficients are high. If the pattern of 'Multicollinearity' in the new data is different from that in the sample data then predictions can be highly erroneous.

Principle Component Regression (PCR) is a method to handle severe 'Multicollinearity' among independent variables. In PCR, instead of regressing the dependent variable on the explanatory variables directly, the principal components of the explanatory variables are used as predictors. This paper analyses performance of predictive models in the presence of 'Multicollinearity' using PCR method. The analysis is based on 10 data sets with varying degrees of 'Multicollinearity'. R program was written to automate the process which can be used for multiple data sets. The performance of PCR method was analysed using 'Root Mean Squared Error' (RMSE).The result showed that RMSE is significantly lower using PCR method than other approaches such as 'Ignore Multicollinearity' and 'Exclude Few Variables'.

It is concluded that PCR method is recommended for dealing with severe Multicollinearity problem. The method also serves as dimension reduction in predictive modelling. In addition to PCR method, partial least square method (PLS) can also be evaluated before the model is finalized for implementation.

BACKGROUND

Predictive modeling in direct marketing is a growing area. Direct marketing function uses predictive models as a vital tool to answer the question: **Which customers are more likely to respond to promotional offers?** Historical data based on past campaigns are used to develop predictive models. Predictive models can help to manage the resources in a more efficient manner for direct marketing.

In direct marketing, predictive models exploit patterns found in historical and transactional data to identify the risks and opportunities. Models capture relationships among many factors to allow assessment of risk or potential associated with a particular set of conditions, guiding decision making.

Multiple linear regression models are built for predicting values of the response (dependent) variable from a collection of predictor (independent) variables. The prediction of the response variable depends on how well the parameters are estimated. Ordinary least squares (OLS) method is a means of getting best linear unbiased estimators BLUEs under the linear set up given by Gauss-Markov. (Montgomery et al., 2001)

The problem arises when the predictor variables are related to one another. This gives rise to a situation called multicollinearity. When there is either an exact or approximately exact linear relationship among the explanatory variables, the BLUE property in multiple linear regression is no longer effective. Use of OLS to estimate the parameters of the response function results in instability and variability of regression coefficients (Cook and Jacoby, 1977). The OLS may result in regression coefficients much larger than the physical or practical situation (Draper and Smith, 1981) and then guide to wrong inferences. Therefore more the multicollinearity the less interpretable are the parameters. In such circumstances principal component regression (PCR) is a technique to handle the problem of multicollinearity and produce stable and meaningful estimates of the regression coefficient.

PCR is a two-step multivariate calibration method: in the first step PCA of the data matrix is performed. The original P variables are transformed into a new set of orthogonal or uncorrelated variables called the principal components of the correlation matrix. This transformation ranks the new orthogonal variables in order of their importance and the procedure then involves eliminating some of the principal components to effect a reduction in variance. And in the second step, after elimination of the least important principal components, a multiple regression analysis of the response variable against the reduced set of principal components is performed using the OLS estimation.

METHOD

We simulated 10 data sets with moderate to strong multicollinearity among independent variables. For each data set, models were developed using linear regression (OLS) and principle component regression (PCR). The numbers of observations in simulated data sets varied from 5,00,000 to 10,20,000.There were six independent variables in each of these data sets. The models were developed on training data sets and performance was evaluated on testing data sets.

The regression analysis was performed using lm function in base R. The principle component analysis was performed using PCR function. The PCR function is available in library 'pls' of R packages.

The two methods were compared using 'Root Mean Squared Error in Predictions' (RMSEP).

R Code for PCR Method

```
#Principal Component Regression
library(pls)
pcrlm<-pcr(Y~X1+X2+X3+X4+X5+X6,ncomp=3,data=data,scale=TRUE)
summary(pcrlm)
p<-predict(pcrlm)
r<-resid(pcrlm)
RMSEP(pcrlm)
```

R Code for OLS Method

```
reg<-lm(Y~X1+X2+X3+X4+X5+X6,data=data)
summary(reg)
p<-predict(reg)
```

```
r<-resid(reg)
predT<-predict(reg,newdata=dataT)
resT<-dataT$SALES-predT
RMSEP<-sqrt(mean(resT*resT))
RMSEP
```

RESULTS AND DISCUSSION

It was observed that RMSEP was less using PCR method as compared to OLS method in 9 data sets out of ten. The RMSEP using PCR method was slightly higher as compared to OLS method in one data set wherein degree of multicollinearity was moderate.

The average RMSEP for PCR method and OLS method were 1.72 and 2.56 respectively.

The results indicate that PCR method gives more stable coefficients in the presence of multicollinarity. The multicollinearity problem can occur many times in the direct marketing scenario as behavioural variables are likely to be correlated.

CONCLUSION

PCR method is recommended for dealing with severe Multicollinearity problem. The method also serves as dimension reduction in predictive modelling in big data. In addition to PCR method, partial least square method (PLS) can also be evaluated before the model is finalized for implementation.

REFERENCES

Cook, E.R. & Jacoby, G.C. Jr. (1977). Tree-ring-drought relationships in the Hudson Valley, New York. *Science, 198*: 399-401.

Draper, N.R., & Smith, H. (1981). *Applied regression analysis*. 2nd ed. New York: John Wiley and Sons. 709 p.

Fekedulegn, B. Desta; Colbert, J.J.; Hicks, R.R., Jr.; & Schuckers, Michael E. (2002). *Coping with Multicollinearity: An Example on Application of Principal Components Regression in Dendroecology*. Res. Pap. NE-721. Newtown Square, PA: U.S. Department of Agriculture, Forest Service, Northeastern Research Station. 43p

Johnson, Richard A., & Wichern, Dean W. (1992). *Applied Multivariate Statistical Analysis* (3rd Edition). Prentice-Hall. ISBN-81-203-1045-4

Montgomery, D. C., Peck, E. A., & Vining, G. G. (2001). *Introduction to linear regression analysis*. 3rd ed. New York : John Wiley and Sons.

PART
TWO-C

SENTIMENT ANALYSIS

Sentiment analysis, or opinion mining, involves the use of natural language processing, text analytics and computer linguistics to mine various sources of data from the Internet to extract subjective impressions and opinions. Governments, politicians and marketers often apply sentiment analysis on reviews and social media to gauge how people feel about them and their products and services. Sentiment analysis aims to decipher the attitude of a writer with respect to a topic or the overall contextual polarity of a document.

The paper," Customer Sentiment Analytics: Leveraging Social Media In Product Marketing", is a case study of how Sentiment Analysis is used strategically on customer opinion expressions leading to better business performance for computer hardware manufacturer, Dell. A machine-learning based sentiment analysis tool is applied to unstructured sources of consumer opinion like social media conversations, technology blogs, editor reviews and ecommerce websites. Actionable insights derived from these large volumes of data help the product and marketing teams to discover customer wants and incorporate them into the next generation of products.

The paper, "Impact of Sentiment Analysis Tools in Application of Integrated Marketing Communication", offers insight into the role of emotions in marketing communications in the Telecom and Insurance service sectors. Cognitive path modeling is used to analyse the impact of gender on emotion in advertisements and the effect of the recall and attentioning processes.

CHAPTER SIX

CUSTOMER SENTIMENT ANALYTICS: LEVERAGING SOCIAL MEDIA IN PRODUCT MARKETING

Case Study of How a Product Marketing Strategy Based on Sentimental Analysis of Customer Opinion Expressions can Lead to Better Business Performance for Dell

Anindita Bhattacharyya and Rishabh Parakh

ABSTRACT

In this paper, we present a scalable approach of how to enable critical business insights into the "Voice of the Customer" by leveraging the users' responses to Dell commercial notebooks, catering to the needs of enterprise business. These consumer opinions are fetched from technology blogs, editors' reviews, fora, and e-commerce retailer websites. We have built a Sentiment Analytics solution based on machine-learning in order to quantify user sentiments and to derive actionable information from large volumes of unstructured conversations happening in the social media space. This solution enables Dell's senior management, and other stakeholders such as sales, marketing and product lifecycle team to identify customer root wants and incorporate those product decisions in the next generation products. This gives us insight into how we compare against the competitors and benchmark our features and services accordingly.

The aim is realized by identifying a potential set of product features from review sites and mining such opinion expressions by associating closely related product features and implementing text-categorization techniques. Subsequently, different rankings or weightages are assigned to these factors to develop the evaluation matrix derived from the frequency of such reviews. Finally, the scores are normalized to a standard scale to present such massive data in easier user-digestible format and eliminate bias due to the disparity in the quantum of customer reviews across different products. While developing this novel framework, the most frequently discussed factors are treated as the most dominant factors to users, allowing top management to make informed business decisions on "what" matters more. Such a business-intelligent framework enables Dell to proactively execute customer-centric go-to-market strategy and facilitate positive change in customer perception over time. Based on this data-driven comprehensive comparison of own product offerings versus those of competitors, businesses can promptly develop effective targeting and product positioning plans, and optimize their product portfolio and enhance their brand reputation.

DELL'S SOCIAL MEDIA JOURNEY

More than ever, hardware has become commoditized. Thus demand for personal computing is linked heavily to the evolving needs of end consumers. For brand differentiation, original equipment manufacturers need to gain a deep insight of customer demand for the products and to advertise their product positioning by using social media space creatively. For example, Dell has more than 21 million connections through fans and followers on Facebook, Twitter, Dell community, and more across the social web.

By leveraging social media sentiment analytics, companies can determine who is creating the buzz: Are they customers, experts, bloggers or others? This valuable data enables enterprises to obtain an outlook into customer issues that can help solve complex business problems. For example, Dell's social media insight report has shown that Twitter was the most preferred channel for all conversations related to Dell's products and accounted for 61.1% of the overall post volume, followed by Facebook and Comments which contributed to 18.5% and 12.2%. Hence, Dell's heritage of direct customer connections underpins Dell's adoption of the social media web as an integrated marketing tool for doing better business.

Dell has always run its business in a customer-focused manner. We strive to empower our customers to do more. We win if the customer does. Hence, it is very important to have meaningful conversations with each of our customers, listen to their needs and issues, and deliver maximum value in the simplest way possible. At the same time, we have to ensure that each one of our millions of customers cherish the relationship they have with our firm. Only such a psychological connect would help us convert each and every customer to a promoter.

Providing support for the customers' need in the digital realm is one of the most vital aspects of Dell's overall social media strategy. What we learn from our customers online helps us to be a better company and deliver the precise products messaging and services our customers need to be successful. Product Marketing managers are an integral part of this process where they create a more sustainable competitive advantage for Dell over its competition and generate greater business benefit to the organization.

The volume of data, rapid pace of social opinions, and the time value of information make the usefulness of social data directly proportional to how swiftly a company acts on it. Customer feedback stems from varying listening posts across the organization, from internal sources like contact-center call logs, 5-star ratings and reviews on the Dell website, to external sources such as social media and expert reviews. This increasingly vital Voice of the Customer (VOC) data often unearths valuable information that can be utilized to drive customer loyalty and retention, increase market share, and grow profitability.

The progress of a sentiment analytics strategy is a journey that originates by listening to online discussions. Then it proceeds to collecting, recording and analyzing the data, and finally monitoring trends. Eventually, heuristics and advanced algorithms are applied to draw business relevance. Gradually, an organization develops analytics maturity and instills a sentiment of analytics culture among its employees.

Product Marketing Solutions – Optimizing Customer Experience

To gain a comparative edge over competitors, Dell has deployed a new 'go-to-market' model empowered with business intelligence and big data analytics. To proactively target the right segment of user profiles by positioning our products effectively and by offering competitive pricing, Dell has effected a paradigm shift in its approach towards product marketing. Product Marketers seek help of social media, technology blogs, editors' reviews and e-commerce retailer websites to gather information about commercial products' feedback generated by end consumers.

To listen to and understand the 25,000 daily mentions of Dell in the English language, Radian 6 and our in-house developed proprietary sentiment analytics tool, Social Net Advocacy Pulse (SNAP) tool, were leveraged. These tools enabled the product team to track a product's performance soon after its launch and obtain actionable insights to plan the next generation product effectively. Social data goes to analysts who review and summarize it for a product roadmap, competitive comparisons, or specific insights into market trends. This analysis may augment the inferences drawn from surveys and focus groups.

Data points thus gathered from usability study and market research of commercial computing products were able to describe in a nutshell how well Dell products are received vis-à-vis competitors. Thus, Dell's senior management, and other stakeholders such as sales, marketing, and branding and product lifecycle team could take well-informed strategic decisions, based on these insights.

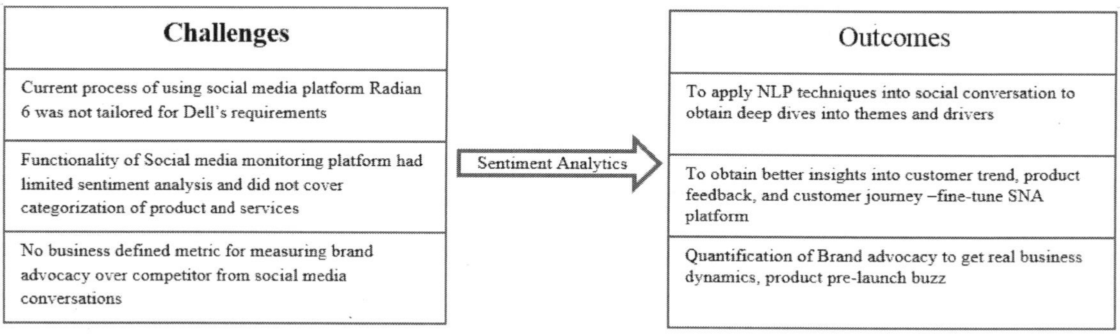

Fig. 1: Challenges and Outcomes

SENTIMENT ANALYTICS – MINING USER OPINIONS AROUND DELL PRODUCTS

Sentiment Analytics or opinion mining refers to a broad area of Natural Language Processing (NLP), computational linguistics and text mining. We used Sentiment Analytics to determine attitudes of end customers with respect to Dell's commercial end products - positive, negative, neutral/mixed. It helped us to describe, evaluate and explain the performance of Dell products over that of competitors. We aggregated user sentiments by various keywords/touch points derived from the input of the product lifecycle management team. Our customized listening technique with drill-down capabilities around various sources was tailored for Dell's social media listening requirements.

We also explored Radian 6 platform's share of voice feature and direct user engagement capabilities. A simple 5-point scale (Negative-Positive) was used as the metric to derive actionable information across the data points of Dell and competitors.

This approach helped us to narrow down the complex linguistics into simple visual and interactive information, facilitating better insights. Thus, opinion mining helps us to give business enough time to manage their brand value and reputation by proactively managing how customers perceive their products/offerings. It also enables us to improve the trajectory of customer perceptions and ratings.

In order to help us effectively differentiate our offerings against those of competitors, it was essential to design a mechanism where unmet customer needs could be identified. The NLP solution provides an effective way to leverage customer feedback and root wants, to address quality problems and improve the quality of the future generation of Dell Consumer products. It enables quick identification of severity levels and digging into specific customer asks, leading to initiation of timely corrective action.

The actions associated with the trends identified from weekly scorecards are long-term solutions to gauge whether our product positioning, pricing and campaigning are working desirably or not. We can also quickly spot irregularities that deserve deeper analyses and probable action.

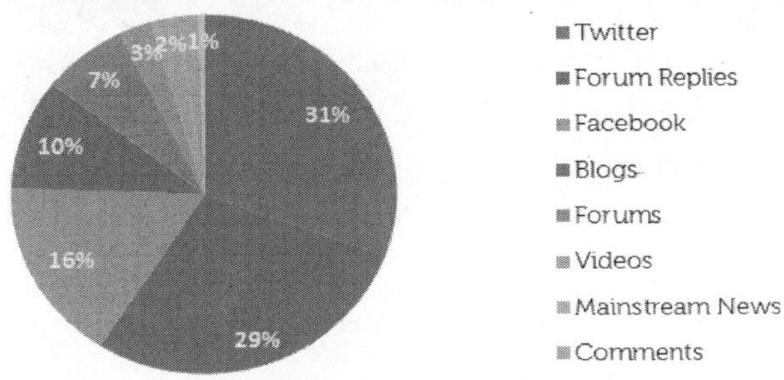

Fig. 2: Latitude in General
Source: Radian 6 July 1 to October 1, 2013.

Discerning Competitors' Product Positioning

Understanding Product messaging of competitors such as Lenovo/HP in the commercial product landscape provides a perspective on the directions taken by competitors in terms of future product planning, design and pricing strategy. By studying the key user sentiment differences between Dell and competitors for commercial products, Dell business managers can identify opportunities for improving Dell commercial products by assimilating best practices of competitive product positioning. Thus competitor analysis provides a defensive strategy to Dell over time in the context of product branding and communication. For example, we can find that Lenovo X1 Carbon (a premium business notebook series equivalent to Dell's Latitude 6430u series) had the highest Share of Voice (SoV) in social conversation. The post volume of Lenovo X1 Carbon was 8.25 times higher than that of Latitude 6430u.

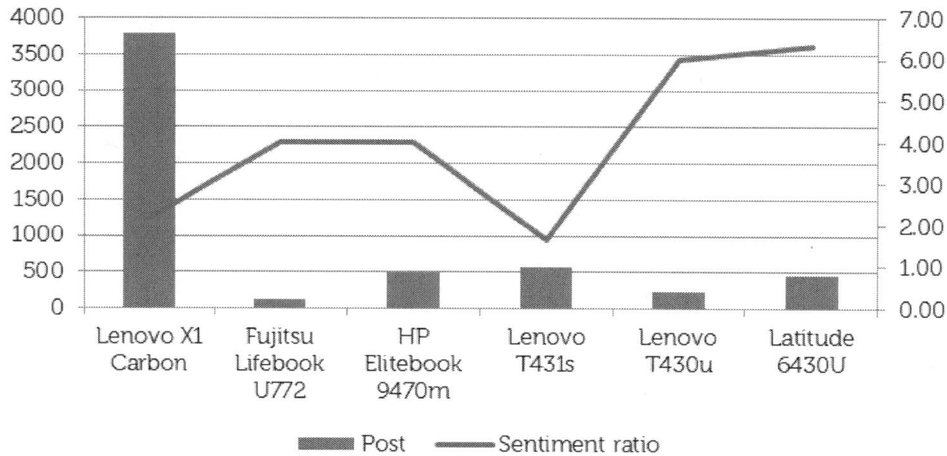

Fig. 3: Post Volume and Sentiment Ratio

Source: Radian 6 July 1 to October 1, 2013.

We drilled down further to locate the media sources and found that an article by industrial analysts caused a spike in social media on the Lenovo X1 Carbon. It suggests that Dell may increase activity in social properties to promote Latitude brand such as having dedicated brand advocates/social media influencers.

Identifying Sample Product from Commercial Product Portfolio

The study was conducted mainly for the Latitude, which is one of the hot selling products that Dell has in its commercial product portfolio. The product line is intended to facilitate maintenance and support tasks for large business houses, allowing its parts to be easily interchanged between different models. Latitude computers are also characterized by their business focused feature sets such as security options. The systems typically consist of Intel processors, ranging from Pentium and Celeron to Core i7 and some models with AMD CPUs as well. The numerous awards and recognitions which Latitude has received is a testimony to the product quality and its specifications.The primary competitors of the Latitude series are the Lenovo ThinkPad line and the HP Elitebook line, both of which offer similar messaging, features and sturdiness as the Latitude line. These competitors' models compete with Latitude in all the areas catering to the product quality, specifications, market segments and price points. The sample space was formed by analyzing the following models:

Latitude 6430u	Lenovo X1 Carbon
Fujitsu Lifebook U772	HP Elitebook 9470m
Lenovo T431s	Lenovo T430u
Latitude 3330/3440/3540	HP Probook Series
Lenovo ThinkPad Essential	Lenovo X131e

Keywords Analyzed

Since Product features were the hottest topics on Latitude product discussions, we picked opinions around keywords such as Keyboard, Touchpad, TrackPoint, Ergonomics, Design, Aesthetics, Materials, Durability, and User Experience. Consumers may not iterate the exact words during their social media conversations; hence we did not limit our research only to this set of touch points. Instead we added in our vocabulary all related words. For example, TrackPoint was associated with words such as Pointstick, point stick, TrackPoint, pointing stick, pointing device etc. to enrich our scope of data gathering. Table 1 below shows the exhaustive set of vocabulary picked during our analysis.

Table 1: Keywords

Keyboard, keyboards, keypad, keypads, type	Touchpad, touchpads, trackpad, trackpads, touch pad, track pad, clickpad, forcepad, input device, mouse
Ergonomic, ergonomics	Usability, user centered design, user experience, easy to use
Design, aesthetic, Materials	Durable, reliable, sturdy

METHODOLOGY

Dell partnered with Clarabridge, a text analytics provider for intelligent sentiment extraction. Their original Natural Language Processing (NLP) engine and machine learning capability uses both pre-established and customizable procedures and dictionaries to disintegrate and examine customer sentiment text, and to deep-dive by scoring it on a scale of -5 to +5.We have also developed in-house a tool called Social Net Advocacy (SNA). This metric identifies purchasing decision, giving us a clear picture of customer promotion of the Dell brand. Dell is using this software (SNA) and incorporating it into all dimensions of the business from product management and marketing to NPS/NSS diagnosis, customer support/service and sales.

Evaluating more than 1 million conversations on an annual basis, the system possesses the capacity to drill down to understand even the minutest details. This enhances Dell's affirmed policy of the customer-centric model and direct feedback. Also, since it apprises in real-time, SNA quickens customer feedback on main topics, facilitating a shorter feedback cycle without negatively affecting the brand equity. Dell uses SNA internally to help the company deliver an enhanced customer experience. SNA is integrated within the Dell Social Media Command Center, which enables the company to monitor and react to online conversations in real time.

We measure SNA at the company level and use this calculation in150+ topics representing various aspects of the business. Online conversations are analyzed for topics including products, features, services, marketing, packaging, customer support and even community outreach efforts. SNA enables organizations to comprehend, calculate and contextualize online feedback, leading to well-informed business assessments and ultimately improving our ratings and reviews. The real time analysis of social information has permitted Dell to proactively suppress any negative publicity before it blows out of proportion.

Machine Learning allowed us to rapidly process large amounts of customer centric data including customer conversations in the form of tweets, posts, reviews etc. Our model was trained on a dataset with a set of input features and a corresponding output. The dictionary was made robust by instructions and sentiment tagging by an initial manual categorization process. We wrote rules and defined conditions that are to be followed for annotation of sentiments to establish a model for extracting the attributes that are talked about in the customer reviews and expert comments. For example, phrases such as beast" were tagged as positive in the context of computers. The word 'hot' has a negative connotation in our industry whereas the word 'sick' has a positive interpretation when referred to laptops. These are exceptions that need to be fed into the model. Also, a string of words may be such that it may not have a single negative word, but still convey a negative meaning. An example is 'could have been' which is a string devoid of any common negative word, but implies negative emotion. Similarly, "I wish" implies neutrality with a tinge of disappointment.

The following phases elaborate the process we followed in implementing the sentiment analytics ecosystem:

Phase 1: Collect – Gather customer feedback from a wide variety of sources

We integrate the widest continuum of customer feedback, regardless of channel, from internal and external sources, in structured and unstructured format, and in any language. This data, both internal and external, represents a complete 360° view of the customers. Within the organization, feedback is targeted from internal sources such as surveys, call center logs, and 5-star ratings and reviews. External

Sources of feedback from social media and other consumer-generated content are also integrated.

Phase 2: Transform – Process, categorize and score different facets of each verbatim

After collecting the feedback, we extract linguistic content, categorize and assign sentiment scores to distinguish the who (Entity Extraction), which (Comparative Analysis), when (Event Extraction), where (Relation Extraction) and why (Intention Analysis) of any customer experience. Real time opportunity was tracked by understanding customer pain points, customer enquiries related to product feature, and the customer's purchase intention.

Simple texts were further churned by a rule parser to perform syntactic linguistic analysis first. Semantic linguistic analysis was carried out to deal with spam detection. Pragmatic linguistic analysis was carried out to extract the intended meaning thus generating more sales opportunity. This exhaustive approach to NLP ensures that the resulting analysis is accurate. The analysis utilized salient features of advanced hybrid machine learning techniques. We perform advanced sentiment scoring for accurately extracting attitudes expressed in the feedback and apply a classification technique for analytical purposes. The different weightages/rankings were assigned across these user's factors/product feature when making evaluations. We logically treated the most frequently discussed (or in some cases the most primitive) factor as the most dominant factor to the users. This further enhanced the results by informing the users on what 'matters' more in latitude product space. Below is an example of how the evaluation matrix was derived from frequency of reviews.

Pros	Cons	Counts	Factors
Great sound quality (13)	Poor sound quality (3)		
Noise isolation (4)	Poor noise isolation/Ambient noise/buzzing (4)	28	Quality of sound
	Cable noise when rubbing (3)		
	Sound leak (1)		
Good fitting (5)	Poor fitting (4)		
	Ear plug easily fall out (1)	21	Ergonomically comfort and fitting
Comfortable (8)	Uncomfortable (2)		
Value for money (5)	Cheaply made (1)		
Durable (3)	Not durable (6)	16	Value and quality
	Packaging protection (1)		
Great functionalities (1)	SW compatibility issues (2)		
Cable management (2)	Short cord (1)	7	Other usability issues
Good control (1)			
Appealing design (3)	Poorly designed (2)	5	Aesthetics

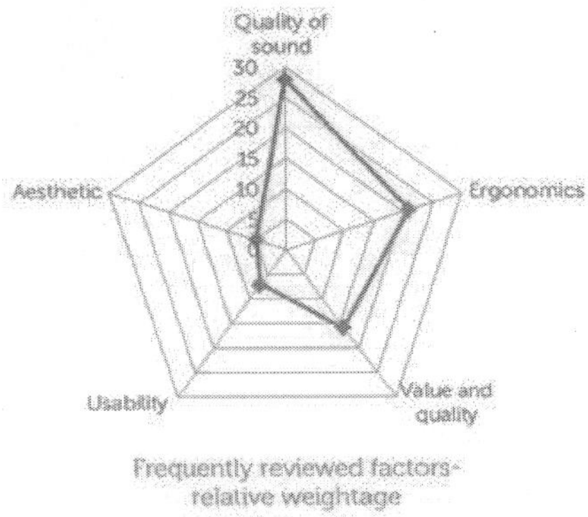

Fig. 4: Derivation of Evaluation Matrix

Phase 3: Deliver – Make actionable insights accessible across the organization

We make the processed data accessible from an internal web-portal so that anyone in the enterprise can receive a critical voice of customer intelligence, when and how they need it. The solution can deliver user-friendly reports and visualizations in a GUI form that make slicing and dicing of the data intuitive and easy. Countless users can quickly spot emerging issues, praises or experiences that are relevant and actionable. We can quickly and securely search, explore, organize, and analyze text from words, linguistic elements, sentiment, and structured data to filter, report, classify and drill into the root cause. We built a sentiment scoring system, taking into consideration the following sentiment ratings:

(+2) emotional positive
(+1) rational positive
(0) neutral
(-1) rational negative
(-2) emotional negative

Provide Strategic Input for the Business

Twitter and technical forums were found to be the main social channels for products belonging to the Latitude line of business. Both Lenovo and HP were active in social posts in the product line. Even Fujitsu came up as the most influential company among all brands in the product line due to its high volume social media presence. We can derive from the facts presented that Dell may increase activity in social properties to promote Latitude series products.

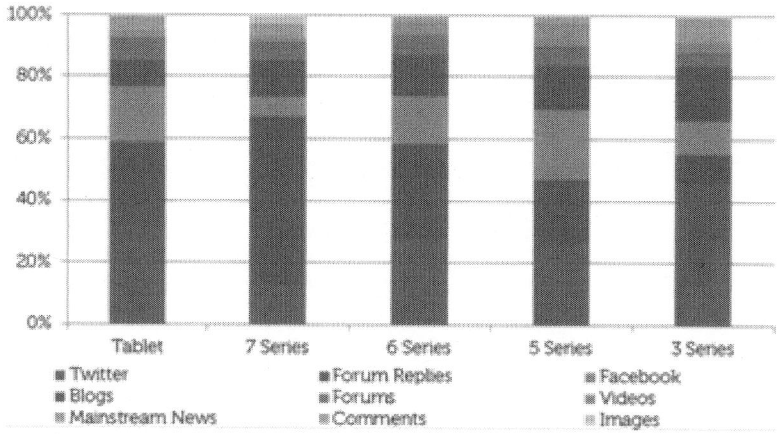

Fig. 5: Media Types (July 1 to October 1, 2013)
Source: Radian 6

For example, the above chart suggests that Dell may need to increase the discussion of its 6 series on Twitter. Dell must also encourage analysts to discuss the 3 series in a technical forum.

Fig. 6: Tag Cloud

The above tag cloud (Fig. 6) obtained from our text analytics on social media suggests that product features were the hottest topics on Latitude products. In general, Latitude products were perceived to have decent features and quality. Processor, battery, RAM, keyboard, and screen were the attributes that customers most associated with the Latitude brand. Hence being more vocal on those product features can win Dell more customer accolades over the competition.

Through social media data, we also discovered that among competitors, the key selling propositions such as Haswell architecture of their CPU were highlighted more, to attract target customer attention. We also realized the importance of industry analysts' articles to mobilize public opinion. As seen in the following chart

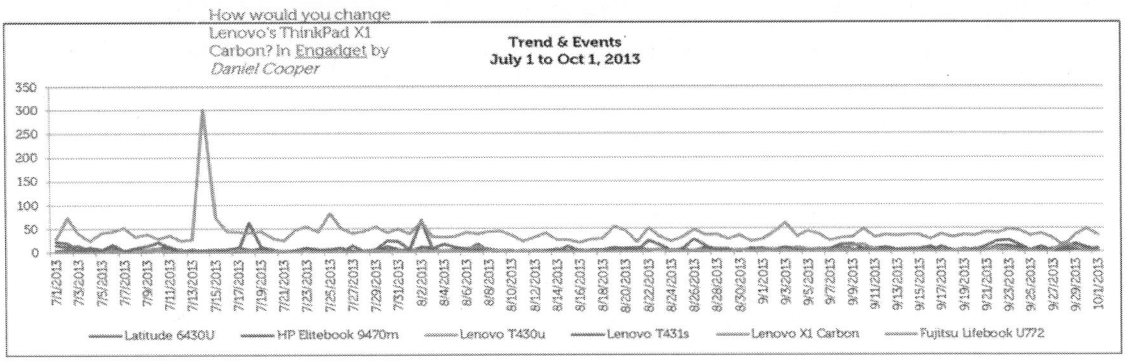

Fig. 7: Effect of an Article

Source: Radian 6

(Fig. 7), an article titled "How would you change Lenovo's Thinkpad X1 Carbon?" in Endgadget, authored by technology expert Daniel Cooper got people talking about this product, thus creating a buzz in the market.

RECOMMENDATIONS

More professionally social media certified and subject matter experts acting as digital advocates can galvanize the customer segments to build a larger Dell loyal customer base. New opportunities to listen, engage, and monitor the future customer base should be tapped into by more engagement in digital advocacy tools such as blogs, website, email, Texts, Facebook etc. Such brand advocates can promote product awareness on a long term basis and can be a part of a sustainable marketing force generating not only a product buzz around but also leading more sales growth and operating profit. Even promotional campaigns like refer-a-friend can amplify the product messages by reaching more target audience profiles and by meaningfully engaging them to reach desired business outcomes. The organization should use the metric, in case of negative review, to determine from which influential people in the industry the content is coming, to understand how far-reachingly the tweet has traveled, and how many people were impacted by this content. This approach will enable reputation management as well. Thus managing social media advocates/influencers analytics alongside sentiment measurement will be able to build a holistic approach towards Dell's social media listening and monitoring.

BUSINESS IMPACT

Measuring, analyzing, and ultimately impacting customer sentiment drives an organization's capability to express and regulate operative social marketing promotions. The data, digital relationships, and resulting analysis inherent in social networks interactions have provided a lasting resource for our business and our customers. And this resource has a growing and lasting impact on many aspects of business - from R&D, to product management, to CRM, to helpdesk, and to sales. As described above, we capture the right sentiment, garner the right insights, and massage the data to ensure that both business and social context information can be brought out in an efficient manner.

And More Meaningful Relationship with Customers

We have created and documented a process in our team to enable continuous application of the sentiment analytics methodology. The purpose is to enable constant structured brainstorming and create new ideas in the organization. IT is a very dynamic industry and impacting innovation processes have created a strategic advantage for Dell. Our process takes a cross-functional and thus interdisciplinary approach to ensure a comprehensive look at the issue to enable optimal insight and decision making. This methodological approach is so simple to follow that it can be applied by other companies in almost any industry apart from high technology. Successful implementation of the methodology of Sentiment analytics, collaborative team work with sales and marketing and product management group, coupled with a procedure of continuous ideation and strategic information can help organizations build better relationships with their customers.

BIBLIOGRAPHY

Baer, Jay. *Social Media Influencers versus Brand Advocates Infographic.* Retrieved from: http://www.convinceandconvert.com/content-marketing/social-media-influencers-versus-brand-advocates-infographic/

Building a Sentiment Analytics Solution Powered by Machine Learning. (2012). Retrieved from: http://www.slideshare.net/ImpetusInfo/building-a-sentiment-analytics-solution-powered-by-machine-learning-impetus-webinar?qid=d534d27d-fbfd-4a14-9b4e-68e1d392b0c9&v=qf1&b=&from_search=3

Clarabridge website. http://clarabridge.com/

CRM 2011. *Geocent White paper.* Retrieved from: http://www.nikolakocic.com/CRM%202011%20Twitter%20Sentiment%20Analysis%20White%20Paper.pdf

Dell's Social Media Strategy (2013). Krista Kotrla, Nov 7th 2013. Retrieved from: http://www.kristakotrla.com/dell-social-media-strategy

Internal Social Advocacy: Unleashing Employees as 'The Next New Product' (2014). Retrieved from: http://www.slideshare.net/dellsocialmedia/activating-employees-as-company-advocates-on-social-media

Kocic, Nikola (2011). *Performing Sentiment Analysis with Twitter and Microsoft Dynamics.* Retrieved from: http://www.nikolakocic.com/CRM%202011%20Twitter%20Sentiment%20Analysis%20White%20Paper.pdf

Opinion Mining, Sentiment Analysis and Opinion Spam Detection. Retrieved from: http://www.cs.uic.edu/~liub/FBS/sentiment-analysis.html

CHAPTER SEVEN

IMPACT OF SENTIMENT ANALYSIS TOOLS IN APPLICATION OF INTEGRATED MARKETING COMMUNICATION

Barnana Sarkar

ABSTRACT

In this age of digital marketing, advertising of brands and products has changed dramatically. Instead of gradually disseminated print ads with delayed responses, the web helps connect consumers with the company through social media marketing. Where impact of print ads to the campaigns exceed days, weeks or months, the instant response of consumers to social networking sites can be measured within clicks. Marketing campaigns today focus on careful consideration of social media, blog spaces, search engine optimization, specific web portals, and search providers. Consumer responses provide an immediate feedback to the company and help the marketing team identify problem areas and barriers to the integrated marketing communication plan, measure the effectiveness and refine the message channels in the promotion mix. Further, based on this feedback they can estimate the sales forecast for the forthcoming quarter.

Social media analytics like Sentiment Analysis record the response of the consumer about how he feels about a certain product. It measures brand association that the consumer feels with a particular brand. Using Sentiment Analysis as a tool we observe in this paper the impact it can have on building a coherent and integrated communication plan set up to market a product. The relevant use of data with measured insight through careful targeting to foremost opinion leaders is the crux of the success of any marketing communication plan. Sentiment analysis helps to integrate the plan, to link marketing activities to sentiments expressed by consumers on relevant websites, blogs, opinion forums, and social networking sites and to link the reliable index to product sales, and most importantly, to put it all together to predict the expected success of a marketing campaign based on the immediate consumer feedback.

INTRODUCTION

This paper studies the emerging interest in emotional aspects of advertising, also studied as a part of consumer behavior (Holbrook & O'Shaughnessy, 1984). We have tried to find answers to questions regarding advertising that include what feelings to invoke in the audience that would convert the attention of the audience to action of purchase as a consumer (AIDA model). On an average the television viewer comes across maximum ads in the following sectors

- Consumer goods (FMCG)
- Automobile
- Telecom Products
- Insurance Sector

In the above sectors, FMCG goods and Automobile sectors are selling *products*, but the latter, Telecom and Insurance are selling *services*. We chose to compare the two sectors – Telecom and Insurance – because both want to consistently invoke similar emotions of Reliability/Security, Commitment, Sincerity and Sensitivity leading up to choosing the Best Plan which is personalized.

We further tried to find out if there is a positive relationship between the gender of the viewer and the emotion felt while watching the same ad and how this relation can be used for application in an Integrated Marketing Plan. One major element of the Marketing Communication Mix is *Advertising*. Emotions in Advertisements allow cognitive processing that helps viewers remember and recall in the long term through relatedness (Friestad & Thorson, 1986). How much advertising influences us has been a topic of discussion among psychologists. We assume for this research that advertising works by persuasion. Persuasion is a rational verbal process that "seduces the subconscious" (Holbrook & Batra, 1987). This study aims at deepening the understanding of the role of emotion in customers by their gender. It has been established by scholars that the personality of the consumer influences Telecom Consumption preference in Nigeria (Aboh, Obi, Agu, & Sydney-Agbor, 2013). We chose to conduct this study on the Indian audience with reference to Telecom and Insurance sector advertising. From a Social Desirability perspective (Fisher, & Dubé,

2005) gender differences have been found in response to advertising with the content of the ad, although it is a controversial assumption that females experience more intense emotional experiences than males. As per our findings of this research, where the audience reaction was recorded in a focus group, we observed that males and females both report similar emotions while viewing ads from Telecom and Insurance sectors.

The purpose behind finding the relation between emotion and gender in ad-viewing is to form a model where emotions can be measured and used effectively during Marketing. This model could be included in an Integrated Marketing Communication Plan, where the use of the right emotion could help selling. As we have observed that advertising is nothing but persuasion at the subconscious level, thus the aim is to develop a Cognitive Path Analysis Model for Sentiments to be used in Ad-making. Through the use of Sentiment Analysis we derived results to establish the relation between emotion and gender, which will be further on used to create the Cognitive Path Analysis Model for Sentiments. The aim is to measure and quantify emotions and use them effectively for the purpose of creating a 360 degree Marketing Communication Plan with one central emotion.

What is Sentiment Analysis? Definitions

An important part of our information-gathering behavior has always been to find out what other people think. With the growing availability and popularity of opinion-rich resources such as online review sites and personal blogs, new opportunities and challenges arise as people now can, and do, actively use information technologies to seek out and understand the opinions of others. Thus, Sentiment Analysis is a Natural Language Processing and Information Extraction task that aims to obtain the writer's feelings expressed in positive or negative comments, questions and requests, by analyzing a large numbers of documents. (Pang & Lee, 2008)

Liu (2010) describes sentiment analysis as a process that categorizes a body of textual information to determine feelings, attitude and emotions towards a particular issue or object. The definition points to the way sentiment analysis works and describes the outcome of polar classification. Kumar and Sebastian (2012) describe sentiment analysis as automated subjectivity analysis similar to opinion mining and appraisal extraction which focuses on extracting and classifying texts with machine language and computer programming. Despite the differences in both perspectives, the general narrative is the same. In other words, sentiment analysis is a data mining technique that uses natural language processing, computational linguistics and text analytics to identify and extract content of interest from a body of textual data. It is a method for determining a sentiment associated with an entity and includes inputting a plurality of texts associated with the entity, labeling seed words in the plurality of texts as positive or negative (Godbole, Skiena, & Srinivasaiah, 2011).

The World Wide Web has dramatically changed the way people express their facts and opinions. People post reviews of products on websites, and express their views about movies, collectively called user-generated response. This has made quick feedback possible about everything. One of the applications for sentiment analysis has been conducted where predicting movie success has been done through sentiment generated on social network websites (Krauss et al, 2008). Various other areas of study have taken opinion-mining or sentiment analysis application with favourable outcomes.

LITERATURE REVIEW

Inter-disciplinary Application of Sentiment Analysis – Uses

Sentiment Analysis cannot be done in isolation. Originally intended to be a part of computational linguistics and research areas of computer science, it has its various applications in many fields of study. A new Web mining approach analyses forum posts of the user-generated responses and predicts trends and real world events in the movie business (Krauss et al, 2008). By analyzing online forum discussions on an internet movie database, Oscar awards were predicted correctly. Also the top 20 highest earning movies were predicted based on the user data. This was called the "wisdom of crowds". In the movie industry, approaches such as "Netnography" (Kozinets, 2002) make use of this fact for marketing research, proposing analysis of statements.

By analyzing sentiments by Cognitive Psychology mainly through the work of Pang & Lee (2008) an accuracy of around 82.8% was achieved in movie reviews.

Pang & Lee (2008) recognize the following subjective signals.

Psychological Verbs, Actions, Adjectives and Perceptual Verbs

1. Psychological verbs (e.g. 'think', 'wonder', 'realize', 'want')
2. Perceptual verbs (e.g., 'see', 'hear')
3. Psychological adjectives (e.g., 'delighted', 'happy', 'jealous', 'scared')
4. Psychological actions (e.g., 'he smiled', 'she gasped', 'she winced')

According to Lipton (2006) in the New York Times, the US government spent approximately $2.4 million dollars in funding research that developed software specifically designed to monitor online activities. According to one official:

> "....sentiment analysis is intended to identify potential threats to the nation. We want to understand the rhetoric that is being published and how intense it is, such as the difference between dislike and excoriate." (Lipton, 2006).

SENTIWORDNET 3.0 is an enhanced lexical resource explicitly devised for supporting sentiment classification and opinion mining applications. (Pang & Lee, 2008) SENTIWORDNET is the result of the automatic annotation of all the synsets of WORDNET according to the notions of "positivity", "negativity", and "neutrality".

Sentiment analysis of natural language texts is a large and growing field. Previous work particularly relevant to our task falls naturally in two groups. The work relates to techniques to automatically generate sentiment lexicons. The second relates to systems that analyze sentiment (on a global or local basis) for entire documents. The present system assigns scores indicating positive or negative opinions to each distinct entity in the text corpus. Our system consists of a sentiment identification phase, which associates expressed opinions with each relevant entity, and a sentiment aggregation and scoring phase, which scores each entity relative to others in the same class. Finally, we evaluate the significance of our scoring techniques over a large corpus of news and blogs and report on our development of a large-scale sentiment analysis system for news and blog entities built on top of the text analysis system and view our daily sentiment analysis report (Godbole, Skiena & Srinivasaiah, 2011)

In recent times we have witnessed an explosion of data availability, the so-called data deluge (Anderson, 2008), determined by an increased amount of electronic action performed (such as using social networks online) and the progressive pervasive reach of IT in all devices. The first of these trends is the so called "open data" movement, characterized by the fact that all across Europe and the US, governments are increasingly publishing their data repositories for other people to access and use.

Another trend concerns the vast amount of data made available by citizens through "participatory sensing": ordinary people play a proactive role in publishing comments and complaints on-line, and increasingly use technology to record additional information, such as photos or audio recordings, typically through smartphones. (Osimo & Mureddu, 2012)

1. Argument mapping software helps in organising these policy statements in a logical way, by explicitating the logical links between them. Under the research field of Online Deliberation, tools like Compendium, Debatepedia, Cohere, Debategraph have been developed to give a logical structure to a number of policy statements and to link arguments with the evidence to back it up.

2. Voting Advise Applications help voters to understand which political party (or other voters) has closer positions to theirs. For instance, SmartVote.ch asks the voter to declare his degree of agreement with a number of policy statements, and then matches its position with the political parties.
3. Automated content analysis helps in processing large amounts of qualitative data. There are today on the market many tools that combine statistical algorithms with semantics and ontologies, as well as machine learning with human supervision. These solutions are able to identify relevant comments and assign positive or negative connotations to it (the so-called sentiment).

Opinion mining is not in itself a new research theme. Automated methods for content analysis have been increasingly used, and have increased at least 6 fold from 1980 to 2002 (Neuendorf, 2002). The research theme is based on long established computer science disciplines, such as Natural Language Processing, Text Mining, Machine Learning and Artificial Intelligence, Automated Content Analysis, and Voting Advice Applications.

However, according to Pang & Lee (2008), since 2001 we see a growing awareness of the problems and opportunities, and "subsequently there have been literally hundreds of papers published on the subject." Several sentiment search engines exist where users run typical queries on any topic of interest, and generate text results. Usually the results are coded and categorized into two or three polar categories. Some examples currently available are:

1. Sentiment 140 - http://www.sentiment140.com
2. Tweetfeel – www.tweetfeel.com
3. Twitrratr – www.twitrratr.com
4. Social Mention – www.socialmention.com
5. Opinmind – www.opinmind.com

However, Pang & Lee (2008) admit that although the content might be skewed, the validity of the process is acclaimed. Another tool in sentiment analysis is word lists or annotated databases which categorize words based on their emotions, for example - attractive (positive valance) or aversive (negative valance). Some examples include: ANEW, General Inquirer and LIWC. Other tools include sentiment analysis programs that are specifically designed to categorize short textural documents. One example is *sentistrength*.

What is new today is the sheer increase in the quantity of unstructured data, mainly due to the adoption of social media that are available for machine learning algorithms to be trained on. Social media content by nature reflects opinions and sentiments, while traditional content analysis tended to focus on identifying topics. (Pang & Lee, 2008)

Keeping in mind the previous studies done in the area of Sentiment Analysis we use this as a tool of application in the area of advertising used for marketing a product. Kennedy & Inkpen (2006) studied Sentiment classification of movie and product reviews using contextual valence shifters that can be applied in the case of advertisements. In a successful advertisement the most important factor calculated in the element of 'recall' (Mehta & Purvis, 2006).

Recall, one of the key metrics in advertising testing, has been criticized over the years as favoring rational advertising over emotional advertising. An analysis and reconsideration of the available evidence show that emotional advertising is not penalized by recall and that emotional content in well-executed commercials can actually boost recall. Strong empirical evidence shows that recall, when used in combination with other measures, is a valid measure of advertising effectiveness and a review of methods utilized in measuring affect, feelings, (Wiles& Cornwell, 1991) as the analysis here illustrates, does not miss the 'emotion in advertising' that builds brands. (Smith, 2012; Agres, Edell, & Dubitsky, 1990; Holbrook& Westwood, 1989; Cho & Stout, 1993)

All major copy testers have their own empirical support demonstrating the validity of their measures. While they often place different emphasis on their measures (particularly among recall, persuasion, and advertising liking), it is nearly universally accepted that recall has value in evaluating advertising effectiveness, with a variety of supplier and independent studies demonstrating its sales validity (Dubow, 1994; also IRI's "How Advertising Works" study by Lodish & Lubetkin, 1992). Although some authors have minimized the findings of this study after removing some of the data points/so-called "outliers," by no means does the research show " . . . no evidence of a relationship between related recall scores and sales effects ..." as Kastenholz and Young (2003) concluded. Additionally, the Advertising Research Foundation Copy Validity Research Project (ARF CRVP) (Haley and Baldinger, 1991) found recall to be a valid measure of advertising effectiveness, second only to advertising liking.

The role of emotions in marketing is not new. To the marketer, customer emotions are indirect motivators of purchase behavior. They shape brand saliency, influence attitudes, beliefs, opinions and perceptions. Links have already been established between emotions and strong brands (Aaker & Keller, 1993; Morrison & Crane, 2007); emotions and consumption; and emotions on product evaluations (Mano & Oliver, 1993). To understand how emotion works in advertising or how it interacts with the recall measure in advertising testing, a basic knowledge of the memory process is useful. Memory is a critical part of consumer behavior and of how advertising influences consumer behavior. Consumers usually do not make brand purchase choices at the time of advertising exposure; rather, it is the memory of the advertising messages that influences consumers. The importance of recall stems from the fact that recall measures some aspect of this memory of the advertising.

Neurologists today are suggesting that the 'attentioning' process is largely out of the conscious control of the individual, and emotion rather than cognitive/rational response guides 'attentioning' (Mast & Zaltman, 2005).

Through this research work we try to measure brand emotion, analyse the relation of gender of viewer and sentiment and hence study the application of the effect of the 'recall' and 'attentioning' process through Sentiment Analysis on our sample for this research. In marketing, research is used for a variety of purposes including: obtaining insights into customer attitudes and beliefs, measuring customer satisfaction, ascertaining the effectiveness of advertising, etc. Some larger companies have their own market research departments whilst smaller companies usually outsource the function to research specialists. Research is carried out in two basic ways: qualitative and quantitative.

RESEARCH METHODOLOGY – DESIGN/METHODOLOGY/APPROACH

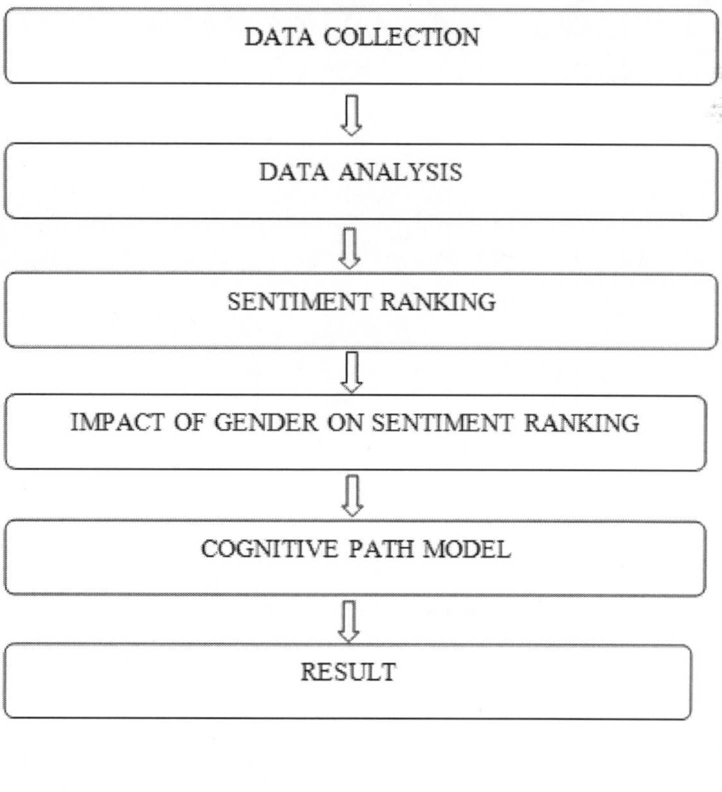

In this study we apply Sentiment Analysis for the study of emotion in advertisements in telecom and insurance sector ads. Ad-viewers in India were interviewed about their habits related to their exposure to media. The interviews were analyzed according to gender and emotion path analysis technique, which divides the sample into different groups in accordance with their gender to the emotion strength or intensity. The ultimate focus is on self-reported emotions embedded in the viewing process.

Primary research was conducted to collect data after ad-viewing by the chosen sample. We applied data processing techniques to all the comments about advertisements shown in a controlled environment. Our purpose was to test whether we could automatically predict audiences' views on a number of ads and emotions from their responses. A machine learning classification approach was chosen in which an algorithm "emotions" was used to classify comments into categories from a given set of ranking of emotions based on their effectiveness. For this research approach we chose a combination of qualitative and quantitative data analysis, we first recorded multiple individual experiences where we tried finding out what people think, how they feel. This kind of information that we recorded was subjective. It involved feelings and emotions that the viewer felt while viewing the ad. Thus a plural research design was followed in this study where qualitative and quantitative research methods were adopted.

DATA ANALYSIS AND FINDINGS

Advertisers have long believed that advertising must arouse some emotion to be effective. This affective response is important for two main reasons. First, the key to branding is the triggering of a meaningful emotional response, which is often, and perhaps always, the major benefit of using the particular product. Second, the process that consumers go through in deciding what brands to buy has a heavy emotion-based dimension to it. In both cases, advertising can be an effective source of enhancement of these emotional responses.

To understand how emotion works in advertising or how it interacts with the recall measure in advertising testing, a basic knowledge of the memory process is useful. Memory is a critical part of consumer behavior and of how advertising influences consumer behavior. Consumers usually do not make brand purchase choices at the time of advertising exposure; rather, it is the memory of the advertising messages that influences consumers. The importance of recall stems from the fact that recall measures some aspect of this memory of the advertising.

Exposure to the medium of advertising was found to be one of the major factors influencing recall of an ad by the viewer. It was found that more male viewers found

How much time do you spend in a day on each of the following media (mention in hours) = 60

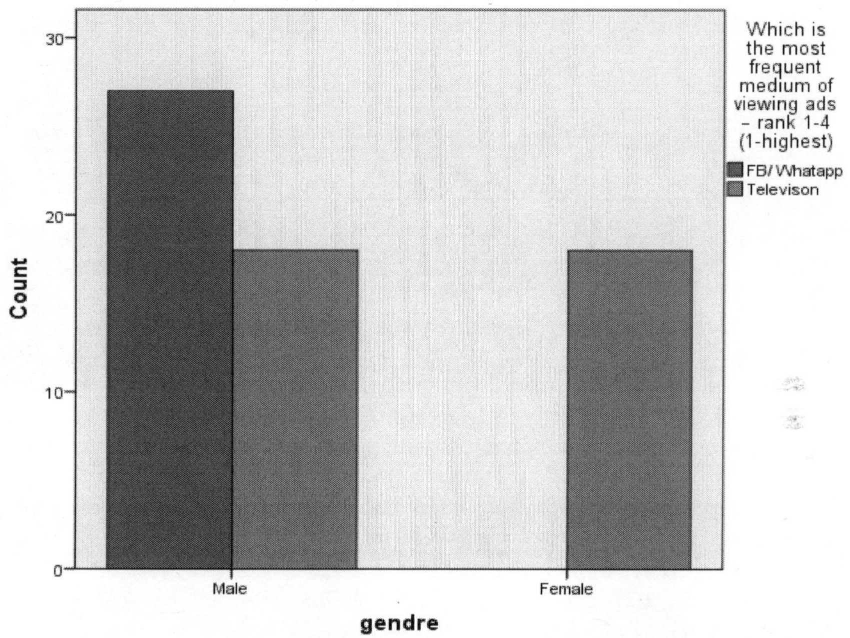

How much time do you spend in a day on each of the following media (mention in hours) = 120

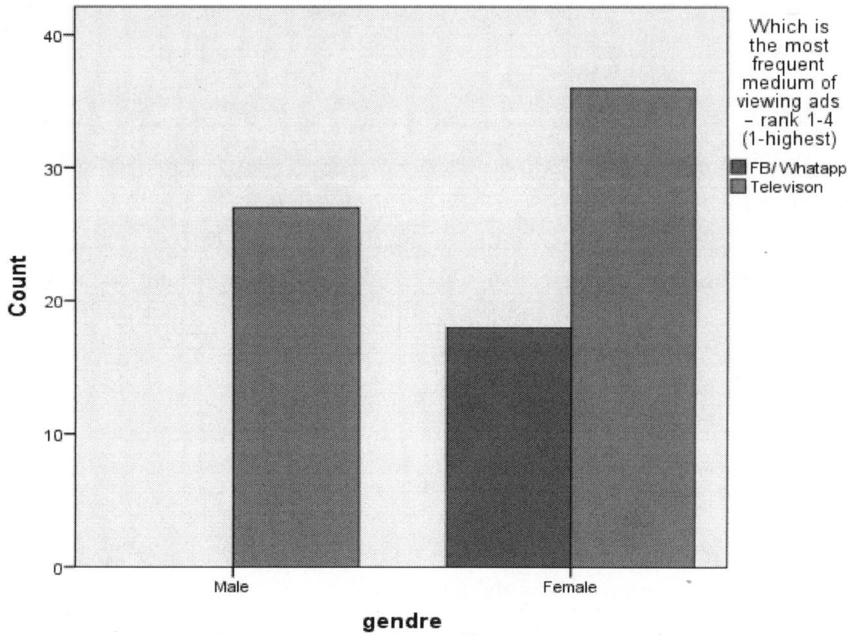

Fig. 1: Comparative time spent on FB/Whatsapp by Males and Females

FB/Whatsapp more preferred over TV viewing. TV viewing was ranked equally for males and females.

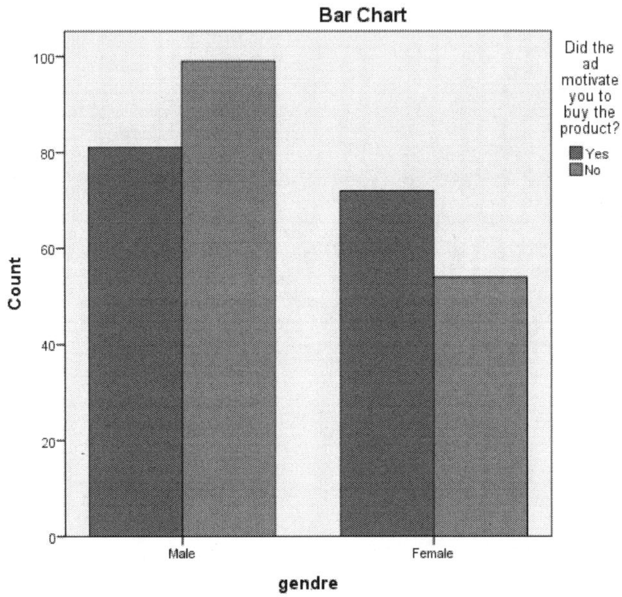

Fig. 2: The Conversion from Attention to Action, Where Viewers were Actually Motivated to Buy the Telecom or Insurance Product

We compared the ranking of emotions that were felt by the audience – out of the following emotions – reliability/security, commitment, sincerity, sensitive/thoughtful. The result that we found was as follows in the telecom and insurance ads.

In both the sectors, commitment was found to be ranked the highest by males and females. The common emotion that was found by both genders in insurance and telecom was Reliability.

After collecting this data we focused on measuring objective facts, where we used Sentiment Analysis to measure the effect of gender on emotion. Subsequently we found that various other results were recorded during data analysis. Sentiment analysis if integrated with quantitative research facilitates more insightful feedback into customer feelings, insights, opinions and sentiments.

A technique called "information gain" was used to reduce the size of the bag-of-words by identifying those words with the lowest certainty of belonging to a given emotion, and then removing them—this is an approach to Cognitive Path Selection. This improves the computation time and also demonstrates the words with highest predictive accuracy. Having calculated the accuracy of our prediction algorithm, the results of the sentiment analysis were then compared with the qualitative data collected for this research.

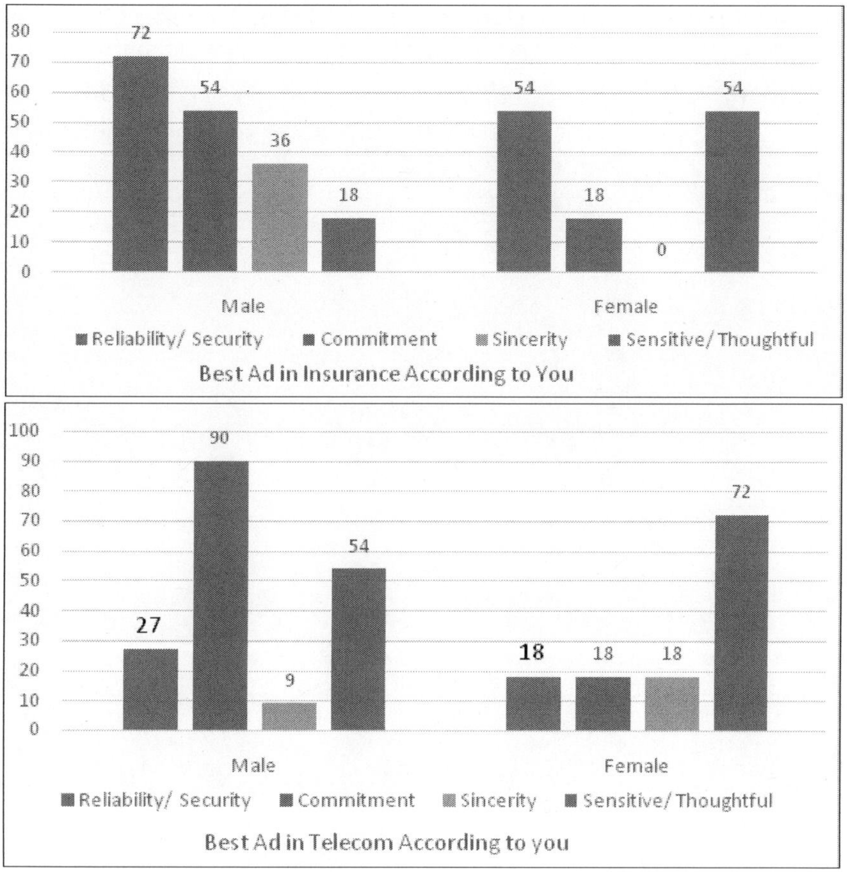

Fig. 3: Comparison of Emotions in Insurance and Telecom Industries by Males and Females

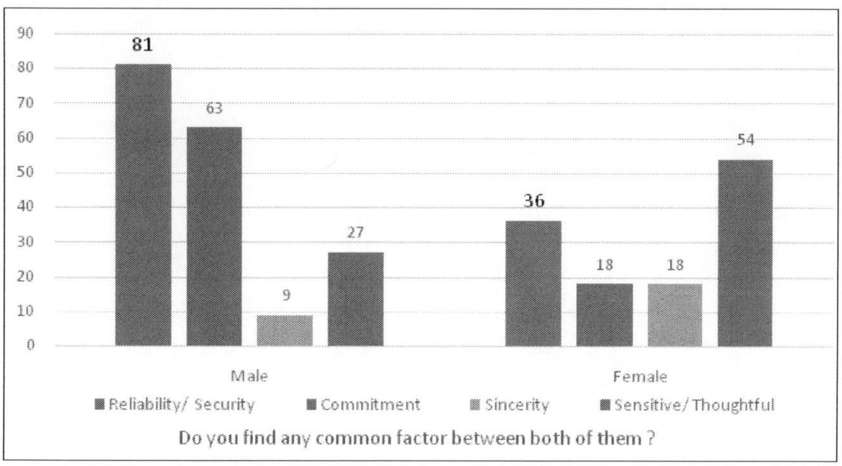

Fig. 4: Common Emotion between Insurance and Telecom as Ranked by Males and Females

Sentiment		*Reliability/ Security*	*Commitment*	*Sincerity*	*Sensitive/ Thoughtful*
Gender	Male	72	54	36	18
	Female	54	18	0	54
Total		126	72	36	72

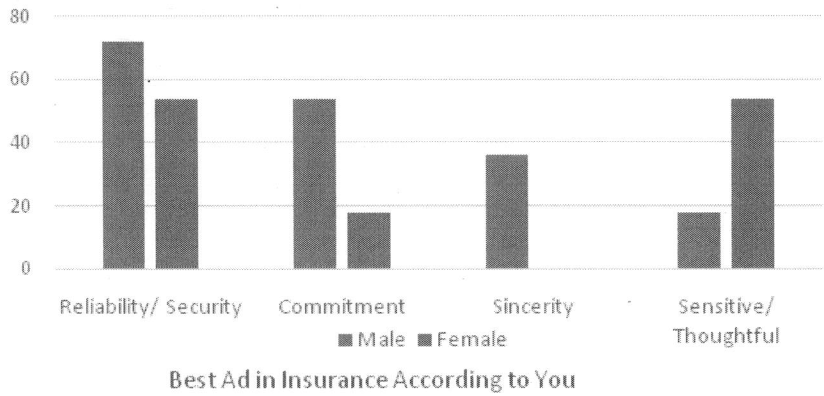

Fig. 5

Relation between Gender and Sentiment Ranking in Telecom Sector					
Sentiment		*Reliability/ Security*	*Commitment*	*Sincerity*	*Sensitive/ Thoughtful*
Gender	Male	27	90	9	54
	Female	18	18	18	72
Total		45	108	27	126

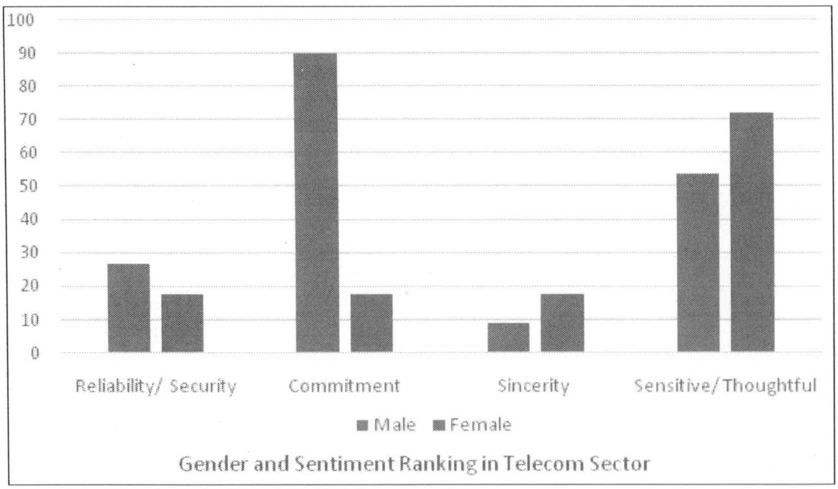

Fig. 6

RESEARCH LIMITATIONS/IMPLICATIONS

The empirical study is conducted within the telecom and insurance industry which may influence the advertising process through Cognitive Path Selection based on analysis of relation of gender of viewer and sentiment felt during Ad-viewing. This interpretation of emotional response and gender difference was based on theoretical assumptions of this particular sample design, where various discrete emotions are located on a continuum.

The controls used in this research were survey questionnaires which were filled by the study group after viewing of ads pre-approved and chosen for this research study. The Cognitive Path Selection model may vary with varying results with different emotions that rank highest.

Originality/Value

The paper offers insight into the role of emotion in advertising and use of that emotion in formulating a relationship using Sentiment Analysis. It forms the ground work to constructing a Cognitive Path Model based on emotion ranking for advertising. It studies the impact of gender on selection of emotion in advertisements. This paper suggests future research areas where the Cognitive Path Model can be applied in real world in Marketing Communication Plan.

BIBLIOGRAPHY

Aaker, D. A., & Keller, K. L. (1993). Interpreting cross-cultural replications of brand extension research. *International Journal of Research in Marketing, 10*(1), 55-59.

Agres, S. J., Edell, J. A., & Dubitsky, T. M. (1990). *Emotion in advertising: Theoretical and practical explorations*. Quorum Books.

Anderson, C. (2008). Wired Magazine, 16(7), 16–07. Retrieved from http://www2.research.att.com/~volinsky/DataMining/Papers/AndersonWired.pdf

Cho, H., & Stout, P. A. (1993). An extended perspective on the role of emotion in advertising processing. *Advances in Consumer Research*, *20*(1), 692-697.

Dubow, J. S. (1994). Point of View: Recall Revisited: Recall Redux. *Journal of Advertising Research, 34*, 92-92.

Fisher, R. J., & Dubé, L. (2005). Gender differences in responses to emotional advertising: A social desirability perspective. *Journal of Consumer Research, 31*(4), 850-858.

Friestad, M., & Thorson, E. (1986). Emotion-eliciting advertising: Effects on long term memory and judgment. *Advances in consumer research*, *13*(1), 111-116.

Godbole, N., Skiena, S., & Srinivasaiah, M. (2011). *U.S. Patent No. 7,996,210*. Washington, DC: U.S. Patent and Trademark Office.

Haley, R. I., & Baldinger, A. L. (1991). The ARF Copy Research Validity Project. *Journal of Advertising Research, 31*(2), Apr-May 1991, 11-32

Holbrook, M. B., & Batra, Rajeev (1987). Assessing the role of emotions as mediators of consumer responses to advertising. *Journal of Consumer Research, 14,* (3), 404-420

Holbrook, M. B., & O'Shaughnessy, J. (1984). The role of emotion in advertising. *Psychology & Marketing, 1*(2), 45-64.

Holbrook, M. B., & Westwood, R. A. (1989). The role of emotion in advertising revisited: Testing a typology of emotional responses. *Cognitive and affective responses to advertising*, 353-371.

Kastenholz, J., & Young, C. (2003). *How Recall Misses the Emotion in Advertising that Builds Brands.* Transcript Proceedings, Advertising Research Foundation, New York.

Kennedy, Alistair & Inkpen, Diana. (2006). Sentiment classification of movie and product reviews using contextual valence shifters. *Computational Intelligence, 22*(2),110–125

Kozinets, R. V. (2002). The field behind the screen: Using netnography for marketing research in online communities. *Journal of marketing research, 39*(1), 61-72.

Krauss, J., Nann, S., Simon, D., Fischbach, K., & Gloor, P. (2008). Predicting movie success and academy awards through sentiment and social network analysis. In *ECIS* (pp. 2026-2037).

Kumar, A., & Sebastian, T. M. (2012). Sentiment analysis on twitter. *IJCSI International Journal of Computer Science Issues, 9*(3), 372-378.

Lipton, Eric (2006). Software Being Developed to Monitor Opinions of U.S. New York Times, October 4, 2006. Retrieved from http://www.nytimes.com/2006/10/04/us/04monitor.html

Liu, B. (2010). Sentiment analysis: A multi-faceted problem. *IEEE Intelligent Systems, 25*(3), 76-80.

Lodish, L. M., & Lubetkin, B. (1992). General truths? Nine key findings from IRI test data. *Admap,* Feb, 9-15.

Mano, H., & Oliver, R.L. (1993). Assessing the dimensionality and structure of the consumption experience: evaluation, feeling, and satisfaction. *Journal of Consumer research,* 451-466. Chicago

Mast, F. W., & Zaltman, G. (2005). A behavioral window on the mind of the market: An application of the response time paradigm. *Brain Research Bulletin, 67*(5), 422-427.

Mehta, A., & Purvis, S. C. (2006). Reconsidering recall and emotion in advertising. *Journal of Advertising Research-New York, 46*(1), 49.

Morrison, S., & Crane, F. G. (2007). Building the service brand by creating and managing an emotional brand experience. *Journal of Brand Management, 14*(5), 410-421.

Neuendorf, K. A. (2002). *The content analysis guidebook* (Vol. 300). Thousand Oaks, CA: Sage Publications.

Nwankwo, B. E., Aboh, J. U., Obi, T. C., Agu, S. A., & Sydney-Agbor, N. (2013). Influence of advertising appeals and personality on telecoms consumption preferences in Nigeria. *International Journal of Academic Research in Business and Social Sciences, 3*(9), 229.

Osimo, D., & Mureddu, F. (2012). *Research Challenge on Opinion Mining and Sentiment Analysis*. Universite de Paris-Sud, Laboratoire LIMSI-CNRS, Bˆatiment, 508.Chicago

Pang, B., & Lee, L. (2008). Opinion mining and sentiment analysis. *Foundations and trends in information retrieval, 2*(1-2), 1-135.

Smith, T. W. (2012). Survey-research paradigms old and new. *International Journal of Public Opinion Research,* eds 040.

Wiles, J. A., & Cornwell, T. B. (1991). A review of methods utilized in measuring affect, feelings, and emotion in advertising. *Current Issues and Research in Advertising, 13*(1-2), 241-275.

PART TWO-D

DATA MANAGEMENT

Customer retention management, and customer churn prediction in particular, is gaining increasing importance in business environments as organizations acknowledge that it is imperative to identify customers who will end their relationship with their brand. Because customer churn is a rare event, undersampling is used to adjust the resulting skewed class distribution. The paper, "A Bagging-Based Undersampling Strategy for Classification: A Customer Churn Prediction Application" investigates the impact of undersampling on customer churn prediction to solve the class imbalance problem and proposes a new undersampling-based algorithm that uses bootstrap aggregation.

Collaborative filtering is a technique that is used to make personalized product recommendations, predicting movie ratings, etc on the Internet. This technique uses algorithms to make customized predictions about a user's likes and interests by consolidating preferences of several users. Online giants like Amazon, Netflix, iTunes, IMDB are examples of websites that employ this technology. Collaborative Filtering is mostly implemented in software like SAS and SQL. The paper, "Collaborative Filtering in Excel" as the title suggests illustrates the implementation of Collaborative Filtering in Excel, a commonly available software. It explains the Excel implementation for 5 different Collaborative techniques – Correlation, Cosine, Jaccard, Dice and Overlap using real-time data.

The paper, "Creating Customer Intelligence through Product-Mix Clustering: Applications & Challenges" discusses business intelligence techniques to have better targeted relationships with customers by making tailored offers basis their historical purchase behavior and also to predict buying behavior of new customers basis the profiles generated. With the advent of big data, many of the classical data clustering techniques such as k-means, rock, rskc and skmeans do not yield correct results due to the large dimension and sparseness of data and therefore need to be tweaked. The paper proposes a new clustering technique CLUTO, which has been tested to yield better quality and more defined clusters.

CHAPTER EIGHT

A BAGGING-BASED UNDERSAMPLING STRATEGY FOR CLASSIFICATION: A CUSTOMER CHURN PREDICTION APPLICATION

Kristof Coussement and Geert Verstraeten

ABSTRACT

Customer retention management deserves a lot of attention in today's business environment. One of the most data-driven tools in the retention toolbox of organizations is customer churn prediction, where one tries to identify customers who will end the relationship with the company by making use of historical information. Often customer churn is a rare event, which results in a skewed class distribution. This paper plunges into the impact of undersampling (ratio) on the customer churn prediction performance and benchmarks a newly proposed undersampling strategy that uses bootstrap aggregation.

Keywords: Undersampling, Churn prediction, Bagging, Ensemble.

INTRODUCTION

Customer retention management is increasingly important for organisations (Ang & Buttle, 2006). In particular, companies confirm that identifying those customers most likely to churn becomes inevitable, especially when markets become saturated (Keaveney & Parthasarathy, 2001). As such, establishing valuable relationships with existing customers rather than attracting new customers who are characterized by a high attrition rate is of crucial importance (Reichheld & Sasser, 1990; Richards & Jones, 2008). The use of information technology that makes it possible to produce and store an ever increasing amount of customer data, and the ever increasing computer performance, shed new light on customer churn prediction through the concept of data mining. Specifically, data mining techniques explore and analyse the huge amounts of available data in order to assist with the selection of those customers at risk (Dierkes, Bichler, & Krishnan, 2011; Hung, Yen, & Wang, 2006). Developments in database processing (Ziarko, 1991), data warehousing (Kelly, 1996), machine learning (Holsapple, Pakath, Jacob, & Zaveri, 1993; Shaw, 1993) and knowledge management (Amidon, 1998), have made data mining an attractive and practical tool to uncover hidden patterns in customer data. An important field in data mining is called classification (Fayyad & Uthurusamy, 1996).

Classification is the procedure where observations are predicted to belong to predefined groups or target classes based on their historical information. Methodologically, a classification model is built on a set of observations where the historical information and the target classes are available (the training set). As such, the classification model tries to link the historical information with the behavioural outcome. Once the classification model is trained, it is evaluated on a set of observations which are not used during the model building phase (the test set). The result is a probability indicating the chance of engaging in that particular behaviour. This classification process is no different for customer churn prediction where one tries to predict whether or not a customer will leave the company in the near future (Au, Chan, & Yao, 2003; Coussement & Van den Poel, 2008). The final outcome is a churn probability for every customer in the test set. Classifying these customers into churners and non-churners based on their probability to leave the company makes it possible to come up with a tailor-made retention program.

However, most of the currently available churn settings represent a highly unbalanced distribution between the churners and the non-churners, given the fact that the churn behaviour is a rare event in the majority of the industries (Neslin, Gupta, Kamakura, Lu, & Mason, 2006). Modelling rare events in marketing settings like customer churn prediction represent opportunities for future research.

> "The models developed in marketing are typically applied to situations where the events of interest occur with some frequency (e.g., customer churn, customer purchases). These models can break down when applied to settings where the behaviour of interest is rare. For example, when modelling the correlates of customer acquisition in a low-acquisition rate setting, the performance of the familiar logit model is often unacceptable. There may be opportunity to gain

valuable insights from the statistics literature on the modelling of rare events." (Gupta et al., 2006)

This paper contributes to the marketing literature by investigating the impact of undersampling as a strategy to solve the class imbalance problem using a large scale experimental setup, and by benchmarking a new undersampling-based algorithm, that combines undersampling with a bagging approach (Breiman, 1996), against related undersampling strategies.

The paper is structured as follows. The next Section describes the class imbalance and the undersampling strategies. Section 3 describes the methodology used throughout the paper, i.e. the newly proposed undersampling algorithm, U-bagging, the standard classifier and the evaluation metric. The next section gives insight into the empirical validation with the datasets description, the experimental setup, and the results. We end this research paper with a conclusion section.

CLASS IMBALANCE AND UNDERSAMPLING

Class imbalance has deserved a considerable amount of attention in the classification literature. Weiss (2004) discovered six problems related to rare event modelling; improper evaluation metrics, lack of data (absolute and relative rarity), data fragmentation, inappropriate inductive bias, and noise. Multiple strategies have been proposed to better address the class imbalance problem amongst which sampling strategies are the most popular in a churn prediction setting (e.g. Burez & Van den Poel, 2009; Verbeke, Dejaeger, Martens, Hur, & Baesens, 2012). The sampling-based strategies change the proportion of churners in the training dataset to make the class distribution more balanced in an attempt to improve churn prediction performance. Two main sampling-based strategies exist, oversampling (i.e. randomly duplicating churning customers to create a more balanced dataset) and undersampling (i.e. randomly deleting non-churners to balance the class distribution). This study focuses on undersampling for the following reasons. First, undersampling is a popular class imbalance technique in churn prediction (Chen, Fan, & Sun, 2012). Second, the effect of undersampling on churn prediction performance is unclear and needs further investigation (Burez & Van den Poel, 2009; Weiss & Provost, 2003). Third, it increases the scalability of the churn prediction modelling setup, as it reduces the, often large, dataset size available for training the churn prediction model. Finally, it is proven that oversampling has no impact on churn prediction performance, while it drastically increases the learning time of classifiers (Bellotti & Crook, 2009; Kennedy, Mac Namee, & Delany, 2013; Verbeke et al., 2012).

METHODOLOGY

U-bagging

This section briefly presents a detailed overview of the U-bagging algorithm. Consider the following notations. X is a set of p independent variables, $X = \{X_1, ..., X_p\}$ and Y is a binary response variable. Denote a training data set by $D = \{(x_i, y_i)\}^n_{i=1}$ with churn incidence, *inc*, consisting of n observations. Each observation (x_i, y_i) is a combination of an input vector x_i and a response y_i with $y_i \in \{0,1\}$. represents the subset of D containing the N_{churn} churners, while is the subset of the $N_{non\text{-}churn}$ non-churners. Training a base classifier C_l involves using the training data to formalize a mapping of the input variable space onto the binary response variable, Y. The prediction of a base classifier C_l is the conditional class membership probability $P(Y = 1 \mid X)$. A bagging ensemble classifier C consists of m base classifiers; $C = \{C_1, C_2, C_3, ..., C_m\}$. The churn incidence after having applied undersampling is represented by u.

The pseudo code of the U-bagging algorithms is given in Figure 1.

Training phase

If $u > inc$ **then do**
For $l = 1$ **to** m **do**
• Undersampling step
  – DNNon-churn|Under = unrestricted random sample from DNNon-churn with a number of observations, so DNChurn / DNNon-churn | Under = u
  – DUnder = DNChurn ∪ DNNon-churn | Under
• Model building step
o Estimate l-th base classifier C_1 using with C_l: $P_l(Y = 1 \mid X)$
end for
end if

Prediction phase
The probability for observation x to belong to the churn class, predicted by the U-bagging classifier C, is $C(x) = \frac{1}{m}\sum_{l=1}^{m} Cl(x)$

Fig. 1: Pseudo Code of the U-bagging Algorithm

Logistic Regression

Logistic regression is used as *standard* classifier throughout this research paper, given its popularity in churn prediction modelling (Neslin et al., 2006). Logistic regression is a well-known classification technique for predicting a dichotomous dependent variable. In running a logistic regression analysis, the maximum likelihood function is produced and maximized in order to achieve an appropriate fit to the data (Hosmer & Lemeshow, 2004). This technique is very popular in churn prediction for mainly three reasons: (1) logit modelling is conceptually simple. (2) a closed-form solution for the posterior probabilities is available; (3) it provides quick and robust results in comparison to other more advanced classification techniques (Neslin et al., 2006; Verbeke et al., 2012).

Variable selection is an important step in the prediction modeling phase, because it highly improves the quality of the final prediction model in terms of generalizability (Kim, 2006). Customer churn datasets usually contain a large number of customer characteristics. In this study, we employ the correlation-based feature selection (CBFS) heuristic of Hall (2000). We argue that CBFS is especially well-suited for churn prediction because it (1) is able to process datasets with both continuous and categorical variables, (2) avoids an expensive estimation of actual prediction model to assess variable candidates within the selection stage, and (3) can remove redundant variables, which alternative approaches to score variables one at a time are unable to detect.

Evaluation Metric

The area under the receiver operating curve (AUC) is used as the evaluation metric throughout this paper. The AUC is a popular evaluation metric in customer churn prediction, while it is used to evaluate the performance of a binary classification system (Hanley & McNeil, 1982). AUC takes into account the individual class performance for all possible thresholds. In other words, AUC will compare the predicted class of an event with the real class of that event, considering all possible cut-off values for the predicted class. The receiver operating curve (ROC) is a graphical plot of the sensitivity – i.e. the number of true positives versus the total number of events – and 1-specificity – i.e. the number of true negatives versus the total number of non-events. The ROC can also be represented by plotting the fraction of true positives versus the fraction of false positives. Intuitively, the AUC represents the probability that a randomly chosen churner will have a higher predicted churn probability than a randomly chosen non-churner.

EMPIRICAL VALIDATION

Data

This research study uses 11 real-life churn datasets originating from a variety of industries like telecommunication, retail, and financial services. The datasets show a variety of characteristics; variables range from 15 to 236, number of customers range from 876 to 74,122, while the churn incidence ranges from 1.76% to 47.37%.

Experimental Setup

This research paper compares the U-bagging algorithm incorporating logistic regression as base classifier against three well-known benchmark algorithms, i.e. a logistic regression without undersampling (Log), a logistic regression with undersampling (LOG+undersampling), and a bagged logistic regression model without undersampling (Bagging). The ensemble models (U-bagging and Bagging) use m equal to 100, while the undersampled churn incidence, u, ranges from 0.1 to 0.9 in steps of 0.1. Moreover, a 5x2 cross-validation is used, and the cross-validated AUC is used as performance metric. In order to test significance, the Wilcoxon signed-rank test with the Bonferroni-Dunn post-hoc test is used (Demsar, 2006; Dunn, 1961; Friedman, 1940; Wilcoxon, 1945).

Results

The contributions fall into four research questions:

- RQ1. What is the impact of the undersampled churn incidence (u) on customer churn prediction performance?
- RQ2. Does undersampling have an impact on customer churn prediction performance?
- RQ3. Does bagging improve the performance of a logistic regression with undersampling?
- RQ4. How does U-bagging perform against a logistic regression and a bagged logistic regression without undersampling?

RQ1. What is the impact of the undersampled churn incidence (u) on customer churn prediction performance?

Log+undersampling and U-bagging are significantly influenced by the undersampled churn incidence, u. Our results indicate that $u = 0.5$, or a balanced distribution between churners and non-churners, is the best undersampling ratio. U-bagging performs best at $u = 0.5$, while the option $u = 0.5$ is not significantly different than the best option for Log+undersampling. These results are in line with the previous undersampling habits in churn prediction literature (e.g. Coussement & Van den Poel, 2008). Moreover, our results indicate that u cannot be too large, because any upper deviations from $u = 0.5$ result in a loss in predictive performance. In detail,

U-bagging with u ∈ {0.8, 0.9} and Log+undersampling with u ∈ {0.6, 0.7, 0.8, 0.9} are significantly less performing than their $u = 0.5$ counterparts. As a consequence, the next research questions are answered under the $u = 0.5$ condition.

RQ2. Does undersampling have an impact on customer churn prediction performance?

Our results indicate that undersampling reduces the churn prediction performance significantly over the different datasets (Signed-rank S = 30, p < .01). This means that in general, the balanced training set ($u = 0.5$) does not increase the prediction performance of the training set with the initial churn incidence.

RQ3. Does bagging improve the performance of a logistic regression with undersampling?

The question remains whether bagging could improve the performance of logistic regression modelling on undersampled training sets. The results guide us to a confirmatory answer that U-bagging significantly improves the prediction performance of Log+undersampling (Signed-rank S = 33, p < .01).

RQ4. How does U-bagging perform against a logistic regression and a bagged logistic regression without undersampling?

The final research question gives insight into how U-bagging performs against a logistic regression without undersampling and bagged version of logistic regression on non undersampled datasets. The results lead to the fact that U-bagging performs significantly better than Log and Bagging (df = 2, $\chi^2 = 15.27$, p < .01, Log = 1.09, Bagging = 2.18, U-bagging = 2.73).

CONCLUSION

Nowadays, organisations realize that the information extracted from the customer database is a valuable tool to leverage their customer knowledge. Consequently, they are forced to shift away from their product-centric strategy and move towards a more customer-centric orientation, taking into account the long-term relationships with their customers, leading to a well-considered CRM strategy. One of the dimensions of CRM is customer churn prediction where one tries to predict whether or not a customer will stay with the retailer based on their historical information. This study validates the impact of undersampling for optimal churn detection and it proposes a new framework that combines bagging with undersampling.

First, the results indicate that undersampling does impact churn prediction performance. In concrete, the balanced distribution that contains as many churners as non-churners is a good option, while extreme undersampling significantly decreases the churn prediction performance. Second, undersampling does negatively impact the churn prediction performance of logistic regression modelling. Third, the newly proposed algorithm, U-bagging, that combines bagging with undersampling for logistic regression modelling, boosts the logistic regression performance whether or not undersampling is employed. Finally, U-bagging speeds up the traditional bagging algorithm, because the logistic regressions are trained on undersampled datasets that are much smaller by definition.

REFERENCES

Amidon, D.M. (1998). Blueprint for 21st century innovation management. *Journal of Knowledge Management, 2*(1), 23-31.

Ang, L., & Buttle, F. (2006). Customer retention management processes - A quantitative study. *European Journal of Marketing, 40*(1-2), 83-99, doi: 10.1108/03090560610637329

Au, W.H., Chan, K.C.C., & Yao, X. (2003). A novel evolutionary data mining algorithm with applications to churn prediction. *IEEE Transactions on Evolutionary Computation, 7*(6), 532-545, doi: 10.1109/tevc.2003.819264

Bellotti, T., & Crook, J. (2009). Support vector machines for credit scoring and discovery of significant features. *Expert Systems with Applications, 36*(2), 3302-3308, doi: 10.1016/j.eswa.2008.01.005

Breiman, L. (1996). Bagging predictors. *Machine Learning, 24*, 123-140.

Burez, J., & Van den Poel, D. (2009). Handling class imbalance in customer churn prediction. *Expert Systems with Applications, 36*, 4626-4636.

Chen, Z.-Y., Fan, Z.-P., & Sun, M. (2012). A hierarchical multiple kernel support vector machine for customer churn prediction using longitudinal behavioral data. *European Journal of Operational Research, 223*(2), 461-472, doi: 10.1016/j.ejor.2012.06.040

Coussement, K., & Van den Poel, D. (2008). Churn prediction in subscription services: An application of support vector machines while comparing two parameter-selection techniques. *Expert Systems with Applications, 34*, 313-327.

Coussement, K., & Van den Poel, D. (2008). Integrating the voice of customers through call center emails into a decision support system for chum prediction. *Information & Management, 45*(3), 164-174, doi: 10.1016/j.im.2008.01.005

Demsar, J. (2006). Statistical comparisons of classifiers over multiple data sets. *Journal of Machine Learning Research, 7*, 1-30.

Dierkes, T., Bichler, M., & Krishnan, R. (2011). Estimating the effect of word of mouth on churn and cross-buying in the mobile phone market with Markov logic networks. *Decision Support Systems, 51*(3), 361-371, doi: 10.1016/j.dss.2011.01.002

Dunn, O. J. (1961). Multiple comparisons among means. *Journal of the American Statistical Association, 56*, 52-64.

Fayyad, U., & Uthurusamy, R. (1996). Data mining and knowledge discovery in databases. [Editorial Material]. *Communications of the ACM, 39*(11), 24-26, doi: 10.1145/240455.240463

Friedman, M. (1940). A comparison of alternative tests of significance for the problem of m rankings. *The Annals of Mathematical Statistics, 11*, 86-92.

Gupta, S., Hanssens, D., Hardie, B., Kahn, W., Kumar, V., Lin, N., . . . Sriram, S. (2006). Modeling customer lifetime value. *Journal of Service Research, 9*, 139-155.

Hall, M.A. (2000). *Correlation-Based Feature Selection for Discrete and Numeric Class Machine Learning*. Paper presented at the Proc. of the 17th Intern. Conf. on Machine Learning, Stanford, CA, USA.

Hanley, J.A., & McNeil, B.J. (1982). The meaning and use of the area under a receiver operating characteristic (roc) curve. *Radiology, 143*, 29-36.

Holsapple, C.W., Pakath, R., Jacob, V.S., & Zaveri, J.S. (1993). Learning by problem processors – Adaptive decision-support systems. *Decision Support Systems, 10*(2), 85-108, doi: 10.1016/0167-9236(93)90032-x

Hosmer, D.W., & Lemeshow, S. (2004). *Applied Logistic Regression*: Hoboken, NJ: Wiley.

Hung, S.Y., Yen, D.C., & Wang, H.Y. (2006). Applying data mining to telecom chum management. *Expert Systems with Applications, 31*(3), 515-524, doi: 10.1016/j.eswa.2005.09.080

Keaveney, S.M., & Parthasarathy, M. (2001). Customer switching behavior in online services: An exploratory study of the role of selected attitudinal, behavioral, and demographic factors. *Journal of the Academy of Marketing Science, 29*(4), 374-390.

Kelly, S. (1996). *Data warehousing: The route to mass customization*: New York: Wiley.

Kennedy, K., Mac Namee, B., & Delany, S. J. (2013). Using semi-supervised classifiers for credit scoring. *Journal of the Operational Research Society, 64*(4), 513-529, doi: 10.1057/jors.2011.30

Kim, Y.S. (2006). Toward a successful CRM: variable selection, sampling, and ensemble. *Decision Support Systems, 41*, 542-553.

Neslin, S.A., Gupta, S., Kamakura, W., Lu, J. X., & Mason, C.H. (2006). Defection detection: Measuring and understanding the predictive accuracy of customer churn models. *Journal of Marketing Research, 43*(2), 204-211.

Reichheld, F.F., & Sasser, W.E. (1990). Zero defections - quality comes to services. *Harvard Business Review, 68*(5), 105-111.

Richards, K.A., & Jones, E. (2008). Customer relationship management: Finding value drivers. *Industrial Marketing Management, 37*(2), 120-130, doi: 10.1016/j.indmarman.2006.08.005

Shaw, M. J. (1993). Machine learning – Methods for intelligence decision support – An introduction [Editorial Material]. *Decision Support Systems, 10*(2), 79-83, doi: 10.1016/0167-9236(93)90031-w

Verbeke, W., Dejaeger, K., Martens, D., Hur, J., & Baesens, B. (2012). New insights into churn prediction in the telecommunication sector: A profit driven data mining approach. *European Journal of Operational Research, 218*(1), 211-229. doi: 10.1016/j.ejor.2011.09.031

Weiss, G. M. (2004). Mining with rarity: a unifying framework. *SIGKDD Explorations Newsletter, 6*(1), 7-19. doi: 10.1145/1007730.1007734

Weiss, G. M., & Provost, F. (2003). Learning when training data are costly: the effect of class distribution on tree induction. *Journal of Artificial Intelligence Research, 19*(1), 315-354.

Wilcoxon, F. (1945). Individual comparisons by ranking methods. *Biometrics Bulletin, 1*(6), 80-83. doi: 10.2307/3001968

Ziarko, W. (1991). The discovery, analysis and representation of data dependencies in databases. In. *Knowledge discovery in databases*. Massachusetts: MIT press.

CHAPTER NINE

COLLABORATIVE FILTERING IN EXCEL

John Dilip Raj, K. Suryaprakasa Rao and Rohit Nair

ABSTRACT

Collaborative Filtering has been used extensively to find similarity in text data, predict movie ratings, and for recommending products online. Many times, this technique is implemented in software like SAS, in SQL or the like. This paper attempts to document the steps required to implement Collaborative Filtering in a tool available to many, Excel.

The first contribution of the paper is that for five different Collaborative Filtering techniques (Correlation, Cosine, Jaccard, Dice and Overlap), formulae have been provided in Excel so that more expensive difficult tools need not be used for this purpose. Using these simple formulae in Excel, it has been shown how this can successfully predict propensity to purchase different product categories at the same time. The second contribution of the paper is that these techniques, requiring just one binary variable per product, have been compared using real-time data. A related, further contribution is that this technique could well do away with a lot of customized, complex models which are time consuming, expensive to build, maintain and thus streamline/rationalize the process, without much compromise on the predictive power.

Keywords: Collaborative Filtering, Excel, Correlation, Cosine, Jaccard, Dice, Overlap.

INTRODUCTION

Similarity measures have been used in a variety of fields, including Biology (Baselga, Jiménez-Valverde and Niccolini, 2007). Both small as well as large companies (Das, Datar, Garg and Rajaram, 2007) also employ these measures in their recommendation engines. The fact that recommendations can both be personalized and largely accurate is one of the reasons why the technique is very popular (Formoso, Fernández, Cacheda and Carneiro, 2013). Collaborative Filtering not just helps business but can also help consumers make better choices (Hennig-Thurau, Marchand and Marx, 2012). A comprehensive review of Collaborative Filtering techniques is given by Su and Khoshgoftaar (2009).

FORMULAE FOR COLLABORATIVE FILTERING IN EXCEL

The data required for Collaborative Filtering can be as simple as historical binary purchase data of consumers. Table 1 details such information for 10 accounts (A1 through A10) across five product categories (PC1 to PC5). The value '1' is entered if an account has purchased the product category in a selected historical time frame and '0' if it has not.

Table 1: Customer Product Matrix

	Observation Time Period				
Account/ Product Category	*PC1*	*PC2*	*PC3*	*PC4*	*PC5*
A1	1	0	1	1	1
A2	1	1	0	1	0
A3	0	1	0	1	0
A4	0	1	1	1	0
A5	1	0	1	1	1
A6	0	1	0	1	0
A7	0	1	0	1	0
A8	0	1	0	0	0
A9	0	1	0	1	1
A10	0	1	0	1	0

Once the account – product category matrix is populated, the next step is finding the similarity between each product category. Five different ways to do this are detailed in the following sections.

Correlation

One of the most common produces in Collaborative Filtering is Correlation. A direct function for the same is available in Excel.

Table 2: Product Similarity Matrix using Correlation

Correlation

	PC1	PC2	PC3	PC4	PC5
PC1	1	-0.76	0.52	0.22	0.52
PC2	-0.76	1	-0.76	-0.17	-0.76
PC3	0.52	-0.76	1	0.22	0.52
PC4	0.22	-0.17	0.22	1	0.22
PC5	0.52	-0.76	0.52	0.22	1

The above table shows the product similarity matrix which is calculated using Table 1 and the value is calculated as below using one simple formula in Excel. For example, to determine the correlation between PC3 and PC4, use the formula,

CORREL(E6:E15,F6:F15)

where E6-E15 is the past customer purchase history for PC3 and F6:F15 for PC4. The similarity in this case is 0.22. In the same way, the similarity between PC1 and PC5 using correlation is calculated using the formula,

=CORREL(C6:C15,G6:G15)

To determine which accounts are most likely to purchase across product categories, a recommendation matrix is needed. This is achieved using matrix multiplication of Tables 1 and 2. The steps in Excel are as given below.

- Select the entire range, i.e. Q6:U15, in this case, and in the function (fx) space on the top of the Excel sheet using the formula as is Figure 1a.

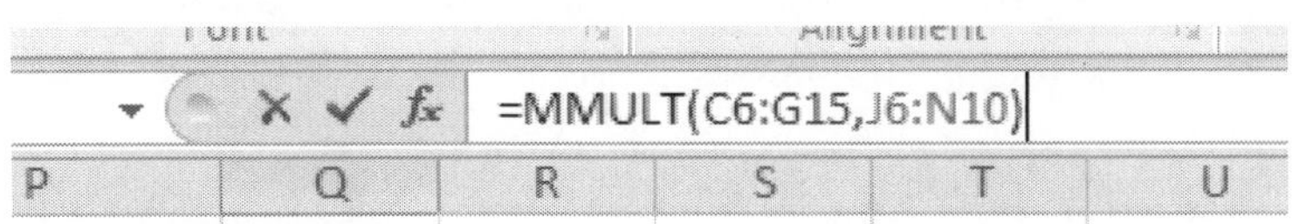

Fig. 1a: First part of Matrix Multiplication Formula in Excel

Here, C6:G15 is the purchase history of all accounts across product categories as in Table 1 and J6:N10 is the product similarity matrix using correlation as in Table 2.

- After entering the formula 'Shift+Ctrl+Enter' buttons are used together, to apply the matrix multiplication to all the cells. The formula now appears as in Figure 1 band Table3 is generated.

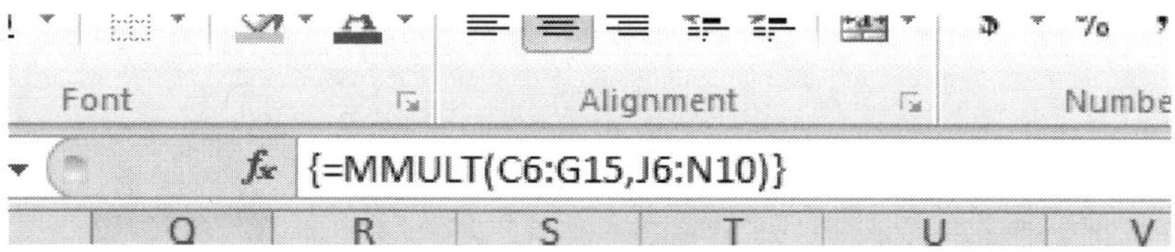

Fig. 1b: Second Part of Matrix Multiplication Formula in Excel

Table 3: Customer Recommendation using Correlation

Customer Recommendation using Correlation

Account/ Product Category	*PC1*	*PC2*	*PC3*	*PC4*	*PC5*
A1	2.27	-2.46	2.27	1.65	2.27
A2	0.45	0.07	-0.02	1.05	-0.02
A3	-0.55	0.83	-0.55	0.83	-0.55
A4	-0.02	0.07	0.45	1.05	-0.02
A5	2.27	-2.46	2.27	1.65	2.27
A6	-0.55	0.83	-0.55	0.83	-0.55
A7	-0.55	0.83	-0.55	0.83	-0.55
A8	-0.76	1	-0.76	-0.17	-0.76
A9	-0.02	0.07	-0.02	1.05	0.45
A10	-0.55	0.83	-0.55	0.83	-0.55

The above table is used for targeting accounts. If the objective is to target the top 10% of accounts for product category 2 (PC2), then account 8 (A8) is chosen. Among the least likely to purchase PC2 would be accounts A1 and A5.

Cosine, Jaccard, Dice, Overlap

Unlike Correlation, the other four techniques, Cosine, Jaccard, Dice and Overlap do not seem to have direct formulae in Excel and therefore the calculation can be split into two parts, the numerator and denominator. The numerator is the same for all these four techniques while the denominator is different for each.

The 'sumproduct' function in Excel, as shown in Figure 3, is used to calculate the numerator for these four techniques. The numerator gives the number of accounts that purchased both the product categories under consideration. For example, to calculate the numerator for similarity between PC1 & PC5 and between PC3 & PC4, the formula is as in Figures 2a and 2b.

Fig. 2a: Numerator for Product Similarity between PC1 and PC5

Fig. 2b: Numerator for Product Similarity between PC3 and PC4

Once these formulae are applied for all the possible product category combinations, Table 4 is generated.

Table 4: Numerator for Cosine, Jaccard, Dice, Overlap across Product Categories

	PC1	*PC2*	*PC3*	*PC4*	*PC5*
PC1	3	1	2	3	2
PC2	1	8	1	7	1
PC3	2	1	3	3	2
PC4	3	7	3	9	3
PC5	2	1	2	3	3

The next step is to determine the denominator for each of the four techniques.

Denominator for Cosine

One of the most popular Collaborative Filtering Technique is the Cosine Similarity Function. PROC IML in SAS achieves this very easily. Similarity, SQL coding can also be written to get the same results.

The denominator in Cosine is calculated using the diagonal value (highlighted in green below) from Table 4 (where the numerator was calculated)

For example, to find the value between PC3 & PC4 and PC1 and PC4, the formulae will be as in Figure 3a and 3b respectively.

=SQRT(L18)*SQRT(M19)

Fig. 3a: Denominator for Cosine – PC3 and PC4

=SQRT(J16)*SQRT(N20)

Fig. 3b: Denominator for Cosine – PC1 and PC4

The same is calculated across all product categories and the denominator as in Table 5 is generated.

Table 5: Denominator for Cosine across Product Categories

	I	J	K	L	M	N
22						
23	**Denominator for Cosine**					
24						
25		***PC1***	***PC2***	***PC3***	***PC4***	***PC5***
26	***PC1***	3	4.9	3	5.2	3
27	***PC2***	4.9	8	4.9	8.5	4.9
28	***PC3***	3	4.9	3	5.2	3
29	***PC4***	5.2	8.5	5.2	9	5.2
30	***PC5***	3	4.9	3	5.2	3

Denominator for Jaccard

Another popular Collabortive Filtering Technique is Jaccard. Here too, like Cosine, calculation of the numerator is the same but the denominator is different. The denominator in this case, for example, between PC1 and PC2 shows the total number who bought PC1, and the total number who bought PC2, but excluding those who bought both. Figures 4a and 4b show the denomintor for product categories PC1 & PC3 and PC4 & PC5 respectively.

=J16+L18-J18

Fig. 4a: Denomintor for Jaccard – PC1 and PC3

=M19+N20-M20

Fig. 4b: Denomintor for Jaccard – PC4 and PC5

Repeating the above across all product categories gives us the denominator for Jaccard, as in Table 6.

Table 6: Denominator for Jaccard across Product Categories

Denominator for Jaccard

	PC1	*PC2*	*PC3*	*PC4*	*PC5*
PC1	3	10	4	9	4
PC2	10	8	10	10	10
PC3	4	10	3	9	4
PC4	9	10	9	9	9
PC5	4	10	4	9	3

Denominator for Dice

A technique very close to that of Jaccard is Dice. In this case, the sum of all who bought the two products (not mutually exclusive) is taken. For example, Figures 5a and 5b give the denominator for product categories PC3 &PC4and PC1 & PC3 respectively.

fx =L18+M19

Fig. 5a: Denomintor for Dice – PC3 and PC4

fx =J16+L18

Fig. 5b: Denomintor for Dice – PC1 and PC3

Replicating the same formulae across all product categories leads us to Table 7.

Table 7: Denominator for Dice across Product Categories

Denominator for Dice

	PC1	*PC2*	*PC3*	*PC4*	*PC5*
PC1	6	11	6	12	6
PC2	11	16	11	17	11
PC3	6	11	6	12	6
PC4	12	17	12	18	12
PC5	6	11	6	12	6

Denominator for Overlap

Among the popular Collaborative Filtering features Simpson Overlap (Nirgude, Sharma and Sedamkar, 2013). It is also one of the easier ones to implement in many tools including Excel. Here, for example, to calculate the denominator for product categories PC2 and PC3 (cell K58 in this case), the minimum number of accounts who have purchased either of the two product categories is taken, as shown in Figure 6a.

Fig. 6a: Denomintor for Overlap – PC2 and PC3

The same when done for all the product categories gives results as in Table 8.

Table 8: Denominator for Overlap across Product Categories

	I	J	K	L	M	N
52						
53	**Denominator for Overlap**					
54						
55		*PC1*	*PC2*	*PC3*	*PC4*	*PC5*
56	*PC1*	3	3	3	3	3
57	*PC2*	3	8	3	8	3
58	*PC3*	3	3	3	3	3
59	*PC4*	3	8	3	9	3
60	*PC5*	3	3	3	3	3

Product Similarity Matrix (Cosine, Jaccard, Dice, Overlap)

With the numerator and denomintor calculated across product categories, the next step is the division of the two. In other words, this product category similarity matrix is similar for all the the techniques and is obtained using the ratio of numerator to the denominator (the denominator which is different for all the four techniques). For example, product category similarity matrix using cosine similarity for PC3 and PC4 (cell L68) is the ratio of L19 to L29. The same ratio holds true for the other three (Jaccard, Dice and Overlap) techniques as well. The product similarity matrix using Cosine Similarity is thereby as in Table 9.

Table 9: Product Category Similarity Matrix using Cosine Similarity Function

Product Similarity Matrix using Cosine

	PC1	*PC2*	*PC3*	*PC4*	*PC5*
PC1	1	0.20	0.67	0.58	0.67
PC2	0.20	1	0.20	0.82	0.20
PC3	0.67	0.20	1	0.58	0.67
PC4	0.58	0.82	0.58	1	0.58
PC5	0.67	0.20	0.67	0.58	1

It is to be noted that only for Dice, post finding the ratio of the numerator and denomintor, it is multipled by '2' to obtain the product similarity matrix.

Customer Recommendation using Cosine, Jaccard, Dice, Overlap

The customer recommendation follows the same process that was followed in Correlation, by multiplying Table 1 with the product similarity matrix of the different techniques.

RESULTS

All these five techniques were compared on real-time data. Given that the data is confidential, the data is masked and displayed. However, the lift charts are comparable to the actual results obtained. Figure 7 shows the results for one product category. The results are of Collaborative Filtering applied on over 4000 accounts and actual purchase behavior in the next few months. The response rate in this case was around 20%. An existing Logistic Regression model was also considered.

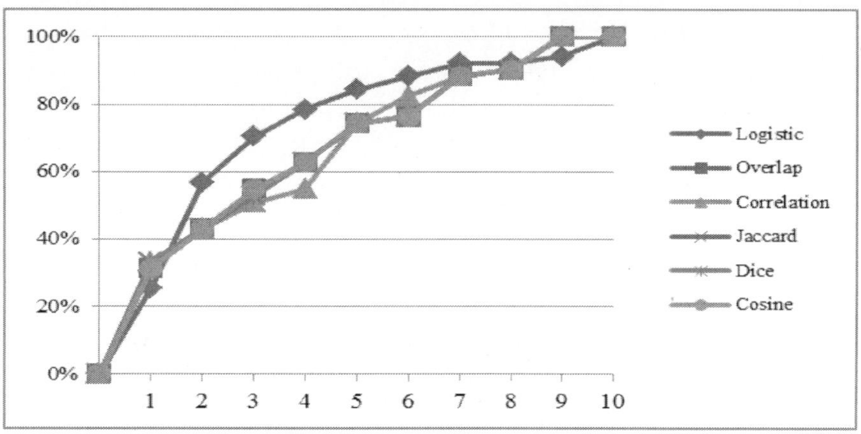

Fig. 7: Decile-wise Cumulative Response Rate across Different Models

Given the regression model had more data to predict performance, it performs better, but it has been seen that Collaborative Filtering also does produce strong results. Regression or many other techniques though may require separate models for each product category whereas in Collaborative Filtering it is just one. In this case, Cosine, Jaccard, Dice and Overlap show very similar performance, as seen in Table 10 and therefore is not seen separately in Figure 7.

Table 10: Performance in Top Deciles across Different Models

Decile/Model	*Logistic*	*Overlap*	*Correlation*	*Jaccard*	*Dice*	*Cosine*
2 (Top 20%)	57%	43%	43%	43%	43%	43%
4 (Top 40%)	78%	63%	55%	63%	63%	63%

These results are only for the data used and can vary by industry, availability, predictability of data and other factors.

CONCLUSIONS, LIMITATIONS AND FUTURE DIRECTIONS FOR RESEARCH

An attempt has been made in this paper to simplify Collaborative Filtering so that the technique can be used even when no high end software like SAS or even SQL coding is available. While there are websites where these calculations can be done, infinite number of accounts and product categories may not be allowed to enter. It is here that providing the formulae for the technique in a widely available tool is of great use. This will be beneficial not only to very small startups, and students who do not have access to much software, but also to businesses who want to use simple tools.

In the paper, there was no issue with non-availability of binary data, whether a customer previously purchased a product category or not. This should not be an issue in either B2B or B2C. However, in case like ratings, where is missing data, more advanced Collaborative Filtering techniques using Genetic Programming (Anand, 2012) and such can be explored.

Goldenberg, Oestreicher-Singer and Reichman (2012) note that websites have started creating a dual-network structure where they offer social networks and user-generated links, along with the product network. The dual network exposure has been empirically shown to increase average product rating and overall satisfaction.

There are more Collaborative Filtering techniques apart from the five covered in this paper. Similar work would help spread the technique more and enable more to learn and apply the same.

REFERENCES

Anand, Deepa. (2012). Feature Extraction for Collaborative Filtering: A Genetic Programming Approach. *International Journal of Computer Science Issues*, *9*(5), 348-354.

Baselga, Andrés, Jiménez-Valverde, Alberto, & Niccolini, Gilles. (2007) A Multiple-site Similarity Measure Independent of Richness. *Biology Letters, 3*(6), 642-645.

Das, Abhinandan, Datar, Mayur, Garg, Ashutosh, & Rajaram, Shyam. (2007). Google News Personalization: Scalable Online Collaborative Filtering. *International World Wide Web Conference*, 271-280.

Formoso, Vreixo, FernáNdez, Diego, Cacheda, Fidel, & Carneiro, Victor. (2013). Using Profile Expansion Techniques to Alleviate the New User Problem. *Information Processing and Management, 49*(3), 659-672.

Goldenberg, Jacob, Oestreicher-Singer, Gal, & Reichman, Shachar. (2012). The Quest for Content: How User-generated Links can Facilitate Online Exploration. *Journal of Marketing Research, 49*(4), 452-468.

Hennig-Thurau, Thorsten, Marchand, André, & Marx, Paul. (2012). Can Automated Group Recommender Systems Help Consumers Make Better Choices? *Journal of Marketing, 76*(5), 89-109.

Nirgude, Vaishali, Sharma, Rekha & Sedamkar, R.R. (2013). A Web Search Engine based approach to Measure the Semantic Similarity between Words using Page Count and Snippets Method (PCSM). *International Journal of Advanced Research in Computer Engineering & Technology,* 2(7), 2252-2257.

Su, Xiaoyuan, & Khoshgoftaar, Taghi M. (2009). A Survey of Collaborative Filtering Techniques. *Advances in Artificial Intelligence*. 19 pages. Retrieved from: www.hindawi.com/journals/aai/2009/421425/

CHAPTER TEN

CREATING CUSTOMER INTELLIGENCE THROUGH PRODUCT-MIX CLUSTERING: APPLICATIONS AND CHALLENGES

Ashish Mahalka

ABSTRACT

Understanding one's customer needs and preferences has become a critical requirement in doing business. One important aspect of customer analytics is clustering or grouping customers based on buying patterns. Both supervised and unsupervised machine learning techniques are available at our disposal to enable grouping of customers. The choice of algorithm depends on the dataset (categorical or numerical fields) on which it is applied. A common problem in clustering large and sparse datasets (observed in retail which has a huge assortment of products at sku level) is that the classical techniques are unable to provide useful results and often does not lead to sufficient dimension reduction to yield informative results. It fails to remove the noise in the dataset and extract relevant information. This paper proposes to tackle the above problem by using an algorithm invariably used in document classification. The paper talks about all the techniques that were used in order to achieve satisfactory results and outcomes and challenges of each of those techniques.

Keywords: Cluster Analysis, Sparse, Large Dimension, Retail, Buying Pattern, Sku Level.

INTRODUCTION

Importance of the Study

The advent of big data and analytics and the tremendous rise of the digital economy have brought in enormous quantities of data which is being generated far more easily and cheaply than ever before. Fast-forward thinking organizations are recognizing data as a strategic asset and leveraging it to make critical business decisions and strengthen their competitive advantage. Retailers, who have long been looking to build customer intelligence so that they can create customized offers and have a better targeted relationship with their customers, are keen to put analytics systems in place. Such business intelligence tools have proven to generate better marketing results and lead to higher sales growth and profitability and to increased customer satisfaction. Many of the available classical techniques failed to yield proper results if the dataset in consideration is of large dimension and sparse. And therefore these techniques need to be tweaked to handle this special dataset and arrive at informative and satisfactory results.

Objective of the Study

The primary objective of the paper is to group customers based on their historical purchase behaviour and derive meaningful and actionable business insights which can then become a framework for measuring results. The clusters are then used to characterize the different customer groups and these characterizations are used in targeted marketing and advertising specific products as directed towards specific customer groups. The characterizations can also be used to predict buying patterns on new customers based on the profiles generated.

Organization of the Sections

The rest of the paper is divided into the following sections. Section II talks about the problem formulation and dataset creation for the various clustering algorithms, Section III deals with references to related research work, Section IV gives details of the methodologies that were used and Section V elaborates on the results obtained from the final algorithm chosen and insights generated from the model. Section VI presents the final conclusions and scope for future work.

PROBLEM FORMULATION

The dataset in consideration is of an Asia-Pacific distributor and the sales transactional data for a period of 16 months is available (approx. 1 million rows). It has mostly business customers belonging to hotels, restaurants, cafes, hospitals, schools, supermarkets, etc. The important fields in the dataset can be divided into 3 categories:

1. **Customer Information** – customerID, customer group, transport zone, menu price, seat capacity

   The whole region is divided into 3 main delivery zones and then into a total of 68 sub-zones. The hotel, café and restaurant customer groups have menu prices which can range from \$50–350 and seating capacity from 50-250. For other groups of customers these fields are "Not Applicable".
2. **Product Information** – item no, segment, product hierarchy, brand, packing size

   The product information follows a hierarchical relationship where "*segment*" is the first level, "*product hierarchy*" second level, "*brand*" and "*packing*" the third and fourth levels.
3. **Transaction Information** – customerID, invoice date, item no, sale amount, cost of goods sold, volume/no of cases

   In order to be able to use the dataset for modelling and insights generation, the transaction data was cleaned and missing values imputed. All the observations related to return of the goods were ignored in the modelling process.

Sparse Matrix

The transactions in the database can be viewed as records with Boolean attributes, each attribute corresponding to a single item. Each record for a customer is represented as a binary vector, the attribute corresponding to an item is *true or '1'* if and only if the customer purchases the item; otherwise, it is *false or '0'*. These Boolean attributes themselves are a special case of categorical variables.

$$[\text{Sparse Matrix}]_{mxn} = \begin{matrix} C_1 \\ C_2 \\ \\ \cdots \\ \cdots \\ C_{m-1} \\ C_m \end{matrix} \begin{bmatrix} 1 & 0 & 0 & \cdots & \cdots & 1 \\ 0 & 1 & 1 & \cdots & 0 & 0 \\ & & & & & \\ \cdots & \cdots & \cdots & \cdots & \cdots & \cdots \\ \cdots & \cdots & \cdots & \cdots & \cdots & \cdots \\ 0 & 0 & 0 & 0 & 0 & 1 \\ 1 & 0 & 0 & 1 & 1 & 1 \end{bmatrix}$$
$$I_1 \quad I_2 \quad \cdots \quad \cdots \quad I_{n-1} \quad I_n$$

Here $C_1, C_2, \ldots, C_{m-1}, C_m$ are 1 to m unique customer accounts and $I_1, I_2, \ldots, I_{n-1}, I_n$ are 1 to n unique items in the database. In the dataset in consideration m = 4467 and n = 2479 with approx. 1% of the cells containing '1' thus leading to 99% sparsity.

RELATED RESEARCH WORK

Many researchers have encountered large dimensions and sparse datasets in document clustering or classification which deals with effective and efficient organization of text documents automatically. Using words as features, text documents are often represented as high-dimensional and sparse vectors – a few thousand dimensions and a sparsity of 95 to 99% is typical. Spherical K-Means algorithm has been often used for clustering such document vectors. (Dhillon, 2001; Shah & Mahajan, (2013). It has also been employed in clustering casino player tracking datasets (Iaci, & Singh, 2012) and in life sciences (Zhao & Karypis, 2005). Therefore the technique has found tremendous acceptance across all such applications which contain high-dimensional sparse data.

REVIEW OF CLUSTERING METHODOLOGIES

Clustering is a powerful technique for identifying data with similar characteristics. Clustering algorithms typically employ a distance or a coefficient similarity measure in order to partition the data. In the following section, we look at how traditional techniques of clustering and some of the new variants such as **rock, rskc, skmeans** and **cluto** perform for a large dimension and sparse dataset.

Shortcomings of Traditional Clustering Algorithms

Given 'm' points in 'n' dimensional space, a clustering algorithm partitions the data into 'k' clusters such that the data points in a cluster are more similar to each other than data points in different clusters. Clustering algorithms can be divided into two categories – hierarchical and non-hierarchical clustering. In non-hierarchical clustering, the entire point space is divided into 'k' clusters that optimize a certain criterion function (minimize the distance of every point from the mean of the cluster to which the point belongs) whereas in hierarchical clustering, each point is treated as a separate cluster and then pairs of clusters whose means are closest are successively merged until the desired number of 'k' clusters remain.

$$E = \sum_{i=1}^{k} \sum_{x \in Ci} | x - \mu_i |$$

It is often seen that the above set of criterion function yields satisfactory results for numeric attributes and is not appropriate for data sets with categorical or Boolean attributes. For a transaction dataset, it invariably leads to long vectors with very few non-zero coordinates. Further a common problem in clustering sparse datasets with very large dimensions when using classical techniques of clustering is failure to provide useful results and latent variables methods used for reduction do not often lead to sufficient data reduction to yield useful and informative results. This has motivated researchers to tweak the traditional algorithms so that a diverse set of datasets can then be handled.

ROCK (RObust Clustering using linKs)

ROCK belongs to the class of agglomerative hierarchical clustering algorithms that employs links and not distances when creating clusters. The research findings indicate that for data with categorical attributes, ROCK generates better quality clusters than traditional algorithms and also exhibits good scalability properties.

ROCK uses similarity measure *Jaccard coefficient* instead of Euclidean distance and since it is not distance measure, centroid-based clustering algorithms cannot be used.

The definition of Jaccard coefficient based on the similarity between two transactions T_1 and T_2 is the following:

$$sim(T_1, T_2) = \frac{|T_1 \cap T_2|}{|T_1 \cup T_2|}$$

where $|T_i|$ is the number of items in T_i. The more items that the two transactions T_1 and T_2 have in common, that is, the larger $|T_1 \cap T_2|$ is, the more similar they are. Thus, the above equation computes the relative closeness based on the items appearing in both transactions T_1 and T_2 and merges the points with most similar pair of points/ highest average similarity.

Guha, Rastogi, & Kyuseok (2000) use a new approach of common neighbours to define links. If point A neighbours point C, and point B neighbours point C then the points A and B are linked, even if they are not themselves neighbours. If two points belong to the same cluster they should have many common neighbours and if they belong to different clusters they will have few common neighbours.

In order to consider any two points as neighbours, $sim\ (p_1, p_2) \geq \theta$ where θ is a user-provided parameter. Then $link\ (p_1, p_2)$ is defined as the number of common neighbours between p_1 and p_2.

The criterion function E – maximise the number of links between pairs of points in each cluster:

$$E_l = \sum_{i=1}^{k} \sum_{p1,p2 \in Ci} link(p_1, p_2)$$

The paper does mention that this criterion function has a good probability of putting

up all points in one big cluster. Hence the authors modified the criterion function and defined a goodness measure based on it:

$$g(C_i, C_j) = \frac{link\left[C_i, C_j\right]}{(n_i + n_j)^{1+2f(\theta)} - n_i^{1+2f(\theta)} - n_j^{1+2f(\theta)}}$$

The ROCK clustering algorithm is present in the "*cba*" package in R.

rockCluster *(x, n, beta = 1-theta, theta = 0.5, fun = "dist", funArgs = list (method = "jacc"), debug = FALSE)*

Results from ROCK Clustering

Table 1: ROCK Clustering Results

Cluster Number	*Cluster Size*	*Cluster Number*	*Cluster Size*	*Cluster Number*	*Cluster Size*
1	15	11	3	21	2
2	5	12	4	22	10
3	3	13	8	23	3
4	4	14	9	24	3
5	9	15	10	25	2
6	3	16	3	26	2999
7	3	17	10		
8	3	18	8		
9	4	19	24		
10	3	20	13		

The two inputs to the algorithm – 'θ' (threshold for neighbours) and 'k' (number of clusters) were varied a lot but the results of the ROCK cluster were no different.

Key Observations from the Results

1. *1 large cluster [cluster number – 26] (approx. 85% of the total data points) and a large number of very small clusters fail to give any satisfactory information*
2. The large dimensions and the sparsity of the dataset cannot be handled by this algorithm
3. This was an indication that a problem of this magnitude required a very different algorithm

Spherical k-Means

Spherical k-Means has been mostly used in clustering text documents employing cosine dissimilarities to perform prototype-based partitioning of term weight representation of the documents. Given such a representation of documents d_i by term weight "feature vectors" x_i, one obvious approach to partitioning the documents into a given number of *k* groups is via minimizing a criterion function of the form

$$E = \sum_i d(x_i, p_{c(i)})$$

over all assignments *c* of objects *I* to cluster ids c(i) ∈ {1,........,k} and over all prototypes (often called centroids) p_1..........p_k in the same feature space as the x_i for a suitable dissimilarity measure *d*, i.e. by performing *k-prototypes partitioning with dissimilarity d.* To mitigate the effect of differing document lengths, Dhillon and Modha (2001) suggest using the Euclidean dissimilarities of the projections of the feature vectors onto the unit sphere, or, employing the so-called *cosine dissimilarity* based on the angle between the vectors.

$$d(x,p) = 1 - \cos(x,p) = 1 - \frac{< x,p >}{\| x \| \| p \|}$$

Hornik et al. (2012) proposed the following extended spherical k-means algorithm in their R package *skmeans* which provides a computational environment for spherical k-means clustering featuring several solvers: a fixed-point and genetic algorithm, and interfaces to two external solvers (CLUTO and Gmeans). The minimization of the criterion function as given below

$$\varphi(M,P) = \sum_{i,j} w_i \mu_{ij}^m (1 - \cos(x_{i,} p_j))$$

skmeans (x, k, method, m = 1, weights = 1, control = list ()) *where*

x – A numeric data matrix with rows corresponding to the objects to be partitioned (zero rows are not allowed)

k – an integer giving the number of classes to be used in the partition

m – number not less than 1 controlling the softness of the partition

weights – a numeric vector of non-negative case weights

method – "genetic", "pclust"

control – list of control parameters ('start', 'verbose', 'maxiter', 'nruns', 'maxchains')

Here "pclust" method was used to perform the clustering. The *heaping* that was observed earlier in the ROCK clustering algorithm was finally removed as *skmeans* is able to neglect the noise features and the results were satisfactory. *However, since the algorithm uses random initial partition, there was a lot of randomness in the results – the sizes of the clusters and the objects in each cluster do not remain fixed. On every run different results were obtained and hence this algorithm was unacceptable.*

Observations and Results

Table 2: Spherical k-Means Clustering Results

Cluster No.	*run1_sizes*	*run2_sizes*	*run3_sizes*
1	163	135	736
2	158	172	185
3	158	108	184
4	190	337	102
5	275	452	189
6	178	295	390
7	185	194	355
8	120	144	86
9	887	420	481
10	434	176	143
11	99	266	396
12	323	194	186
13	144	117	194
14	431	882	174
15	237	90	181

The above results from 'skmeans' run for k = 15 shows how the cluster sizes change on each run of the algorithm. On digging deep, it was also observed that approx. *50% of the data points shifted from one cluster to another in every run. This led to the instability in the clustering output.*

CLUTO (using skmeans package)

The *skmeans* package discussed before also provides an external interface to the **vcluster** partitional clustering program from **CLUTO**, the **CLU**stering**TO**olkit by George Karypis (Karypis, 2003; Zhao & Karypis, 2001). **CLUTO** is a comprehensive package for partitional and hierarchical clustering which provides algorithms "optimized for operating on very large datasets both in terms of the number of objects as well as the number of dimensions" and has been reported to perform very well in many application contexts. Moreover, since most high-dimensional datasets are very sparse, CLUTO directly takes into account this sparsity and requires memory that is roughly linear on the input size. The partitional algorithms of CLUTO use a "randomized incremental optimization algorithm that is greedy in nature, has low computational requirements, and has been show to produce high quality clustering solutions".

Cluto contains partitional, agglomerative, and graph-partitioning based clustering algorithms. Bisecting k-means is the default option from the partitional class of algorithms. In addition, Cluto offers multiple distance (similarity measure) functions like cosine, Euclidean, correlation coefficient and jaccard coefficient. Cluto has an option to select one of several clustering criterion functions from four categories: internal, external, hybrid and graph-based.

There are a total of 18 different optional parameters that control how *vcluster* computes the clustering solution. Some of the important ones that were used:

- **clmethod**(clustering method) = rb, rbr, direct, agglo, graph
- **sim** (similarity measure) = cos, corr, dist, jacc (applicable when *clmethod* = *graph*)
- **crfun** (criterion function) = $I_1, I_2, E_1, G_1, G_1', H_1, H_2$

There are a whole lot of options which control the output information and visualization of the clusters (Karypis, 2003).

In the paper, we have used -**clmethod** = **rbr** (similar to repeated bisection but overall solution globally optimized) and **bagglo**(similar to agglomerative method but the process is biased by a partitional clustering solution), -**sim** = **cos** (cosine of the angle between the two vectors)and **corr** (pearson correlation coefficient between the two vectors) and –**crfun** = $\mathbf{I_2}$ and $\mathbf{H_2}$ (I_2 and H_2 generally lead to very good clustering solutions).

Two cluster statistics are used to decide on the optional parameters mentioned above and also on the value of '*k*' (number of clusters/partitions) – average silhouette width and Pearson-Gamma. **Silhouette width** is defined as follows:

$$s(i) = \frac{b(i) - a(i)}{\max(a(i), b(i))}$$

Where a(i) = average dissimilarity between i and all other points of the cluster to which i belongs. For all other clusters C, d(i,C) = average dissimilarity of i to all observations of C. The smallest of these d(i,C) is b(i) = $\min_c$ d(i,C) and can be seen as the dissimilarity between i and its 'neighbour' cluster, i.e. the nearest one to which it does *not* belong. Observations with a large s(i) are very well clustered and a small s(i) means that the observation lies between two clusters.

Pearson-Gamma is defined as the correlation between distances and a 0-1 vector where 0 means same cluster, 1 means different clusters. In order to select the input parameters to the algorithm, both average silhouette width and Pearson-Gamma are looked at in unison.

Vcluster executable can be downloaded for Linux, Sun, OSX and MS Window platforms from http://glaros.dtc.umn.edu/gkhome/cluto/cluto/download. CLTUO's stand-alone library is also available which can be accessed directly from a C or C++ program. However we have used '*skmeans*' package in R which provides a CLTUO interface.

skmeans(x,k, method='CLUTO',
control=list(vcluster='D:\\Tools\\cluto2.1.1\\Win32\\vcluster.exe',
control=c("-clmethod=rbr","-sim=corr","-crfun=h2","-clabelfile=col.clabel","-cstype=best","-nfeatures=10"),verbose=TRUE))

Selection of Input Parameters

As mentioned above, in order to find the best input parameter combination, we execute an automation program for all values of 'k' ranging from 15 to 30. We

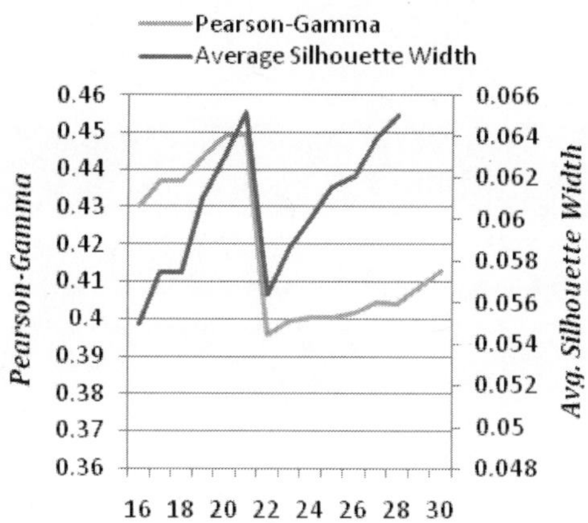

Fig. 1: -clmethod=rbr, -sim=cos, -crfun=H2-sim

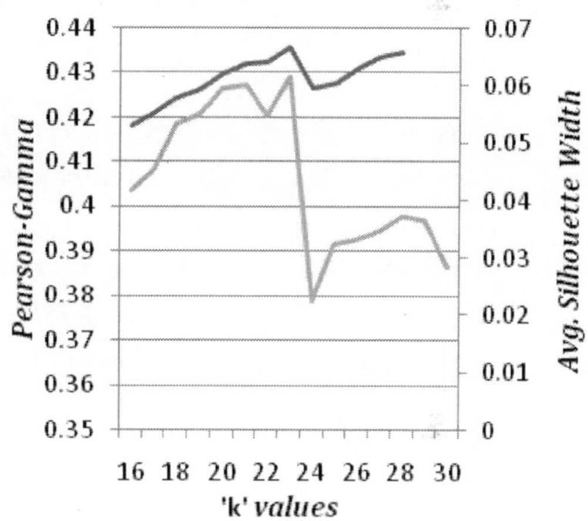

Fig. 2: -clmethod=rbr, -sim=corr, -crfun=H2

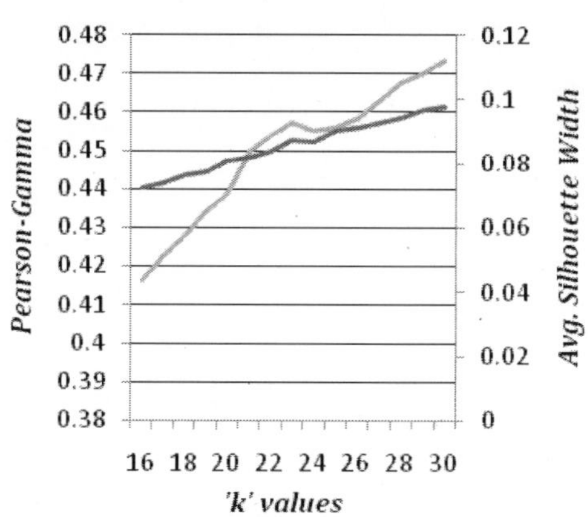

Fig. 3: -clmethod=rbr, -sim=cos, -crfun=I2

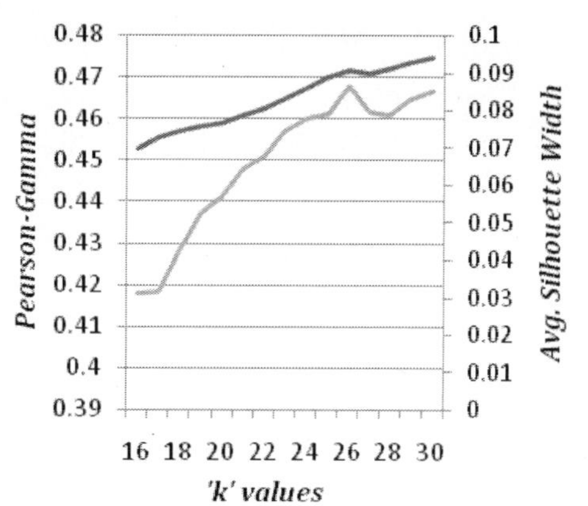

Fig. 4: -clemethod=rbr, -sim=corr -crfun=I2

look at cluster quality statistics average silhouette width and Pearson-Gamma which increase to a certain point and then decrease. A continuous increasing trend is not desirable. A sample output of the program is shown Fig.1 to 4.

From the charts, it is clearly visible that the overall values of average silhouette width and Pearson-Gamma is greater when **–clmethod= rbr** than when **–clmethod=bagglo**. Hence repeated bisection gives better results than agglomerative clustering method.

Within the repeated bisection method, **similarity measure=corr** and **criterion function=H2** does not follow a monotonic trend and we have an inflexion point at **k=23**.

Sample Output from CLUTO

vcluster (CLUTO 2.1.1) Copyright 2001-03, Regents of the University of Minnesota
Matrix Information --
Name: C:\Users\ashish.m\AppData\Local\Temp\RtmpSACZnv\file1c8042de1559,
#Rows: 4467, #Columns: 2479, #NonZeros: 117421
Options ---
CLMethod=RBR, CRfun=H2, SimFun=CorrCoef, #Clusters: 23
RowModel=None, ColModel=None, GrModel=SY-DIR, NNbrs=40
Colprune=1.00, EdgePrune=-1.00, VtxPrune=-1.00, MinComponent=5
CSType=Best, AggloFrom=0, AggloCRFun=H2, NTrials=10, NIter=10
Solution --
23-way clustering: [H2=1.57e-003] [4467 of 4467]

----

cid SizeISimISdevESimESdev |

----

0 141 +0.274 +0.171 +0.013 +0.014 |
1 161 +0.230 +0.110 +0.008 +0.012 |
2 242 +0.223 +0.155 +0.004 +0.010 |
3 517 +0.167 +0.056 +0.007 +0.009 |
4 310 +0.198 +0.039 +0.039 +0.008 |
5 132 +0.171 +0.073 +0.021 +0.012 |
6 146 +0.169 +0.068 +0.024 +0.012 |
7 152 +0.176 +0.046 +0.032 +0.014 |
8 158 +0.166 +0.070 +0.023 +0.012 |
9 150 +0.143 +0.055 +0.017 +0.008 |

RESULTS AND ANALYSIS

Table 3 CLUTO: Cluster Sizes (in %age of total)

Cluster No.	*Size*	*Size (in % total)*
1	141	3.16%
2	161	3.60%
3	242	5.42%
4	517	11.57%
5	310	6.94%
6	132	2.96%
7	146	3.27%
8	152	3.40%
9	158	3.54%
10	150	3.36%
11	143	3.20%
12	183	4.10%
13	218	4.88%
14	143	3.20%
15	190	4.25%
16	112	2.51%
17	136	3.04%
18	134	3.00%
19	133	2.98%
20	198	4.43%
21	283	6.34%
22	179	4.01%
23	306	6.85%

The clustering results obtained using CLUTO and the input parameters selected previously show that the heaping problem is resolved and exactly similar results are obtained on executing the algorithm again and again. The min. cluster size is 2.51% and max. cluster size is 11.57% which are very good results for any clustering technique.

In order to generate more insights about the clusters obtained in the previous step, we make use of the categorical and numeric variables as mentioned in section II. We look at the top 2* customer-groups, menu price and seat capacity for top 5 clusters and also the top products purchased for each of these clusters such that their combination is unique to a cluster.

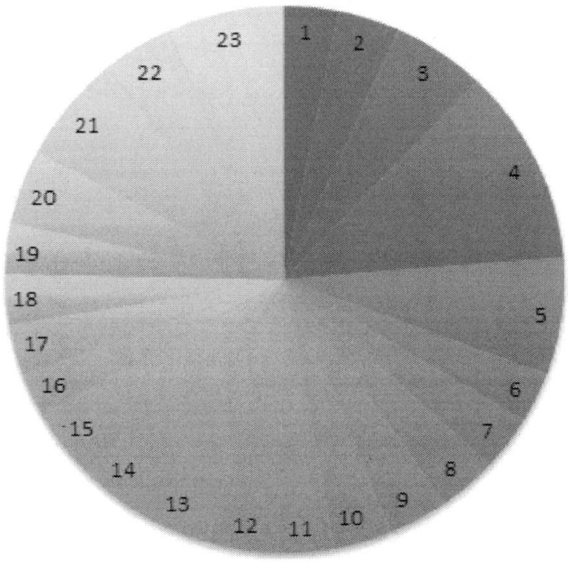

Fig. 5: Cluster Sizes Distribution

Table 4: Profiling Top 5 Clusters Based on Categorical Attributes*

Cluster No.	*Customer Group*		*Menu Price*		*Seat Capacity*	
4	European Rest.	Bar & Rest.	$51-150	$151-250	51-100	Less than 50
5	Rehabitation Centre	Elderly Home	Not Applicable	-	Not Applicable	-
23	Japanese Rest.	Café & Dessert	Not Applicable	$51-150	Not Applicable	Less than 50
21	Activity Centre	District Organization	Not Applicable	-	Not Applicable	-
3	Japanese Rest.	HK Style Café	$51-150	Less than $50	51-100	Not Applicable

* The profiling of all the clusters based on these categorical attributes is available in Appendix I

Table 5: Key Products Purchased by Customers in Top 5 Clusters*

Cluster No.	*Key Products Purchased (segments/prod hierarchy)*
4	SPICES & HERBS, SAUCES, BAKING PRODUCTS
5	VEGETABLES, SUGAR, DRIED FRUIT
23	BEER, WINE, SEAFOOD, OIL
21	BISCUIT, NOODLES, OATMEAL, READY DRINK
3	TISSUES & NAPKINS, WIPERS, GLOVES

*The key products for all the clusters is available in Appendix II

The results from the 3 clustering algorithms used in the paper and the limitations/ challenges posed by each of them is summarised in the table below:

Table 6: Results summary of the Clustering Algorithms

Serial No.	*Clustering Algorithm*	*Similarity Measure*	*R-packages Used*	*Results*
1	ROCK (Robust Clustering using Links)	Jaccard coefficient	cba	Heaping and large number of clusters with very small sizes
2	Spherical k-Means	Cosine	skmeans	Heaping resolved but lot of randomness in the clusters
3	CLUTO	Correlation coefficient	CLUTO	Both heaping and instability removed

In order to generate business insights, all the clusters are plotted on a business metric of number of orders and volume of goods purchased. The **"# of cases"** on the y-axis indicates the average volume of all the customers belonging to that cluster. The **"# of deliveries"** on the x-axis refers to average number of orders of all customers in that cluster. The **"blue"** dotted line represents the average orders and average volume

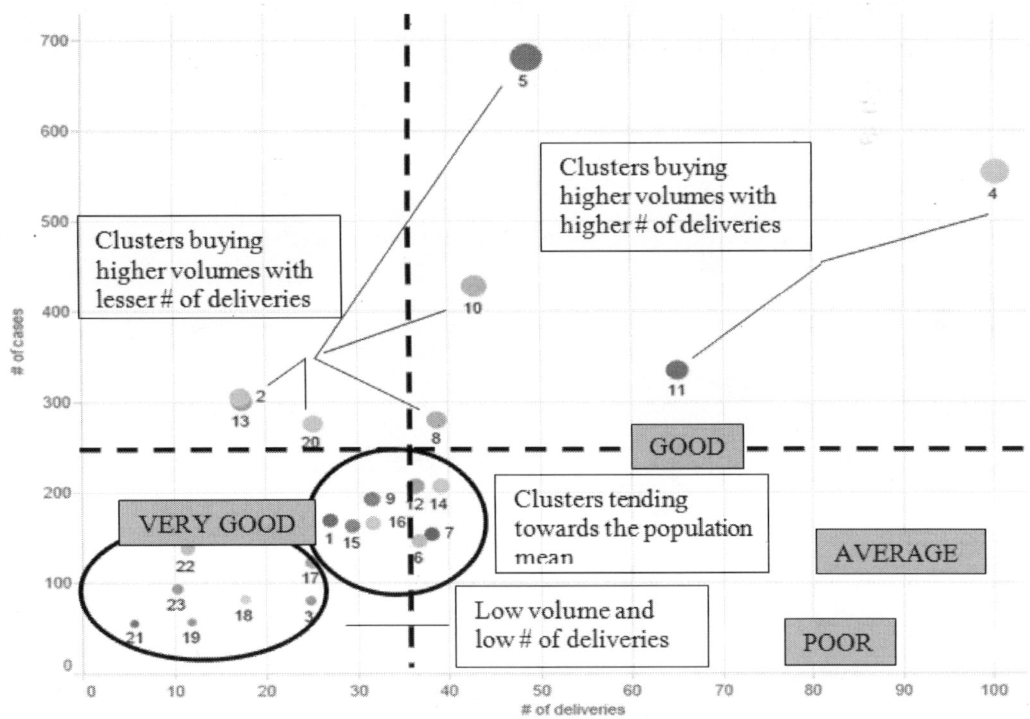

Fig. 6: Grouping of Clusters using Business Metrics

for the entire dataset. It can be seen that the clusters are well arranged in 4 different groups. And on the basis of low/high orders and low/high volumes, can be labelled into 4 different categories – **very good, good, average** and **poor**. This categorization helps businesses to generate intelligence about their customers and then focus their scarce resources appropriately on those customers who give more value. We have further used the clustering result to do a Market Basket Analysis on the top 20 SKUs of each cluster and identify strong association between products. It mainly helps in increasing sales per customer and thereby adds to overall profitability as well.

CONCLUSIONS AND FUTURE WORK

In this paper, we have seen the challenges that present themselves when clustering of a large dimension and highly sparse (approx. 99%) dataset is attempted. The traditional clustering techniques such as k-means fails to yield proper results when the dataset contains categorical/boolean attributes and also is unable to remove the noise features in a large dimension dataset. The new variants such as rock, rskc and skmeans suffer from heaping and/or instability problems.

However the results of our experiment with CLUTO are very encouraging. There are significant differences in the sizes of the clusters found and also the quality of the clusters are very good. The fact that each cluster can be defined by different set of products solves the business problem that led to the genesis of this paper.

The future work would involve checking the scalability of this algorithm in terms of dimensions going to many thousands and the objects or data points in millions. Though this algorithm is known to work excellently in document classification, it will be an interesting read in retail transactions or any other application.

REFERENCES

Dhillon, Inderjit S., & Modha, Dharmendra S. (2001). Concept Decompositions for Large Sparse Text Data Using Clustering. *Machine Learning, 42*(1-2), 143 – 175

Guha, Sudipto, Rastogi, Rajeev, Shim, Kyuseok. (2000). ROCK: A Robust Clustering Algorithm for Categorical Attributes. *Information Systems 25* (5), 345-366

Hornik, Kurt; Feinerer, Ingo; Kober, Martin, & Buchta, Christian (2012). Spherical k-Means Clustering. *Journal of Statistical Software, 50* (10, September 2012). Retrieved from: http://statmath.wuwien.ac.at/~hornik/ software.html

Iaci, R., & Singh, A. K. (2012). Clustering High Dimensional Sparse Casino Player Tracking Datasets. *UNLV Gaming Research & Review Journal, 16*(1). Retrieved from http://digitalscholarship.unlv.edu/grrj/vol16/iss1/2

Karypis, G. (2003). *CLUTO: Clustering Toolkit.* Technical Report 02-017, Department of

Computer Science, University of Minnesota. Retrieved from: http://glaros.dtc.um.edu/gkhome/fetch/sw/cluto/manual.pdf

Kondo Yumi (2011). *Robustification of the sparse K-means clustering algorithm.* [M. Sc. Thesis]. Vancouver: The University Of British Columbia.

Shah, Neepa, & Mahajan, Sunita. (2013). Document Clustering with CLUTO. In *Proceedings of National Conference on New Horizons in IT*. Mumbai: MET League of Colleges.

Zhao, Y., & Karypis, G. (2001). *Criterion functions for document clustering: Experiments and analysis*. Technical Report TR #01–40, Department of Computer Science, University of Minnesota, Minneapolis, MN. Available at http://cs.umn.edu/~karypis/publications.

Zhao, Ying, & Karypis, George. (2005). Data Clustering in Life Sciences. *Molecular Biotechnology, 31,* 1-26.

APPENDICES

APPENDIX I

Cluster Distribution Based on Customer-Group, Menu Price and Seat Capacity

Cluster No.	*Customer Group*		*Menu Price*		*Seat Capacity*	
1	Japanese Rest.	-	\$51-150	\$151-250	51-100	Less than 50
2	Gasoline Station	General Trade	Not Applicable	-	Not Applicable	-
3	Japanese Rest.	HK Style Café	\$51-150	Less than \$50	51-100	Not Applicable
4	European Rest.	Bar & Rest.	\$51-150	\$151-250	51-100	Less than 50
5	Rehabilita-tion Centre	Elderly Home	Not Applicable	-	Not Applicable	-
6	Japanese Rest.	Fast Food	\$51-150	Less than \$50	Less than 50	51-100
7	Bakery	European Rest.	Less than \$50	\$51-150	Not Applicable	101-150
8	Wholesaler-Major L	Chinese Rest.	Not Applicable	\$51-150	Not Applicable	151+
9	European Rest.	Bar & Rest.	Not Applicable	\$151-250	Not Applicable	51-100
10	HK Style Café	Western Rest-Gen	\$51-150	Less than \$50	Less than 50	Not Applicable
11	Western Rest-Gen	Japanese Rest	\$51-150	Less than \$50	51-100	Less than 50

Cluster No.	Customer Group		Menu Price		Seat Capacity	
12	Chinese Rest.	Bakery	Less than $50	$51-150	Not Applicable	Less than 50
13	General Trade	Frozen Meat Retailer	Not Applicable	-	Not Applicable	-
14	Japanese Rest.	Café and Dessert	$51-150	Less than $50	Less than 50	Not Applicable
15	Chinese Rest.	European Rest.	$51-150	$151-250	51-100	Less than 50
16	Japanese Rest		$51-150	Less than $50	51-100	Not Applicable
17	Café & Dessert	Japanese Rest.	Less than $50	$51-150	Less than 50	Not Applicable
18	School	Pantry	Not Applicable	Less than $50	Not Applicable	Less than 50
19	Western Rest-Gen	Japanese Rest.	$51-150	Less than $50	Not Applicable	Less than 50
20	Chain-General Trade	Chain-Supermarket	Not Applicable	Less than $50	Not Applicable	Less than 50
21	Activity Centre	District Organization	Not Applicable	-	Not Applicable	-
22	HK Style Café	School	Not Applicable	Less than $50	Not Applicable	51-100
23	Activity Centre	District Organization	Not Applicable	-	Not Applicable	-

APPENDIX II

Cluster Distribution Based on Key Product Segment or Product Hierarchy

Cluster No.	Key Products Purchased
1	SAUCE, SUGAR, CREAM, BEER
2	SEAFOOD, OLIVE OIL, PASTA, SNACKBAR
3	TISSUES & NAPKINS, WIPERS, GLOVES
4	SPICES & HERBS, SAUCES, BAKING PRODUCTS
5	VEGETABLES, SUGAR, DRIED FRUIT
6	SEAFOOD, SUGAR, SAUCE, VEGETABLES
7	FRUIT, VEGETABLES, SAUCE, JAM
8	MILK, FLOUR, SPICES, CHEMICALS

Cluster No.	*Key Products Purchased*
9	TEA, MILK, SAUCE, SUGAR, FRUIT
10	VEGETABLES, WINE, PASTA, BAKING PRODUCTS
11	SAUCE, HEALTH DRINK, SPICES, BAKING PRODUCTS
12	FLOUR, BAKING PRODUCTS, MILK, SUGAR
13	SAUCE, VEGETABLES, SOUP
14	SPICES, HERBS, NUTS, CHEESE
15	SOFT DRINK, JUICE, BEER
16	PLASTICS, FOIL, CHEESE, OILS
17	CREAM, CHEESE, SUGAR, SOF TDRINK
18	JELLY, HEALTH DRINK, JUICE, MILK
19	CREAM, CHEESE, SAUCE, MEAT
20	RICE, OILVE OIL, NOODLES, SAUCE
21	BISCUIT, NOODLES, OATMEAL, READY DRINK
22	OATMEAL, JUICE, SEAFOOD, BUTTER/ MARGARINE
23	BEER, WINE, SEAFOOD, OILS

CLOSING NOTE

CASE

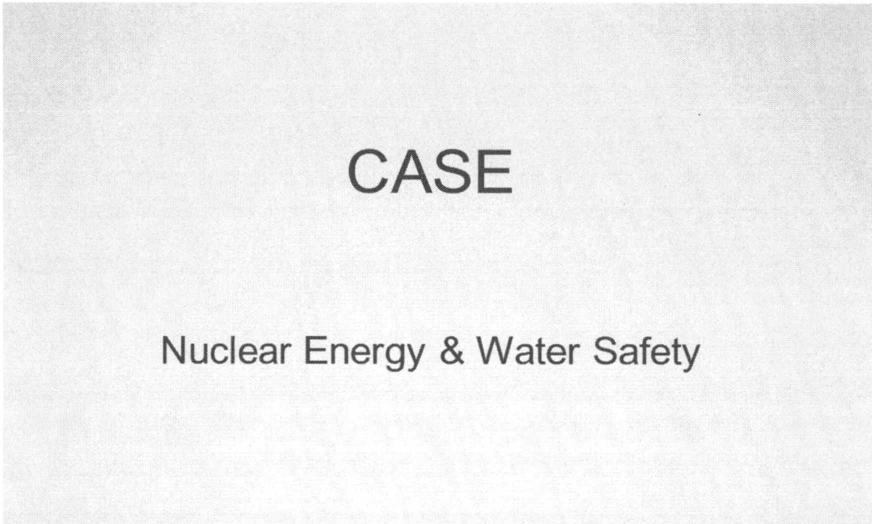

We've talked about a lot of marketing implications of big data analytics in the cases discussed previously - implications like re-designing cars, selling breakfast cereals, etc. I'll start with a case study about how big data is helping to figure out the relationship between nuclear energy and water safety. We already know that radiation and radio activity seep into the groundwater which imposes a very strict penalty on the availability of ground water for other uses. There is a lot of evidence to show and big data, in addition to everything we seem to know, also tells us something we don't know.

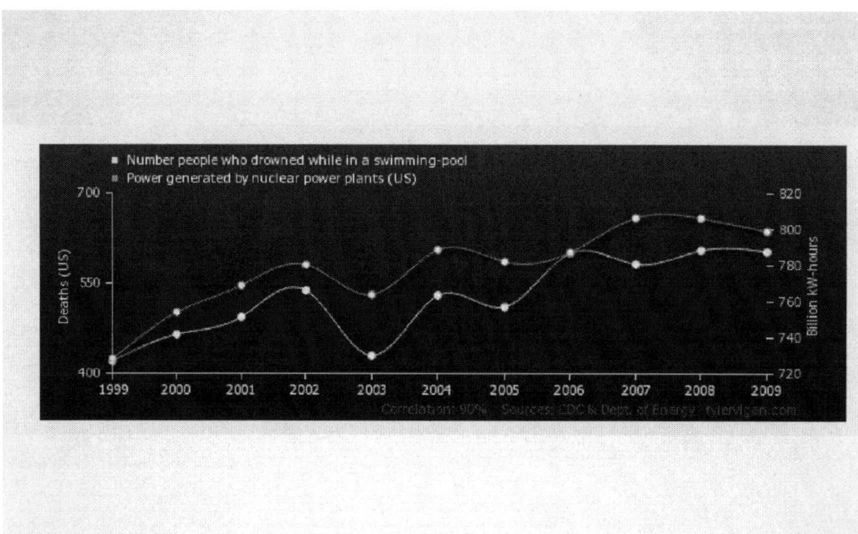

The red graph line shows how much power is generated in the US through nuclear power plants and the green one shows how many people are drowning in swimming pools. So, in addition to radioactive material in ground water, nuclear energy probably seems to be changing the water current, water density, etc because of which people seem to be drowning.

CORRELATION EXAMPLES

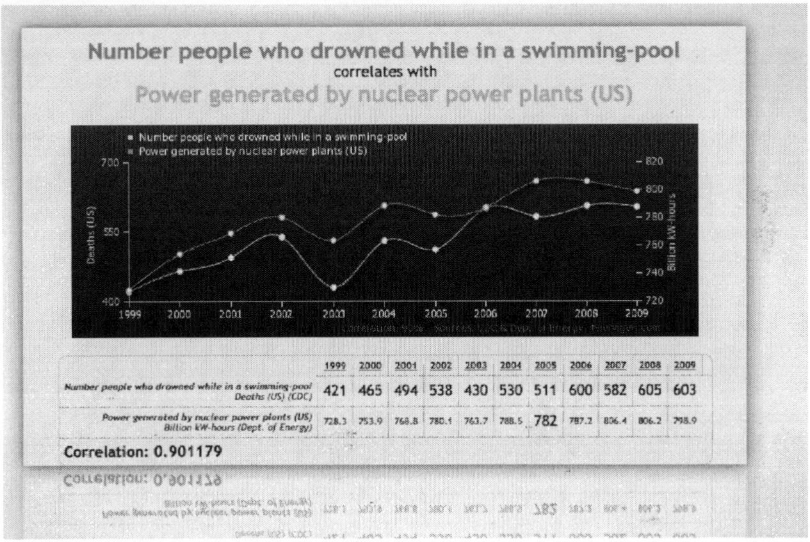

	1999	2000	2001	2002	2003	2004	2005	2006	2007	2008	2009
Number people who drowned while in a swimming-pool Deaths (US) (CDC)	421	465	494	538	430	530	511	600	582	605	603
Power generated by nuclear power plants (US) Billion kW-hours (Dept. of Energy)	728.3	753.9	768.8	780.1	763.7	788.5	782	787.2	806.4	806.2	798.9

Correlation: 0.901179

Even though this seems to be a trivial fact, the correlation is about 0.9. This data is from a website for spurious correlations.

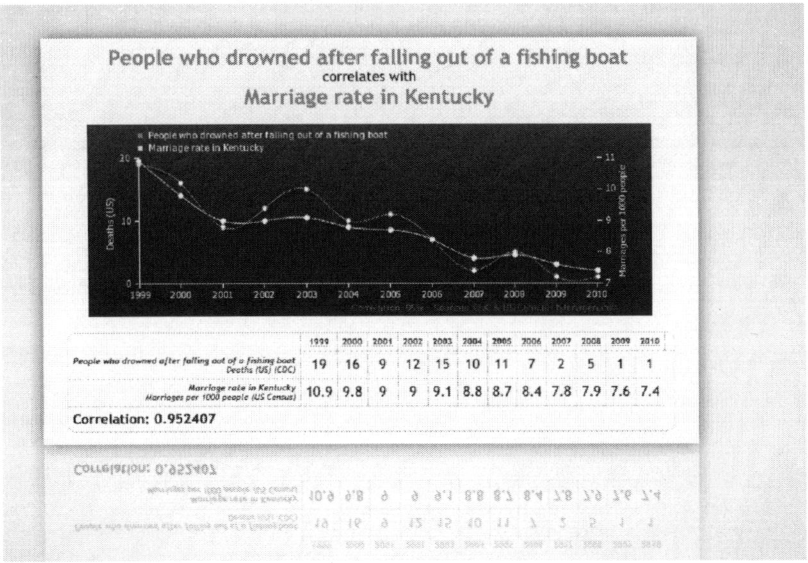

	1999	2000	2001	2002	2003	2004	2005	2006	2007	2008	2009	2010
People who drowned after falling out of a fishing boat Deaths (US) (CDC)	19	16	9	12	15	10	11	7	2	5	1	1
Marriage rate in Kentucky Marriages per 1000 people (US Census)	10.9	9.8	9	9	9.1	8.8	8.7	8.4	7.8	7.9	7.6	7.4

Correlation: 0.952407

Another example from the spurious correlation website; people who drowned after falling out of a fishing boat is correlated with the number of marriages in Kentucky.

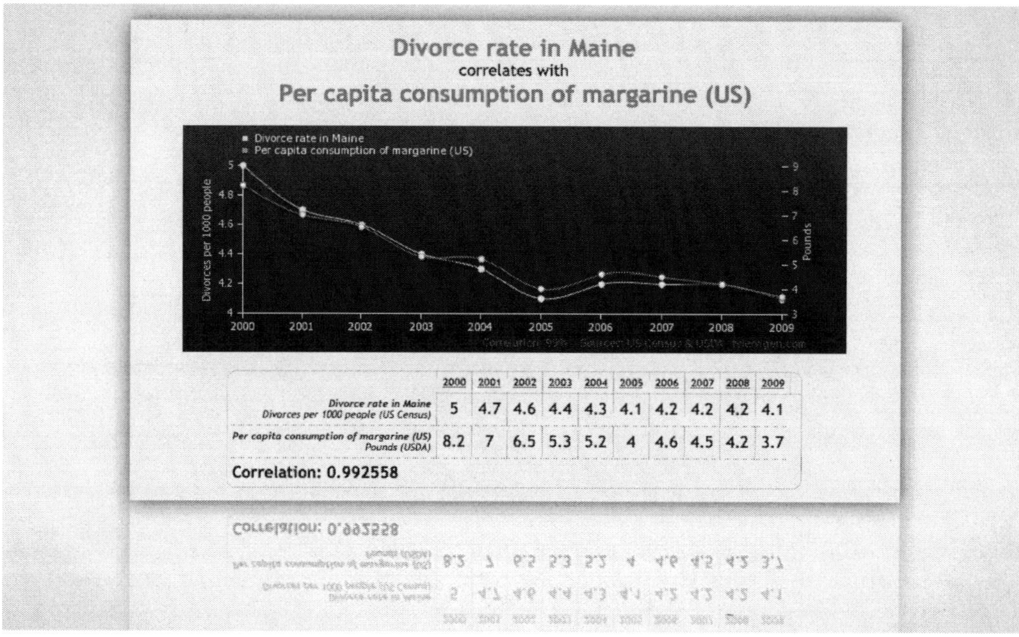

Another spurious correlation example is how the divorce rate in Maine is completely correlated with the per capita consumption of margarine.

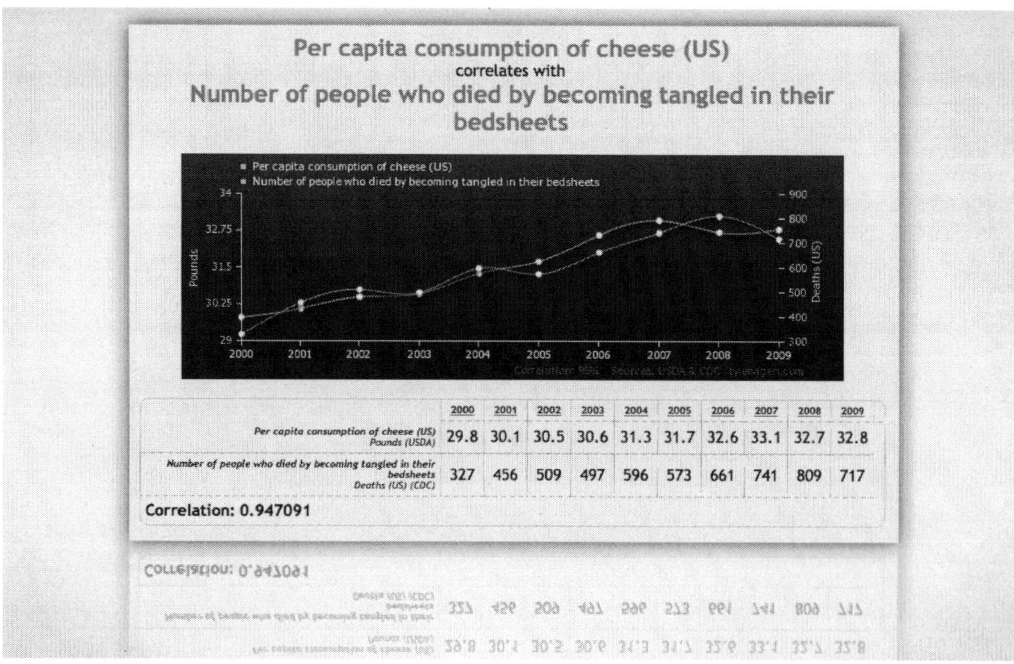

Another very interesting correlation is that when you start having more cheese it increases your chances of dying by entangling in your bed sheet.

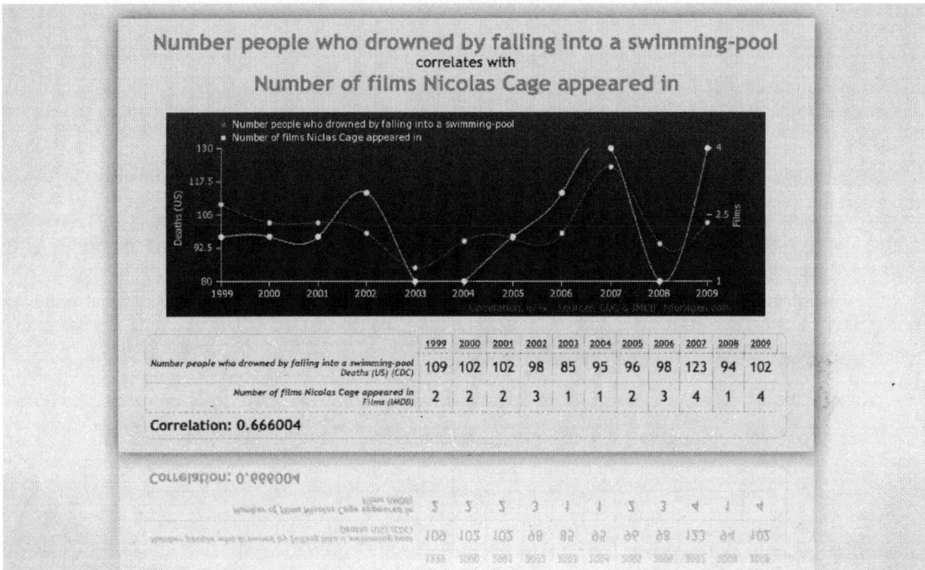

The last one, my favorite of all the spurious correlations is the number of people who drowned by falling into a swimming pool is directly correlated with the number of films in which Nicolas Cage has acted. So what we could take away from conferences like these is that there is so much data to be analyzed. We think we are missing out and make fatal flaws like reading information like this.

PREMISE

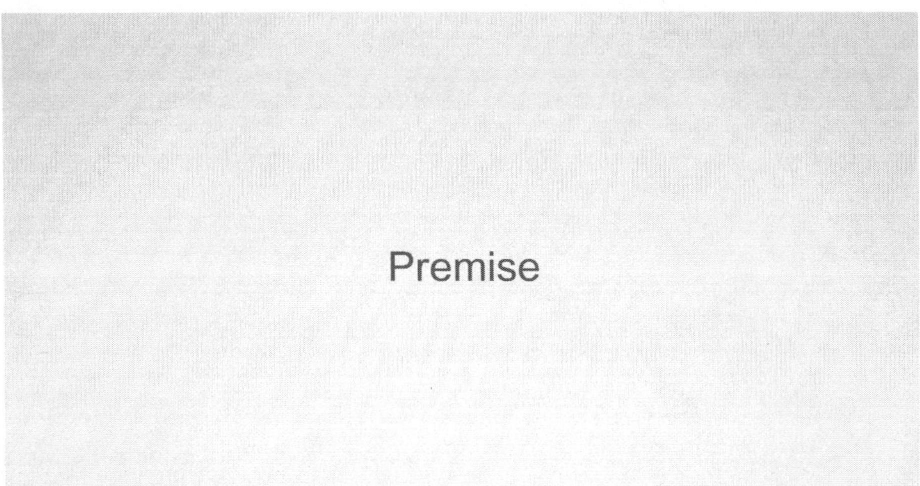

There has been a high level of attention, interest and almost a reverence for data because we believe it cannot be incorrect because it is big data obviously. The anchor point is that the difference between having a tremendous amount of reverence and a complete disdain for it, is that you, as a listener or a reader, have to figure out where you fall. The common mistake a lot of people make, including the users of big data, is that they fall on the other spectrum which means that we assume that if they are numbers they must be right. I have been in market research for about 25 years and if you tell me what findings you want, I will write a questionnaire, do the field work, you can get someone to analyze the data and you will get the findings you want. Therefore, we know that as people who work with data, we have tremendous power and ability to manipulate and move things. One of the common things you hear in market research is when in doubt, lean in favor of the ad i.e. if something looks ambiguous just focus on the positives. So, we as people who work with data should never forget our responsibilities because the onus is on us to make sense of the big data.

ANXIETY OF INFLUENCE

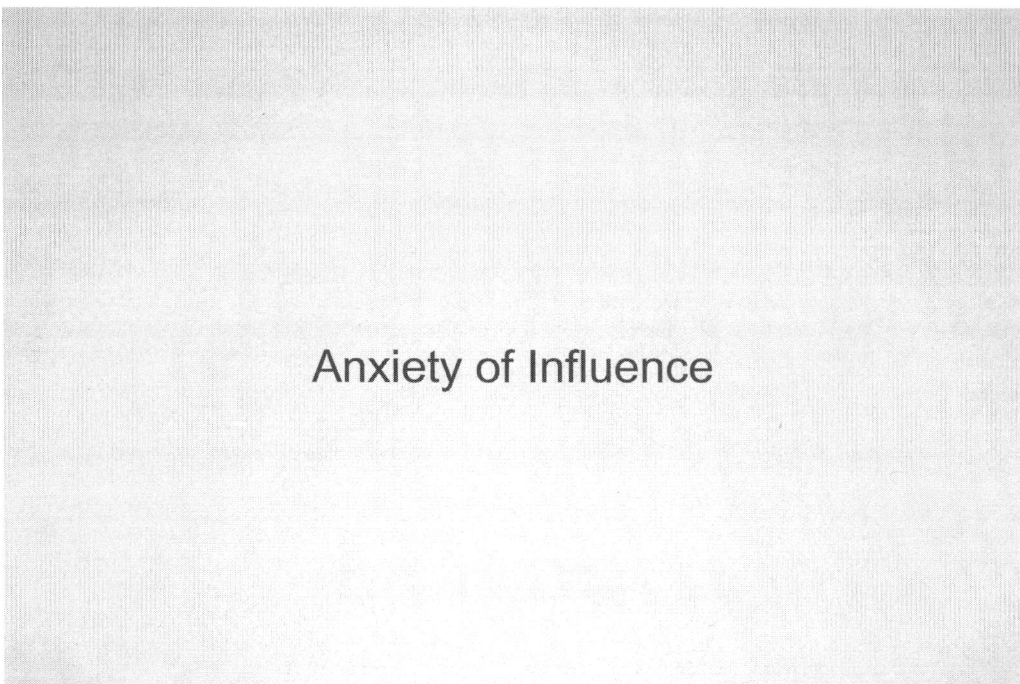

Anxiety of Influence is a simple concept in the domain of literature and specifically in the sub-domain of poetry. If you are a poet you want to be informed by the poets who preceded you, which means you are trying to be different from the poems previously written but at the same time you don't want to be influenced by the poems you have previously read. If you are not sufficiently informed you might repeat a poem and if you are sufficiently informed, that conditions you and you might repeat the poem. Creating art like a story or a poem is an incredibly stressful thing because it imposes anxiety of influence. It is a very broad concept because it applies to various fields including marketing and businesses. In this day and age we have nice things like high speed internet, high definition TV, etc but the big problem of living in this day and age is that everything interesting or important that has to be said has already been said. For the last 50 years, in my opinion, we haven't said anything new. If you read the marketing books by Roe Anderson from way back in the 50's and 60's, you'll see that there isn't a single idea that hasn't been covered. What we have been able to do is be very clever about the same things e.g., The 4 Cs became 5 Cs and eventually 6 Cs now. We don't want to get caught doing something that is simple and not complex. In fact if it is simple probably it is not important because if it is not simple it won't get communicated or understood. If it isn't understood then it doesn't really matter because it won't be used and implemented. In the history of literature and dissemination of knowledge, simpler ideas crack faster, complex ideas get stuck.

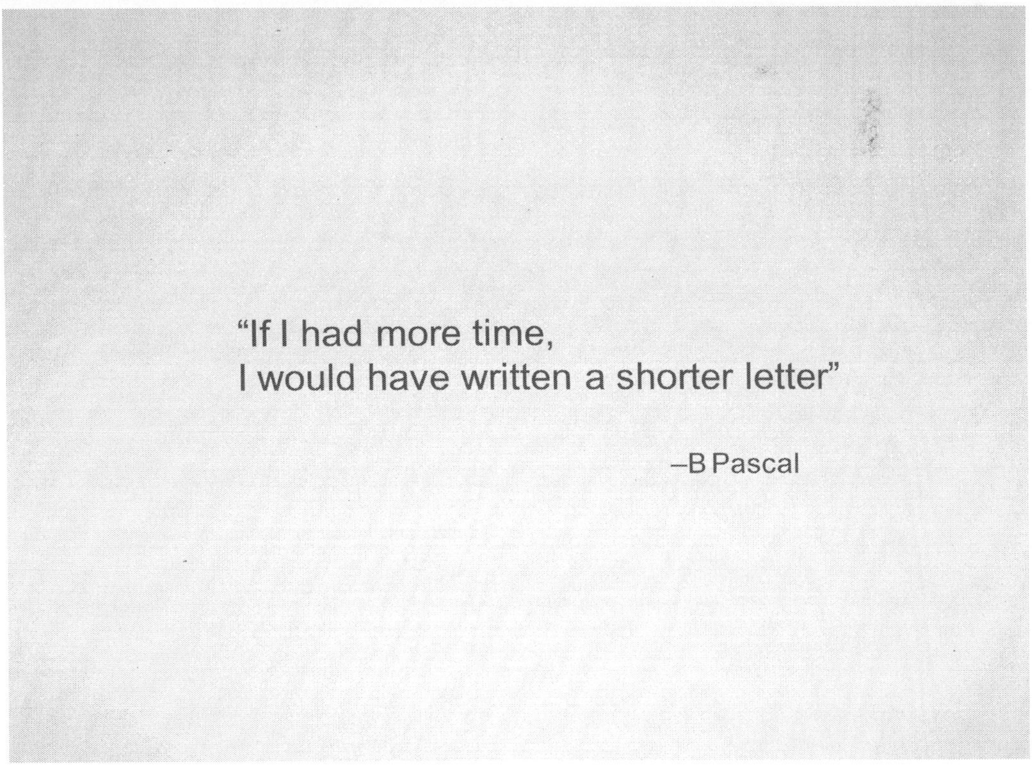

Pascal is famously known to have said 'If I had more time I would have written a shorter letter'. Simplicity is very crucial in ideas and when I look at an idea there should be some benefit I derive from it in a simple manner. Cerebral hygiene is a concept in social psychology, i.e. what you put in your mind essentially is like a hygiene. If you put junk in there your brain becomes junky it starts stinking over time, but if you put good ideas there it becomes cleaner and sharper. As listeners we need to have a strong filter for what we allow to come in. If trivial ideas start going in, 15 years from now we all become a trivial civilisation.

FOCUS ON PROFITS

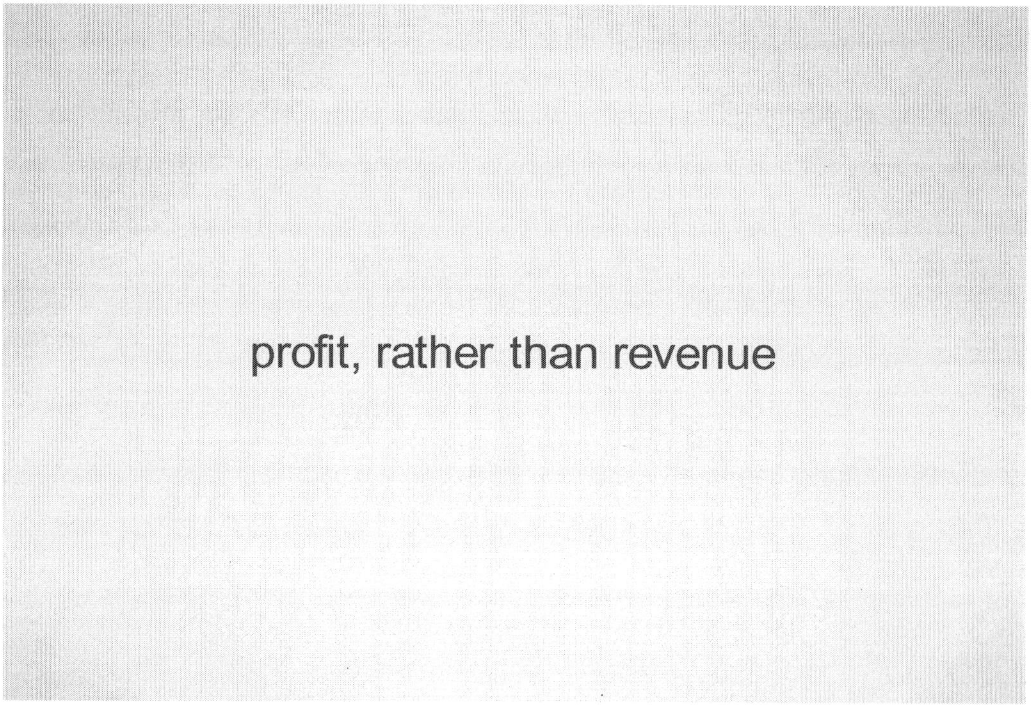

If your organization has nothing to do with customer safety and if it is not non-profit, then profits really are everything. If you look at the books and the statements showing revenue and profit and numbers of ideas in which big data was used, we realize it simply doesn't matter. For instance, there are ideas about cars prompting you to have coffee, giving you hugs, etc. A better predictor of driver's safety is to ensure that the cell phone is not in the driver's hand. Because, after putting all this technology in cars, are we making more money? The answer is no and therefore these ideas don't matter. On the other hand, big data has benefits in so many other areas like teaching. Teaching has changed so much over the last five years. Today, for example, when I go into a class I know exactly what percentage of the class has actually read the material. If 50% of the class hasn't read it, you approach the topic differently than if 80% has read it. When you are in front of an intelligent audience, you don't want to bore them and if 80% has read it then you don't want to talk about what they already know. How do we do this? When you send information to people you can put beacon images and when the image launched, it pings the sender of the information. Through this you know exactly which 45%, for example, has read it and if you don't want to put anybody on the spot you know exactly who to call because you know this person has read the article. Of course, they can still open the article and not read it, but the chances are much better. This improves ROI because it reduces the speaker's stress level which increases productivity. We should remember that there is a sizzle factor in all this, but we should also remember that we have a responsibility to the shareholders and other stakeholders who rely on us to make a profit.

OPPORTUNITIES

New Sources of Data

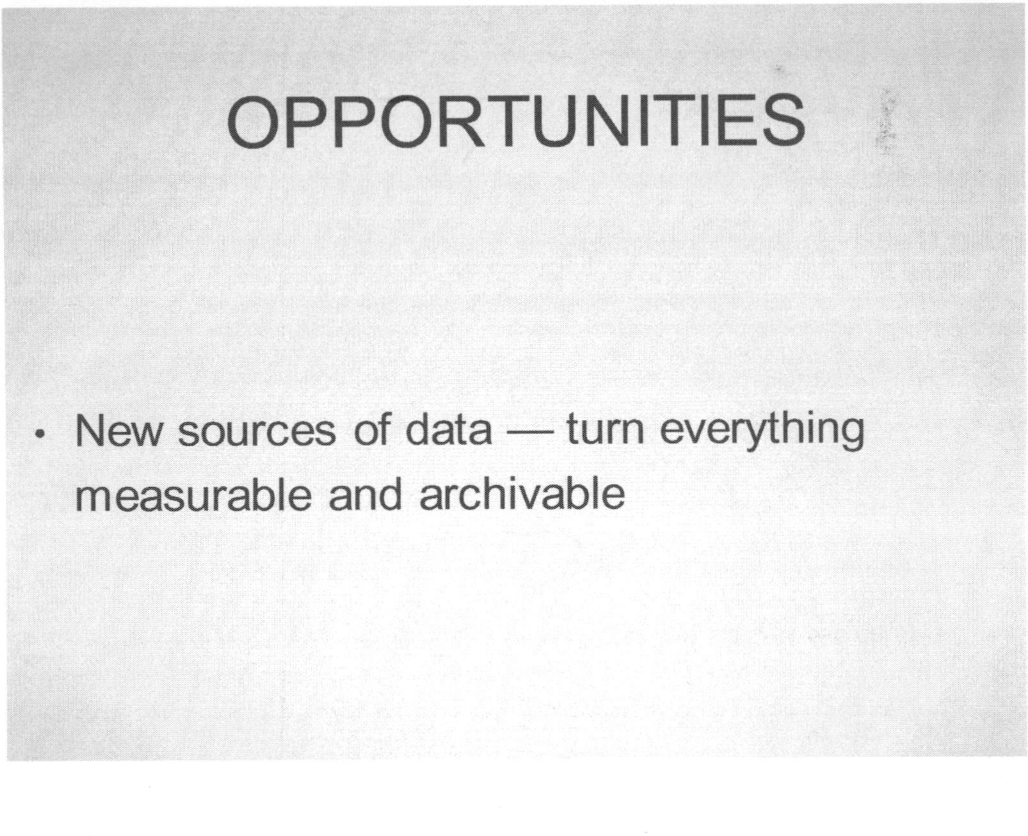

One of the big areas in big data analytics which hasn't really been spoken about much is new sources of data. Some of the most exciting opportunities in big data analytics is how to turn non-digital data points into digital data points.

For example, how can a completely non-digital experience where somebody goes to a store, looks at a shampoo and puts it back be turned into something digital? This is where there are a lot of opportunities especially in a market such as the Indian subcontinent where there are a lot of rural markets. Simply making sure that when somebody is entering a store they get a small card that they have to drop off into a bin before they can access a product that they want to touch and hold, is a very simple technology that can give phenomenal results because you know right away which product has been lifted off the shelf. It makes somebody's propensity to like the product a little complex but if you don't use this technology there is no data. The choice that managers have to make is no data versus some data. There are tremendous opportunities to convert non-digital footprints into digital footprints, QR codes, beacon images, etc.

Source Credibility

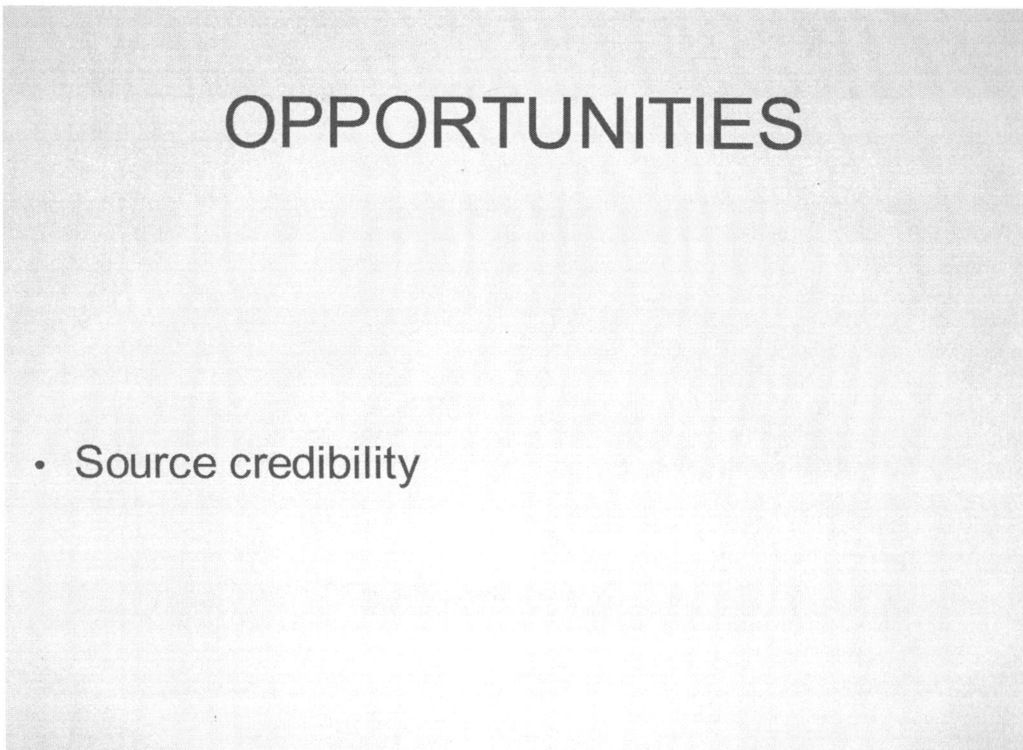

One of the most important topics is the whole issue of source credibility. When I consult with companies, I see that people are not questioning the credibility of the source of data. We look at people tweet, post on Facebook and treat this as compulsive data that we put in large bins, wrangle it, structure it, analyze it and then draw inferences, without questioning the credibility of this data. There are some active users on Twitter who talk about things like the printers that they have used, refrigerators they have bought, etc. If we look at their consumption pattern of these products and how much they spend on them, they could be richer than Bill Gates. So, if they are not buying these products, how are they reviewing them? These reviews are garbage because they are made up. There are ways by which we can question the credibility of data, for example rather than putting all data and start data wrangling, you need to first wrangle the data per user. This is hardly done by anybody, in fact most of the data visualization apps used for big data analytics don't even allow you to analyze the data by user. You need to specifically query for each user and assign 2 to 3 people in the company to allow you to sort it by user. The effort is worth it because when you realize that maybe 40-45% of the data is not credible, it enables you to decide whether make a strategic decision or not based on poor quality data.

Boundary Conditions

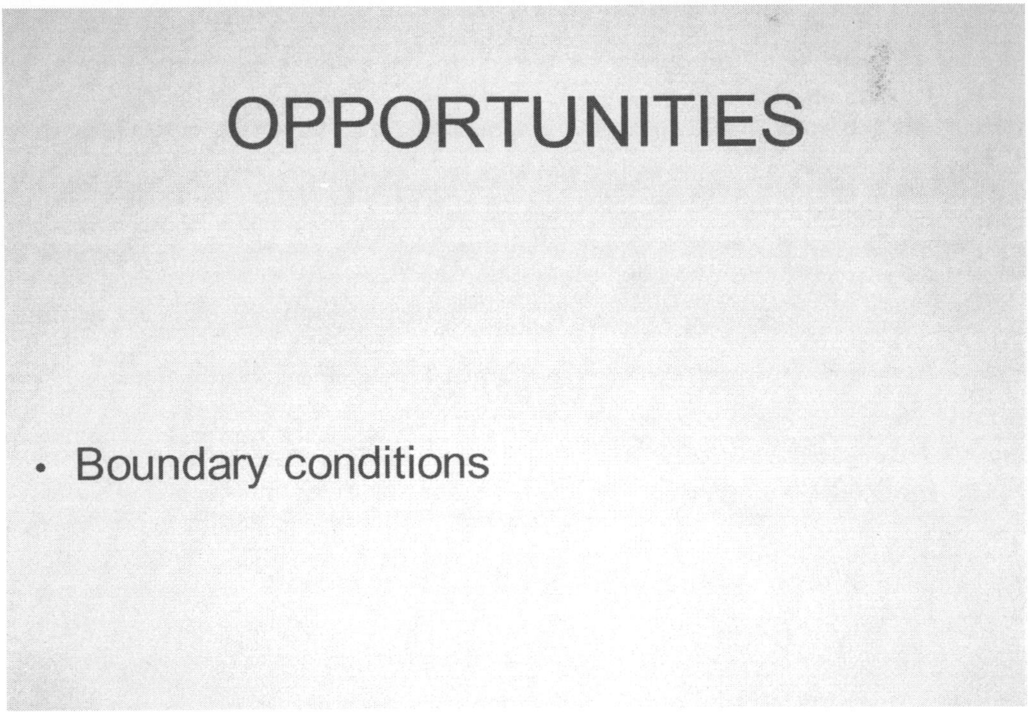

The third one is boundary conditions; again many of the previous papers have been looking at the problem one way versus the other. But one of the things we forget to ask is what the boundary conditions are, which means at what point will big data analysis stop becoming relevant and the hypothesis start breaking down.

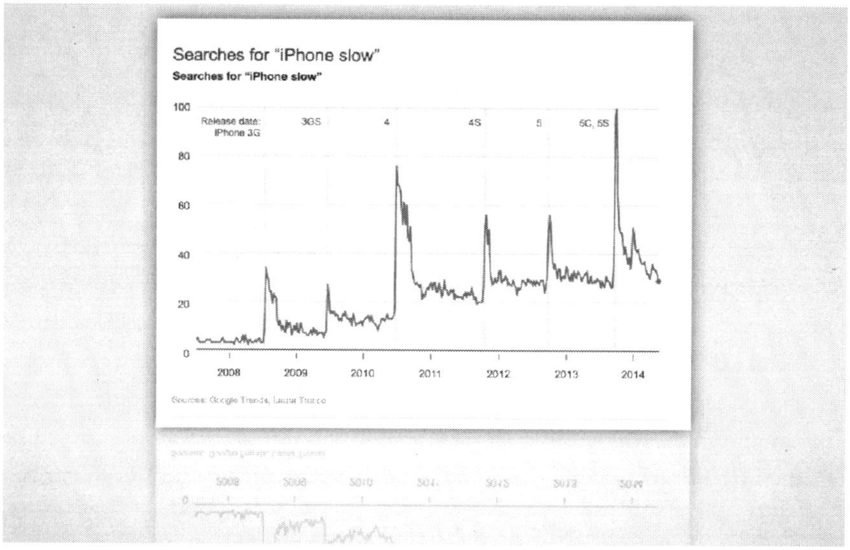

This chart shows the Google Search queries for I-Phone becoming slow. If you map it up it actually peaks every time there is a new model of I-Phone launched. So when I-Phone 3GS came there was a peak in the searches for why I-Phone has become slow, similarly there are peaks for I-Phones 4, 4S, 5 and 5S. After every launch users start thinking their current phone has become slow. There are various hypotheses for it, for example, people suddenly realize that their product is outdated and is becoming slower.

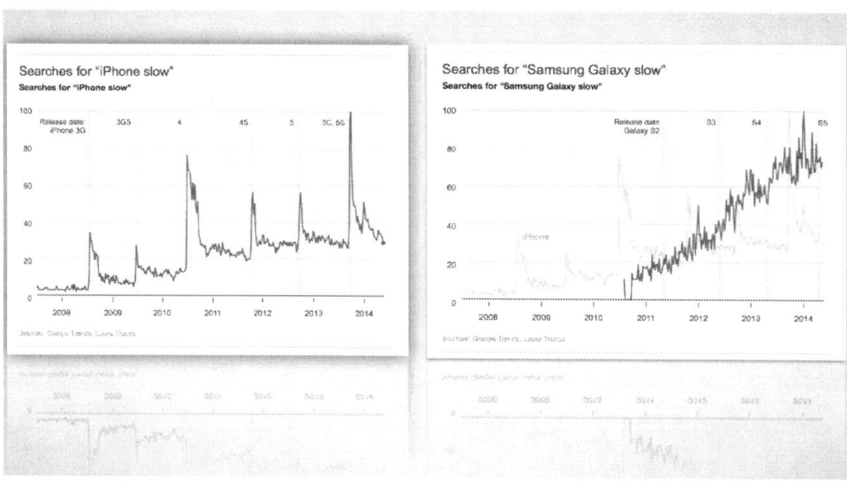

However, it does not happen for Android. For the searches of a Samsung Galaxy getting slower, there is a steady rise because as phones get older, search for the phones getting slower goes up but it doesn't peak like in the case of I-Phone. What's the difference between the two? That's a boundary condition. As analysts of big data, we have to figure out when the data in the chart becomes irrelevant. Sometimes, the insights are so enticing that we forget or ignore that there are boundary conditions. The difference between Apple and Samsung is that the adoption of the latest version of the operating system in Apple is 90% whereas for Samsung it is 120%. New versions of the operating system make higher demands on the hardware than the older versions. In Apple's case, if you are not using the latest version of the OS the hardware becomes obsolete because the demands on the hardware are high. The reason the number of searches peak is because Apple launches software and hardware at the same time. It has nothing to do with Apple users or Samsung users, it's simply got to do with the adoption and launch cycles. In Android the device launch and the software launch are different and penetration of the latest software is lower than in the case of Apple. There is always greater variation within data than between data and there are boundary conditions which we absolutely have to respect.

Secondary Use of Data

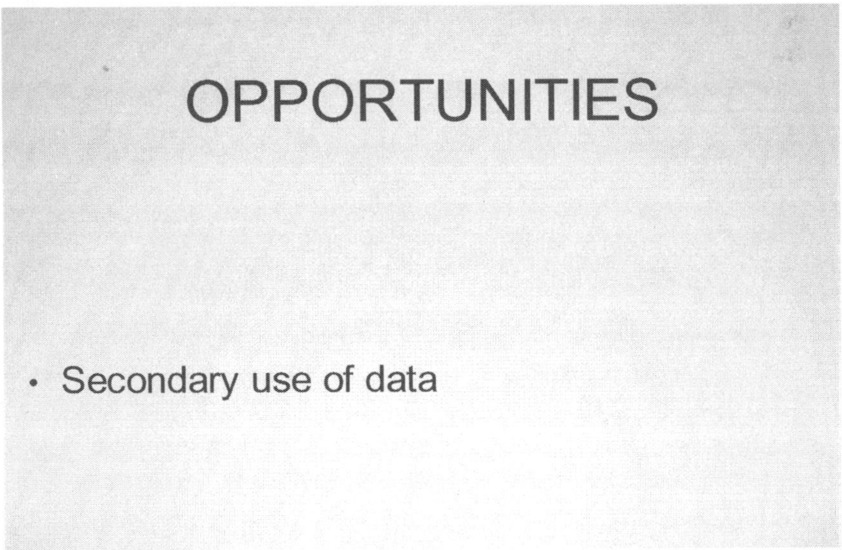

As big data analysts we have a responsibility to worry about the secondary use of data, which simply means that if data has been collected and everyone involved knows it is going to be used in a certain way but when you start using it for something else, that's called secondary use of data. For example, optimized Google Searches based on your history is primary usage, but when we analyze it, like in the previous chart, that is considered secondary usage. In most countries and markets, secondary usage of the data requires you to have a different contract with the provider of the data, which means users must understand that the footprint they leave has a secondary usage, if they don't understand that we are in breach of privacy. We must always remember to respect privacy because historically secondary uses of data have gotten us into a lot of trouble. For example, in Europe, way back before Hitler came, one of the problems they had during war was when somebody died they didn't know how to give them the proper burial rites because they didn't know what their religious beliefs are. So they decided to keep records of ethnicity and religion so that if anyone were to die in a tragic incident they could look up the records and give them proper burial rites. After a few years, when the Nazis came rolling into town all they had to do was get this book, look up all the Jews. That is the secondary use of data. In the moment the data can look trivial but out of context it can be deadly. Big data is leaving very little room for people to be private and as people who are asking other people to trust us and get involved, we have a responsibility. Secondary usage of the data is when things start spiraling out of control and the onus is on us to realize that that has to happen.

Internet of Things

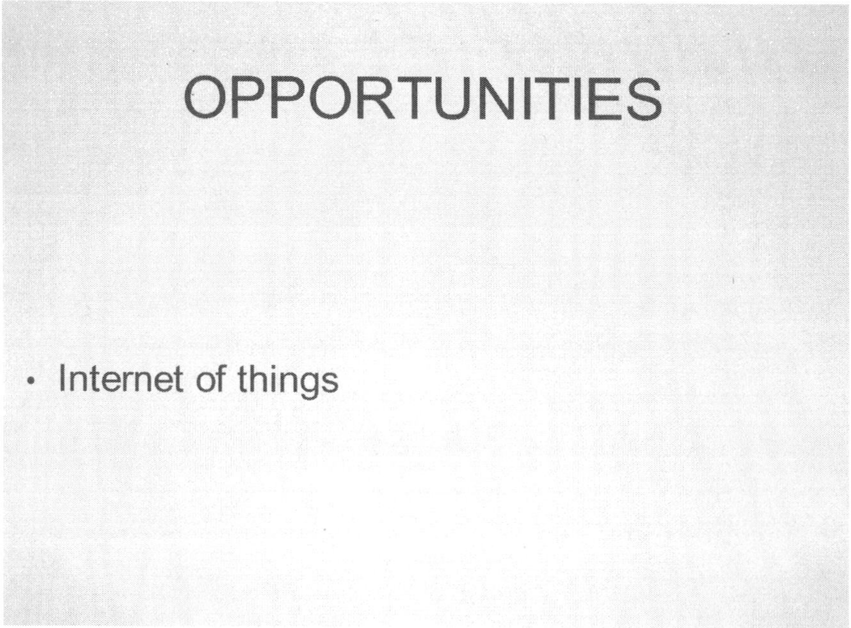

Big data analytics hasn't moved into the realm of the Internet of things yet, but the most exciting opportunity is not necessarily the analysis of internet of things, but the analysis of the interface of the user and the internet of things. For example, the interaction between the wearer of the smart watch with the smart person is one of the major areas where there is a tremendous opportunity.

SUBJECT INDEX

APPENDIX

Affiliations of the Conference Paper Contributors

Anthony Thomas – *Vodafone India*
Satish Mittal – *Vodafone India*
Sunder Muthuraman – *Meritus India Analytics Pvt Ltd.*
Manoj Kumar – *Meritus India Analytics Pvt Ltd.*
T. Sujit Kumar Dora – *Meritus India Analytics Pvt Ltd.*
Kavya Madhava – *Meritus India Analytics Pvt Ltd.*
Thayagarajan Subramanian – *Meritus India Analytics Pvt Ltd.*
Mansi Madan – *Jagan Institute of Management Studies*
Vibhati Sharma – *Blueocean Market Intelligence Pvt Ltd.*
Swaroop Johnson – *Blueocean Market Intelligence Pvt Ltd.*
Ayan Ghosh – *HP Global Analytics*
Archana Menon – *HP Global Analytics*
S. Ravi Kumar – *Genpact India Pvt Ltd.*
Sameer Malhotra – *Pwc LLP.*
Anand S. Rao – *Pwc LLP.*
Joseph Voyles – *Pwc LLP.*
Anjali Malik – *SP Jain Institute of Management and Rsearch*
Rajiv Kumra – *IIM Lucknow*
Lalit Sharma – *Rocketalk*
Akshatha Krishna – *Genpact India Pvt. Ltd.*
Ani babu – *Genpact India Pvt Ltd.*
Rajkumar Dan – *Dell International Services India Pvt Ltd.*
Dinesh RC – *Dell International Services India Pvt Ltd.*
Kristof Coussement – *IESEG School of Management*
Paul Harrigan – *The University of Western Australia*
Tim Daly – *UAE University*
Julie Lee – *The University of Western Australia*
Geoff Soutar – *The University of Western Australia*
Nitin Kumar – *Genpact India Pvt Ltd.*
Deepali Nair – *Mahindra Holidays and Resorts India Ltd.*
Surabhi Verma – *Nitie Mumbai*
Som Sekhar Bhattacharyya – *Nitie Mumbai*
Subin Sudhir – *IIM-Kozhikode*
Anandakuttan Unnithan – *IIM-Kozhikode*
Veena Ranjith – *Dell International Services India Pvt Ltd.*
Praveen Srinivasan – *Cognizant Technology Solutions India Pvt Ltd.*
Ramya Chittigala – *Cognizant Technology Solutions India Pvt Ltd.*
Aparna Mukherjee – *Genpact Sales and Marketing Solutions*
Snigdha Pain – *Lady Brabourne College*

Vinayak Deshpande – *Sankhya Analytical Research Pvt. Ltd.*
Anindita Bhattacharyya – *Dell International Services India Pvt Ltd.*
Rishabh Parakh – *Dell International Services India Pvt Ltd.*
Barnana Sarkar – *Guru Nanak Vidyak Society Institute of Management*
Geert Verstraeten – *Python Predictions*
John Raj – *Dell International Services India Pvt Ltd.*
K. Suryaprakasa Rao – *Anna University*
Rohit Nair – *Marketelligent &* Co. *Ltd.*
Ashish Mahalka – *Blueocean Market Intelligence Pvt Ltd.*